Afoot & Afield Portland/Vancouver

Douglas Lorain

WILDERNESS PRESS
BERKELEY

FIRST EDITION June 2003

Cover and book designer: Jaan Hitt
Book Production: Archetype Typography, Berkeley, California
Editor: David Kolodney, Thomas Winnett
Assistant Editor: Jessica Benner
Proofreader: Peter Feng
Managing Editor: Jannie Dresser

Original maps by the author
Maps digitized: James Ragsdale
Map design: Jaan Hitt

All photographs by the author except where otherwise indicated.

Front cover photo: © 2003 Douglas Lorain, Abiqua Falls, near Scotts Mills, OR
Frontispiece photo: © 2003 Douglas Lorain, Jagged spine of Mitchell Point
            (looking north), Oregon, Columbia Gorge, OR
Back cover photo: © 2003 Douglas Lorain, Mitchell Point, Columbia Gorge, OR

ISBN 0-89997-289-6
UPC 7-19609-97289-1
Manufactured in the United States of America

♻ Print on recycled paper

Published by Wilderness Press
            1200 5th Street
            Berkeley, CA 94710
            Phone (800) 443-7227
            Fax (510) 558-1696
www.wildernesspress.com   mail@wildernesspress.com

Contents

Difficulty Ratings: *   Easy   ⌂ Good cloudy weather hike
                   **   Moderate
               ***   Difficult
            ****   Strenuous

The Best Hikes by Theme

Urban and Suburban Hikes

Portland and Willamette Valley

Mountain Hikes

Mount Hood

Waterfall Hikes

Southwest Washington

Portland and Willamette Valley

Columbia River Gorge

Salmon–Huckleberry Area

Saddle Mountain, Oregon State Park

View Hikes

Wildflower Hikes

Bird and Wildlife Hikes

Old-Growth Forest Hikes

Mountain-Biking Routes

Locator Map

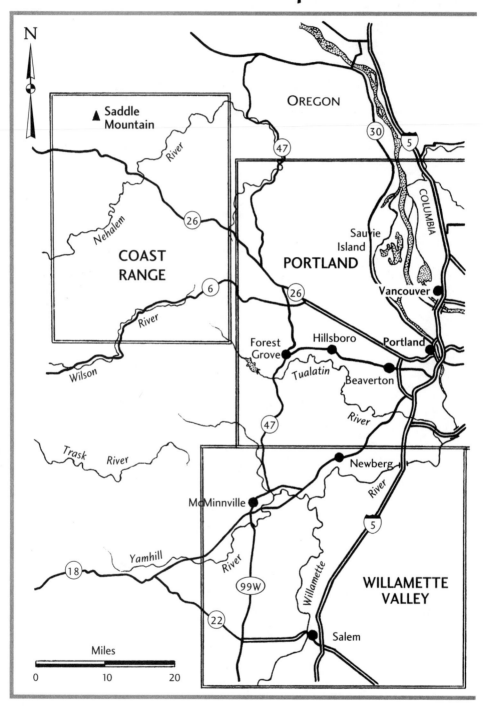

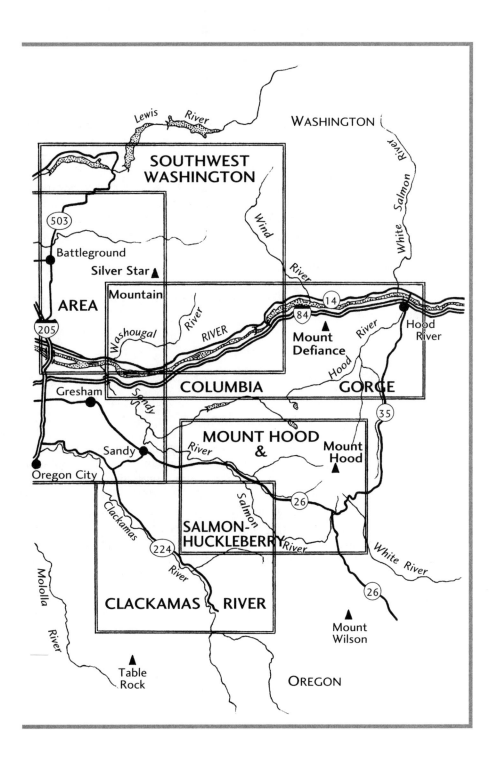

Acknowledgments

I have no scapegoat to take the blame for the inevitable mistakes that occur in the preparation of any guidebook. All errors and omissions fall entirely at my own booted feet. Nonetheless, a few people deserve to be mentioned for their help in making this book happen.

For her assistance with all things botanical and for putting up with me as a sibling, I thank Christine Ebrahimi.

For introducing a fresh perspective on useful outdoor books, my appreciation goes to Trevor and Kathy Todd.

I also thank Brianna James, without whose friendship and support this book (and many other things) would not be possible.

Finally, thanks to the people at Wilderness Press who, to my amazement, were nice enough to publish my books in the first place. Special mention must go to Tom Winnett, Mike Jones, Jannie Dresser, and Jaan Hitt. Also, thank you to David Kolodney, the freelance editor for this book, and Peter Feng, the proofreader. They all deserve more recognition than they usually get for turning the author's preliminary efforts into something that is readable, useful, and attractive for you, the reader.

Safety Notice

While hiking is not an inherently dangerous sport, there are certain risks you take when you venture away from the comforts of civilization. Some of the trips described in this book go through remote wilderness terrain. In an emergency, supplies and medical facilities will not be immediately available. The fact that a hike is described in this book does not mean that it will be safe for you. Hikers must be properly equipped and in adequate physical condition to handle a given trail. Because trail conditions, weather, and hikers' abilities all vary considerably, the author and the publisher cannot assume responsibility for anyone's safety. Use plenty of common sense and a realistic appraisal of your abilities so you can enjoy these trips safely.

Preface

Outdoor lovers in the Portland/Vancouver metropolitan area are among the most fortunate in the country. Within a one-hour drive from their homes they can hit the trail through dense old-growth forests, walk beside spectacular waterfalls, climb to viewpoints above massive glaciers, explore wetlands that are home to waterfowl and bald eagles, traipse through wildflower-covered meadows, or wander through the quiet forests of a 5000-acre park right in the city of Portland. Few other cities in the country have such a wide assortment of opportunities.

My goal in writing this book was to provide the first comprehensive guide to every worthwhile walk of at least 1 mile, on still-wild public lands, and accessible within a one-hour drive from Portland. The one-hour driving-time is from somewhere in the major cities and suburbs of the greater Portland/Vancouver area. That does not mean that every drive will be less than one hour for every resident. If you live in Hillsboro, it may take you up to 45 minutes just to get to Gresham, on the other side of the metro area, before you start the one-hour drive to Mt. Hood. Nonetheless, every trip has a short enough drive time to qualify as a good spur-of-the-moment adventure.

The hikes range in difficulty from simple strolls through urban preserves to rugged climbs in the Columbia River Gorge and on glacier-clad Mt. Hood. There are paths here familiar to every Portland hiker as well as dozens of new routes never covered in any guidebook. They have in common a convenient proximity to Portland and a wild character that allows city residents to "get away from it all."

A large percentage of these hikes are open year-round. So this guide also serves as a winter hikes manual. The northwest's notoriously soggy winters often make trails muddy. With waterproof boots and the proper attitude, hikers can enjoy many fine trails all year.

Many worthwhile urban and semi-urban walks have been excluded because they don't qualify as "wild." If you are looking for a quick leg-stretcher, and don't mind a landscape that features manicured lawns or picnic tables, then try any of the many easy hikes in city parks and greenways. Often these routes follow paved trails that hikers share with joggers and bicyclists. Among the best of these options are the **Fanno Creek Greenway** in Beaverton, the network of trails around **Washington Park's arboretum**, the riverside path in **Willamette Park**, and the **Salmon Creek Greenway** in Clark County.

Trails that do not qualify as "wild" also include pleasant routes that feature wild scenery but are located near major roads or go through and around golf courses, such as those at Skamania Lodge or at Glendoveer and Rose City golf clubs.

I have hiked every trip in this book at least once and most of them several times. However, roads and trails do constantly change. New routes are built, old trails cease to be maintained or are simply abandoned, and floods and landslides obliterate some routes. Your comments on recent developments or changes are welcome. Please write to me in care of Wilderness Press, 1200 5th Street, Berkeley, CA 94710.

Hidden Falls along Tarbell Trail, Washington

Introduction to the Portland/Vancouver Area

IN MOST CITIES, A BOOK LIKE THIS WOULD BEGIN WITH SOMETHING LIKE "WELCOME TO THE WILDLANDS BEYOND THE CITY'S FAMILIAR CONCRETE JUNGLE." But no Portland/Vancouver resident would recognize or agree with that characterization, because this is a city still firmly tied to Mother Nature. One reason for this, of course, is that often Ma Nature literally hits you in the face with rain as soon as you walk out the door—an experience that is both humbling and a useful reminder of just who's in charge here. But even when it isn't raining, the natural world is still constantly in evidence. It's just a short drive from anywhere in the greater Portland area to forests so wild that elk are more likely to be seen than people. On the city's skyline sits not only Mt. Hood, the signature landmark of our region, but four other wild volcanic peaks. Parts of the Columbia River Gorge, only 30 minutes from the downtown skyscrapers, remain as wild today as when Lewis and Clark passed through in 1805.

But Portland is not only *surrounded* by wild country, it manages to include wilderness right in the city limits. The enormity of Forest Park, the largest forested city park in the world, provides country that is wilder than many designated wilderness areas. In the towering evergreens that stand in virtually every city neighborhood live gray squirrels, raccoons, great horned owls, and other wildlife. Endangered peregrine falcons live amid the downtown buildings and bridges. People even fish for salmon in the Willamette River in downtown Portland. So Portland is truly a city where you can never really escape the natural world—and that's just the way we like it.

Every Imaginable Shade of Green—The Local Flora

I once had a friend who moved from the Pacific Northwest to Phoenix, Arizona. He liked his new environment, but would constantly comment about how much he missed the color *green*. All the rain we get ensures that even in the dry months of late summer the Portland area always stays green. Washington may officially be the Evergreen *state*, but it's Portland that takes the honor as the Evergreen *city*.

All that greenery is composed of thousands of plant species inhabiting dozens of different environments. Professional botanists recognize a wide range of plant communities throughout our area. The average hiker, however, won't notice most of these, because the same species are predominant through-out the region. Once you learn to recognize these relatively few species, you are well on your way to feeling like an expert and getting more enjoyment from your travels.

As all of us umbrella-toting Portlanders already know, we live in a virtual rainforest. That forest is made up of a canopy of big trees with several layers of understory species.

Douglas-fir is by far the most abundant species on the forest's top floor. Point at any random conifer on most of the trails in this book and there is roughly a 75% chance that the tree is a Douglas-fir. At lower elevations the second most common species is the western hemlock, a beautiful evergreen with tiny needles and drooping limbs. At the highest elevations of

Cache Meadow, Clackamas River Country, Oregon

Wahclella, Columbia Gorge, Oregon

the Cascade Mountains, the hemlock family banner is taken up by a close relative, the mountain hemlock. A similar thing happens with cedars. At lower elevations look for western red cedar, while in the high country Alaska yellow cedar takes over. With the true firs you should recognize grand fir down low, Pacific silver fir and noble fir at mid elevations, and subalpine fir up high. Other evergreen species of note include Engelmann spruce, western white pine, and lodgepole pine.

Deciduous trees are less common than conifers, but they mix with the evergreens at all lower elevations, and in some areas leafy trees actually outnumber those with needles. Especially abundant are bigleaf maple and red alder. On the drier hills you will find woodlands of Oregon white oak, while in the wet bottomlands of the river valleys there are black cottonwoods. From mid-October to mid-November both bigleaf maple and black cottonwood grace the area with their bright yellow leaves.

Get off the elevator at the second floor of our forests and the doors will open up to a whole array of smaller tree species. Most notable of these is the vine maple, another great fall-color species. This short understory tree has many-pointed leaves that turn a striking reddish-orange color in October. Another second-story species is the Pacific yew, a fascinating conifer that lives in shady forests and uses red berrylike fruits, instead of cones, to reproduce. Pacific dogwood, with its showy white blossoms in April and May, also deserves mention. Other common small trees on the second story include Pacific willow, Sitka alder, black hawthorn, and Oregon ash.

Below these small trees is a layer of large and small shrubs. Once again, unless you want to be an expert, you need only to learn a handful of the most common species. Many of the larger shrubs are berries, like salmonberry, thimbleberry, and blackberry, all of which have tasty edible fruit in season. Other common large shrubs include elderberry (both red and blue varieties), serviceberry, snowberry, and devils club. Probably the most abundant large shrub at mid elevations in the Cascades is the Pacific rhododendron. From May to early July, the showy pink blossoms of this evergreen plant put on displays that can even make clearcuts look good . . . well . . . *almost.*

Moving down to the forest's ground floor takes us to the low-growing shrubs. The most important member of this group, especially for your taste buds, is the huckleberry. From mid-August to mid-September the positively delicious berries of this abundant mid- to high-elevation plant will slow the berry-picking hiker's progress to a crawl. Other common low shrubs include kinnnikinnick, salal, and, in the alpine zone, both pink and white heather. No list of low shrubs would be complete without mentioning one of the most abundant members of the group, the yellow-blooming Oregon grape.

The plants most closely associated with the bottom floor of our forests are ferns. Experts recognize numerous species but, once again, the novice needs only to know four or five common varieties. Sword fern, easily the most common type, is a hardy but strikingly beautiful evergreen fern that is so abundant in this area we often take its beauty for granted. Sunnier areas will invariably feature bracken fern, while wetter places have lots of maiden-hair and lady fern. The final fern species that the average hiker will want to learn is the licorice fern. This common species is what botanists term *epiphytic,* which means that instead of growing out of the ground, like its relatives, the licorice fern grows directly out of tree trunks and rocks.

Everybody loves flowers and many people go hiking specifically to enjoy the sight and smell of blossoms. From March through September, there are always flowers to enjoy somewhere in our region. Wildflowers, however, are difficult to categorize, because so many different kinds of plants, including many listed above, produce flowers. If we restrict this group to just the smaller, ground-level types (as most people do), then you can look like an expert by knowing just a few dozen species. When hiking in dense forests, you won't see great displays of wildflowers, but you will find scattered blooms that help to brighten the shady forest floor. Look for yellow wood violet, the relatively rare pink calypso orchid, and several varieties of white flowers, including trillium, queens cup, bunchberry, twinflower, and vanilla leaf.

If you want to see great wildflower displays, then get out of the forest and head for the meadows. In the lower-elevation valleys, you need to find one of those increasingly rare places that have yet to be paved over or plowed under. The most striking flower in these fields is blue camas, a plant that was once an important food source for Native Americans.

There is greater variety in the mountains. Depending on the elevation, the higher meadows will provide spectacular displays any time from mid-June to mid-August. Just as the snow melts, the ground will come alive with

1 Silver dollar plant (a type of mustard)
2 Trillium
3 Oregon grape
4 Grass widow
5 Tall larkspur
6 Camas
7 False Solomon-seal
8 Corydalis
9 Balsamroot
10 Beargrass

11 Oak and licorice fern
12 Teasels
13 Grasses
14 Licorice fern
15 Big leaf maple
16 Ferns and mosses on talus slope
17 Wind contorted fir tree
18-20 Varieties of fungus
21 Author beside old cedar tree

the blossoms of glacier lily, avalanche lily, and western pasque flower. A little later, you will enjoy cinquefoil, lupine, paintbrush, spiraea, shooting star, yarrow, and, perhaps most notable of all, beargrass. By the end of summer, the meadows will still have some flowers, especially asters, goldenrods, and blue gentians, which bloom well into September.

The banks of creeks feature lush vegetation and a unique array of water-loving flowering plants. Of particular note are yellow monkeyflower and pink Lewis monkeyflower, false solomon seal, and bleeding heart. Dry and rocky places have wildflowers better adapted to these environments. Here you may find yellow stonecrop, blue larkspur, lavender cliff penstemon, and the whites of pearly everlasting, prairie star, and cats ear, among others.

If wildflowers lead the brigade of popular plants, then the least popular plant, poison oak, also deserves mention. This species is most common in dry, sunny places, but it can also be found in denser forests. You should be especially wary of this rash-producing menace when you are hiking in the eastern Columbia River Gorge. Poison oak comes in a variety of forms, sometimes growing as a vine and sometimes as a low bush, but it always has lobed, often shiny leaves, that grow in groups of three. Hikers who travel with the family pet need to remember that, no matter how smart you think Rover is, he probably isn't bright enough to recognize and avoid poison oak. Many unsuspecting pet owners have picked up a nasty rash from merely petting their dog after a hike in poison-oak country.

Various species of moss grow abundantly in our forests. Trying to identify these species is beyond the interest level of most hikers. It's worth pointing out, however, that the old adage about moss growing only on the north side of a tree does not work around here. If you get lost and try to navigate by this old trick, you'll be in big trouble, because in this wet environment moss grows on *all* sides of the trees.

Mushrooms and fungi are an area of special interest for many Northwest hikers. Our forests feature several dozen varieties growing out of the ground, out of old stumps, and even out of living trees. Many species are edible, and collecting mushrooms is a fun activity. **Do not**, however, eat any mushrooms unless you are experienced and completely confident in your ability to identify the various species. There are several poisonous types in our area, and every year people get sick, and some even die, from eating the wrong mushrooms.

Fur, Feathers, Scales, and Slime—The Local Fauna

Hikers aren't the only creatures leaving footprints on our area trails. By far the most common large mammal you will encounter, apart from *Homo sapiens* and their canine companions, is the black-tailed deer. Even on trips within the city limits, you are likely to see deer tracks and every hiker who spends time in the backcountry will see lots of deer. Next on the list of large mammals is the Roosevelt elk. It's always a thrill to catch a glimpse of these large, impressive animals. The most likely area to observe elk is in the Coast Range. Other large

Beaver dam

mammals prowling area forests include black bears and mountain lions, but the average hiker would be extraordinarily fortunate to see either.

Smaller mammals are another story. In the right habitat, every hiker will see chipmunks, Douglas squirrels, and pikas. Some representative examples of the other common smaller mammals in our area are porcupine, beaver, raccoon, skunk, coyote, red and gray fox, marmot, and snowshoe hare. Hikers who are quiet stand a better chance of seeing these, and all other, wildlife.

As is true throughout the world, insects are, by far, the most common form of wildlife in our area. Apart from admiring butterflies, however, most hikers think of insects only when they are forced to swat bothersome mosquitoes. Higher on the food chain are spiders. The thick vegetation and the abundance of insects for prey ensure that spiders are quite common. The most important result of this fact is that the first person to hike a trail in the morning must negotiate an obstacle course of webs. You will spend considerable time (and a lifetime's vocabulary of swear words) wiping the webs off your face, hair, and clothing. My advice is to wave a walking stick in front of you or, better yet, convince your hiking partner to take the lead. Another good option is to hike in the winter, when spiders are less active and build fewer webs.

After insects, our most common and conspicuous form of wildlife are birds. The feathered menagerie includes a wide range of colors, sizes, and forms. Tiny rufous hummingbirds zip past looking for flowers to visit, while various species of chickadees, wrens, warblers, and sparrows, among others, fill the forests with song. Easily the most common bird in the mountains is the dark-eyed junco, formerly called the Oregon junco and still termed that by the average proud Oregonian. During the winter months, these happy, clicking birds with black heads come down to the valleys and are among the most common residents at backyard feeding stations.

Great-blue herons are probably the most conspicuous large birds in the Portland area. Every Portlander is familiar with this, the city's official bird. These tall and delicately beautiful avians are often seen flying overhead, prowling for food along streams or beside ponds, or just standing around in dry fields hunting for mice. Other large birds of note include Canada geese and various species of ducks, which spend their winters in the mild climate of the Willamette Valley; ospreys and bald eagles, which can often be seen on larger lakes and rivers; and red-tailed hawks, easily our most abundant flying predators.

The Pacific Northwest is home to eight salamander species, one of the highest such concentrations in the world. Our wet forests host some fascinating and beautiful species, including the long-toed salamander, the tiny Oregon ensatina, and the aptly named Pacific giant salamander, which actually *barks*. Due to their secretive nature, however, you will rarely see any salamanders. The sole exception to this rule is the rough-skinned newt, an interesting and abundant representative of the group that can be found in almost any pond, lake, or slow-moving stream. A fact unknown to even most experienced outdoor lovers is that the rough-skinned newt is poisonous. Their skin emits a toxin that, if ingested, can be deadly. Fortunately, the poison cannot penetrate your skin. But be sure to wash your hands after handling a newt.

Other amphibians also take well to this damp environment. You will encounter several species of frogs, the most common of which are the Pacific treefrog, the western toad, and the red-legged frog. Sadly, frog populations have been declining in recent years. This is a worldwide problem, the reasons for which are not well understood. In our area, probably the leading cause of this decline is the unfortunate introduction, and population explosion, of the bullfrog. This non-native predator feeds on smaller frogs, as well as baby turtles, birds, and other unfortunate victims.

In this wet climate, reptiles are less common than amphibians. Lizards, for example, are fairly common east of the Cascades, but they are very rare in the area covered by this book. You are likely to see them only on the drier slopes on the Washington side of the Columbia River Gorge. Snakes are much more common. In and around Portland there is no need to worry about rattlesnakes, except perhaps at places like Dog Mountain in the eastern Gorge. What you *will* encounter throughout this area are various species of harmless garter snakes and racers.

No list of area wildlife would be complete without mentioning one of the most famous, and strangely popular, residents of the Pacific Northwest—the lowly banana slug. Mollusks aren't generally the most beloved of organisms and, even here in the slug capital of the world, area gardeners have been in a long-standing war with the creatures (usually a *losing* battle, or so my gardening friends lament). One of the most memorable encounters you will have on a rainy day in the woods is with the banana slug. The first tell-tale sign is the famous slime trail crossing your path. Follow this sticky slime and you will soon come across the source, a surprisingly colorful, and almost frighteningly large, slug. The banana slug comes in an array of colors, mostly greenish-yellow with black spots, and can be up to 10 inches long (the average is about 6 or 7 inches). People from other parts of the country find this to be evidence that all the rain up here has made Portlanders a bit addled, but many Northwest residents have a strong affection for the slug. One town in western Washington holds an annual slug festival, and it is even possible to purchase various souvenir items featuring the banana slug.

Welcome to the Pacific Northwet—The Local Weather

RAIN. Anyone who lives in this part of the world knows that there's no getting around it. For eight or so months of the year it rains . . . a lot . . . in Portand. But there is much more to the climate story than just precipitation. Each season has its own weather-related quirks, and all the hills, canyons, river valleys, and mountains in our area help to create numerous *microclimates*. Once you master these local weather idiosyncrasies, you'll stay drier and have more fun in the outdoors.

Ferns, moss-covered trees and rocks, and running streams are among the beneficiaries of Oregon's heavy rainfall (Ruckel Creek).

Summer in the Pacific Northwest is just about ideal. From mid-July until early October rain is unusual, despite all those stories we tell out-of-staters in an effort to keep them out. This is not to say that we never get clouds in the summer months. In fact, morning clouds are quite common. One of the best times to go hiking is when clouds cover the Willamette Valley. A large percentage of summer days in our region begins with a layer of marine air, which pushes in from the Pacific Ocean carrying low clouds with it. What far too many hikers in Portland and Vancouver fail to realize is that once you climb above about 2000 feet, you leave the clouds and fog behind and enjoy brilliant sunshine. A great aesthetic advantage of hiking in such weather is that you can climb to a viewpoint and look *down* on the billowy white fog that covers the valleys with its delicate fingers that creep through low passes in the ridges. The fog also hides most of the clearcuts, and it helps to ensure greater solitude, because outdoor lovers in the socked-in Portland/Vancouver lowlands look out their windows, see the low clouds, and wrongly assume that it's too gloomy to go hiking.

Despite being farther north than Minneapolis, Portland's proximity to the Pacific Ocean keeps the winter weather relatively mild. It may rain a lot, but severe winter weather is rare. Generally we get only two or three days of snow per year, and even that usually melts away in a day or two. The mountains, of course, get lots of snow, and with several feet piling up every winter, it takes many months for all that white stuff to melt away. Precisely when trails open for travel varies from year to year, but a pretty good rule of thumb is that trails below 1000 feet remain open all year. At 2000 feet, trails begin to open by mid-March. With every 1000 feet of elevation, it takes an additional month for the snow to melt. Thus, by mid-April the snow line will be around 3000 feet; by mid-May it's 4000 feet, and that number becomes 5000 feet by mid-June. The highest trails open some time in July. Sunnier south-facing slopes melt out sooner than north-facing ones. This is true everywhere

in the country, but it is probably less pronounced here than elsewhere, because the heavy tree cover keeps the snow well shaded, even on south-facing slopes.

Don't let yourself and your hiking boots go into hibernation just because it's winter. Despite all that famous rain, every wet season features at least some welcome sunshine and, if you are properly equipped, many trails are a joy to hike even in the rain. Usually you can rely on any trail below 1000 feet to be open all year.

Fall and spring weather is less predictable than winter and summer. There is a local joke that you can tell it's spring in Portland when the rain starts to get warmer. By the time May and June roll around, the skies are still all too often covered

In early summer, you may still find winter snow clinging to mountain lakes (Mazama Trail looking toward Mt. Hood, Oregon).

with clouds, and people start to get frustrated. Statistically, there are a lot more sunny days at this time than we've had in the previous six or seven months. Taking advantage of these welcome brighter days is highly rewarding. Spring hikers will be treated to a natural world positively bursting with new life that has definitely noticed the increase in life-giving sunshine.

Autumn in the Portland/Vancouver area produces weather that is best described as variable. In some years, it starts raining in September and everyone knows that it won't really let up until next June. In at least one year in three, however, we enjoy a glorious Indian summer, with nice weather extending all the way into October. This is one of the best times to go hiking, because the temperatures are cool, the bugs are gone many areas feature wonderful fall colors. After Labor Day the trails are virtually deserted. On a day just after the first light dusting of snow in early October, be sure to make a trip to the high trails on Mt. Hood. The mountain really comes alive with this first covering of snow. You can also take some spectacular photographs of the snow-dusted peak, over the golden meadows framed by the red splashes of huckleberry bushes. Down in the valleys, and especially in the Columbia River Gorge, the fall colors remain excellent into mid-November. Be aware, however, that in the deep, shady canyons on the Oregon side of the Gorge, the sun goes down very early. In November, you should expect darkness by about 3:00 P.M. Bring fast film and a tripod to take photographs in this low light, and carry plenty of warm clothing for the hike back out.

The mountains and valleys surrounding the Portland/Vancouver area cause different wind and precipitation patterns that create localized climates. One of these so called *microclimates* is the small, but noticeable, rainshadow just east of the Coast Range. The downsloping hills of Yamhill and western Washington counties get noticeably less annual rainfall than do the upsloping hills in eastern Clackamas, Multnomah, and Clark counties.

The most important microclimate in our region is the Columbia River Gorge. As everyone already knows, the Gorge is almost always windy. The violently twisted trees and the abundance of windsurfers attest to the strength of the winds here, so hikers must come prepared for often bitter wind chills. For most of the year, the prevailing wind is from west to east. But during the winter months, the Gorge often acts as a funnel for cold air from east of the Cascade Mountains. As a result, the almost-sea-level Gorge stays much colder than anywhere else in our region. Consequently, the Gorge gets a lot more snow and freezing rain than do neighboring Portland and Vancouver. An inch of cold rain in Portland may fall as a foot or more of snow in Cascades Locks, even though Cascade Locks is only about 20 feet higher in elevation. This means that the aforementioned elevation rules for snow-free hiking generally don't apply in the Gorge. The much sunnier Washington side melts out a lot faster and, in fact, it often provides the nicest early-spring hiking in our region. For photographers, and those who can stand bitterly cold temperatures, it's also fun to visit the Gorge during a mid-winter cold spell. With luck, the waterfalls will be encased in a spectacular coating of ice.

Trail Safety
and Courtesy

ALTHOUGH GENERALLY VERY SAFE, THE SPORT OF HIKING DOES INVOLVE A CERTAIN LEVEL OF RISK. In the Portland/Vancouver area the risks are relatively minor, but they are real, and good preparation is important to help minimize the potential dangers.

Preparation and Equipment

The most important preparation for a hiking trip is being in good physical condition. The trips in this book range in difficulty from quite easy to extremely strenuous. Each trip is rated from * to ****. Trips rated as * are the easiest and should be enjoyable to anyone, although a small degree of conditioning is always helpful. Trips rated as ****, on the other hand, are beyond the abilities of all but a handful of the best-conditioned hikers. Before selecting a hike, be honest about your physical condition. Don't overextend yourself by taking a trip that is beyond your fitness level. After all, you go hiking to *enjoy* yourself, not *exhaust* yourself, and, most importantly, a wilderness trail miles from your car is *not* the place to suddenly realize that your body is not prepared for strenuous activity. On average, about one hiker a week has to be rescued on the backcountry trails of the Portland/Vancouver area. Don't let yourself become a statistic. There are plenty of hikes in this book at every ability level. Work your way up to the more difficult trips, so you can enjoy every outing comfortably and safely.

Although the weather in the Portland/Vancouver area is often cold and wet, we humans are most comfortable, and perform best when we stay warm and dry. The proper clothing is the best way to resolve this discrepancy.

For strenuous activities like hiking, your best bet is to wear several layers of synthetic or wool clothing. It is relatively easy to regulate your temperature by simply adding or removing layers. Years ago hikers had only two options for clothing fabrics—cotton and wool. Wool kept you warm, but was scratchy and uncomfortable. Cotton was comfortable, but provided no insulation when it got wet—a certain recipe for hypothermia in our rainy climate. The science of fabrics has come a long way since then. Today there is a dizzying array of synthetic fabrics and special wool blends that wick moisture away from your body, are lightweight, feel comfortable against your skin, keep you warm on cold, rainy days, and help you stay comfortably cool in hot weather. More new fabrics come out all the time.

The first layer against your skin should be something like capilene or coolmax which are warm, comfortable, and wick away your perspiration on hot summer days. The next layer will depend on the season. In colder winter weather, opt for a long-sleeve wool or synthetic shirt. On warm summer days, you may go for cotton. Regardless of the season, you should carry or wear some sort of outer shell. A waterproof windbreaker is ideal. In the Columbia River Gorge, where the wind never seems to stop blowing, a windbreaker is practically indispensable. In winter, you'll also need to carry a warm coat. A fleece jacket is a good choice, because it provides insulation with minimal weight.

Below the waist, forget cotton jeans and go instead for lightweight nylon pants, which stop the wind and provide insulation even when they get wet. In winter, you might consider wool pants to keep your legs warmer. Few local hikers travel in shorts, but on hot summer days you might do so, as long as you also carry long pants should the weather turn ugly or the trail turn out to have lots of brush or poison oak.

Gaiters are also nice to have along, and some hikers wear them all the time. These cover from your shoe tops to just below the knees. They keep your feet and lower legs dry, especially when you are traveling through brushy or grassy areas that are often covered with dew or water from the last rain shower. Gaiters also keep snow and mud from crawling over the tops of your boots and getting your feet wet and uncomfortable.

The miracle fabrics discussed above have also done wonders for socks. Today's hi-tech hiking socks provide cushioning comfort while wicking moisture away from your feet to reduce the chance of blisters. I usually wear two pairs of socks. The first is a synthetic wool blend and the second is made of thick, cushy wool. With this system, and comfortable boots, I haven't had a blister in almost a decade of rugged hiking.

As for footwear, the debate about hiking boots versus lightweight shoes has gotten an amazing amount of attention in recent years. For decades, the standard advice was to wear heavy leather hiking boots to keep your feet dry and your ankles supported, and to protect your feet on rough wilderness trails. Proponents of super lightweight hiking, on the other hand, scoff at this advice and wouldn't hike in anything but comfortable running shoes. Today, you don't have to make this choice, because there are a whole range of lightweight hiking boots that rely on synthetic fabrics instead of heavy leather to keep water out. They also provide necessary traction, with soles designed to grip the ground. A good pair of these will meet your needs for most trails. If you are backpacking or traveling on particularly rough or muddy trails, however, you will probably want to rely on your tried-and-true leather boots.

Being Properly Equipped

Except when hiking on gentle trails in city parks, hikers should always carry a pack with certain essential items. The standard "Ten Essentials" have become well known. They are commonly listed as:

1) water-repellent coat
2) drinking water
3) extra food
4) pocket knife
5) waterproof matches
6) firestarter
7) first aid kit
8) flashlight
9) map
10) compass

I strongly advise adding a small plastic signaling whistle and a warm knit cap to this list.

Just carrying these items, however, doesn't make you "prepared." Unless you know things like how to apply basic first aid, how to build an emergency fire, and how to read a topographic map or use a compass, then carrying these items doesn't do you a bit of good. These skills are all fairly simple to learn and at least one member of your group should be familiar with all of them.

More important to your safety and enjoyment than any piece of equipment or clothing is exercising common sense. When you are far from civilization, a simple injury can be life-threatening. Don't take unnecessary chances. Never, for example, jump onto slippery rocks or logs, or crawl out onto dangerously steep slopes in the hope of getting a better view. Fortunately, the vast majority of wilderness injuries are easily avoidable.

Some Special Hazards

Sadly, venturing out into the natural world doesn't guarantee an escape from the problems of civilized life. Car break-ins and vandalism are regular occurrences at trailheads, so hikers need to take reasonable precautions. Don't encourage the criminals by providing unnecessary temptation. Leave your shiny new car at home and drive a beat-up older vehicle instead. Leave nothing of value in your car, and especially not in plain sight. My car has been broken into three times over the years. The last two times, the thieves only took home some pairs of ratty old tennis shoes, to which they were welcome. If all trailhead vehicles held only items of similar value, the criminals would soon seek out more lucrative targets.

In general, all water in the backcountry should be considered unsafe to drink. Dayhikers can carry all the water they need. Backpackers will have to purify the water. Boiling is the most effective way to kill the nasty little micro-organisms that cause the problems, but the simplest purification methods are filtering and chemical treatments like iodine.

A special hazard in the autumn is hunting season. Hikers need to advertise themselves with a bright red or orange cap, vest, pack, or other conspicuous article of clothing to avoid being mistaken for a suitable target. Hunting is prohibited in state and city parks and in some wildlife refuges. It is very popular, however, in state and national forests. Oregon's general deer-hunting season usually runs from the first weekend of October to early November. In Washington the season usually starts one week later and runs further into November. In both states, the elk-hunting season is in late October or early November.

Ticks are a minor annoyance in spring and early summer, especially in grassy or brushy areas and in the Columbia River Gorge. Ticks in other parts of the country often carry serious diseases such as Rocky Mountain spotted fever and Lyme disease. Fortunately, only a handful of cases have been reported in Oregon and Washington, so ticks here are more disgusting than dangerous. Still, it's wise to check your body and clothing regularly when in tick habitat, and to remove the little buggers quickly.

Also not terribly dangerous, but extremely bothersome, are mosquitoes. These annoying invertebrate vampires can be numerous enough to ruin your trip if you're not prepared with bug repellent, long pants, and a long-sleeve shirt. The flying blood suckers are most abundant around lower elevation marshes and near lakes and ponds in the Cascades. At low elevations, they are at their worst from spring to midsummer. At higher elevations, they peak for a period of about three weeks following the snowmelt at any given elevation.

Two other bits of common wisdom also deserve mention. The first is that you should never hike alone. This is probably good advice on rarely traveled wilderness trails, but I would never forego a trip just because I couldn't find a hiking partner. You can simply choose a more popular trail. These routes invariably have a fair number of other hikers around, so you're never really alone.

The second bit of advice is that you should let a responsible person know where you're going and when you expect to return. That will greatly aid in any search-and-rescue efforts, should they become necessary. If you stay on the trail and stick to popular areas, this caution may not be necessary, but it never hurts, and it's a good habit to develop.

Being a Good Neighbor

All hikers take with them a responsibility not only for their own safety, but for being good stewards of the natural environment. Be respectful of the land you are visiting, and leave it in the same condition as you found it. Common sense should make the following rules obvious: never litter; never pick wildflowers; never cut switchbacks; and never let your dog or children chase wildlife. Less obvious guidelines help not only to preserve the resource but to leave it in even better shape than before you arrived. One easy thing to do is to pick up any litter left by others. You should also do some minor trail maintenance as you hike by removing rocks, limbs, and debris from the path.

These rules are either common courtesy or carry the force of law: avoid disturbing other hikers and wildlife with shouts or any other unnatural sounds; leave all plants, mushrooms, logs, and even rocks where nature put them; do not damage or remove any item of historic or archeological interest, such as Native American vision-quest sites or pits, old trapper cabins , pottery, or arrowheads, since they are protected by federal law; stay on the trail and avoid trampling plants, especially delicate meadows and streamside locations that tend to draw crowds.

If you are backpacking, be especially scrupulous to follow the "no-trace" principles. Camp well away from water on an established site that won't be further damaged by your tent and your activity around camp. In wilderness areas, the rules generally require that all camps be at least 200 feet from any trail or water source. Leave the site in as natural a condition as possible. Avoid building a campfire and rely instead on a small backpacking stove to cook your food. Finally, deposit human waste in a small "cat hole" about 6 inches deep, then cover it.

Cliffs below summit of Hamilton Mountain, Washington

How to Use this Book

I HOPE THAT THIS BOOK WILL SERVE AS BOTH A FIELD REFERENCE AND A CATALYST FOR DREAMING ABOUT THE OUTDOORS. On those all-too-frequent dismal days of winter you can pick up this guide and read about the beautiful places you hope to enjoy as soon as the rain stops. You don't need any explanation for how to use a book for dreaming, so this section will focus on the best ways for using it as a planning tool and a field guide.

For hikers unfamiliar with our region and for outdoor veterans looking for new places to explore, I suggest that you start with the **Best Hikes** listing following the table of contents. Based on thousands of miles of hiking in and around Portland, this list gives the reader my recommendations for the best walks to see waterfalls, wildflowers, great views, and other attributes popular with hikers. Armed with this information, you can rapidly narrow down your options to a hike that meets your preferences. Keep in mind, however, that *every* trip in this book is worth hiking. Some may be better than others, but there isn't a dud in the lot, so you really can't go wrong.

After scenery, the second most important consideration of most hikers is location. This book covers only trails within a one-hour drive of the Portland/Vancouver area, so every hike is close enough for that spur-of-the-moment outing. To narrow things down even further, the trips have all been organized by their general geographic region (Coast Range, Columbia River Gorge, etc.). Each region begins with an overview map that shows the location of major highways, towns, and natural features. From there, individual hikes or hiking areas are covered by detail maps that show particular trails described in the text. The numbers on these maps correspond to the hike numbers in the text.

Each major hiking area includes a brief introduction giving information about the region's general character, terrain, and other notable features. More detailed information is available in the introductory paragraph for each hike.

Capsulized Summaries

Each hike begins with a summary chart giving you overview information that allows you to immediately see if the trip fits your current interests, your fitness level, and the time of year. Here is what each line in the summary tells you.

Distance

This is the total round-trip distance of the hike to the nearest 0.1 mile. For the few hikes that are recommended as one-way trips, the mileage is labeled accordingly.

Elevation Gain

This is the *total* (not the net) elevation gain for the round-trip hike. Once again, one-way hikes are specifically identified as such. Keep in mind that for most hikers the difficulty of a trail is determined at least as much by how far *up* they go as by simply how far they go.

Hiking Time

This is the approximate time it will take the average hiker to complete the round-trip hike. If a trip is recommended as a one-way adventure, it is so identified, and the hiking time will correspond to the one-way distance.

Optional Map

For many hikes, the map in this book will suffice for your trip. However, you may want to carry a contour map of the area to help pick out landmarks and to more closely follow your upward, or downward, progress. This entry identifies the best available contour map for each hike. In many areas the privately produced Green Trails maps are the best, because they are specifically designed for hikers, are reasonably up-to-date, and use an ideal scale for pedestrians. When USGS maps are recommended, the listed maps are in the 7.5' series.

Usually Open

This tells you when the trail is typically snow-free enough for hiking.

Best Times

This is my subjective judgment of the time(s) of year when a trip is at its best for hiking. In general, this will be when the flowers are at their peak, the fall colors at their best, the wildlife most abundant, and so on.

Agency

This refers to the government agency that manages the area covered by the hike. It never hurts to call ahead to the appropriate agency for the latest information about trail conditions, closures, regulations, etc. See Appendix B for a complete list of addresses and phone numbers for each agency.

Difficulty

This is an overall rating of how difficult this trip is relative to other hikes. The four categories use astericks to signal the relative difficulty of the trip.

* **Easy**. Relatively short hikes over gentle terrain. These trips are suitable for hikers of any age or ability.

** **Moderate**. Hikes of moderate length or short hikes that go over more difficult terrain. Most reasonably fit people should be able to take these hikes, although they may need to take several rest breaks.

*** **Difficult**.   Hikes that are a good workout for even fit hikers. They combine longer distances with a fair amount of elevation gain.

**** **Strenuous**. Very challenging hikes that are very long and/or cover rough terrain with great changes in elevation. Only very fit hikers should attempt these trips.

In general, each higher level represents a doubling of difficulty level. On average, trips with two astericks ** are twice as difficult as trips with one, and so on.

Cloudy Weather Options – ☁

Let's face it, the Portland/Vancouver area gets more than its share of gloomy, overcast days. Fortunately, you don't have to forego an enjoyable day on the trail just because the sun is hiding. Unlike viewpoint hikes, the forests, waterfalls, and other features of trips marked with a ☁ are just as good in the gloom as they are under clear skies.

Other Useful Information

Many hikers prefer loop trips, because they allow one to sample a greater variety of scenery on the hike. All hikes that are recommended as loop trips are so named.

Looking north from northern ridge of Silver Star Mountain, Washington

Every hike in this book follows either established trails or unmaintained hiking routes that are easy to navigate. The forests and thick undergrowth that cover virtually all of the Portland/Vancouver area make cross-country travel somewhere between very difficult and impossible. In general, off-trail routes should be left exclusively for very experienced travelers. The Portland/ Vancouver area has more than enough worthwhile destinations that can be reached by trail. There is no need to resort to bushwhacking.

Until recently, one joyful aspect of hiking was that it was an outdoor activity you could do for free: You didn't have to buy a fishing license, pay for a lift ticket, or even get expensive lessons. You could just drive or hitch a ride to the nearest trailhead and take off. Today, however, most public land agencies require that you pay a fee of some kind to use their trails. In the national forests, all cars parked within 0.25 mile of any trailhead must display a trailhead parking pass. In 2003, daily permits cost $5, and an annual pass, good in all the forests of Washington and Oregon, was $30. The permits can be purchased at all ranger stations and many sporting goods stores in the Portland area. Many, but not all, state parks also require that visitors pay an entrance fee, whether or not they are hiking. Finally, on Sauvie Island, the Oregon Department of Fish and Wildlife requires a day-use pass for hikers, bird-watchers, and all other users.

If you want to avoid paying for the privilege of going for a hike, then your options are more limited, but not zero. To date, anyway, state forests and most national wildlife refuges in Oregon and Washington do not charge fees. In addition, all city parks in the Portland area are free. You can also visit the less popular state parks, which generally don't charge a fee.

Trail bridge below Wahkeena Falls, Columbia Gorge, Oregon

Northern Oregon Coast Range

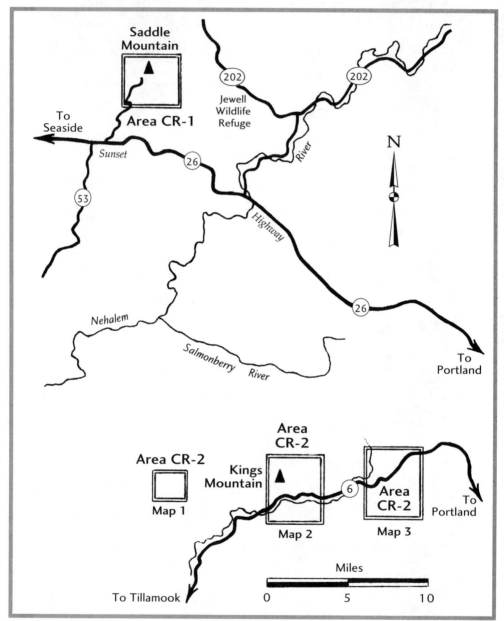

Northern Oregon Coast Range

Area CR-1: Sunset Highway Corridor

U.S. HIGHWAY 26, BETTER KNOWN AS THE SUNSET HIGHWAY, LEADS NORTHWEST FROM PORTLAND ON ITS WAY TO THE POPULAR COASTAL RESORTS OF SEASIDE AND CANNON BEACH. Before it reaches the Pacific Ocean, the road passes through a recreation area whose attractions aren't as well known as those along the coast but are still well worth exploring.

The Coast Range here is a rolling sea of second-growth forests that spreads across a contorted land of gnarled hills and stream canyons. Those streams support precious runs of steelhead and salmon, while Roosevelt elk wander the hills providing sport for hunters in the fall and viewing pleasure for visitors throughout the year. Sad to say, there are only a handful of trails. Most of the land is either privately owned or is in Clatsop State Forest, which has practically no maintained trails, so visitors in search of exercise must look for other options.

For a mustn't miss opportunity to see elk, visit the Jewell Wildlife Refuge off State Highway 202 about 10 miles north of the Sunset Highway. Nearby Fishhawk Falls provides a chance to stretch your legs, but since the unsigned path to it is only 0.2 mile long, it doesn't really qualify as a hike.

Two other short trails take off directly from Highway 26. One trail visits a small plaque marking the only spot in Oregon where four counties meet. The other is a nature-trail loop at the Sunset Rest Area that explores the logging history of the region. Neither of these paths is either long enough or interesting enough to be included in this book as a separate trip. Fortunately for the devoted pedestrian, there is at least one place in this area where you can go for a nice hike, and it's a doozy.

Trip 1

Saddle Mountain

(Map Area CR-1)

Distance	Elevation Gain	Hiking Time	Optional Map	Difficulty
6.1 miles	1700 feet	3.5 hours	None needed	***

Usually Open	March to November
Best Times	Late May to mid-June
Agency	Oregon State Parks – Tillamook Region

Saddle Mountain is undoubtedly the premier destination for pedestrians in the northern Oregon Coast Range. The open slopes near the top of this prominent landmark are home to a wide array of colorful wildflowers, including several rare species found virtually nowhere else in the world. But you don't have to be a botanist to enjoy this outing. Anyone who likes fine vistas will be thrilled with this hike because it provides the best views in this part of the state.

Directions: Drive U.S. Highway 26 to near milepost 10, about 65 miles west of downtown Portland. Turn north on the narrow paved road for Saddle Mountain State Park and drive 7.0 miles to its end at a parking area that serves both the trailhead and a small walk-in campground.

The popular path up Saddle Mountain starts at the east side of the parking lot and climbs gently through a thick forest of red alder and bigleaf maple. Head-high salmonberry bushes crowd the edges of the trail, giving it something of a tunnel-like feeling. After 0.2 mile a side trail leaves the main route to your right. Take the time to do this very worthwhile side trip, as it climbs to a small knoll with terrific views of Saddle Mountain from an angle that really shows how the mountain got its name.

Back on the main trail, you climb a series of irregularly spaced switchbacks through attractive woods of mixed conifers and deciduous trees. In several places you'll notice where other hikers have cut switchbacks, causing erosion and needlessly trampled vegetation. Please stick to the official route and don't add to the problem. Geology buffs will be fascinated by a prominent basalt dike a bit west of the trail at about the 1-mile point.

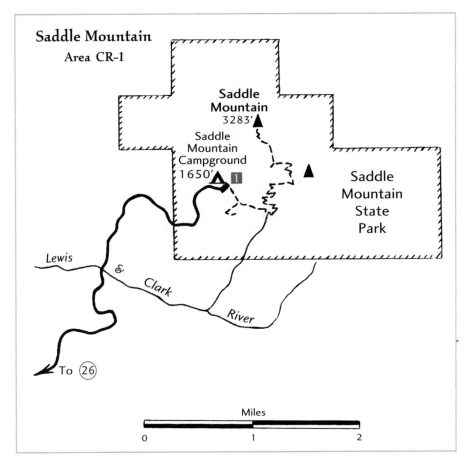

Continuing uphill, mostly in the shade of evergreens, you reach the wonderful meadows that cloak the upper slopes of the mountain. From March to September you can always enjoy at least some flowers here. The peak blooming season comes in early June, when a whole array of colors are there to enjoy, including blue larkspur and iris, red paintbrush, yellow buckwheat, and white chickweed.

Shortly before you reach the low point of Saddle Mountain's saddle, a path drops down a meadowy ridge to your left. A side trip here reveals outstanding views of the open, rounded slopes around the summit of Saddle Mountain, your next goal. To reach that goal, go across a narrow walkway through the mountain's saddle, then climb steeply up the final 0.4 mile on a rocky trail with poor footing. You can gain greater stability by hanging on to a cable handrail.

The view from the often windy summit includes Cascade snow peaks as far north as Washington's Mt. Rainier, the shimmering Pacific Ocean to the west, and even (with the aid of binoculars) the 125-foot-high Astoria Column on a hill in the town of the same name to the northwest. Return the way you came.

View west from Cedar Butte

The Coast Range

Area CR-2: Upper Wilson River

Unlike the virtually trail-free Clatsop State Forest to its north, the Tillamook State Forest has several options for putting miles on your hiking boots. A network of uncrowded hiking trails mounts steep ridges, wanders through attractive second-growth forests, and visits scenic waterfalls.

All this comes as something of a surprise to most Portland/Vancouver residents, who generally think of the Coast Range as nothing but hills covered with clearcuts. The range has the misfortune to be the best place in the world to grow evergreen trees, so the mountains have suffered centuries of abuse from logging. As a result, most outdoor lovers simply ignore this land, heading instead for the Cascade Mountains or the coast. The Tillamook State Forest is a real hidden treasure because it is virtually free of clearcuts. This circumstance is not due to magnanimous timber companies, but rather to a series of massive fires that occurred during the 1930s and 1940s. These fires blackened over 350,000 acres of productive timberland, sending up smoke clouds that were visible for hundreds of miles, and leaving behind a charred landscape with nothing standing but a few silver snags.

The massive replanting effort that followed this series of conflagrations has yet to produce trees large enough to harvest, so hikers can climb to viewpoints in this forest and look down on a green landscape free of the unnatural outlines of clearcuts. Wildlife has returned with the trees. Elk are now abundant, as are all the other animals that formerly roamed these hills. The often steep system of trails here visits most of the best that this area has to offer. It will delight hikers looking for a change from the usual destinations in the Columbia River Gorge and the Cascade Mountains.

Trip 1

Cedar Butte

(Map Area CR-2, Map 1)

Distance	Elevation Gain	Hiking Time	Optional Map	Difficulty
2.2 miles	750 feet	1 hour	*Tillamook State Forest*	**

Usually Open	Late March to November
Best Times	Late May to mid-June
Agency	Tillamook District (Tillamook State Forest)

Here is a chance to explore a part of the Coast Range that very few hikers ever visit. The rugged scenery in this part of the state will come as a welcome surprise to most Portland hikers, because the view from the summit doesn't include a single clearcut! Also of interest are the rock-garden wildflowers encountered atop the scenic ridges.

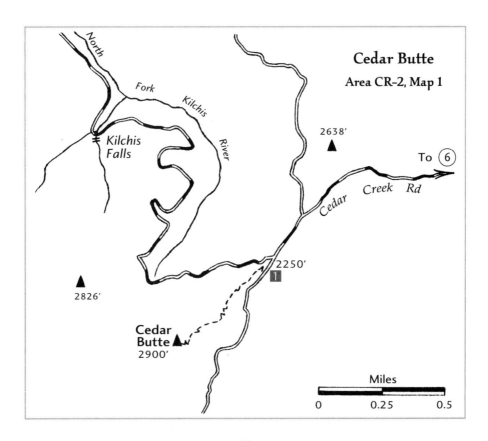

Directions: Drive west on State Highway 6 toward Tillamook. At milepost 22.6 (about 1.0 mile west of the small store at Lees Camp) turn right on North Fork Road at the sign for Jones Creek Campground. Go straight after 0.3 mile, now following gravel Cedar Creek Road. At a junction about 3.0 miles from Highway 6 keep straight on the main road and begin a very steep climb to a junction at a pass 6.5 miles from Highway 6. You bear slightly left and just 0.3 mile later reach a fork at a saddle below prominent Cedar Butte. The unsigned trailhead is about 100 yards down the left fork. Look for a sketchy path climbing diagonally up the roadcut.

The unmaintained footpath up Cedar Butte climbs along the top of a narrow ridge covered with young Douglas-fir. The ground cover, typical of mid-elevations in the Coast Range, is a mix of Oregon grape, sword fern, and salal. Like most Tillamook State Forest trails, there is nothing subtle about this path as it charges steeply up the ridge with a half dozen very short switchbacks providing only limited relief. Several confusing elk trails cross the route, but you can't go wrong by simply following the steepest way up the spine of the ridge. After 0.7 mile you level off on a rocky ridgecrest with lots of June-blooming beargrass and several species of smaller alpine wildflowers.

The climb isn't over yet. After a brief 50-foot drop, you resume the steep ascent on a semi-open hillside. The best route is often hard to determine, but it is impossible to get lost, because the goal, the top of Cedar Butte, is clearly in sight. The small flat spot you eventually reach situated atop Cedar Butte with its shattered bits of glass is the former site of a fire lookout.

Because the expansive view from this summit includes many unfamiliar landmarks, it's a good idea to bring along a contour map and a copy of the BLM Salem District—Westside map to help identify the convoluted assortment of jagged peaks and ridges.

Truly dedicated scramblers can continue west cross-country from Cedar Butte along the mostly open but very rugged ridge to reach more high viewpoints and rock gardens. Solitude is virtually guaranteed. After about 2 miles you will reach a deep little pass beyond which travel becomes impossible.

While in the area it's worth your time to check out the wispy 80-foot drop of Kilchis Falls. From the road junction near the trailhead, drive 2.1 miles down the right fork to where a tiny creek plummets over a sheer rock face just above the left side of the road.

Trip 2

Kings Mountain

(Map Area CR-2, Map 2)

Distance	Elevation Gain	Hiking Time	Optional Map	Difficulty
5.5 miles	2800'	3 hours	*Tillamook State Forest*	***

Usually Open	Late March to November
Best Times	Mid-May to mid-June
Agency	Forest Grove District (Tillamook State Forest)

If you take only one hike in the upper Wilson River drainage, make it the trail up Kings Mountain. The peak is one of the highest in the northern Oregon Coast Range, and the views from the open meadows atop its 3226-foot summit are terrific. On a clear day you can see not only the extensive green hills of the Coast Range, but also the Pacific Ocean and even distant snow peaks in the Cascades, including Mounts Hood and Jefferson. The advantage of this hike over neighboring Elk Mountain is that while the total elevation gain is greater, the grade, while still steep, is less exhausting and the trail is better maintained. Finally, the flowers are more abundant in the large meadows atop this peak, so you can luxuriate in views and in the smell and color of the blossoms.

Directions: Drive west from Portland on State Highway 6 toward Tillamook. Near milepost 25, look for the brown sign with a hiking figure on it, and the small trailhead parking lot for the Kings Mountain trailhead on the right.

Like so many other paths in western Oregon, this trail begins in a lush forest of Douglas-fir, western hemlock, and red alder whose branches are draped with mosses. The forest floor is covered with sword fern and a low carpet of oxalis and candyflower, both of which feature small white flowers in spring. Just 0.2 mile from the start is an unmarked but obvious junction with the Wilson River Trail, which forks off to the right (Trip 4).

To continue up to Kings Mountain, bear left and make an irregular but usually gentle climb through attractive woods. At first there are small creeks in the gullies on either side of the trail, but afterwards the trail is entirely dry. About 1 mile from the trailhead the forest gets drier and the slopes steeper as you begin to tackle the worst of the climb. As with all paths in this area, you will notice blue paint markings on the trees along the route. These aren't really necessary, as the trail is obvious throughout. The uphill climb is uneventful (and unrelenting) except near the 2000-foot level. There you'll find two places where the path stays nearly level for a couple of hundred yards as it follows sections of very old roads that seem to come from nowhere and end for no apparent reason.

Fairly steep climbing eventually leads you to a picnic table right beside the trail, just 0.3 mile from the top. You can stop here for a rest, but save your longer lunch break for the very top, where the view is far superior. The final climb to the summit is quite steep in some sections, with loose gravel that can be a bit dangerous on the way back down. On the plus side, most of the final 0.2 mile is a joyous route through open meadows that are ablaze with wildflowers in early June.

Very adventurous hikers can continue this hike over the rugged path that connects Kings Mountain with Elk Mountain to the east. For a description of this difficult route, see Trip 3.

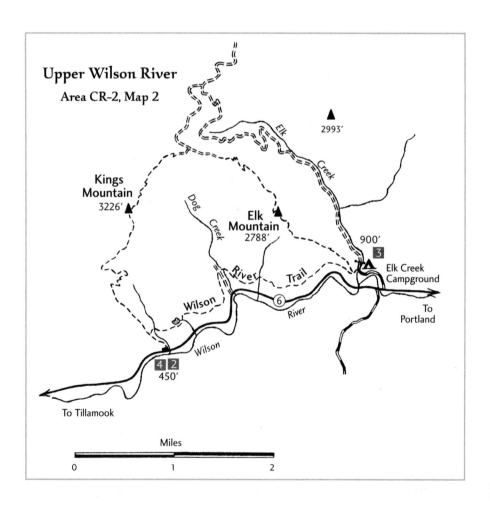

Upper Wilson River

Area CR-2, Map 2

Trip 3

Elk Mountain Loop

(Map Area CR-2, Map 2)

Distance	Elevation Gain	Hiking Time	Optional Map	Difficulty
8.5 miles	2500'	4 to 5 hours	*Tillamook State Forest*	***
(shorter loop)	(shorter loop)	(shorter loop)		

Usually Open	Late March to November
Best Times	Mid-May to mid-June
Agency	Forest Grove District (Tillamook State Forest)

All your hard work on that stairmaster at home will come in handy on this thigh buster. The trail up Elk Mountain is short, but it's brutally steep. Fortunately, the flower show is excellent, and inviting views stretch over hundreds of square miles of hills and valleys. Be aware that this trail can be treacherous, especially downhill, because of loose gravel and extremely slippery mud. Boots with good traction are a necessity. There is no drinking water along the route, and since you will do a lot of sweating, you'll need to carry at least two quarts of water on a hot day.

Directions: Drive west on State Highway 6 toward Tillamook. Near milepost 28, turn right on the well-marked gravel access road to Elk Creek Campground. The trailhead is at the end of this 0.3-mile road, just after you cross a bridge over Elk Creek.

The trail starts with a moderately steep climb of 0.1 mile in mixed coniferous and deciduous forest to a junction at a saddle. The path going straight is the newly constructed Wilson River Trail (Trip 4). For Elk Mountain you turn right on a trail marked with a large blue dot painted on a tree. The path climbs steeply, sometimes through red-alder and Douglas-fir forests, but mostly up open, rocky areas on the spine of a narrow ridge. The views are frequent and superb, especially looking down the Wilson River Canyon and up to the ramparts of Elk Mountain. Flowers are numerous in May and June. Look for starflower, salal, paintbrush, lomatium, wild rose, thimbleberry, and a host of others.

At several points this ridgetop route loses elevation, but it is quickly regained. Steep climbs are the hike's dominant feature. The terrain is very wild, although you never fully escape the sounds of well-traveled Highway 6, almost directly below.

The route continues to resemble going the wrong way on a very steep downhill ski run, until the 2500-foot level. Here you level off a bit and pass a small, waterless camp, then traverse the west side of a rocky spine. Another

View of Kings Mountain from north ridge of Elk Mountain

series of steep uphills and open ridgetop viewpoints finally take you to a small open spot atop 2788-foot Elk Mountain. As expected, the views are terrific, for the most photogenic look west to craggy Kings Mountain. In early June wildflowers abound, including penstemon, lupine, arnica, beargrass, paintbrush, and Washington lily.

You can turn around here and return the way you came, but if you aren't exhausted from the climb, there are two loop options you might consider. Both loops begin by dropping very steeply down a trail on the northwest side of Elk Mountain. This path, appropriately marked with signs stating CAUTION—STEEP AREAS, is narrow, challenging, and rugged. Subtlety was clearly not the goal of the trail builders, as they scornfully bypassed obvious opportunities for gentle sidehill traverses, opting instead for dangerous routes along the up-and-down, knife-edge ridge. Fortunately, these difficulties end within a mile, as you hit an old road that wanders pleasantly through shady forests. This overgrown road is also well-traveled by wildlife, as frequent elk droppings and piles of bear scat attest. You make several short and gentle uphill switchbacks, then follow a view-packed ridge crest to a saddle and an unmarked T-junction with another closed road.

For the shorter loop, turn right at the saddle and in just 0.4 mile you reach a junction with the road leading back down to Elk Creek Campground. This old logging road often runs near Elk Creek, whose clear, cascading waters are a nice diversion from the otherwise rather monotonous red-alder forest. The total length of this shorter loop is about 8.5 miles.

More athletic hikers looking for a real challenge can turn left at the T-junction and head west to Kings Mountain. This longer loop initially follows a closed road, which soon turns to trail and gets fairly nasty. You must negotiate about 1 mile of very steep ups and downs as you skirt the north side of some sheer cliffs and rock pinnacles. Expect to use your hands and probably your backside from time to time, to safely negotiate this section. As compensation for your efforts, exceptional views to the north are frequent and flowers are abundant. In addition to the previously mentioned species, look for wallflower, phlox, larkspur, clover, stonecrop, bunchberry, and dandelion. Finally, the rough scramble eases off, as you enter the gorgeous open meadows atop Kings Mountain.

From here, the loop follows the trail down from Kings Mountain (Trip 2) and returns to Elk Creek Campground via the Wilson River Trail (Trip 4). The total length of this very difficult loop is 12.0 miles. Since there are no reasonable campsites along the way, the loop must be completed in one day.

Trip 4

Wilson River Trail

(Map Area CR-2, Map 2)

Distance	Elevation Gain	Hiking Time	Optional Map	Difficulty
3.4 miles (one way)	700' (one way)	1.5 hours (one way)	*Tillamook State Forest*	**

Usually Open	All year (except during winter storms)
Best Times	April to June / Mid to late October
Agency	Forest Grove District (Tillamook State Forest)

This newly constructed path provides a welcome link allowing hikers to make a challenging loop hike that connects Kings and Elk mountains (Trips 2 & 3). As a separate hike, this lower-elevation trail is a pleasant leg-stretcher with attractive forests, several splashing creeks, and some nice viewpoints. Since it is at such a low elevation, this trail provides a nice alternative for hikers looking for a scenic place to walk in early spring or even midwinter, although the path will be muddy then.

To do this hike as a one-way trip, it is better to begin from Elk Creek, as that involves a total elevation loss of about 400 feet. As part of the Kings and Elk mountains loop trip, however, it is more likely that you will do this trail from the Kings Mountain end, so that is the way it is described here.

Directions: Drive west on State Highway 6 toward Tillamook. Near milepost 25, look for the brown sign with the hiker on it and the parking lot for the Kings Mountain trailhead on the right. For the upper trailhead at Elk Creek, turn north off Highway 6 near milepost 28 and drive the gravel access road to Elk Creek Campground for 0.3 mile to its end just beyond a bridge over Elk Creek.

The Kings Mountain Trail begins in a lush forest of Douglas-fir, western hemlock, and red alder most of whose branches are covered with hanging mosses. Just 0.2 mile from the start is an unsigned but obvious junction. The Kings Mountain Trail veers off to the left, while the Wilson River Trail goes to the right.

The trail almost immediately hops over a small creek, then begins the gentle ascent that will dominate the entire route. An abundance of vine maple in the understory makes this section particularly attractive in mid-to-late October. The path goes around the south side of a small pond and marshy area, then crosses the outlet creek for the marsh. There was no bridge in the summer of 2000, but a bridge is planned.

As you hike you will probably see the knobby tire tracks of mountain bikes and the paired crescents of deer hooves. You may also see the makers of these tracks, the former more common on weekends, the latter on quiet weekdays. As for sounds, in addition to birds and wind in the trees, you will often hear traffic on Highway 6 to the right, but the noise is never terribly intrusive.

Beyond the pond you make an extended contour of a forested hillside above the road, then dip into a canyon to cross a jeep road and rock-hop across good-sized Dog Creek. Two switchbacks and more climbing now lead you to a rocky, open hillside above the highway. As you hike, keep an eye out for large, old stumps, many still showing where loggers cut slots for springboards. The daring woodsmen then stood on the precarious springboards so they could cut higher on the tree trunk.

The rest of this easy trail alternates between forested hillsides overlooking the road and small side canyons with trickling creeks that provide opportunities to cool off by dunking your head. The trail ends with a short climb to a saddle where there is a poorly marked junction with the Elk Mountain Trail. You continue straight and drop a few hundred yards to the Elk Creek Trailhead.

Trip 5

Southern Gales Creek Trail & University Falls

(Map Area CR-2, Map 3)

Distance	Elevation Gain	Hiking Time	Optional Map	Difficulty
4.2 miles (combined)	800' (combined)	2 hours	*Tillamook State Forest*	**

⌂

Usually Open	All year (except during winter storms)
Best Times	April to mid-June
Agency	Forest Grove District (Tillamook State Forest)

For a comprehensive history of Oregon's Coast Range forests you can't do any better than the Gales Creek Trail. For countless centuries the trees here grew undisturbed, reaching sizes that boggle the mind. Sadly, none of these magnificent giants remain, but you will pass many old stumps testifying to the grandeur of the forests that once covered these hills. In many of those stumps you will see evidence of the loggers who brought an end to these great trees, in the form of slots that these hardy workmen cut to support their springboards, allowing them to cut through the tree farther above the ground.

More history is embodied in the trail itself. A short part of the route follows an abandoned logging railroad, an example of the transportation of choice for rugged Pacific Northwest lumbermen. Later history is demonstrated by fire-scarred snags that still stand following the historic Tillamook Burn fires of the 1930s and 1940s. After these fires, a replanting effort of equally historic proportions replaced the lost trees, so that now a healthy, second-growth forest covers these hills.

All in all, the perceptive hiker will find this to be an interesting lesson in history. For those not interested in history, the hike is still an enjoyable outing through an attractive Coast-Range forest.

The Gales Creek Trail ends at Rogers Pass. Beyond this point you can connect with an intricate network of roads and trails south of the pass. These routes explore the second-growth forest and cross pretty little creeks, so you might expect that this easily accessible area would provide good hiking opportunities. Sadly, it doesn't because this is also a major playground for off-road enthusiasts. Even on rainy days in midwinter it is impossible to escape the noise of ATVs. If you visit on a summer weekend, earplugs are essential equipment. Not only is peace and quiet impossible, the machines also rip the trails into a muddy mess.

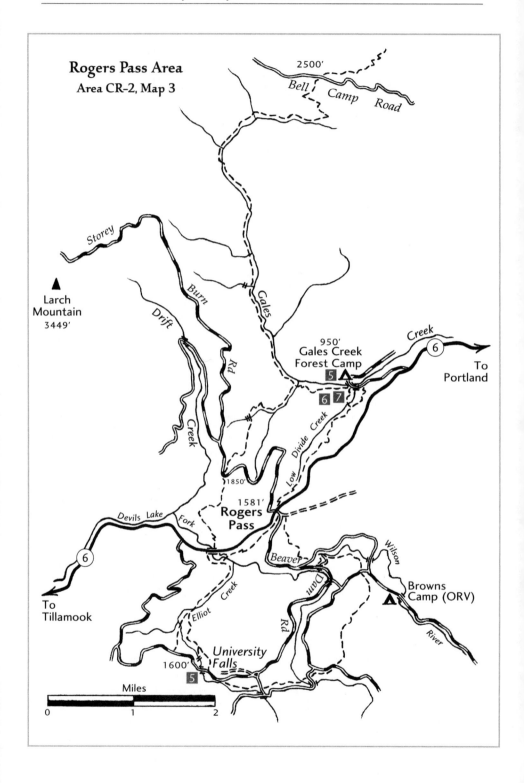

Rogers Pass Area
Area CR-2, Map 3

2500'

Bell   Camp   Road

Storey

▲
Larch
Mountain
3449'

Burn

Drift

Gales

Rd

Creek

Creek
⑥

950'
Gales Creek
Forest Camp
5 ▲

6 7

To
Portland

Low   Divide Creek

1850'

1581'
**Rogers
Pass**

Devils Lake   Fork

Beaver

Wilson

6

Elliot   *Creek*

Dam

Rd

Browns
Camp (ORV)
▲

To
Tillamook

River

1600'
*University
Falls*
5

Miles
0   1   2

Stump with old springboard hole

Fortunately, many of the former multiple-use trails have now been closed to vehicles, and new routes carved out of the forest for the ATVs. By and large the trail closures are respected by the two- and four-wheeled terrors, but I still cannot recommend hiking beyond Rogers Pass for anyone who values peace and quiet.

The Gales Creek Trail is one of the routes that is closed to motor vehicles and is in a quieter area that provides a respite from the noise. While you are in the area, however, you should at least take the opportunity to visit University Falls, a spectacular destination that is worth at least some aggravation. By driving to the University Falls trailhead, just 0.2 mile from the falls, you will bypass the worst of the race-track cacophony.

Directions: Drive west on State Highway 6 toward Tillamook. Just before you reach milepost 35, turn right on the well-signed road to Gales Creek Forest Camp. After 1 mile you come to the trailhead on the left side of the road just before a culvert spanning Low Divide Creek. This campground is closed in winter, so in the off season you will either have to walk the gated access road or start this hike from Rogers Pass.

To reach the University Falls trailhead, continue west on Highway 6 to Rogers Pass and turn left (south) on gravel Beaver Dam Road, following signs for Browns Camp. In just 100 yards you turn right at a junction, following signs for University Falls trailhead. At 0.7 mile and 1.2 miles, you bear right at two Y-junctions, in both cases following signs for University Falls trailhead. After another 1.5 miles you bear right at a final Y-junction, although this one lacks a sign, and drive 0.7 mile to the small trailhead on the right.

From Gales Creek Forest Camp the trail of the same name climbs a woodsy hillside to join a short section of an old logging railroad. With careful analysis you may even be able to pick out the regular moss-covered bumps of the old railroad ties in the middle of the trail.

You soon leave this gentle section in favor of a roller-coaster route that follows the hillside above rollicking Low Divide Creek. At 0.2 mile from the trailhead, you go straight at a junction, then cross several marshy areas and seasonal creeklets, usually employing boardwalks for this purpose. In April, expect to see lots of blooming skunk cabbage in these boggy areas. The large yellow blossoms of these plants almost offset the impact of their unpleasant odor.

In general, the forest is a nice mix of Douglas-fir, western red cedar, and western hemlock on the hillside, with red alders dominating the wet areas near the creek. The most abundant plants on the forest floor are salal and sword fern. The trail itself is less pleasant than the surrounding forest, because the clay soils are often very slippery when wet. Even boots have a hard time providing a good grip, so bring a walking stick.

The last third of the hike is a consistent uphill that winds away from the creek and makes a moderately steep climb in a few short switchbacks to the small gravel parking area just east of Rogers Pass on Highway 6.

If you decide to tack on a visit to University Falls, return to your car and drive to the University Falls trailhead as described above. The 0.2-mile footpath begins by climbing briefly, then it crosses two ATV tracks and begins to descend. At the bottom of a short descent is a junction beside a horse hitching post.

From here you turn left and walk about 100 yards to the base of University Falls. This 100-foot cascade is most impressive in winter and spring when the water is high, but it is worth a visit even in late summer when the falls are only a trickle.

Blooming rhododendron near Mt. Jefferson, Oregon

Trip 6

Central Gales Creek Trail

(Area CR-2, Map 3)

Distance	Elevation Gain	Hiking Time	Optional Map	Difficulty
10.1 miles	1200'	4 to 6 hours	*Tillamook State Forest*	**

Usually Open	All year (except during and shortly after winter storms)
Best Times	April to June
Agency	Forest Grove District (Tillamook State Forest)

This new trail is not yet known to most Portland area hikers, but it's bound to draw more admirers as word spreads about this attractive and relatively easy creekside ramble through the second-growth forests of the Tillamook State Forest. **Note:** Despite heavy rainfall, this is a good winter hike, because the tread drains well and remains in good shape with relatively few mud problems.

Directions: Drive west on State Highway 6 toward Tillamook. Just before you reach milepost 35, turn right on the well-signed gravel road to Gales Creek Forest Camp. After about 1 mile, pull into the day-use parking area on the left just before the road crosses a bridge over Gales Creek. **Warning:** This campground is closed from November to May when a gate blocks the access road from Highway 6. The gate is sometimes open during the off season, but even if it is, DO NOT drive through it—it may close at any time without warning.

Take the Gales Creek Trail to the right (north) from the parking area and begin a slow steady climb. For the next 0.7 mile you travel across a hillside about 50 feet above Gales Creek generally staying near the transition line between the second-growth coniferous forests on the slopes above you and the alder woodlands near the stream. The forest floor beneath these trees is covered with a dense mat of sword fern, which grows so profusely it forces out nearly all other understory species.

After 0.8 mile you will take a narrow log bridge over an unnamed side creek, then immediately reach a junction with the Storey Burn Trail (see Trip 7). Turn right and travel up and down on a trail that alternately hugs 15-foot-wide Gales Creek or traverses the woodsy hillside above the water. Much of the time the trail follows an old road, long since abandoned and now just a wide, well-graded trail. A little over 1 mile from the Storey Burn junction, the trail crosses a small side creek. Look left to see a 20-foot-tall, sliding waterfall.

The author on a log bridge over Gales Creek, Oregon

Falls along Gales Creek Trail,
Tillamook State Park, Oregon

In winter or early spring when the water runs high and the waterfall is not obscured by foliage, it's at its best.

The forest scenery remains unchanged as you continue up the canyon of Gales Creek for another mile to a sturdy log bridge that takes you over the creek. After another 0.5 mile, you come to a second log bridge and cross the flow again. As it slowly gains elevation, the trail goes over several side creeks. Quaint wooden bridges sometimes convey you, but more often you simply hop over. Although these side creeks are small, they make up a large percentage of Gales Creek's volume, so the main stream gets noticeably smaller as you continue up the canyon.

Near the 4.5-mile point, you pass a nice campsite after which the creek and accompanying trail curve to the east and the canyon narrows. The ascent now gets more strenuous as the grade becomes moderately steep. Just beyond the 5-mile point, Gales Creek has diminished to the point where it barely deserves to be called a creek. Here the trail pulls away from the water to ascend a woodsy hillside. Most hikers will want to turn around here, because the scenery is less interesting away from the creek. If you prefer to make this a longer one-way hike, however, stay on the trail as it climbs another mile to a wide, forested ridgeline where it crosses remote Bell Camp Road. The trail then descends a final 2 miles to a developed trailhead on the Cochran Road, just a few miles west of the town of Timber.

Trip 7

Storey Burn Loop

(Area CR-2, Map 3)

Distance	Elevation Gain	Hiking Time	Optional Map	Difficulty
8.1 miles	1500'	4 hours	*Tillamook State Forest*	***

☁

Usually Open	March to December
Best Times	May and June
Agency	Forest Grove District (Tillamook State Forest)

This accessible hike is a welcome addition to the rapidly developing system of hiking and biking trails in Tillamook State Forest. Although less attractive than the route along Gales Creek, which starts from the same trailhead, this circuit gives you a better workout and views from the wooded ridges north of Rogers Pass.

Directions: Drive west on State Highway 6 toward Tillamook. Just before you reach milepost 35, turn right on the well-signed gravel road to Gales Creek Forest Camp. After about 1 mile, pull into the day-use parking lot on the left just before the road crosses a bridge over Gales Creek. **Note:** This campground is closed from November to May when a gate blocks the access road from Highway 6. If you are hiking in the off season, start at the busier Summit Trailhead on the east side of Rogers Pass another 2 miles up Highway 6 from the Gales Creek turnoff.

For a counterclockwise loop, take the Gales Creek Trail to the right (north) from the parking area and begin a slow steady climb. After traversing the woodsy hillside above Gales Creek for 0.8 mile, a narrow log bridge will take you over an unnamed side creek. You immediately reach a junction with the Storey Burn Trail.

Turn left (uphill) and begin a steady climb that keeps pace with the small cascading creek on your left. You travel through second-growth forests composed of the usual Coast Range mix of Douglas-fir, western hemlock, western red cedar, bigleaf maple, and alder. Although the forest canopy is quite dense in places, it allows ample sunshine to reach the forest floor in order to support a thick growth of sword fern and Oregon grape. About 1 mile after starting on the Storey Burn Trail, you splash across a small creek right beside a pretty, stair-step waterfall—a great place for a leisurely rest stop. Above this point the trail slowly winds uphill through a partially logged area to a junction with the gravel Storey Burn Road.

To relocate the trail, find a dirt jeep track directly opposite where you hit the road; walk 80 yards up this track to the large gravel parking lot for the little-used Storey Burn Trailhead. Your signed trail loop continues on the west side of this parking lot.

The Storey Burn Trail now travels gently up and down for 0.5 mile taking you past forest openings offering good views of heavily forested Larch Mountain to the north and the upper reaches of the Wilson River Canyon to the west. Past these openings the well-graded trail winds down through attractive woods to Highway 6. You avoid the traffic by crossing under a tall road bridge. About 0.2 mile later is a signed junction with an ATV trail.

Go straight. For the next 0.3 mile you cross the flats beside Devils Lake Fork Wilson River. These often-muddy flats are covered with a tangle of mixed deciduous trees. Look for the tracks of elk, deer, raccoon, and black bear. After leaving the flats, the trail climbs a hillside for 0.1 mile to a junction. Turn left (uphill) taking a wide and noisy ATV route for 0.5 mile to Highway 6, where there is a large Oregon State Highway Department facility at Rogers Pass. **Note:** A quieter foot trail paralleling this ATV route is being planned and will make this short walk more pleasant. After you hike around the highway facility, go 300 yards east along the shoulder of the busy highway to a large gravel pullout signed as the SUMMIT TRAILHEAD.

The trail angles down from this pullout and drops fairly steeply for 0.4 mile through relatively dense woods. When the reddish-orange clay becomes wet—a depressingly high percentage of the time in this rainforest—it is difficult for hikers to maintain their dignity on the slippery surface. After the steep section ends, the trail goes up and down (mostly down) beside small Low Divide Creek for another 1.3 miles to a signed junction. Either direction will take you back to Gales Creek Forset Camp; the most direct route is to the one on the left. This trail soon crosses a wooden bridge over Low Divide Creek, then continues another 200 yards back to the day-use parking lot and your car.

Falls along Storey Burn Trail, Tillamook State Park, Oregon

Southwest Washington

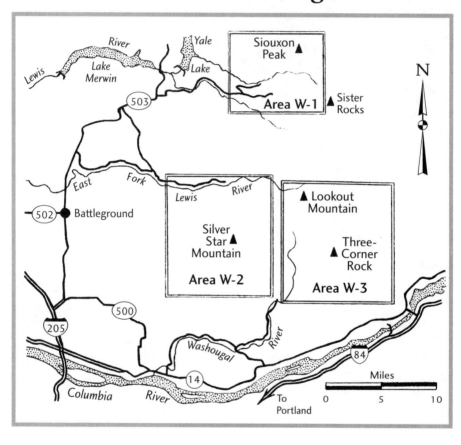

Southwest Washington

Area W-1: Siouxon Creek Area

SIOUXON CREEK (PRONOUNCED SOO-SON) FEEDS INTO THE LOWER END OF YALE LAKE AND IS A MAJOR TRIBUTARY OF THE LEWIS RIVER. The most notable thing about this stream, however, is that its deep canyon is the only major unlogged basin in this part of the Washington Cascades. Most of the trees are second growth, although not as a result of logging. Rather, fires in the early twentieth century led to a naturally renewed forest.

More enchanting than the forests, however, are the creeks. The crystal-clear waters splash over gentle riffles, pause in quiet eddies, drop over scenic waterfalls, and slide through slot canyons, all of which adds up to a superbly scenic hiking experience.

If forests and waterfalls aren't your cup of tea, then you can also make the stiff climb from the canyon bottom up to Huffman Peak, where you'll enjoy wonderful perspectives of nearby Mt. St. Helens.

The area provides something for just about every category of outdoor lover: There are opportunities for anglers along the stream; backpackers find joyous camps perfect for a quiet night in the woods; mountain bikers use the lower trail for scenic one-track riding; families with children saunter along the easy canyon trails, while hard-core hikers get a real workout on steep viewpoint paths; and photographers find plenty to keep themselves occupied. All this is in an easily accessible little paradise with paved-road access all the way to the trailhead.

Trip 1

Huffman Peak Loop

(Map Area W-1)

Distance	Elevation Gain	Hiking Time	Optional Map	Difficulty
14.5 miles	3000'	7 to 8 hours	*Green Trails – Lookout Mountain*	***

Usually Open	May to October
Best Times	Mid-June
Agency	Wind River Ranger District (Gifford-Pinchot National Forest)

So you've come to the Siouxon Creek area and you say that the Siouxon Creek Trail, while beautiful, just doesn't provide enough exercise. Well, there's another worthy option here for athletic hikers looking to pump up that heart rate. The climb to Huffman Peak will satisfy the cardiovascular needs of the most avid hiker and has the added benefit of providing a first-rate view of Mt. St. Helens.

By making a loop out of the trip and returning on the Siouxon Creek Trail, you won't even miss the waterfalls and forests that are the area's main attraction. In addition to strong lungs and thighs, this hike requires an unusual piece of equipment—a pair of wading shoes. You'll need them to make the bridgeless lower crossing of Siouxon Creek.

Directions: Begin by driving to Battleground, either by going north on State Highway 503 from Interstate 205, or by going east on State Highway 502 from exit 9 off Interstate 5. From the intersection of the two state highways in the middle of Battleground, proceed north on Highway 503 for 16.8 miles and turn right on N.E. Healy Road just after you pass the Mt. St. Helens National Volcanic Monument headquarters.

After 9.2 miles on N.E. Healey Road, bear left at a poorly signed junction and travel on single-lane, paved Forest Road 57. Drive another 1.3 miles, then turn sharply left on often unsigned Forest Road 5701. Follow this rough, paved road for 3.7 miles to its end at a trailhead parking lot.

View of Mt. St. Helens from Huffman Peak, Washington

The trail departs near a large signboard about 100 yards west of the parking area. You hike just 50 feet and turn left (west) at a signed junction. For the next couple of miles you follow an easy trail that parallels the road, staying some distance below it in a lovely western-hemlock forest. Along the way you splash across three small side creeks that won't even get the tops of your boots wet, but which provide enough water to satisfy an array of riparian plants like devils club and maiden-hair fern.

After 1.9 miles the trail splits, and you go right on a path that winds steadily downhill for 0.2 mile to a good camp beside a ford of Siouxon Creek. This is where you need to break out the wading shoes. The stream is about

30 feet wide and calf-to-thigh deep, depending on the season. The ford isn't particularly dangerous, but until late summer you can expect it to be chilly.

Pick up the trail above a little gravel bar on the opposite bank and quickly climb away from the water. The trail uses several short switchbacks and a couple of fairly steep traverses to reach the rounded crest of a forested ridge.

This forest is a good example of the succession process that takes place at low elevations of the western Cascades. The high canopy of the forest is made up of tall Douglas-firs, while beneath this canopy grow shade-tolerant western hemlocks. If this forest manages to avoid logging or fires for the next couple of centuries, the firs will die and the hemlocks will take over as the climax species. But since you don't have time to wait for this process to take place, pick up your pack and push on northeast up the ridge.

For almost a mile the going is very easy as you stay level or gradually climb in a dense forest, then the uphill grade picks up a little as you climb near the southern edge of the rim. Along the way you often come to open areas where you have to push through thickets of Oregon grape and salal, but which give you frequent views over the deep, green depths of the Siouxon Creek drainage. The trail gets steeper as it works away from the rim and traverses the heavily wooded north side of the ridge. This steeper grade lasts for almost 1 mile before you level off and contour across the ridge's south side. As you go higher, wildflowers become more common, especially lupine, beargrass, bunchberry, and white anemone. When the uphill finally ends, the trail curves to the left and crosses a partly forested slope with lots of huckleberries and good views east to Huffman Peak, then you come to a saddle and a junction with the North Siouxon Trail.

If you are up for a cross-country scramble, take the time from this saddle to visit the top of Huffman Peak. The climb initially goes through forests, then up an open rocky slope. The way is often steep and requires some rock scrambling, but it is not dangerous. The reward for this effort comes in the form of extensive views from the rocky summit. Several roads and clearcuts spoil things a bit, but the fine views of massive Mt. Rainier, truncated Mt. St. Helens, and bulky Mt. Adams more than make up for it.

After returning to the main trail at the saddle, you turn east and traverse the steep slopes on the shady north side of Huffman Peak. The trail goes through the saddle east of the peak, then stays level or goes gradually downhill for a little less than a mile before reaching a small brown sign marking the junction with Wildcat Trail 156.

The recommended loop turns sharply back to the right here, climbing very steeply for a few hundred yards to the top of a viewless knoll, then descending a little ridge to the south. The downhill along this ridge is gentle for most of the first 0.5 mile, but as the little ridge peters out, the pace of the descent quickens. A few miniature switchbacks help somewhat, but generally you steeply descend the forested hillside. For a short time the pace lessens as the ridge reappears, but this respite is followed by nine very steep switchbacks. You know you are near the bottom when you start to hear the sound of crashing Wildcat Falls, in the canyon on your left, and come to a rocky overlook above the falls. From this viewpoint the trail descends six more switch-backs to a stunning viewpoint near the base of the falls' 100-foot sheer drop. From here the trail follows the creek downstream for 0.2 mile to a junction just above Siouxon Creek.

The trail to the right goes down 50 yards to a knee-deep ford of Siouxon Creek. Since you still have those wading shoes, this ford should be no problem. A short distance up the south bank is a campsite and a junction with the Siouxon Creek Trail. If you want to extend the trip a bit, bear left at the junction on the north side of Siouxon Creek, hop across Wildcat Creek, and then climb upstream for 0.5 mile through lovely forests to a junction with the Chinook Trail. Bear right (downhill) and drop to a rockhop crossing just below 50-foot-high Chinook Falls. To close out the loop, walk downstream past a couple of campsites and across a wooden bridge over Siouxon Creek. Turn right at a junction on the opposite side of the bridge and walk 3.7 miles along the scenic Siouxon Creek Trail back to your car.

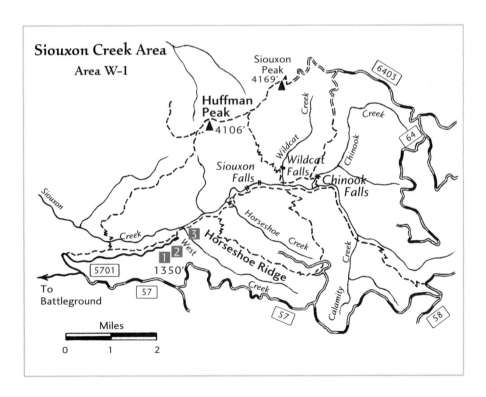

Trip 2

Siouxon Creek Trail

(Map Area W-1)

Distance	Elevation Gain	Hiking Time	Optional Map	Difficulty
7.6 miles	700'	3.5 to 4 hours	*Green Trails –* *Lookout Mountain*	**

Usually Open	March to November
Best Times	Mid-May to mid-June
Agency	Wind River Ranger District
	(Gifford-Pinchot National Forest)

This is the premier hike in the Siouxon Creek drainage. There are no grand viewpoints, but the glories of two Pacific Northwest trademarks, forests and streams, are nowhere on better display than here. A cloudy day is as good as a clear one, because the forests and waterfalls are spectacular even in the gloom.

Directions: Begin by driving to Battleground, either by going north on State Highway 503 from Interstate 205, or by going east on State Highway 502 from exit 9 off Interstate 5. From the intersection of the two state highways in the middle of Battleground, proceed north on Highway 503 for 16.8 miles and turn right on N.E. Healy Road just after you pass the Mt. St. Helens National Volcanic Monument headquarters.

After 9.2 miles on N.E. Healey Road, bear left at a poorly signed junction and travel on single-lane, paved Forest Road 57. Drive another 1.3 miles, then turn sharply left on often unsigned Forest Road 5701. Follow this rough, paved road for 3.7 miles to its end at a trailhead parking lot.

The trail departs from the north side of the lot and drops 50 feet to an intersection with the Siouxon Creek Trail. You turn right and descend through a lovely forest composed predominantly of western hemlocks. On the forest floor are lots of downed nurse logs, mosses, sword fern, and oxalis. After 0.1 mile of downhill, you reach the creek bottom and cross West Creek on a flat-topped log bridge. The walls of the lush side canyon holding this creek are draped with mosses and ferns. Immediately after the bridge, you pass the first of many excellent creekside campsites. After this camp, the trail travels in small ups and downs, gradually making its way uphill but staying about 50 feet above the clear waters of Siouxon Creek. About 0.9 mile from the trailhead is the signed junction with the Horseshoe Ridge Trail (Trip 3).

The Siouxon Creek Trail goes straight and does a series of small ups and downs, alternating between creek-level flats covered with a tangle of jungle-like vegetation, and hillsides sprouting tall cedars, firs, and hemlocks. Several tiny tributary creeks cross the trail, providing ample water for plants like devils club and salmonberry. You cross Horseshoe Creek on a plank bridge just above lacy Horseshoe Creek Falls and, about 100 yards later, come to a junction with a 180-yard spur trail to a viewpoint at the base of the falls.

About 0.2 mile after Horseshoe Creek Falls is a camp with a little wooden bench where you can sit and enjoy a classic view of nearby Siouxon Falls, a twisting cataract with a deep swimming hole at its base. A short distance further upstream is a smaller waterfall with an equally good but not-as-popular swimming hole. At both locations the water is very cold. As you continue hiking on this lovely path, you pass numerous unsigned side trails leading to terrific campsites and lunch spots that are perfect places for the kids to play or for adults to quietly contemplate nature.

About 0.8 mile above Siouxon Falls is the unsigned junction with the upper end of the Horseshoe Ridge Trail bearing uphill to the right. You stay straight on the lower path and walk 0.7 mile to a second junction right next to a bridge. The official Siouxon Creek Trail continues straight, reaching Forest Road 58 in about 4.5 miles. A more attractive route turns left and crosses the bridge above a deep pool of water. You then climb past two excellent camps and follow Chinook Creek upstream to the base of Chinook Falls, a 50-foot drop over a sheer cliff.

You can turn around here, but for even more scenery, you can cross Chinook Creek and traverse a hillside to a junction with the Chinook Trail. Turn left here and travel downhill for 0.5 mile to a simple crossing of Wildcat Creek, a little above where this stream joins Siouxon Creek. To visit 100-foot-high Wildcat Falls, turn right at a junction and climb 0.2 mile to a viewpoint at the base of this falls. To close out the trip, either return the way you came, or, if it is late summer and you are willing to get wet, turn left at the junction below Wildcat Falls and drop to a knee-deep ford of Siouxon Creek. Wading shoes and a walking stick may come in handy, depending on the water level. On the opposite bank, an obvious use trail climbs about 100 feet back to the Siouxon Creek Trail.

Trip 3

Horseshoe Ridge Loop

(Map Area W-1)

Distance	Elevation Gain	Hiking Time	Optional Map	Difficulty
10.4 miles	2700'	6 to 7 hours	*Green Trails – Lookout Mountain*	***

Usually Open	April to early November
Best Times	May and June
Agency	Wind River Ranger District (Gifford-Pinchot National Forest)

Exercise is the principal attraction of this hike. There are only infrequent views, and these are generally limited to ridges covered with clearcuts. So this is a good hike to tackle in gloomy weather, as you won't feel like you missed anything. The relatively low elevation ensures that this trail opens earlier in the season than most others in the Cascades.

Directions: Begin by driving to Battleground, either by going north on State Highway 503 from Interstate 205, or by going east on State Highway 502 from exit 9 off Interstate 5. From the intersection of the two state highways in the middle of Battleground, drive north on Highway 503 for 16.8 miles and turn right on N.E. Healy Road just after you pass the Mt. St. Helens National Volcanic Monument headquarters.

After 9.2 miles on N.E. Healey Road, bear left at a poorly signed junction and travel on single-lane, paved Forest Road 57. Drive another 1.3 miles, then turn sharply left on often unsigned Forest Road 5701. Follow this rough, paved road for 3.7 miles to its end at a trailhead parking lot.

The trail departs from the north side of the lot and drops 50 feet to an intersection with the Siouxon Creek Trail. You turn right here and drop to a bridged crossing of West Creek, then continue another 0.8 mile through lovely creekside forests to a signed junction with the Horseshoe Ridge Trail.

You turn right here and climb away from the creek on a grade that starts off fairly steep but soon becomes very steep. Over 20 switchbacks of varying length help to lessen the grade slightly, but at other times the trail simply goes directly up the extremely steep slopes. The trail is also quite narrow, so watch your step. After about 1.5 miles you reach a minor ridgecrest, after which things get a lot easier.

The trail turns left to follow the ridge, sometimes climbing in steep sections and sometimes going along at a welcome level grade. Most of the trees are either western hemlock or Douglas-fir, while salal, beargrass, and Oregon grape cover the ground. You pass a small rocky overlook with a decent view to the west, then travel on or near the narrow crest of woodsy Horseshoe Ridge.

The gentle path along this ridge does some short ups and downs to avoid rock outcrops, but mostly stays level. Along the way you leave the forest three times and go through small, sloping meadows with lots of ground-hugging juniper bushes and a few scattered wildflowers.

After a long, very gradual climb you eventually make a couple of small switchbacks just before the ridge widens and the trail curves to the left. From here the path gradually loses about 200 feet and comes to the end of a dirt road where there is a small hunter's camp. Pick up the trail on the opposite side of the camp and follow it over a low rise then down a short distance to a second isolated gravel road.

To resume the trail, turn left on the road and 25 yards later bear right onto a signed foot trail. Staying on the east side of the ridgeline, this generally level route goes along a viewless ridge with lots of beargrass. After about 1 mile you begin to descend very steeply for 0.6 mile. Once you reach the first of four long switchbacks, the trail is much better graded. It remains that way all the way down the densely forested slopes to an unsigned junction with Siouxon Creek Trail.

To return to your car, turn left and walk this easy and very scenic route for 2.1 miles, as it passes Siouxon and Horseshoe Creek falls back to the lower junction with the Horseshoe Ridge Trail.

Along Horseshoe Ridge Trail, Gifford Pinchot National Forest, Washington

Southwest Washington

Area W-2: Silver Star Mountain

Most Portlanders recognize Silver Star Mountain, although few know its name. As seen from the city, Silver Star Mountain is a long ridge to the northeast that obscures the view of Mt. Adams in the distance. But from atop the ridge itself there is nothing to obstruct the terrific views, not only of Mt. Adams, but also of several other impressive peaks, as well as the patchwork of farms and cities to the west.

But Silver Star Mountain offers much more than just views. Although not terribly high in elevation, the peak has an alpine feel. The trees that once grew on Silver Star Mountain have never grown back from the massive Yacolt Burn of 1902. As a result, the high ridgeline of this mountain is surprisingly open, providing a wealth of outstanding views and some equally outstanding wildflower displays in June and July.

The mountain itself is part of the Gifford Pinchot National Forest, but most of the adjoining lands are in the Yacolt State Forest. To follow ecological rather than administrative boundaries, the entire connected complex is treated here as one area.

Trip 1

Tarbell Trail to Hidden Falls

(Map Area W-2)

Distance	Elevation Gain	Hiking Time	Optional Map	Difficulty
10.0 miles	1100′	5 hours	*Yacolt Burn State Forest*	**

Usually Open	Mid-March to November
Best Times	April to June
Agency	Yacolt State Forest

More than one hundred years ago, a man named George Tarbell lived alone in the roadless forests northwest of Silver Star Mountain. He made a living by farming and mining for gold. His isolated cabin was connected to the outside world only by a narrow 6-mile-long trail that led to the nearest wagon road. Today that trail has been reopened and you can walk in the hermit's footsteps. They lead you to a spectacular waterfall that remains nearly as unknown today as it was in Tarbell's time.

Directions: Begin by driving to Battleground, either by going north on State Highway 503 from Interstate 205, or by going east on State Highway 502 from exit 9 off Interstate 5.

The two state highways intersect in the middle of Battleground. From here drive north 5.7 miles on Highway 503. Turn right on N.E. Rock Creek Road, which soon becomes Lucia Falls Road. After 8.5 miles turn right on N.E. Sunset Falls Road. Go another 2.0 miles on this road, then turn right again onto N.E. Dole Valley Road. Exactly 2.4 miles further on turn left onto gravel Road L 1100, which is marked with a small brown sign for the Tarbell Picnic Area. After 2.2 miles, turn right at a junction. Fifty feet later, park in the signed lot on the left side of the road.

You begin by a sign saying that Hidden Falls is 4¾ miles away. Walk through a pleasantly rustic picnic area, then turn right at an unsigned junction. Soon thereafter you come to a second junction—this one with a horse trail. The sign here says that Hidden Falls is now

5.8 miles away. Apparently the falls is not only hidden, it is also a moving target! Actually neither sign is correct. Hidden Falls is actually 4.9 miles away.

Turn left onto the horse trail, which wanders gradually uphill in a typical, second-growth, Douglas-fir forest. With just 100 years of growth since the 1902 Yacolt Burn, most of the trees are little more than 1 foot thick, but a few are as much as 3 feet thick and nearly 100 feet tall. Vegetation covers almost every square inch of the forest floor, especially Oregon grape, oxalis, thimbleberry, salal, false lily-of-the-valley, and sword and bracken fern. There are also lots of vine maples, whose leaves turn scarlet and orange in late October.

Two switchbacks climb past the edge of a clearcut and take you up to a crossing of a narrow gravel road. The small seam of sunlight created by this road is just enough for June-blooming iris to thrive. Continuing past this junction, you make a series of gentle climbs and level walks through dense foliage that creates a sort of living tunnel. In places horse hooves have churned the tread into a muddy mess, so wear boots rather than tennis shoes.

After topping a low rise, you turn east and cross a very isolated old road in the middle of an equally old clearcut. Trailside thimbleberry and the enormous spreading fronds of bracken fern are racing to capture as much light as possible before the rapidly regrowing Douglas-firs cover them with a shady canopy. Shortly after reentering an older forest, you cross a rarely used motorcycle track, then wander along the south side of low and rounded Squaw Butte. Several openings in the forest provide room for flowers like vetch, iris, golden pea, dandelion, beargrass, and wild rose. There are also some partially obstructed views of Silver Star Mountain to the southeast and Larch Mountain to the south. The trail loses some elevation among the trees and crosses more partially forested slopes before making a long, looping contour into a densely forested valley on the northwest side of Silver Star Mountain.

You should eventually come to a junction with a newly constructed route that is part of the planned Chinook Trail, which will one day make a circle route along both sides of the Columbia River Gorge. This section of it leaves the Tarbell Trail and goes to the left on its way to Silver Star Mountain. The signs here give distances to various destinations, but like the signs at the trailhead, these are not to be trusted. One sign claims that it is only 2 miles back to the Tarbell Picnic Area where you started. The actual distance is close to 3.5 miles.

In any case, the trail stays level for a short distance before it descends six quick switchbacks and makes a bridged crossing of North Fork Coyote Creek. After this, it contours around a forested ridge and switchbacks downhill to take you into the next creek canyon. This canyon holds South Fork Coyote Creek and 92-foot-high Hidden Falls, just above a log bridge.

A wooden bench at the base of this lacy falls makes an ideal lunch spot and turnaround point. Beyond the falls, the trail makes a tough switchbacking climb onto a shoulder of Silver Star Mountain. Since you can reach this area more easily from Grouse Vista (see Trip 5), be satisfied with the falls and return to your car the way you came.

Trip 2

Cold Creek to Larch Mountain

(Map Area W-2)

Distance	Elevation Gain	Hiking Time	Optional Map	Difficulty
12.0 miles	2400'	6 to 7 hours	*Yacolt Burn State Forest*	***

Usually Open	May to early November
Best Times	Mid-May to June
Agency	Yacolt State Forest

Located a little to the southwest of Silver Star Mountain, Larch Mountain is lower in elevation, but it features many of the same attributes of its larger neighbor: open wildflower meadows, good views, and wildlife. There are two good trails to this high point, the more interesting of which is the long climb up the valley of scenic Cold Creek.

The trails here are used mostly by mountain bikers and equestrians, but why should they have all the fun? Hikers are also welcome, and it's high time we came to see what everybody else has kept secret. As always, be sure to give horses the right of way by stepping off the trail on the downhill side to let them pass. Motor vehicles are prohibited from most of the recommended trails, although you will cross several motorcycle tracks. Many riders seem to view the official trail restrictions as merely *optional* and routinely ignore the rules, so you can expect the quiet of your wilderness experience to be rudely broken by the noise of motorbikes, especially on weekends.

Directions: Begin by driving to Battleground, either by going north on State Highway 503 from Interstate 205, or by going east on State Highway 502 from exit 9 off Interstate 5.

The two state highways intersect in the middle of Battleground. From here drive north 5.7 miles on Highway 503. Turn right on N.E. Rock Creek Road, which soon becomes Lucia Falls Road. After 8.5 miles turn right on N.E. Sunset Falls Road. Go another 2.0 miles on this road, then turn right again onto N.E. Dole Valley Road. Stay on this road for 3.9 miles to the end of pavement and continue another 1.3 miles to a prominent intersection. Veer right, following signs for the Larch Corrections Center, and drive exactly 0.9 mile before parking in an unsigned pullout on the left, just before a culvert over Cold Creek.

 Pick up the wide trail that crosses the road just a few feet west of the creek culvert and turn left (south). In a few yards you come to a large sign giving the mileage to various destinations, including the 6.0 miles to Larch Mountain. The walk begins in a lush Douglas-fir forest not far from splashing Cold Creek, which has mostly red alder and western red cedar near its banks.

The forest floor is almost completely covered with bracken and sword fern, bleeding heart, oxalis, salmonberry, thimbleberry, and other common species in various shades of green. The "river music" of cascading water and the songs of birds, especially those of the ever-present American robin and winter wren, provide audio stimulation and enjoyment.

Cross Cold Creek on a plank bridge, then continue uphill near the creek. The trail does lots of small ups and downs but gradually gains elevation. At about 1.5 miles you go straight across an unsigned junction where an unofficial mountainbike trail comes in from the left. Shortly thereafter, you again cross Cold Creek on a plank bridge. A horse hitching post and two wooden benches make this a good rest stop.

Continue hiking amid increasing numbers of lovely, droopy-limbed western hemlocks. You briefly pull away from the creek and switchback up a heavily forested hillside. After this you make bridged crossings of two branches of Cold Creek about 0.4 mile apart. At the second crossing are a decent campsite and an unsigned trail heading downstream. You go straight on the main trail and switchback uphill, gradually leaving behind the sounds of "river music."

About 0.4 mile after the last creek crossing, you pass diagonally through a confusing and unsigned junction with a motorbike track, then switchback to the right on top of a wide, forested ridge. More climbing takes you up to and around a small rockslide and cliff where red paintbrush, purple penstemon, white beargrass, and yellow golden pea grow profusely.

After climbing a bit more in forest, you come to a lovely open slope of shale rock with lots of June-blooming lupine, lomatium, and beargrass. There are also fine views here, especially northeast to bulky Silver Star Mountain and north to Mounts Rainier and St. Helens. Several roads and clearcuts mar the scene somewhat, but it is still very attractive. A lone picnic table just below the trail is signed as the FLINTSTONE PICNIC AREA. It provides Fred and Wilma, or any other visitors, a first-rate lunch spot, although this exposed location is often windy.

Above the rocky slope you enter open, mid-elevation forests of Douglas-fir and Pacific silver fir, with lots of star-flowered smilacina and bunchberry covering the ground. Go straight through an unsigned four-way junction and 100 yards later you will come to a signed fork in the trail. The path to the left goes down to Grouse Vista (see Trip 3), but your route turns right and climbs 0.2 mile to a junction with another motorcycle track.

The only sign here says HORSE TRAILS, and it points to the trail you came in on. To reach the top of Larch Mountain, bear left and walk uphill on the motorcycle track past a large beargrass meadow on your right and through nice forests to the rather disappointing summit. There is a nice view southwest to Vancouver and Portland, but most of the scene is despoiled by a clearcut right at the top, as well as by a gravel road, and microwave and cellular-phone towers—the modern plague of so many mountain tops. To enjoy your lunch where the views are better, go back to the meadows you passed near the junction below the summit.

Trip 3

Larch Mountain from Grouse Vista

(Map Area W-2)

Distance	Elevation Gain	Hiking Time	Optional Map	Difficulty
6.0 miles	1200'	3 hours	Yacolt Burn State Forest	**

Usually Open	May to early November
Best Times	Mid-May to June
Agency	Yacolt State Forest

For a shorter approach to the meadows and the views on Larch Mountain, try this route from Grouse Vista. The distance and elevation gain are only about half as much as the Cold Creek Trail (Trip 2), and the views from the meadows near the top are just as spectacular.

Neither this Larch Mountain nor the more famous one in Oregon have any larch trees growing on them. The western larch grows only east of the Cascade divide. The name comes from early loggers who used the term "larch" to refer to the noble fir. The two species actually have little in common.

Directions: Begin by driving to Battleground, either by going north on State Highway 503 from Interstate 205, or by going east on State Highway 502 from exit 9 off Interstate 5.

The two state highways intersect in the middle of Battleground. From here drive north 5.7 miles on Highway 503. Turn right on N.E. Rock Creek Road, which soon becomes Lucia Falls Road. After 8.5 miles you turn right on N.E. Sunset Falls Road. Go another 2.0 miles on this road, then turn right again onto N.E. Dole Valley Road. Stay on this road for 3.9 miles to the end of pavement and continue another 1.3 miles to a prominent intersection. Turn left on Road L 1200 and climb for 5.2 miles to the pass at Grouse Vista. The best parking is on the right.

Three routes leave from the right (west) side of the pass. The two southernmost are motorcycle tracks, which are nothing but an annoyance for hikers. Instead, take the northernmost of the three routes and very soon you will come to a brown sign giving distances to various points along the trail. After an all-too-brief warm up, the trail starts to climb steeply on a wide, rocky tread. While you climb, the rocks and boulders on the trail are merely a nuisance, but on the way back down they can easily twist your ankle, so be extra careful on the return trip.

Views here are generally obstructed by trees, mostly short Douglas-fir, grand fir, and western hemlock. As you climb, the sounds of rushing water from Grouse Creek in the canyon on your right gradually grow louder as the creek gets closer.

After a little over 1 mile, the trail is joined by an unsigned motorbike track coming in from the left. But 0.2 mile later this track splits off again. Shortly after this, you pass an active beaver pond and large dam on your right. If you arrive here in the early morning, take some time to scan the pond for the busy builders of this impressive construction project.

Above the pond, you make a bridged crossing of Grouse Creek, loop back to the right, and traverse up the increasingly open hillside. When the trail tops a ridge, the views improve greatly, as most of the trees disappear and you stand in an open meadow. Bulky Silver Star Mountain lies to the northeast, but the best views look to the distant snow peaks of Oregon's Mt. Hood and decapitated Mt. St. Helens in Washington. You can also see the region's better known Larch Mountain, on the Oregon side of the Columbia River.

The trail turns west and follows the ridge up through more meadows and strips of trees. Wildflowers abound here, including such colorful favorites as beargrass, lupine, iris, queens cup, and golden pea. This is the most attractive part of the hike, although the trail is a bit rocky and deeply gouged by motorcycles.

About 2.5 miles from the trailhead is a junction with the trail coming up from Cold Creek (Trip 2). To reach the top of Larch Mountain, you bear left here and climb 0.5 mile past a beargrass meadow and through several confusing junctions with motorcycle routes. The mountaintop is rather ugly, however, with a clearcut and electrical towers, so for better views return to the meadows below.

With a car shuttle you can make a long one-way trip by going down the Cold Creek Trail. See Trip 2 for details.

Trip 4

North Silver Star Mountain Loop

(Map Area W-2)

Distance	Elevation Gain	Hiking Time	Optional Map	Difficulty
5.0 miles	1700'	3 hours	*Green Trails – Lookout Mountain & Bridal Veil* (some trails not shown)	**

Usually Open	Mid-May to October
Best Times	Mid-June to mid-July
Agency	Wind River Ranger District (Gifford-Pinchot National Forest))

No matter how you get to the top of Silver Star Mountain, you will enjoy expansive views and abundant wildflowers. The easiest of the direct hiking routes to the summit is from the north along either an abandoned road or a wildly scenic new trail, which passes a series of jagged rock formations and goes through some of the best wildflower meadows in this book. The two routes can be easily combined into a spectacular, relatively easy, and surprisingly little-traveled loop.

Directions: Begin by driving to Battleground, either by going north on State Highway 503 from Interstate 205, or by going east on State Highway 502 from exit 9 off Interstate 5.

The two state highways intersect in the middle of Battleground. From here drive north 5.7 miles on Highway 503. Turn right on N.E. Rock Creek Road, which soon becomes Lucia Falls Road. After 8.5 miles turn right on N.E. Sunset Falls Road. Go another 2.0 miles on this road, then turn right again onto N.E. Dole Valley Road. Exactly 2.4 miles further on turn left onto gravel Road L 1100, which is marked with a small brown sign for the Tarbell Picnic Area. After 2.2 miles, go straight at a junction beside the picnic area and drive 2.1 more miles to a fork. Bear left here and go 3.4 miles to a four-way junction. Turn right and drive steeply uphill on bumpy, gravel Road 4109 for 2.6 miles to the road-end turnaround.

There is no trail sign visible from the trailhead, and several old roads and trails look equally promising. The proper route leaves from the west end of the parking area and goes about 25 yards to a trail sign identifying this as Silver Star Trail 180. If you don't hit this sign very soon after starting to hike, go back and try again.

The Silver Star Trail switchbacks four times up a slope covered with brushy vine maple, then comes to a junction with a closed jeep road. Bear right (uphill) and walk about 150 yards to a large gravel turnaround in the road.

The scenery here, and for some time to come, is truly outstanding. The entire area is surrounded by huge sloping meadows that are carpeted with wildflowers in late June and early July. There are dozens of varieties, but the most common kinds are beargrass, lupine, wild carrot, paintbrush, iris, yarrow, valerian, tiger lily, and golden pea. Scattered about the open slopes are perky little noble fir trees, which look for all the world like Christmas trees, a popular use for this evergreen.

In addition to the flowers and trees, there are terrific views. Most impressive are Mt. St. Helens and Mt. Rainier, peeking over forested ridges to the north, and Mt. Adams to the east. Southward, Mt. Hood makes an almost perfectly framed appearance in a low point in the ridge east of Silver Star Mountain.

To hike the new scenic trail, leave the road at this turnaround and bear left at a sign identifying Ed's Trail. This extremely scenic route is rough and narrow, and open only to hikers. The trail ascends steeply at first, then more gradually near the edge of a drop-off. The huge meadows here boast even more flowers than those you passed below. Added to the previous mix are columbine, wallflower, penstemon, fireweed, lomatium, and bistort—all looking for their place amid the other blossoms. You round a small ridge and the scenery improves yet again, as the rocky spine of Silver Star Mountain's summit ridge becomes visible directly ahead.

Still crossing open slopes, you climb gradually and come to the ridgecrest, where you join an ancient two-rut road. Turn left and in just 100 feet you will come to a signed junction with the Chinook Trail going down the meadows to the right. Continue straight and keep climbing as the trail skirts to the left of several jagged rock outcroppings on the spine of the ridge. Along one of these detours, you will go through a natural, keyhole-shaped rock arch, before having to work your way around the base of some massive cliffs.

From here the trail goes very steeply up some improvised rock steps, climbs to a notch in the cliff, then descends a bit through more meadows. The floral display in this higher meadow is still magnificent, with pink spiraea, yellow woolly daisy, and three kinds of light pink flowers—phlox, lewisia, and saxifrage—joining the color show. Once the trail finally leaves the meadow, it enters a forest of Pacific silver fir and soon comes to a major ridgetop junction.

The jeep road you have been paralleling meets your route here, as does the Bluff Mountain Trail (Trip 6), which angles in from the left. There is also an unsigned trail directly across the road from you, which goes southwest toward Sturgeon Rock. To reach the summit, you turn left on the jeep route and climb for 200 yards to a road junction where you should bear left. In about 0.2 mile this rock-strewn, old road works its way up to the saddle between the twin summits of Silver Star Mountain. There are trails going up to both high points. On the clearest days you can see not only the nearby volcanic peaks already mentioned, but also Mt. Jefferson and the Three Sisters in Oregon, and the Olympic Mountains to the northwest in Washington.

Since this is the easiest route to the top of Silver Star Mountain, you might still have some extra energy to do some exploring. One of the most scenic and interesting side trips is a visit to some rock pits once used by Native American boys during their spiritual vision quests. To reach it, take an obvious boot path from the more southern of the two summits of Silver Star Mountain, then drop very steeply down an open hillside to an unsigned junction with a better-graded official trail. Go left here and walk about 0.8 mile up and down through beargrass meadows. Watch out for a patch of thick brush here that may scratch your legs if you are wearing shorts. The rock pits are on a small talus slope near the end of the ridge. Please do not disturb this important religious and archeological site.

To return, walk back on the trail past the junction with the boot path up Silver Star Mountain. You will soon come to a four-way junction with a jeep road. Turn right and climb a short distance back to the junction just below the summit. Go straight and walk 200 yards down to the junction with Ed's Trail. For variety on the way back, you can stay on the old jeep road and walk this route as it gently descends for 2.0 miles through view-packed meadows back to the trailhead.

Trip 5

Silver Star Mountain from Grouse Vista

(Map Area W-2)

Distance	Elevation Gain	Hiking Time	Optional Map	Difficulty
7.5 miles	2300'	4 hours	*Yacolt Burn State Forest*	***

Usually Open	May to October
Best Times	Mid-May to June
Agency	Yacolt State Forest & Wind River Ranger District (Gifford-Pinchot National Forest)

This is the most popular route to the top of Silver Star Mountain, perhaps because it has the easiest road access and lends itself perfectly to a loop. Although the hike is very attractive, it is neither as scenic nor as abundant in wildflowers as either the northern loop (Trip 4) or the Bluff Mountain Trail (Trip 6). Nonetheless, it is an enjoyable hike with glimpses of a towering waterfall to go along with the extensive views from the top. Although the old jeep roads which form most of this loop were closed to motor vehicles in 1984, old habits apparently die hard. You will still encounter the occasional noisy intruder on the quiet of the land.

Directions: Begin by driving to Battleground, either by going north on State Highway 503 from Interstate 205, or by going east on State Highway 502 from exit 9 off Interstate 5.

The two state highways intersect in the middle of Battleground. From here drive north 5.7 miles on Highway 503. Turn right on N.E. Rock Creek Road, which soon becomes Lucia Falls Road. After 8.5 miles turn right on N.E. Sunset Falls Road. Go another 2.0 miles on this road, then turn right again onto N.E. Dole Valley Road. Stay on this road for 3.9 miles to the end of pavement and continue another 1.3 miles to a prominent intersection. Turn left on Road L 1200 and climb 5.2 miles to the pass at Grouse Vista. The best parking is on the right.

The trail on the east side of the pass starts as an old jeep track blocked by berms intended to keep motor vehicles out. After about 0.1 mile, there is a junction with the Tarbell Trail, a narrow foot trail that bears off to the left. Take this pleasant little trail that goes up and down through woods that come alive in May with small pink blossoms of bleeding heart.

After rounding a ridge, you contour across intermittently open slopes on the walls of a huge forested canyon. As you get close to the head of the canyon, you will be able to glimpse a towering 100-foot waterfall on Rock Creek to your left. Unfortunately, you never get a really good look at the falls from the trail, and there is no easy scramble to a better viewpoint. Cross the wooden bridge over Rock Creek and begin your climb out of the canyon at a moderate grade. A mix of eight switchbacks and long traverses eventually leads up heavily wooded slopes to a junction with an old road near a saddle in the ridge.

Turn right on this bumpy and rocky track and climb steeply through viewless forests on the south side of the ridge. After a little over a mile, check carefully on the left for a look at the sheer columnar basalt cliffs of Sturgeon Rock. For a better look, you can scramble off the trail to some excellent viewpoints at the base of the cliffs, where you can sometimes see climbers inching their way up the rock face.

An unsigned footpath veers off to the left near the east end of Sturgeon Rock, but you should stay on the road, as the uphill grade lessens somewhat for the final 0.3 mile to the junction. About 80 feet before you reach this junction, an unsigned trail goes left for about 100 feet to a piped spring with refreshingly cool water.

The return route to Grouse Vista goes right at this junction, but you can take a scenic side trip to the summit by turning left. After 20 feet, a foot trail cuts sharply right on its way out to some Native American rock pits (see description in Trip 4). For the summit, you go straight and climb to a little saddle where there is a final junction. Turn right (uphill) and climb for 0.2 mile on a rock-strewn old jeep road to the saddle between the two summits of Silver Star Mountain. Both summits have terrific views and are well worth visiting. Views extend for hundreds of miles over large parts of two states, but some of the most interesting views are of the nearby ridges and canyons of Silver Star Mountain itself. Flowers are also abundant, including paintbrush, beargrass, pink heather, and avalanche lilies near the top.

To return to your car, go back to the road junction near the spring and follow the old jeep track downhill to the southwest. This fairly steep route travels through extensive meadows with good views and lots of flowers. The tread is very rocky, so watch your step to avoid turning an ankle. At a little saddle about halfway down, there is a junction with an abandoned track that goes left. It's worth exploring this track for a short distance to check out the cliffs of prominent Pyramid Rock. Once you've had your fill, return to the main trail and drop down the ridge to the trailhead.

Trip 6

Bluff Mountain Trail

(Map Area W-2)

Distance	Elevation Gain	Hiking Time	Optional Map	Difficulty
13.2 miles	2600'	6 to 7 hours	Yacolt Burn State Forest & Green Trails – Lookout Mountain	***

Usually Open	Mid-May to early November
Best Times	Mid-to-late June
Agency	Wind River Ranger District (Gifford-Pinchot National Forest)

The summit of Silver Star Mountain is a worthwhile destination by any route, but for great scenery nothing can compare to the approach from the east along the Bluff Mountain Trail. The drive here is fairly long. In fact, at almost 1.5 hours from Portland the drive is longer than the rule for inclusion in this book allows. The hike is included because it is one of the author's favorites. The well-graded trail is rarely crowded, has fine wildflower displays, and almost nonstop fabulous views. On a clear day, and you should definitely save this outstanding hike for a clear day, views extend from Oregon's Three Sisters to Washington's Mt. Rainier, and even down to the skyline of downtown Portland (usually hidden beneath a haze of pollution). Carry an extra quart of water, as the route is dry and exposed to the sun over its entire length.

Directions: Begin by driving to Battleground, either by going north on State Highway 503 from Interstate 205, or by going east on State Highway 502 from exit 9 off Interstate 5.

The two state highways intersect in the middle of Battleground. From here drive north 5.7 miles on Highway 503. Turn right on N.E. Rock Creek Road, which soon becomes Lucia Falls Road.

After 8.5 miles turn right on N.E. Sunset Falls Road and follow this route about 7.4 miles to Sunset Campground. Turn right and drive through the camp to a bridge over the East Fork Lewis River. Immediately on the other side of the bridge turn left onto gravel, pothole-filled Forest Road 41. Stay on this narrow route as it climbs 9.0 miles to a saddle. The trailhead parking area is on the right.

The Bluff Mountain Trail starts as an old jeep road, now closed to motor vehicles. The old road undulates along a scenic ridgetop, where in the century since the 1902 Yacolt Burn only scattered Pacific silver firs have grown back and the tallest have yet to attain a height of 20 feet. As a result, you can enjoy extensive views, not only of the region's recognizable snow peaks, but also of Little Baldy and distant Silver Star Mountain along a rugged ridge to the southwest. The open ridge is carpeted with a delightful mix of huckleberry, beargrass, and serviceberry bushes, along with a wide array of wildflowers.

After 2.0 up-and-down miles, you descend about 350 feet to a small saddle where the road ends, and the trail veers off to the right. The path loses 150 feet in one long switchback to another, more prominent, saddle. It then cuts across the north side of Bluff Mountain. Along this traverse, you cross one strip of larger trees where in early summer you may encounter lingering snow patches and small runoff creeks.

Initially, this section provides excellent views west to the open talus slopes of pointed Little Baldy. Later, you can look north for views of the truncated summit of Mt. St. Helens and part of Mt. Rainier. Wildflowers on this cool slope include yellow glacier lily and wood violet, pink bleeding heart, and white false solomon seal and avalanche lily.

The trail now climbs to and crosses another saddle, this one in dense timber, then traverses the open, view-packed talus slopes on the south and west sides of Little Baldy. Here you get great looks at the impressive crags of your destination, Silver Star Mountain. Still traveling west toward that goal, the well-graded trail uses a couple of short switchbacks to work its way gradually up an open ridge with lots of beargrass. You go straight at the signed junction with the rarely-maintained Star Way Trail #175 before you make the final push to the mountain.

The last bit snakes up the ridge, then cuts into the trees on the north side of the peak, where snowdrifts usually remain into late June. The trail ends at an intersection where a closed jeep road and several foot trails all meet. To reach the summit, turn left on the jeep road and 200 yards later bear left (uphill) at another road junction. The final 0.2 mile is a climb on a rock-strewn road to the high saddle between the dual summits of Silver Star Mountain, both of which are easily accessible.

Once at the top, just sit back and enjoy the view. To the north and east are the great volcanic snow peaks of Washington (St. Helens, Adams, and Rainier), while to the south are the more dainty but equally impressive peaks of Oregon (Hood and Jefferson). In the distance to the south, some 125 miles away, are the Three Sisters. People familiar with this area will also be able to spot lesser landmarks such as Three-corner Rock, Larch Mountain, Tanner Butte, the Goat Rocks, and Mt. Defiance, to name just a few. Although this is usually a dayhike, those willing to spend the night here will be rewarded with spectacular sunsets and views down to the city lights of Portland.

Southwest Washington

Area W-3: Three-Corner Rock Area

Three-corner Rock's summit pinnacle is an unmistakable landmark visible from highpoints in all directions. More often than not, however, when hikers see this distant rocky outcropping, they are forced to ask: "what's that?" The question is usually accompanied by a vague feeling of embarrassment that they are not already familiar with such an obvious feature. Surprisingly few hikers follow up on their natural curiosity to seek out the trails exploring the

Three-corner Rock, Washington

scenic routes to and around Three-corner Rock. That is a shame, because the rock sits at the hub of a very attractive region of second-growth forests, stream canyons, and view-packed ridges, which encompasses miles of little-known trails.

The biggest obstacle to exploring here is that the area's dirt and gravel roads are poorly signed, confusing, and very often rough. The Yacolt State Forest manages most of the land, but their maps omit crucial information like locked gates and many road junctions. Bring along either plenty of patience or someone familiar with the area and you will enjoy your trip much more. Once on the trails, however, you can forget the driving difficulties and simply savor the scenery. Views, of course, include a few too many clearcuts and logging roads, but they are grand nonetheless. On a more intimate scale, the delicate wildflowers, bubbling creeks, and lush forests are as fine here as they are throughout our region.

Trip 1

Snag Creek Trail

(Map Area W-3)

Distance	Elevation Gain	Hiking Time	Optional Map	Difficulty
4.6 miles	1300'	2 to 3 hours	*Green Trails – Lookout Mountain* (trail not shown)	**

Usually Open	Mid-March to early December
Best Times	Mid-April to May
Agency	Yacolt State Forest

This fun trail was originally built by the Civilian Conservation Corps in the 1930s, but was abandoned for several decades and fell into disrepair. Then in 1981 an industrious Boy Scout troop in Washougal took on the project of reopening the old trail. They have done an admirable job, so today this rarely traveled route provides a nice outdoor experience and deserves more attention from hikers.

Directions: Go 1.5 miles east of Bridge of the Gods on State Highway 14 and turn left on Rock Creek Drive. After about 0.4 mile you pass the turnoff to Skamania Lodge. Immediately thereafter, turn left on Foster Creek Road. Drive 0.9 mile to a set of powerlines and turn left again on paved Red Bluff Road. In just 0.4 mile the road turns to gravel at a fork. Here you bear right on Road CG 2000. After another 2.1 miles go left at another fork to continue on Road CG 2000, which gets narrower and a bit bumpy with lots of potholes.

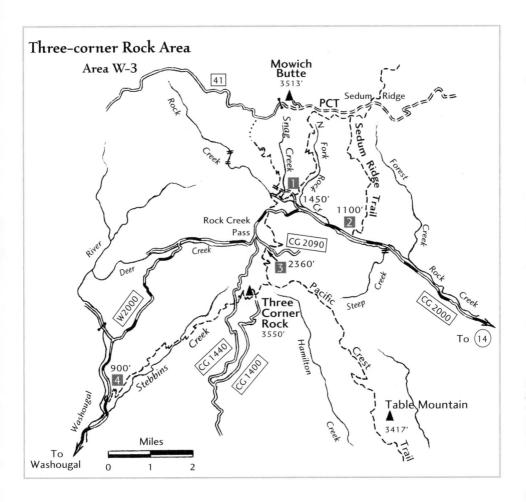

Three-corner Rock Area

Area W-3

Mowich Butte 3513'

41

PCT

Sedum Ridge

Snag Creek

N Fork Rock Cr

Sedum Ridge Trail

Forest

Creek

1450'

1100'

Rock Creek Pass

CG 2090

2360'

Creek

Rock Creek

River

Deer

W2000

Pacific

Steep

Creek

CG 2000

To 14

Three Corner Rock 3550'

Crest

Creek

Hamilton

CG 1440

CG 1400

Stebbins

900'

Creek

Table Mountain

3417'

Trail

Washougal

Creek

Miles

0   1   2

To
Washougal

About 3.3 miles later, at a bridge over Rock Creek, take a moment to admire Steep Creek Falls, a lovely cascade on a tributary stream that tumbles directly into Rock Creek. To reach the Snag Creek trailhead, keep driving another 2.4 miles, then turn right on dirt Road CG 2070. After 0.4 mile, park on the very narrow shoulder of this rough road at the signed crossing of the Pacific Crest Trail (PCT).

You begin the hike by veering left off the road onto the south-bound PCT. The trail contours across a brushy hillside above Rock Creek in a second-growth forest of small Douglas-firs and bigleaf maples. This area was logged in 1973 and replanted in 1975, which gives you a chance to see the rate at which the land recovers from logging activity. After 0.2 mile you cross cascading Snag Creek on a wide plank bridge and enter older and more attractive woods. Just 150 yards after the bridge is a junction with Snag Creek Trail, where you turn right.

Just above the PCT, the trail passes a nice campsite, then climbs moderately steeply through a pleasant western-hemlock and Douglas-fir forest. The wide path is so lightly traveled that it is now being invaded by bracken fern. Based on the amount of elk droppings on the trail, the route seems to be used more by hoofed creatures than booted ones. For the first 0.1 mile you follow splashing Snag Creek. When you come to a junction with a washed-out jeep road, turn left on this road and walk uphill about 150 yards. Then switchback to the right at a brown sign for the Snag Creek Trail.

The trail now ascends a ridge under the shade of tall hemlock trees before coming to the edge of a clearcut, which is a bit unsightly but provides nice views up to Mowich Butte and Sedum Ridge. You climb steeply past this logging scar, then make one long switchback, followed by seven short ones, to the top of a ridge. At this point there is a break in the trees that provides an unusually good perspective of the rocky pinnacle and microwave tower on Three-corner Rock to the southwest. You can also see a portion of Mt. Hood and several high points in the Columbia River Gorge. Two wooden benches here allow you to enjoy the view in comfort.

Just 0.1 mile past this view the trail leaves Yacolt State Forest land and enters the national forest. After this change in stewardship, the trail deteriorates rapidly. The path formerly extended for another 1.3 miles to Mowich Camp on Forest Road 41, but it is now too rough a bushwhack to be recommended. So be satisfied with the viewpoint and return the way you came.

Trip 2

Sedum Ridge – Mowich Butte Loop

(Map Area W-3)

Distance	Elevation Gain	Hiking Time	Optional Map	Difficulty
11.3 miles	2700'	5 to 7 hours	*Green Trails – Lookout Mountain & Wind River* (part of route not shown)	***

Usually Open	Late April to November
Best Times	Mid-May to June
Agency	Yacolt State Forest & Wind River Ranger District (Gifford-Pinchot National Forest)

The old Sedum Ridge Trail climbs a woodsy ridge that would, by itself, be a pleasant if unremarkable hike, but when you combine it into a loop with the Pacific Crest Trail you have a full day of scenic hiking. To make the trip even better, add a side trip to Mowich Butte, a viewpoint with far-ranging vistas across forested hills and valleys and to distant volcanic snow peaks.

Directions: Go 1.5 miles east of Bridge of the Gods on State Highway 14 and turn left on Rock Creek Drive. After about 0.4 mile you pass the turnoff to Skamania Lodge. Immediately thereafter, turn left on Foster Creek Road. Drive 0.9 mile to a set of powerlines and turn left again on paved Red Bluff Road. In just 0.4 mile the road turns to gravel at a fork. Here you bear right on Road CG 2000. After another 2.1 miles go left at another fork to continue on Road CG 2000, which gets narrower and a bit bumpy with lots of potholes.

About 3.3 miles later, at a bridge over Rock Creek, take a moment to admire Steep Creek Falls, a lovely cascade on a tributary stream that tumbles directly into Rock Creek. To reach the Sedum Ridge trailhead, keep driving for exactly 0.9 mile and park in a large, unsigned pullout on the left.

The trail starts beside an inconspicuous brown sign on the north side of the road. You begin climbing almost immediately on a slope covered with dense forests of Douglas-fir and western hemlock. After a few hundred yards, the path ducks into a little gully with a seasonal trickle of water, then leaves it and traverses a hillside to the east.

When the trail turns left, the effort of the climb really picks up as you ascend a wide, steep, woodsy ridge. Views are generally blocked by trees, but you get occasional looks at the Rock Creek Valley, which drops further and further below you as you hike. The trail receives only intermittent maintenance, but remains reasonably easy to follow without excessive blowdown to hamper your progress. After almost 2 miles the trail levels off a bit and goes around the east side of a high point on the ridge, then drops slightly into a wide saddle.

Above this saddle, the uphill resumes as you make a fairly steep traverse of the west side of a ridge. You then go through an almost imperceptible saddle on a side ridge, after which the steep uphill is over. From here you go up and down (mostly up) along the west side of the narrowing ridge and end with a mostly level section to a possibly unsigned junction with the Pacific Crest Trail. Just a few feet above you is the closed, dirt Forest Road 41, which hugs the crest of Sedum Ridge.

You turn left on the PCT and parallel Road 41 through a forest of small Douglas-fir, Pacific silver fir, and western hemlock. After a short distance, you come to the base of a basalt cliff where you gain good views to the south toward the Rock Creek Valley and several highpoints in the Columbia River Gorge. From here you walk west to a saddle and work around the south side of a knob in the ridge. Then you will drop a bit to cross some steep slopes just below a saddle and Road 41.

To make the recommended side trip to Mowich Butte, find a place to scramble up to Road 41, noting carefully for the return trip where you'll need to turn off the road, and follow the road uphill for about 0.4 mile to a junction. Turn right and walk up a narrow dirt road to the top of Mowich Butte. A lookout once stood atop this 3513-foot peak, so, not surprisingly, the views are excellent.

To the northeast are the Wind River Valley and distant Mt. Adams. To the northwest is the recently active Mt. St. Helens. To the west is Silver Star Mountain, and to the south is distinctive Three-corner Rock, with Mt. Hood in the distance. Fast-growing trees will eventually block this view. Although the road is closed to cars, it is often used by mountain bikers, so you may have some company. Given all the hoof tracks in the road and trail, it should come as no surprise that *mowich* is the Chinook language word for *deer*.

To make the return leg of the loop, return to the PCT and hike southward. The trail is well graded, as most sections of this famous trail are, so the downhill will be easier on your knees than the relatively steep Sedum Ridge Trail. First, this wide trail wanders almost due south, then it rounds a ridgeline and turns west. You cross a usually dry gully, where there are dense thickets of salmonberry, ferns, and devils club, then continue downhill. You descend by four switchbacks to cross a usually flowing little creek beside a small falls. Follow the slopes about 80 feet above this creek to its confluence with North Fork Rock Creek.

Now in lower-elevation forests of large hemlocks and firs, you stay on woodsy slopes above North Fork Rock Creek for a little less than 1 mile, then veer away and cross a partially open hillside to a trailhead on Road CG 2070.

To get back to your car, turn left and walk 0.4 mile along this rough gravel road over a bridge on Rock Creek and up to a junction with Road CG 2000. Turn left and walk this pothole-filled road for 1.5 miles back to your car.

Trip 3

Three–Corner Rock via PCT

(Map Area W-3)

Distance	Elevation Gain	Hiking Time	Optional Map	Difficulty
4.8 miles	1200'	2 to 3 hours	*Green Trails – Bridal Veil*	**

Usually Open	Mid-April to November
Best Times	Mid-May
Agency	Yacolt State Forest

If the long trail to Three-corner Rock from Stebbins Creek (Trip 4) is more than you want to tackle, then you'll be glad to know that there is a much easier alternative. The driving access is a bit tricky, but the trail is easy and the views from the destination are always spectacular.

Directions: Drive 10 miles east on State Highway 14 from its intersection with Interstate 205, then turn left at the traffic light onto 15th Street in Washougal.

Go straight through two traffic lights in town as the road changes its name, first to 17th Street, then to Washougal River Road. Stay on this good paved road for 17.8 miles past several intersections to a bridge over the river and the end of the pavement. Take a moment to stop here for a look at Dougan Falls, a popular swimming hole in summer.

After the bridge, turn right on pothole-filled, gravel Road W 2000. After 3.4 miles you pass the lower Three-corner Rock trailhead. Continue driving for 7.2 miles, staying on the main road past several intersections, and follow signs where existing for Rock Creek Pass. At the pass is a four-way junction. To reach the Pacific Crest Trail, take the second right, onto Road CG 2090, and drive up this rocky route for 0.3 mile to a saddle and the unsigned trail crossing. There is room here for about three cars to park beside the road.

The southbound trail heads to the right (southwest) and begins a well-graded climb in dense mountain-hemlock and Pacific silver fir forests. The route is unremarkable as you gradually ascend near a woodsy ridge on three irregularly spaced switchbacks, the highlights being a couple of decent viewpoints where you can see parts of Mounts Adams, Hood, and St. Helens. After 1.7 miles there is a junction with the spur trail to Three-corner Rock. The sign for this junction may be missing, but the trail is obvious.

Turn right and wander very gradually uphill on a rocky trail through an open meadow with decent views and lots of colorful wildflowers. Blue lupine and white beargrass are the dominant species, with some red paintbrush, yellow lomatium, and orange tiger lily offering a smattering of other colors. After 0.3 mile, and just 50 yards before you join a jeep road, look for a spur trail going to the right, which goes about 100 feet to a small spring with a possible campsite and a watering trough for horses.

After this spur trail, you follow the road for about 0.2 mile to a four-way junction. To your right is the large rockpile at the summit of Three-corner Rock. Take the time to scramble to the top of this rockpile to enjoy unrestricted views of all the major snow peaks in our region, as well as most of the major high points in the Columbia River Gorge. You can even see a small portion of the shimmering Columbia River. The extensive view explains why this location was once the site of a fire-lookout building, but all that remains of that historic structure are some concrete foundations. In modern times, mountaintops that formerly featured picturesque old wooden lookout buildings now sprout unsightly metal microwave and cellular-phone towers. Unfortunately, one of these structures is just a few hundred yards to the south.

If this hike is too short for you, you can extend the trip by continuing south on the PCT toward Table Mountain. This route parallels a jeep road for part of the way, but features extensive views as it follows a scenic ridge. Table Mountain is about 5.5 miles away, including a short cross-country scramble to the plateau on top.

Trip 4

Three-Corner Rock via Stebbins Creek

(Map Area W-3)

Distance	Elevation Gain	Hiking Time	Optional Map	Difficulty
4.2 or 18.4 miles	3800′	2 or 10 hours	*Green Trails – Bridal Veil*	** or ****

Usually Open	April to November
Best Times	Mid-May
Agency	Yacolt State Forest

This hike gives you the choice between a long, tiring approach on a quiet trail and a relatively short walk from a higher trailhead. Either route ends at the views and flowers around Three-corner Rock, which by themselves justify any amount of effort. The short route is fun and scenic but somehow feels like cheating. After all, reaching the destination isn't the only reason people go hiking. Perhaps more than any other activity, hiking is about the journey itself.

Directions: Drive 10 miles east on State Highway 14 from its intersection with Interstate 205, then turn left at the traffic light onto 15th Street in Washougal. Go straight through two traffic lights in town. The road changes its name, first to 17th Street, then to Washougal River Road. Stay on this good paved road for 17.8 miles past several intersections to a bridge over the river and the end of the pavement. Take a moment to stop here for a look at Dougan Falls, a popular swimming hole in summer.

After the bridge, turn right on pothole-filled, gravel Road W 2000 and drive a final 3.4 miles to a large trailhead parking lot on the left. This is the lower trailhead for those wishing to take the long hike.

To reach the upper trailhead, continue driving for 7.2 miles on Road W 2000, staying on the main road through several intersections and following signs, where existing, for Rock Creek Pass. At the pass is a four-way junction. Take the first right turn onto Road CG 1440 and drive on this rough road for exactly 2.3 miles. Park just after a small sign saying TRAIL CROSSING and before the road crosses a gully.

From the lower trailhead, the trail leaves from the southwest corner of the lot and drops past an outhouse to a plank bridge over a trickling creek. From here it parallels the road for a few hundred yards on river-level flats covered with red alder and Douglas-fir. You cross the access road and pick up the trail on the opposite side as it goes up a wide gravel path that was once a road.

Climb this old road for about 50 yards, then turn off on a foot trail to the right that ascends six quick switchbacks to a ridgecrest. The trail rounds this ridge and works its way along the hillside above Stebbins Creek in the canyon on your right. For the next 3 miles the trail makes a series of frustrating ups and downs, most of which would have been unnecessary had the trail been better engineered.

Fortunately, the scenery is pleasant as you walk through attractive second-growth forests of Douglas-fir, western hemlock, bigleaf maple, and red alder. The route begins to go slightly downhill for about 0.2 mile, then crosses a seasonal creek and makes a series of traverses and short uphill switchbacks. After crossing beneath a bouldery rockslide, you ascend six switchbacks, then immediately lose most of this hard-won elevation. You make a downhill traverse to a nice viewpoint of Three-corner Rock and the Stebbins Creek Valley, then descend five rough switchbacks to a camp next to a bridge over Stebbins Creek.

Now that the ups and downs are over, the trail crosses the bridge, then ducks into and climbs out of a side canyon on eight switchbacks that lead to the crest of a small ridge. For the next couple of miles the trail follows this ridge, rather steeply uphill at first, then more gently. Spur trails lead to decent viewpoints that make good rest stops, although the views don't compare to those from Three-corner Rock. Eventually you make a final fairly steep uphill push and come to a rough road. This is the upper trailhead described earlier.

The trail resumes just north of a little gully and makes 18 fairly long switchbacks through increasingly interesting and open country. There are several small rockslides and brushy areas on this slope, and the partially obstructed views improve as you climb. Finally, you top the ridge in a flowery meadow and meet a small road near a microwave tower. To reach the top of the rockpile at the summit, simply walk over to its base and scramble up the boulders to the old lookout site. Views extend to Mounts Adams, Hood, and St. Helens and include countless forested ridges and valleys in all directions.

Portland and the Willamette Valley

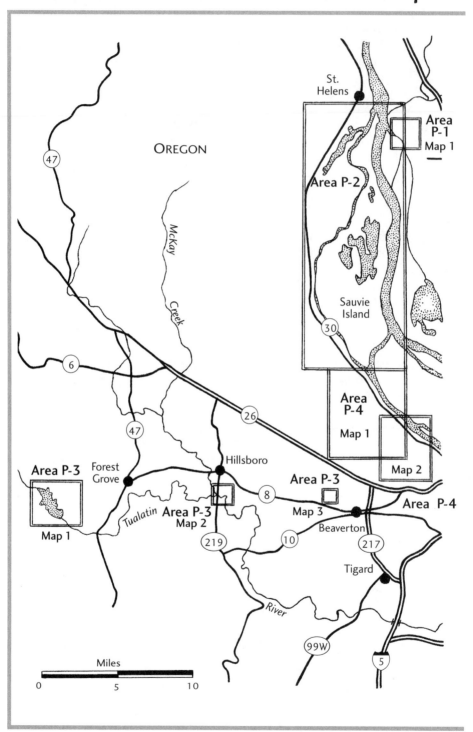

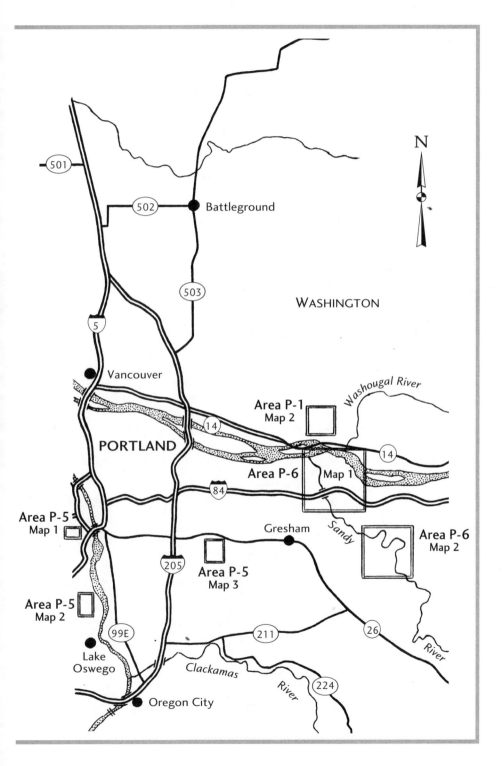

N

501

502 Battleground

503

WASHINGTON

5

Vancouver

Washougal River

Area P-1
Map 2

14

PORTLAND

Area P-6   Map 1

14

84

Area P-5
Map 1

Gresham

Sandy

Area P-6
Map 2

205

Area P-5
Map 3

Area P-5
Map 2

99E

211

26

River

Lake
Oswego

Clackamas

River

224

Oregon City

Oak trees stand along the Wetlands Trail in Ridgefield National Wildlife Refuge, Washington

Iron Mountain Bridge, Tryon Creek State Park, Oregon

Portland
and the
Willamette Valley

Area P-1: Around Vancouver

FAST-GROWING VANCOUVER SITS JUST NORTH OF THE COLUMBIA RIVER FROM PORTLAND AND IS THE SECOND LARGEST MEMBER OF THAT CITY'S METROPOLITAN COMPLEX. Even though artificial lines on a map put Vancouver in a different state than Portland, the city is effectively tied much more closely to Portland than to other Washington metropolises like Seattle and Spokane. The two cities are so similar in fact that for most residents the biggest clues that you are even *in* another state (apart from that big river you have to cross) is that in Washington you'll have to pay sales tax and to pump your own gas.

Outdoor lovers on either side of the river can easily drive back and forth to enjoy the highlights of both states, but for some reason people from Oregon rarely do so, opting instead to stick with the familiar destinations in their home state. This is a big mistake. Southwest Washington has a lot to offer, and some of those outdoor attractions are very close by. While Vancouver has no wild city parks to compare with Portland's Forest Park, a smaller city nearby does. In Lacamas Creek Park the small city of Camas has an outdoor treasure equal to anything you can find in more distant locations, with scenic hiking trails that take you to all of the many attractions. For wilder adventures, head just 15 minutes north of Vancouver to Ridgefield National Wildlife Refuge, one of the best wildlife-viewing areas in the Portland region. The refuge has only one developed hiking trail, but most of the land is open to the public, and many explorations are available to the adventurous walker.

Trip 1

Ridgefield Refuge – Oak to Wetlands Trail

(Map Area P-1, Map 1)

Distance	Elevation Gain	Hiking Time	Optional Map	Difficulty
2.1 miles	150'	1 hour	Use trailhead handout	*

⌂

Usually Open	All year
Best Times	Winter for wildlife; Late April for flowers
Agency	Ridgefield National Wildlife Refuge

This fine wildlife trail hits the most diverse and scenic terrain in Ridgefield National Wildlife Refuge, a generally overlooked local resource. Its easy circuit travels through habitat of a rich array of wildlife, including large concentrations of waterfowl in fall and winter. A visit in late April will delight you with colorful wildflowers. In winter and spring, the trail is often very muddy, so wear boots. Pets are not allowed on the refuge.

Directions: Take exit 14 off Interstate 5 north of Vancouver, and drive west on State Highway 501 for 3 miles to the community of Ridgefield. At the west end of town, turn right at a T-junction with Main Street. After 1.1 miles, turn left on a well-signed gravel road that in 200 yards arrives at a large parking area at the trailhead.

A paved trail drops from the parking lot to an information kiosk where you can pick up a map and interpretive brochure for the nature trail. From here the trail climbs over an elaborately large, arcing bridge that spans three sets of railroad tracks. Immediately on the other side of the bridge, turn right at a junction and follow the Oak to Wetlands Trail through country that is entirely true to its name. Initially, the path wanders through grassy areas punctuated by large specimens of Oregon white oak, tangles of blackberries, and a wide variety of birds. Look for rufous-sided towhees, various sparrows, black-capped chickadees, ring-necked pheasants, and the ubiquitous American robin.

Soon the path drops to a viewing area for Duck Lake and its surrounding marshes, where the abundant avian life changes to such species as mallards, red-winged blackbirds, and marsh wrens. Unfortunately, another form of flying wildlife, mosquitoes, also make their home here. Other animals to look for are painted turtles and nutrias, which look like large muskrats, as they sun themselves on the opposite bank of the lake.

Past Duck Lake the trail returns to the oaks, crosses a small creek on a bridge, and shortly thereafter arrives at a fork. Both directions are part of the loop, but for now bear left and hike through a swath of blackberry brambles, whose rapidly growing vines have sharp thorns that rip through both skin and clothing, so keep your distance. Soon after entering a forest of Douglas-fir, you veer left at another trail junction and continue to a 150-foot side trail to nature-trail site #9, on a little bluff overlooking part of the marsh. The main trail goes through lush forests with an understory of sword ferns and spring wildflowers like wood violet, twinflower, Oregon grape, and star-flowered smilacina.

Just as you emerge from the trees, you arrive at a junction with a trail that leads to a very worthwhile side trip visiting the most attractive terrain on this

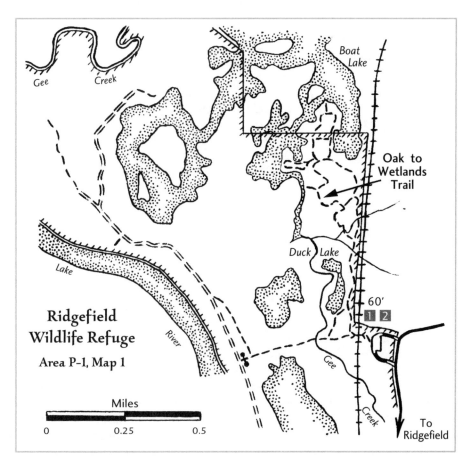

Gee   Creek

Boat
Lake

Oak to
Wetlands
Trail

Duck Lake

Lake

River

60'
1 2

Ridgefield
Wildlife Refuge

Area P-1, Map 1

Gee

Miles

0   0.25   0.5

Creek

To
Ridgefield

hike. To explore this area, go left at the junction. Some 10 feet later you will arrive at another junction with a smaller side loop to site #11 on the nature trail. This side route leads to a nice overlook of the marsh, where you may see a great blue heron or double-crested cormorant. In late April, this overlook supports an abundance of wildflowers, especially yellow buttercups and pink onions.

To see the trip's best scenery, return from site #11 and turn north on a trail that soon comes to a detour route which avoids the private property you are about to enter. The detour is mandatory from October 1 to the end of February, when the private property is closed to the public. In spring and summer, continue straight and hike up to site #12, an open knoll with fine views of lakes, marshes, and woodlands. The knoll is carpeted with wildflowers in late April, especially blue camas and pink onion. This is indeed a choice lunch spot.

To return to your car, first complete the side loop that goes up and down along the shores of tranquil Boot Lake, then turn left at the junction with the main loop and wander through lush, dense woods of Douglas-fir, bigleaf maple, western red cedar, and Oregon white oak. You may hear trains going by on the nearby railroad tracks, but otherwise this is a pleasant, woodsy walk that takes you back to the junction with the return trail near Duck Lake.

Trip 2

Ridgefield Refuge – Gee Creek Exploration

(Map Area P-1, Map 1)

Distance	Elevation Gain	Hiking Time	Optional Map	Difficulty
3.7 miles	100'	2 hours	None	**

Usually Open	All year (sometimes flooded in winter)
Best Times	Winter for wildlife; Late April for flowers
Agency	Ridgefield National Wildlife Refuge

If you didn't get enough exercise on the Oak to Wetlands Trail (Trip 1) or you're simply looking for a change of pace from established paths, try this excellent route. The trail here isn't officially maintained for hikers, but this entire portion of the refuge is open to the public. By exploring away from established routes, you can enjoy more solitude in a scenic setting. This area was originally set aside for the benefit of the many wildlife species that live here. To protect that wildlife, pets are strictly prohibited from the trail.

Directions: Take exit 14 off Interstate 5 north of Vancouver, and drive west on State Highway 501 for 3 miles to the community of Ridgefield. At the west end of town, turn right at a T-junction with Main Street. After 1.1 miles, turn left on a well-signed gravel road that in 200 yards arrives at a large parking area at the trailhead.

A paved trail drops from the parking lot to an information kiosk, then climbs over a large, arcing bridge that spans three sets of railroad tracks. Immediately on the other side of the bridge, the Oak to Wetlands Trail goes off to the right, but to explore the Gee Creek area you turn left.

The trail goes past some restrooms, then drops to a plank bridge over sluggish Gee Creek. From the bridge the path goes along the north shore of a marshy lake, where you are likely to see several species of water birds. In winter, look for ducks like mallard, pintail, and wigeon, as well as tundra swan and the ubiquitous great blue heron. In the adjoining marsh grasses and willow hedgerows are song sparrows and red-winged blackbirds. Much of this section will be muddy, and in some years it may even be flooded at this time of year, so rubber boots are best.

Where the trail comes to a gate, you turn right and parallel a brushy fence line. Follow this fence for several hundred yards to where you merge with a refuge maintenance road coming in from the left. Follow this rarely used road as it travels beside a thick hedgerow of blackberries, willows, and large cottonwood trees. The road goes through a usually open gate, cuts to the left

Gee Creek, Ridgefield National Wildlife Refuge, Washington

through the trees, and emerges at an open area. From here, a 50-yard side trail on the left goes to an overlook of Lake River, a backwater slough of the Columbia River, where you may see double-crested cormorants, red-tailed hawks, and northern harriers.

This overlook is an acceptable turnaround point, but a much better one is still ahead. About 0.1 mile past the side trail, the rapidly diminishing road splits. The route to the left heads through more wet fields and hedgerows before petering out altogether amid grasses and scattered oak trees. The more interesting and attractive option from the road split goes to the right and travels through a strip of trees to reach a larger meadow with a nice view of snow-capped Mt. St. Helens.

Continue hiking northeast on the overgrown road to a fence, which you climb over on a metal ladder, then ascend a bit to a small, grassy, oak-covered knoll. The trail disappears here, but take the time to explore the many nearby oak-covered hills. Your efforts will be well rewarded with photogenic trees, spring wildflowers, and fine views of a large lake to the south. Birds you may see on this lake include great egret, hooded merganser, tundra swan, and various species of ducks. Bring a blanket, binoculars, and a sack lunch to sit in the grass under the shade of the oak trees and watch the wildlife in style. Once you've had your fill, just return the way you came.

Trip 3

Lacamas Creek Park Loop

(Map Area P-1, Map 2)

Distance	Elevation Gain	Hiking Time	Optional Map	Difficulty
3.4 miles	400'	2 hours	Use trailhead signboards	*

Usually Open	All year
Best Times	Late April to early May
Agency	Clark Parks & Recreation Department

Camas is a small, unassuming mill town on the Washington side of the Columbia River that most outdoor lovers drive right past on their way to better-known attractions in the Columbia River Gorge. But the 6000 or so residents of this town have a secret that outsiders have yet to discover. Lacamas Creek Park, a 325-acre preserve, is one of the wildest and most attractive city parks in the country. Hidden in this park are unusually varied and attractive woods, beautiful waterfalls, a tranquil lake, lots of birds, and some of the best low-elevation wildflowers in the Portland area. This loop hike visits all of the park's numerous highlights and is one of the author's favorite easy hikes in the Portland/Vancouver area. It is the perfect option for you to showcase the subtle charms of our region to people visiting from out of town.

Directions: From Vancouver, drive east on State Highway 14 about 6 miles past the junction with Interstate 205 and take exit 12 to Camas. Drive the exit road for 1.4 miles, then turn right at a four-way flashing stoplight. After three blocks, turn left on N.E. 3rd Avenue and 0.8 mile later, just before you cross Lacamas Creek, turn left on an unsigned lane that looks like a private drive-way. About 50 yards down this road is a small trailhead parking lot. Be sure not to block a small, private, gravel driveway when you park.

Walk north past a house and go around the park's entry gate to a trailhead signboard. The wide gravel path wanders north, stay-ing above the rushing waters of Lacamas Creek and traveling through bigleaf-maple woods that in April and May come alive with the sounds of songbirds. Under the maples are common shrubs like holly,

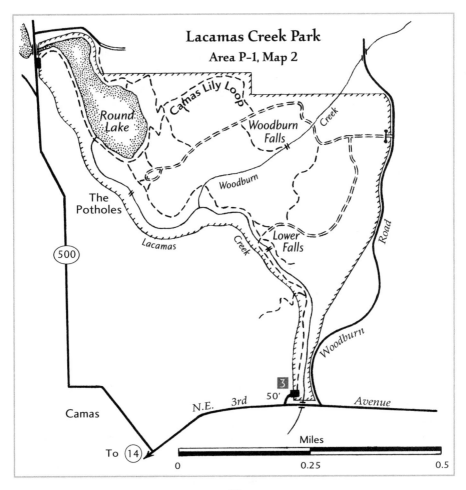

Lacamas Creek Park
Area P-1, Map 2

Camas Lily Loop

Round Lake

Woodburn Falls

Creek

Woodburn

The Potholes

Lacamas

Creek

Lower Falls

Road

500

Woodburn

3

N.E.   3rd   50'   Avenue

Camas

Miles

To 14

0   0.25   0.5

Lacamas Creek, Lacamas Creek Park, Camas, Washington

salmonberry, and thimbleberry, while the forest floor features the blossoms of false solomon seal, wild strawberry, bleeding heart, and fairybells.

After 0.25 mile you go straight at a junction with a side trail that goes off to the left and climbs to a residential area. The main trail rolls up and down through a forest where the bigleaf maples are joined by stately Douglas-fir and western hemlock. The forest floor is crowded with at least four different types of ferns: lady fern, maiden-hair fern, bracken fern, and sword fern. A little over 0.3 mile from the last junction, the trail comes to a pair of picnic tables, then crosses Lacamas Creek on a sturdy metal bridge just upstream from Lower Falls, an impressive sliding cascade.

On the east side of the bridge is an unsigned four-way junction. To the right, a winding, unofficial trail goes downstream along the east bank of Lacamas Creek providing some decent views of Lower Falls. To begin the loop, you turn left and walk upstream beside the beautifully cascading creek to a wooden bridge across smaller Woodburn Creek. Above this bridge you go through a grove of lovely western red cedar before climbing a bit to an open rocky meadow. In late April this meadow is filled with perky blue camas. Take the time to sit in this scenic meadow and look down on a short but impressive waterfall on Lacamas Creek called The Potholes.

Just a few feet past the meadow, you reach the end of a gravel service road and skirt around the left side of the road's turnaround loop. The path goes north for about 100 yards, past several unmarked side trails, to a junction with a wide path beside tranquil Round Lake. Turning left here takes you to a busy, manicured playground and picnic area typical of most city parks. For a wilder experience, turn right, and you will soon reach a junction at the southeast corner of the lake. You turn left here and make two short switchbacks up a hillside covered with vine maple and Douglas-fir, to a junction near the top of the hill.

Turn left at the junction and after 100 yards turn right on the Camas Lily Loop. Although most trails in this park are open to mountain bikers, the Camas Lily Loop goes through a designated natural area that is open only to foot travel. The path climbs steeply but briefly to an open meadow surrounded by Oregon white oak and white avalanche lilies. In the meadow itself is an abundance of blue camas. This is probably the best place in the Portland area to enjoy this lovely flower, which in the centuries before pavement and plowed fields was very common in the natural meadows of the Willamette Valley.

There are many side trails exploring the meadow, all of which are worthwhile, but for the loop you stay left at all questionable junctions. The main path skirts the outside edge of several meadows, then descends through evergreen woods to a junction with a closed gravel access road. For a fine short side trip here, go right about 100 yards, then turn left and walk downhill on a 0.2-mile side trail that dead-ends at the base of joyful Woodburn Falls, which cascades over a mossy rock ledge.

To complete the loop, return to the closed gravel road and walk east. The road loops down to the right to cross small Woodburn Creek on a wide bridge before ascending briefly to a junction. You turn right and walk a narrow gravel route through strikingly attractive mixed woods. In the spring, you might hear the eerie, high-pitched cries of ospreys, which live in this area. Here they find good nest sites in the tall snags, and plenty of fish to eat from Lacamas Creek, Round Lake, and the nearby Columbia River. The trail drops to a poorly marked junction with a wider gravel path, where you turn right and almost immediately return to the bridge just above Lower Falls. Cross the bridge and return the way you came.

Portland and the Willamette Valley

Area P-2: Sauvie Island

Located just downstream from the confluence of the Willamette and Columbia rivers, Sauvie Island is a mostly flat expanse of farms, marshes, and woodlands that has long been popular with visitors from Portland. They come to this, the largest island in the state of Oregon, for a variety of reasons, including pumpkin picking in the fall, berry harvesting and beachgoing in the summer, and wildlife watching in the winter. While the island is not particularly scenic, it is a great place to go birding, so if you must choose between carrying a camera and toting binoculars, go for the latter.

The northern half of the island is a state wildlife refuge open to hikers and other outdoor enthusiasts. Much of the refuge is closed to travel between October 1 and April 15, to protect wintering wildlife. There are no overnight camping facilities, and day visitors must purchase parking permits, which in 2001 cost $3.50 per day or $11 for an annual pass.

Trip 1

Warrior Rock

(Map Area P-2)

Distance	Elevation Gain	Hiking Time	Optional Map	Difficulty
6.8 miles	None	3 to 4 hours	None needed	**

Usually Open	All year
Best Times	All year
Agency	Sauvie Island Wildlife Area

At the northern tip of Sauvie Island is a quiet sandy beach that is ideally suited for watching ocean-going ships sail past while enjoying views of the city of St. Helens just across the water. In season, the hike provides opportunities either to observe wildlife (winter) or to pick delicious blackberries (summer). If you bring the family pet, keep in mind that all dogs must be on leash.

Directions: Drive U.S. Highway 30 northwest from downtown Portland about 10 miles to a traffic light where you turn right and immediately cross a bridge onto Sauvie Island. Once across the bridge, the road curves north and in 0.2 mile reaches Sam's Grocery, where you can purchase a day-use parking pass. Now that you can legally park on the island, continue north on Sauvie Island Road 1.8 miles, then turn right on Reeder Road. Stick with this road for 4.2 miles through a few minor intersections to a stop sign. Go straight, still on Reeder Road, and follow it for 8.6 miles until the road ends at a gravel turnaround. The last 2.3 miles of Reeder Road have a gravel surface.

You go through a fence stile on the west side of the parking lot, then follow an overgrown jeep track that loops north through a pasture where you'll have to step carefully to avoid smelly cow pies. In addition to cows, this grassy field often accommodates a flock of geese in winter. If you see the birds suddenly scatter for no apparent reason, be sure to check the skies for one possible cause: bald eagles, several of which spend the winter here.

At the north end of the field, go over or around another gate and pick up the rough refuge-maintenance road that you will follow for the rest of the hike. Much of the route is lined with huge cottonwood trees and a tangle of blackberry brambles. In mid-to-late August, the abundant berries of these thorny plants afford an irresistible temptation to turn your tongue and fingers purple, so allow plenty of time for picking and eating.

At several points along the way unsigned side roads and trails go off to the left, visiting various lakes and small ponds. At all junction stick to the main road, which always stays straight or bends to the right. In the spring, the mud along the road is a good place to look for the tracks of deer and raccoons.

After nearly 3 miles, the narrowing road fades away as it enters a small grassy meadow and comes to a fork. A couple of hundred yards to the right is a tiny lighthouse (closed to the public) and a secluded beach. This is the ideal spot for watching freighters go by. If you go left at the fork, you follow a foot trail beside a beach on the north shore of the island. After 0.5-mile you'll find some pilings where there is a nice view of the historic town of St. Helens to the west.

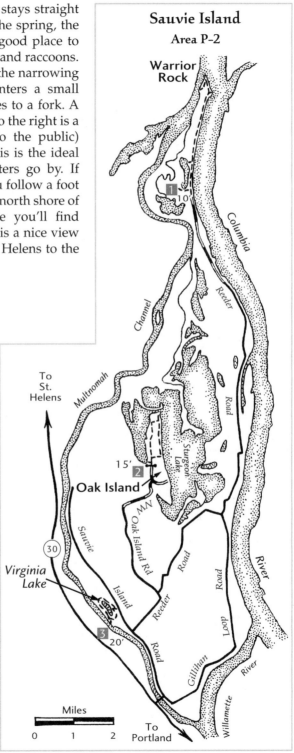

Trip 2

Oak Island Loop

(Map Area P-2)

Distance	Elevation Gain	Hiking Time	Optional Map	Difficulty
2.4 miles	None	2 hours	None needed	*

☁

Usually Open	April 16 to September 30
Best Times	Any time its open
Agency	Sauvie Island Wildlife Area

Oak Island *isn't* technically an island, because the shallow, murky waters of Sturgeon Lake surround only three sides. But why worry about technicalities when you can enjoy such a splendid spot? This easy nature trail is probably the nicest hike on Sauvie Island, because of the diversity of habitats, the good views, and the abundant wildlife. You can even learn something by picking up the trailhead handout, which explains the natural and the Native American history at various marked stops along the way. Dogs must be on leash.

Directions: Drive U.S. Highway 30 northwest from downtown Portland about 10 miles to a traffic light, where you turn right and immediately cross a bridge onto Sauvie Island. Once across the bridge, the road curves north and in 0.2 mile reaches Sam's Grocery, where you can purchase a day-use parking pass. Now that you can legally park on the island, continue north on Sauvie Island Road for 1.8 miles, then turn right on Reeder Road. Drive this route 1.1 miles, then veer left onto N.W. Oak Island Road. Follow this road 3.1 miles to the end of pavement at a gate that is closed at 10:00 P.M., to enforce the refuge's day-use only policy. Go straight through the gate and drive 1.0 mile further, following signs for a nature trail, to the roadend parking lot beside a second gate and signboard.

After walking around this gate you will immediately come to a fork in the road. Bear left onto a lesser-used jeep route signed with a small yellow hiker symbol. This route goes north through oak woodlands, past lots of blackberry brambles, and into some open areas where a few blue camases bloom in late April and May. As you hike, you may enjoy the sight of cute little cottontail rabbits or fast-running California quail scurrying away into the brush. Also making their home here are black-tailed deer, northern flickers, song sparrows, various warblers, mourning doves, and other wildlife.

At a junction after about 0.2 mile, the trail forks to form the loop. For a clockwise loop, go straight and hike beside a large cultivated field on the left and a wild oak woodland on the right. After going north for about 0.8 mile, the trail goes through a small stand of cottonwoods, where colorful northern orioles nest, then turns right. The route now heads east for a short distance to the shores of Sturgeon Lake. To the northeast, snowy Mt. St. Helens looms like a conical, flat-topped cloud. In the shallow waters of the lake, large carp rise to the surface and make quite a ruckus with their splashing.

The trail turns south at the lake and follows its shore for about 0.8 mile to a small, rocky beach. Here the trail veers to the right at a yellow hiker sign and closes the loop with an easy stroll through oak woodlands to the junction north of the parking lot.

Trip 3

Virginia Lake Loop

(Map Area P-2)

Distance	Elevation Gain	Hiking Time	Optional Map	Difficulty
2.2 miles	None	1.5 hours	None needed	*

Usually Open	April 16 to September 30
Best Times	Any time it's open
Agency	Sauvie Island Wildlife Area

This is a very easy loop that goes around a marshy, wildlife-rich lake and visits Multnomah Channel, where anglers can try their luck in the Columbia River backwater. Like all trails on Sauvie Island, this is a good choice for hikers with children, as the trail gains no elevation and sports lots of wildlife. In August, both kids and parents will enjoy eating the delicious blackberries that ripen there. Dogs must be on a leash.

Directions: Drive U.S. Highway 30 northwest from downtown Portland about 10 miles to a traffic light, where you turn right and immediately cross a bridge onto Sauvie Island. Once across the bridge, the road curves north and in 0.2 mile reaches Sam's Grocery, where you can purchase a day-use parking pass. Now that you can legally park on the island, continue north on Sauvie Island Road for 1.8 miles to a junction where you go straight. After 0.6 mile you turn left into a small gravel parking lot for the Wapato Greenway Access.

You hop over a gate across a maintenance road and hike west 100 yards on a jeep route beside a hedgerow. At an unsigned junction a hiking trail veers to the left, while the jeep road goes right. For a clockwise loop, follow the trail to the left, which goes along the edge of a

Virginia Lake, Sauvie Island

grassy field beside a brushy area of blackberry brambles and cherry trees. As you hike, listen and watch for song sparrows, western meadowlarks, American robins, rufous-sided towhees, yellowthroats, and a variety of other songbirds. After 0.1 mile you hit a junction with a wide gravel track and turn left.

This trail stays in the shade of tall black cottonwoods as it loops around the edge of a large marsh called Virginia Lake. Along the way you pass a wildlife-viewing blind, a little before crossing over the end of the marsh. Then you wander through a cottonwood forest to the next unsigned junction, where a 150-yard dead-end trail goes off to the left to Hadley's Landing, a fishing pier and boat dock on Multnomah Channel.

If you go right at the loop trail junction, you travel north through a shady strip of cottonwoods and brush. Multnomah Channel is on the left and Virginia Lake on the right. Although poison oak is rare here, there are more than enough thorny blackberry vines and stinging nettles to discourage off-trail exploration. In the spring, this stretch of trail is especially nice early in the morning when all the birds are singing.

After about 1 mile, the trail curves right and crosses the end of the Virginia Lake marsh on a short boardwalk. Now you climb very briefly, then turn south on slightly higher ground past farms, grassy fields, and scattered oaks and Douglas-firs. If you brought binoculars, you will have the chance to search the marsh for great blue herons, cinnamon teals, red-winged blackbirds, mallards, and other water-loving birds that make the marsh home. After about 0.6 mile, you come to a junction beside a covered picnic shelter, where you turn left and close out the loop with a short stroll back to your car.

Portland and the Willamette Valley

Area P-3: Washington County

Although thousands of outdoor lovers live in Washington County, and there are plenty of things to see, the county boasts very few hiking trails. The majority of the county's land lies in the fertile flatlands of the Tualatin Valley. Until recently, most of this was farmland. Although it was privately owned, it was at least rural and attractive.

Today, tens of thousands of acres in this, Oregon's fastest growing county, have been paved over and developed into subdivisions, strip malls, and high-tech enterprises. While these provide necessary employment and housing, they lack natural appeal. The wildest country still in public hands is in the western part of the county, in the foothills of the Coast Range. But even here there are virtually no trails. The only hiking opportunities are in isolated regional parks and nature preserves.

The study of economics informs us that one of the things that makes an item valuable is scarcity, so Washington County's few wild trails are all the more valuable due to their rarity. Each of the three trails described in this book is fairly new, and each explores very different sorts of terrain.

At Henry Hagg Lake, you can walk a meandering shoreline path that circles a surprisingly attractive reservoir in the foothills of the Coast Range. In the Jackson Bottom Wetlands Preserve, a trail explores the bird-rich marshes and riparian areas near the Tualatin River south of the bustling city of Hillsboro. Finally, in the Tualatin Hills Nature Park, the wild crown jewel of a system of parks run by the Tualatin Hills Park and Recreation District, you can explore dense forests and small ponds. Hopefully the popularity of these new trails should inspire the development of more parks and preserves for Washington County hikers.

South Shore Henry Hagg Lake

Trip 1

Henry Hagg Lake Loop

(Map Area P-3, Map 1)

Distance	Elevation Gain	Hiking Time	Optional Map	Difficulty
13.1 miles	250'	6.5 hours	Not really necessary	***

Usually Open	All year
Best Times	Early-to-mid April
Agency	Bureau of Reclamation

The trail around Henry Hagg Lake, a man-made reservoir built in 1975, comes as something of a surprise to wilderness lovers. You'd never expect to find such a pleasantly wild footpath around a reservoir, especially one with a good paved highway circling it. But the trail builders did such an admirable job of routing this path that hikers can enjoy something close to a wilderness experience, despite nearby distractions.

If you visit in the first part of April, when the developed recreation sites surrounding the lake are not yet open, the wilderness feeling is greatly enhanced. Fortunately, early April is also a particularly scenic time to make this hike because of the abundance of forest wildflowers and the budding leaves on the trees. You will have to carry all of your own water at this time of year, however, because the piped water sources at the picnic areas will not yet be available. The path is closed to horses, but is open to mountain bikes and, in fact, the circuit is a wonderful trip for bicyclists.

Directions: Drive State Highway 47 south from Forest Grove almost 4 miles and turn right (west) on the well-signed road to Scoggins Valley Park and Henry Hagg Lake. Continue for 4 miles to the large earthen dam that creates the reservoir. An elaborately large fee booth collects a day-use charge from late April through September. There are at least a dozen places you could start this loop trip, but if you visit before the recreation sites are open, you'll have to park at one of the lots beside the main road or, as recommended here, at the gravel parking lot below the dam just south of the entrance booth.

From the lower lot you follow a narrow gravel road up a grassy slope to the top of the dam. For a counterclockwise loop, cross the road atop the dam and follow a fence line about 0.2 mile to a paved road that is gated and closed in the off season. As at all places where the trail touches a road, the trailhead is marked by a rust-red-colored post.

To pick up the trail, walk down toward the lake and look for the path leaving the parking area about 100 yards north. The surprisingly quiet trail goes up and down as it zigzags in and out of forested side canyons with pic-

Henry Hagg Lake
Area P-3, Map 1

turesque bridges over trickling creeks. The forests are surprisingly open, and feature pretty April-blooming wildflowers like wood violet, trillium, and slender toothwort. The murky, greenish waters of the lake are almost always visible through the trees, and you will often hear waves lapping up against the shore. As you hike this circuit you will pass dozens of short spur trails (far too many to list in this text) that take off to the right leading to the road, but in all cases the proper route for continuing to circle the lake is unmistakable. Somewhat less frequent, but more worthwhile, are the many short routes leading down to the lake. Almost all these paths end at choice picnic spots.

After 1.3 miles, you cross a paved boat-ramp parking area. The trail resumes at the west end of the lot as an all-accessible paved trail. You walk past a couple of scenic picnic sites, then return to dirt path and make a long detour through pleasant forests around a large arm of the reservoir. In these woods listen for the surprisingly loud song of winter wrens and, in the spring, the drumming of ruffed grouse. You can see an inviting and attractive grassy hillside on the opposite shore of the lake. The trail continues to the end of the lake arm, where you cross a small creek over a culvert, then briefly touch the road at a trailhead.

The path now passes several sturdy picnic tables before emerging on the grassy hillside you saw from the opposite shore. This is a fine place to lazily lie in the grass and enjoy a tranquil view. From this grassy area you return to a second-growth forest of western red cedar, Douglas-fir, red alder, grand fir, and bigleaf maple, as the up-and-down trail alternates between woods and grassy overlooks framed by oak trees. After passing through more woods, the path travels just below the road, along the edge of a marshy area, before climbing briefly to the road shoulder.

The route then follows the road shoulder for about 250 yards to cross a bridge over Tanner Creek, where you return to a true trail. This path travels through more scenic grassy areas and marshes alive with red-winged black-birds. You must negotiate several muddy spots as you round two small arms of the lake, before coming to a large gravel parking area. Follow the road for 0.4 mile past the attractive Scoggins Creek Picnic Area, then go over a road bridge that spans clear, rushing Scoggins Creek.

Not far from this creek, you turn left onto a footpath, then make several steep little ups and downs near the lake in a pleasant mix of woods, artificial rocky areas, and grassy slopes. You then come to a large boat ramp and picnic area, which are very busy in the summer months. You cross two large parking lots before returning to the trail. Another 0.3 mile of hiking takes you to the more intimate Sain Creek Picnic Area, after which you round yet another arm of the reservoir and follow the road again to cross Sain Creek itself.

The final segment of the path is more of the same — skirting arms of the lake, passing through woods alive with flowers like calipso orchid and wood violet, and crossing grassy areas. You often approach but never quite reach the road. The footpath ends about 0.2 mile before you reach the south end of the dam. From here you follow the road past a large gravel parking area, then over the dam and back down to your car.

Along the north shore of Henry Hagg Lake

Trip 2

Kingfisher Marsh Loop

(Map Area P-3, Map 2)

Distance	Elevation Gain	Hiking Time	Optional Map	Difficulty
1.8 miles	100'	1 hour	Trailhead handout	*

Usually Open	All year
Best Times	November to April (for wildlife)
Agency	Jackson Bottom Wetlands Preserve

As science increases human understanding of natural ecosystems, our appreciation of what used to be considered *wasteland* has changed. For example, what used to be worthless *jungles* are now seen as invaluable *rainforests*, the loss of which is now widely considered a global crisis. On a domestic level, there once were *swamps*, which had to be drained and put to more "productive" uses. Now they are *wetlands* with recognized value as wildlife habitats, flood-control areas, and natural filters for water pollutants. Like tropical rainforests, the loss of wetlands is now seen as a matter of grave concern.

Jackson Bottom is a precious remnant of the Willamette Valley's once extensive wetlands. With all but a few such areas long since filled and converted into shopping malls or agricultural land, wildlife is increasingly dependent on the tiny wetlands that remain. A visit to this 650-acre preserve gives hikers a chance to see a great blue heron colony, rafts of waterfowl, and aquatic mammals such as muskrats, beavers, and river otters. Pets are not allowed on the trails in this wildlife preserve.

Directions: Begin by driving to downtown Hillsboro, about 15 miles west of Portland. Turn south on State Highway 219 (S. First Avenue) and 1.4 miles later look for a marked trailhead parking lot on the left, immediately before the bridge over the Tualatin River.

From the southwest corner of the parking area, the trail drops on wooden steps into dense riverside vegetation and turns downstream. For tangible proof of the abundance of wildlife in Jackson Bottom, take some time to look beside the slow-moving water in search of tracks in the mud. In the spring, warblers fill the air with their distinctive songs, and in winter the sounds of honking geese give hikers a thrill.

The dirt path (sometimes muddy in winter) follows the river to a junction with a trail that is covered with wood chips to reduce the mud problems. You turn right at this junction and travel between the dense riparian vegetation on your right and grassy Kingfisher Marsh on your left. Numerous interpretive

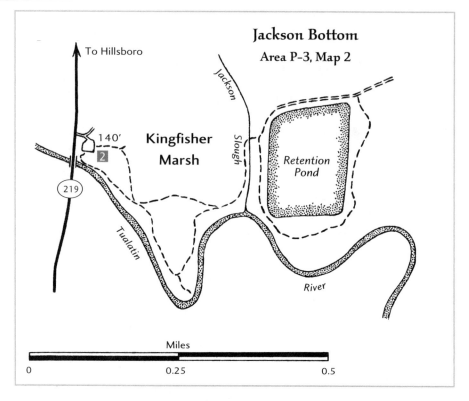

Jackson Bottom
Area P–3, Map 2

To Hillsboro

Jackson

Jackson Slough

140'

Kingfisher
Marsh

Retention
Pond

219

Tualatin

River

Miles

0   0.25   0.5

signs, all drawn and written by local elementary-school children, add to the enjoyment of this hike, as do the many benches where you can rest and listen to the birds. Another nice feature are the hundreds of bird houses erected by local wildlife enthusiasts, which are clearly appreciated by our feathered friends, who happily make use of these nesting sites.

The level path comes to a dead end at a viewing platform at a curve in the Tualatin River. To return to the loop trail, retrace your steps about 100 feet, then turn north on a trail that soon reconnects with the woodchip-covered route you left earlier. The trail now travels north beside small Jackson Slough, and soon comes to a viewing shelter that overlooks Kingfisher Marsh to the west and a large retention pond to the east. You will cheer for the swallows that zip past your head here in search of insects, as there seems to be no shortage of blood-sucking mosquitoes.

The trail crosses a bridge over Jackson Slough, where you may hear the raucous call of marsh wrens. It then splits to loop around the retention pond. Turn right and walk through the tall grasses back to the trees beside the Tualatin River, then curve left and pass between the river and the retention pond through an area of overgrown shrubbery. After leaving the trees, you come to another viewing shelter, then zigzag through grassy areas to a junction with a maintenance road at the northeast corner of the pond. Turn left and walk the sometimes muddy road back to the junction at the bridge over Jackson Slough.

For variety on the return trip, you can skip the riverside path and take the trail in the grasses north of the river. This path passes a spur to yet another viewing platform, shortly before ending at the southeast corner of the parking area.

Trip 3

Tualatin Hills Nature Park Loop

(Map Area P-3, Map 3)

Distance	Elevation Gain	Hiking Time	Optional Map	Difficulty
2.1 miles	50'	1.5 hours	Use trailhead handout	*

Usually Open	All year
Best Times	All Year
Agency	Tualatin Hills Park & Recreation District

The Tualatin Hills Nature Park does not provide a wilderness experience. At just 195 acres, this little suburban oasis is too small to truly escape the sights and sounds of the outside world. In addition, the park is so popular you are almost constantly in the company of other park users pushing baby carriages, jogging, or quietly enjoying the trails. But the park itself and its landscapes are still quite wild, and in at least one way they are even *more* natural than many locations farther from the city. In the park, efforts have been made to remove non-native plants like English ivy, so the mosaic of species here consists primarily of native vegetation. There is also a wide assortment of wildlife to enjoy, including muskrats, beavers, rough-skinned newts, and dozens of species of birds. Bring a pair of binoculars and several nature guides to fully enjoy this hike.

Directions: The best access is from the Interpretive Center in the southeast corner of the preserve. To reach it, take Murray Boulevard either 0.3 mile north from State Highway 8 (the Tualatin Valley Highway) or 2.1 miles south from the Murray Road exit off U.S. Highway 26. In either case, you reach a traffic light and turn west on Millikan Way. Take this route 0.7 mile past a traffic light and turn right at the well-signed turnoff into the parking lot.

The trailhead on the north side of the interpretive center is marked by a large signboard, where you can gather general information about the park and pick up a trail map. The paved trail goes for about 200 feet to a junction which, like all the junctions in the park, is marked by a small post identifying the trails and distances. There are many good options from this point. For the recommended loop, turn right on the

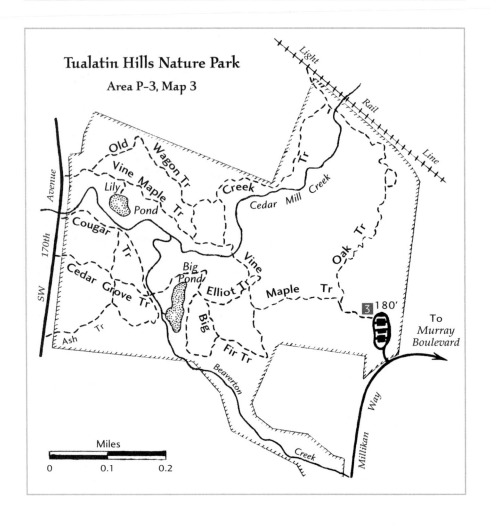

Tualatin Hills Nature Park

Area P-3, Map 3

paved Oak Trail and wander this circuitous path through lovely second-growth forests.

The trees are a mix of Douglas-fir, red alder, Oregon white oak, western red cedar, Pacific yew, and grand fir. Not far into the hike you come to some out-of-place ponderosa pines, a very unusual species for the west side of the Cascades. In early April the park features a variety of woodland wildflowers, as well as numerous migrating and resident birds, most prominently black-capped chickadees, winter wrens, and rufous-sided towhees. Many benches and interpretive signs along the trail offer good opportunities to stop and to enjoy both flowers and birds.

The remarkably level, paved route uses boardwalks to cross marshes and wet areas. The most extensive network of these boardwalks takes you over Cedar Mill Creek, where a spur from the main trail leads to a romantic little gazebo overlooking the marsh. In this area you will probably hear the trains of Portland's light-rail transit system zipping past, but fortunately these intrusions are brief and the trains remarkably quiet, compared to typical trains.

Just after the end of the last boardwalk is a junction. To do the full loop, leave the paved trail here and turn left onto Creek Trail, a woodchip-covered path that is often muddy and may be closed in winter. This trail follows the edge of a marshy area where thick-stalked rushes line the path. The calls of red-winged blackbirds draw your attention away from the warehouse complex just outside the preserve, on your right.

You soon turn away from the warehouse area and reenter wilder woods, just before coming to a junction with the Old Wagon Trail. Turn right on

Sword fern in Tualatin Hills Nature Park

this woodchip- and gravel-covered path and less than 0.1 mile later turn left on Coyote Trail, which goes a short distance to a junction with the paved Vine Maple Trail.

At this junction you have the option of returning to the Interpretive Center by turning left, but for more exercise and a longer loop, turn right. This pleasant route goes 0.2 mile to where the pavement ends at a short spur to Lily Pond. After taking this side trip, you follow the main route, which goes straight and soon reaches busy S.W. 170th Avenue. You turn left, following the road shoulder. At the south end of the bridge over Beaverton Creek, look for the Cougar Trail back into the park. In winter, avoid this path because it is usually flooded.

As an alternate route you can continue on the highway shoulder for another 0.1 mile, then take the much drier Cedar Grove Trail to rejoin the loop. In drier conditions, follow the Cougar Trail as it goes through muddy areas beside the creek to a junction, where you go straight and continue near the creek to a four-way junction next to a bridge. A 100-yard walk up the trail that goes straight here takes you to a good view of Big Pond, where you are likely to see ducks, geese, great blue herons, belted kingfishers, and other water-loving birds.

Back at the bridge, you cross the creek, then skirt the marsh of Big Pond to a junction with the Elliot Trail. From here you can follow either the woodsy Big Fir Trail to the right, or follow the Elliot Trail directly back to the paved Vine Maple Trail. In either case, once you reach the Vine Maple Trail, turn right and join the legions of joggers and baby strollers heading back to the Interpretive Center.

Portland and the Willamette Valley

Area P-4: Forest Park

Most backcountry hikers scoff at the words "city park." That's where you go with the kids on a lazy afternoon to toss the Frisbee on a manicured lawn or to watch junior's little league baseball game. City parks certainly aren't the destination for a *real* wilderness experience. Well it's time to adjust your attitudes, because Portland's Forest Park is no ordinary city park.

First of all, it's *huge*. Covering fully 5000 acres, Forest Park is the largest forested city park in the United States. Secondly, it's *wild*. There are no manicured lawns, ball fields, or man-made improvements of any sort, other than trails and a few old roads. The place is wild enough, in fact, that the woods are home to elk and the occasional black bear. Right here in the city limits is a bona fide wilderness.

Exploring this gigantic preserve is made relatively easy by an intricate network of hiking trails. Walking these trails is not only good exercise, it's fun and attractive. The paths travel through miles of mixed woods, cross numerous small creeks, lead past tiny woodland wildflowers, and prowl ridges where bigleaf maples display their lovely fall colors.

It is true that, were it not for its easy access, Forest Park would not be the much-loved place that it is. With no identifiable destinations, your goal here is simply to enjoy walking in a quiet and beautiful forest, not getting from Point A to Point B as quickly as you can. Every mile of every trail is equally attractive and can best be described as continuously pleasant rather than spectacular. There are no real *highlights*, but there are still a lot of worthwhile trail miles, and the best part is that you don't have to leave the city limits to enjoy them.

Trip 1

Far North Forest Park

(Map Area P-4, Map 1)

Distance	Elevation Gain	Hiking Time	Optional Map	Difficulty
5.1 miles	300'	2.5 hours	None needed	**
(one way)	(one way)	(one way)		

☁

Usually Open	All year
Best Times	April / early November
Agency	Portland Parks Bureau

Starting in Washington Park near the Oregon Zoo, the Wildwood Trail has been gradually extended over the years so that it now travels almost 30 miles through the wilderness parks in the hills of northwest Portland. The entire route is a joy, and any section makes an excellent option for Portlanders seeking exercise and the quiet contemplation of nature. The last section to be completed was the 5.1 miles through the far northern part of Forest Park.

This hike is pleasant in any season, but the trail is most enjoyable in April, when the forest flowers are in bloom, or in November, when the bigleaf maples put on a fine fall-color display. In theory, the route is open only to pedestrians, although in practice you will see lots of mountainbike tracks.

Directions: To reach the N.W. Germantown Road trailhead, follow U.S. Highway 30 (N.W. St. Helens Road) through northwest Portland to the St. Johns Bridge. Just north of the bridge, turn sharply left at a traffic light and follow the bridge-access road 0.1 mile to the junction with N.W. Germantown Road. Here you turn right and drive 1.5 miles to the small trailhead parking area on the left. Unless you are just being dropped off, don't start this hike from its north end at N.W. Newberry Road, since there is no parking or identifiable trailhead.

The northbound Wildwood Trail starts from a log-lined parking pullout about 100 yards downhill from the signed parking area. The remarkably level route immediately begins the pattern it will retain throughout its length—zigzagging into little gullies and around small ridges on a quiet forested hillside. Light-blue diamonds painted on tree trunks mark the route, but really are unnecessary, as the route is always evident.

The woodsy scenery rarely changes, but it is not monotonous—unless you don't like lush forests, delicate ferns, stately trees, and forest wildlife.

Remarkably, even though you never leave Portland's city limits, you rarely hear the sounds of traffic or anything else unnatural. The forest alter-

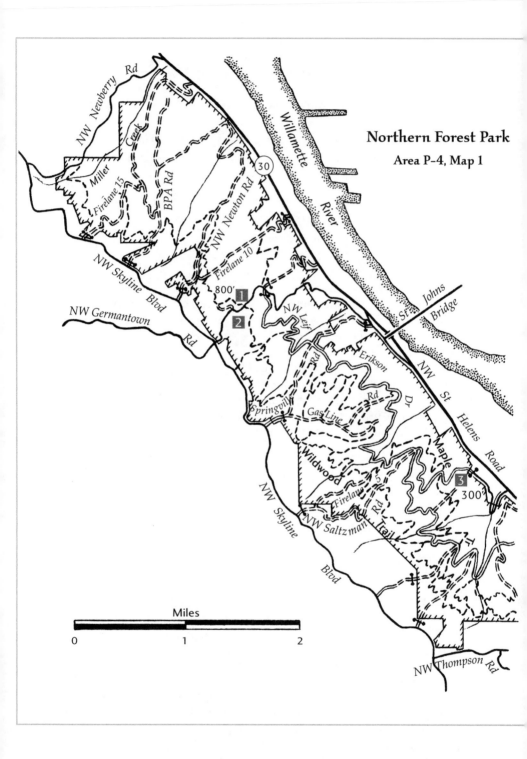

Northern Forest Park

Area P-4, Map 1

nates between areas dominated by evergreens like western red cedar, Douglas-fir, and western hemlock, and those places dominated by deciduous trees, especially bigleaf maple and red alder.

Ferns are abundant throughout and always lovely. The most common variety is sword fern. Bracken fern predominates in areas that get a bit more sun, and maiden-hair fern on the wetter slopes. Delicate licorice fern hang from the trunk of almost every tree. Other forest-floor species include native Oregon grape and thimbleberry, and non-native blackberry and English ivy, which grow out of control and are slowly taking over everything.

Since this description applies to every mile of this hike, all that remains is a listing of the other landmarks and junctions. Major junctions are marked with signs showing a map and distances to the nearest .01 mile, (as if it really mattered whether a trail is 5.12 or 5.13 miles long).

After 0.8 mile, you cross Fire Lane 10, one of several former roads now used as trails. In another mile, more woodsy zigs and zags take you to abandoned N.W. Newton Road. Another mile, mostly a gentle uphill, brings you to a powerline and the BPA Road. One more gentle mile, and you cross Fire Lane 15 and a second set of powerlines. You finish off with a mile of attractive forest walking and a quick trip into the headwaters of Miller Creek. Done as a one-way car shuttle, this trail makes a very easy dayhike.

Trip 2

Northern Forest Park Loop

(Map Area P-4, Map 1)

Distance	Elevation Gain	Hiking Time	Optional Map	Difficulty
16.1 miles	500'	6 to 8 hours	None needed	***
(with many shorter options)				

Usually Open	All year
Best Times	April / early November
Agency	Portland Parks Bureau

Don't be put off by the long mileage of this trip. The total shown is only a suggestion. The Wildwood Trail and N.W. Leif Erikson Drive, which form the outgoing and returning legs of the loop, run parallel to one another, and there are numerous connecting routes, so there is always an option for crossing over and shortening this hike. Like other trails in Forest Park, this loop keeps to deep woods. The forest is always shady and enjoyable, with lots of lush greenery in spring and early summer. In early November, the less popular northern parts of Forest Park are more attractive than the southern regions, because more of the trees are deciduous, and the fall colors are on display.

Directions: To reach the N.W. Germantown Road trailhead, follow U.S. Highway 30 (N.W. St. Helens Road) through northwest Portland to the St. Johns Bridge. Just north of the bridge, turn sharply left at a traffic light and follow the bridge-access road 0.1 mile to the junction with N.W. Germantown Road. Turn right here and drive 1.5 miles to the small trailhead parking area on the left.

As it does elsewhere in Forest Park, the Wildwood Trail here contours across steep, forested hillsides, extending to the ends of minor ridges and down the little gullies and canyons of seasonal trickling creeks. Small woodland wildflowers brighten the forest floor in the spring, especially white trillium and yellow wood violet in April. Taller shrubs include Oregon grape and salmonberry, with an abundance of sword fern scattered throughout.

How far you go depends entirely on how much exercise you want and the time available. There are many points where your route intersects trails or old roads and you can cut it short by descending about 150 feet to go back on N.W. Leif Erikson Drive. The first of these comes after just 0.6 mile, at the intersection with the Waterline Trail. After this the Wildwood Trail continues into deep little canyons lush with maiden-hair fern and tiny creeks spanned by quaint little bridges. About 1.5 miles further on comes your next opportunity to turn left, on Springville Road, a closed dirt and gravel route.

About 0.8 mile beyond the Springville Road junction, deep-forest travel takes you to the Hardestry Trail, which is your next opportunity to drop down to N.W. Leif Erikson Drive. Taking this left turn and looping back to your car ends a good short dayhike of about 5.6 miles. If you continue on the Wildwood Trail, you wind back and forth in attractive woods for 1.7 miles to Gas Line Road, yet another dirt road that can be used to close a moderately long loop.

If you push even further on the Wildwood Trail, you cross Oil Line Road after 0.5 mile. From there 2.8 miles of wild zigs and zags bring you to the last recommended turnaround point, at the end of Firelane 5. To close the loop here, turn left and walk the 0.3 mile down to N.W. Leif Erikson Drive. This junction is only a few hundred yards from the Maple Trail. If you have two

White trillium

cars, you can make this hike a fun one-way trip by ending at the N.W. Saltzman Road trailhead, described in Trip 3. N.W. Leif Erikson Drive here is relatively free of joggers and bicyclists, so the gentle walk along this overgrown old route is quiet and pleasant. It is about 7 miles along N.W. Leif Erikson Drive back to N.W. Germantown Road, where you turn left and walk uphill 0.3 mile back to the Wildwood trailhead.

Trip 3

Central Forest Park Loop

(Map Area P-4, Map 1)

Distance	Elevation Gain	Hiking Time	Optional Map	Difficulty
8.2 miles	500'	4 hours	None needed	**

Usually Open	All year
Best Times	Late March to mid-April
Agency	Portland Parks Bureau

This loop hike, through the central part of the preserve, is the wildest option in Forest Park. Other hikes require using the biker-and-jogger thoroughfare of N.W. Leif Erikson Drive on your return. On this outing, however, almost all of the route keeps to hiker-only trails by linking the Maple Trail with a typically attractive section of the Wildwood Trail, which makes for a beautiful and quiet circuit through the hills.

Directions: Drive on U.S. Highway 30 from northwest Portland toward St. Helens. Just past milepost 5, turn left on N.W. Saltzman Road and drive 0.9 mile to a gate. Be sure not to block the gate when you park.

You begin with an easy uphill walk of 0.4 mile on N.W. Saltzman Road to a junction with the Maple Trail, where the loop begins. For a clockwise loop, turn left and follow the narrow footpath as it ascends through a forest of western hemlock, Douglas-fir, and—true to the trail's name—bigleaf maple, which put on a nice show of bright yellow leaves in early November. Down on the forest floor is the characteristic assortment of sword fern, Oregon grape, and the invasive English ivy, along with a smattering of forest wildflowers, such as trillium, wood violet, and vanilla leaf, which peak in early April.

You cross a jeep track beneath a set of powerlines, then wind very gradually uphill as the trail explores these heavily forested ridges and creek canyons. The trickling creeks are spanned by quaint little wooden footbridges. Since you're not heading to an end point at some lake, viewpoint, or waterfall, take the opportunity to clear your mind of the hiker's disease of *destinationitis*. Enjoy the glories of the hike itself, especially the subtle charms and intimate beauty of this quiet forest. It won't be long before you realize that the white blossom of a trillium, the mosses and licorice ferns hanging onto the limbs of a maple tree, or the deep-green fronds of a sword fern afford as much beauty as more "spectacular" mountain lakes or vistas.

Stay on the Maple Trail, keeping left at one possibly unsigned junction, all the way to N.W. Leif Erikson Drive. Since it is far from the nearest trailhead, this part of the closed road sees fewer joggers and only a handful of bicyclists. Your route crosses the road, staying to the left with the Maple Trail, rather than the parallel old fire road on the right. You then climb a bit to the crossing of a tiny creeklet and a junction with the Wildwood Trail.

To do the recommended loop, turn right on the Wildwood Trail and amble along this famous path as it contours across the forested slopes of the park. As usual, the Wildwood Trail rarely gains or loses any noticeable elevation, featuring only brief ups and downs for the next 3.2 miles. You'll cross several creeklets, a small clearing beneath a powerline, and three old jeep roads, but the basic forest scenery remains unchanged throughout, and the proper course is always well marked. At one of the many small ridges along the way, you reach the end of Firelane 5, a closed jeep road going up to the left. Turn right onto a possibly unsigned but obvious foot trail that loses about 150 feet in 0.3 mile before arriving back at N.W. Leif Erikson Drive. You turn right on this closed road, and a little less than 0.2 mile later, you turn left at a small grassy area, returning to the Maple Trail. This path goes 1.2 miles through more of the same kind of uneventful but pleasant forest scenery back to the junction with N.W. Saltzman Road.

Trip 4

Southern Forest Park Loop

(Map Area P-4, Map 2)

Distance	Elevation Gain	Hiking Time	Optional Map	Difficulty
8.6 mile	700'	4 hours	None needed	**

Usually Open	All year
Best Times	Late March to mid-April
Agency	Portland Parks Bureau

Even if Forest Park lacks any really spectacular scenery, you can't beat it for convenience. With less than a five-minute drive you can go from the hectic world of downtown traffic and skyscrapers to the quiet woods of this massive park. Outdoor-loving office workers come here for a short hike or a jog during their lunch break, while others take advantage of the long evenings of early summer to go for a hike after work.

This route in the southern part of the park is especially convenient, since it has the shortest street access to the big city. Interestingly, most visitors aren't hikers at all; N.W. Leif Erikson Drive is closed to cars but hosts a cross section of Portland's fitness fanatics, joggers, bicyclists, and inline skaters, all taking advantage of this scenic, traffic-free opportunity to pursue their chosen form of exercise. But don't be dissuaded from a visit just because part of the loop is heavily traveled by nonhikers. The upper segment of the route, along the Wildwood Trail, is for pedestrians only and therefore much less crowded than other parts of the park.

Directions: From Interstate 405 in downtown Portland, take exit 3 for U.S. Highway 30 toward the town of St. Helens. From this off-ramp you immediately exit onto N.W. Vaughn Street, which you follow for 0.3 mile to the traffic light at N.W. 26th Street. Turn left, then two blocks later turn right onto N.W. Thurman Street. Follow this road uphill over a tall bridge and through a quiet neighborhood for 1.2 miles, then keep going straight where the road swithchbacks to the left. In about 100 yards you'll reach a small parking area and a gate across the start of N.W. Leif Erikson Drive.

Begin your hike by going around the gate and gradually climbing the wide surface of the partly paved, partly gravel road. After 0.3 mile you part with the stream of joggers and bicyclists in favor of the hiker-only Wild Cherry Trail, which goes off to the left. This pleasant path climbs moderately steeply on a sometimes muddy tread to a signed junction with the Wildwood Trail. Turn right and follow this practically level path as it wanders along the heavily forested hillsides of Forest Park. The route is very easy, and since there are no viewpoints or other highlights causing you to linger, the miles go by quickly.

The forest here is predominantly Douglas-fir, with some western red cedar, Pacific yew, and bigleaf maple for a bit of variety. The forest floor affords plenty of variety, but it is dominated by the usual sword fern and Oregon grape. Just 0.6 mile beyond the Wild Cherry Trail you come to a four-way junction with the Dogwood Trail. For a very short loop, you can turn right here, and drop to N.W. Leif Erikson Drive to return to your car. For more exercise and forest scenery, however, go straight and continue the level hike on the Wildwood Trail. The path comes within spitting distance of a trailhead on N.W. 53rd Drive, then takes you to a junction with the Alder Trail, another option for a shortened loop.

For the full recommended trip, veer left, sticking with the Wildwood Trail a bit below the ridgecrest on your left, for another uneventful but soothing 1.8 miles. Along the way you pass through several nearly pure stands of bigleaf maple, which are particularly fetching with the new green leaves of spring or the old yellow leaves of early November. Eventually, the nearly level, wandering Wildwood Trail comes to a junction with Firelane 1, a closed dirt road. The Wildwood Trail crosses this road, but a better option is to turn right and follow the fire lane downhill for a little over 100 yards, then bear left onto the Nature Trail.

This trail switchbacks downhill for 0.4 mile before arriving at a small open spot, the site of now dismantled Rocking Chair Shelter. Beyond this point the Nature Trail continues a short distance to a junction where you turn right (downhill) and descend along small but attractive Rocking Chair Creek, past an old dam site to a junction with NWLeif Erikson Drive. To complete the loop, turn right and follow this attractive winding road as it goes past a couple of decent viewpoints of the city. It gets steadily more crowded with other visitors. In the 3.4 miles from Rocking Chair Creek, you pass junctions with Firelane 1, Alder Trail, Dogwood Trail, and finally Wild Cherry Trail, all the way back to the starting point.

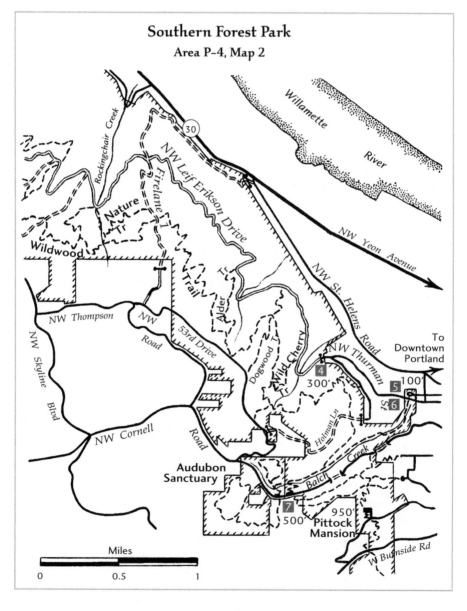

Trip 5

Balch Creek – Wildwood Trail Loop

(Map Area P-4, Map 2)

Distance	Elevation Gain	Hiking Time	Optional Map	Difficulty
4.8 miles	700'	2 to 2.5 hours	None needed	**

☁

Usually Open	All year
Best Times	Late March to mid-April
Agency	Portland Parks Bureau

This easy loop provides a perfect sampling of the charms of Forest Park. You start by hiking up a first-rate urban stream canyon, then follow a particularly attractive segment of the Wildwood Trail across heavily wooded slopes, and finish with a short walk through a quiet city neighborhood. Probably no other major city in North America can match this type of wild variety within its city limits.

While this path is open and enjoyable in any season, it is most attractive from late March to mid-April, when the forest floor comes alive with wildflowers. Most abundant are Oregon grape, trillium, twinflower, and wood violet—which, despite that old rhyme about violets being blue, are mostly yellow in this area. Wear boots or shoes that you don't mind getting muddy, as the path is usually a sloppy mess in winter and spring.

Directions: From Interstate 405 in downtown Portland, take exit 3 for U.S. Highway 30 toward the town of St. Helens. From this off ramp you immediately exit onto N.W. Vaughn Street, which you follow for 0.3 mile to the traffic light at N.W. 26th Street. Turn left, then right in less than a block, onto N.W. Upshur Street. Follow this road for 0.5 mile to its end at a small parking lot and turnaround, directly beneath a tall suspension bridge on N.W. Thurman Street.

The paved trail starts by going through a small picnic area under the imposing bridge. This bridge is a favorite roosting and nesting site for pigeons, so you will probably be serenaded with their soft cooing sounds as you hike. You pass a catch basin where the waters of Balch Creek, flowing towards you, disappear beneath the pavement, then continue along the lovely wild creek above. In the 19th century, this stream was used as a water source for the city, and even though it flows entirely within the city limits, it remains clean enough today to provide habitat for native cutthroat trout.

The trail crosses the creek on a bridge, shortly after which the pavement ends and the scenery changes suddenly from city to wilderness. Though you are only a few hundred yards from the street grid, homes, and apartments of the big city, that all seems worlds away as the forested canyon effectively shields you from the man-made sights and sounds. Just a few steps into your hike and you are already enjoying the sounds of birds and a bubbling creek, happily enclosed in a wilderness.

After the first crossing of Balch Creek, the wide path parallels the stream, which tumbles over rocks and small waterfalls under an overhanging canopy of salmonberry and western red cedar. The cliffs and tree trunks near the stream are covered with mosses and ferns, while the forest floor is carpeted with sword fern, Oregon grape, and trillium.

You recross the creek on a bridge just below a particularly fetching little falls, then pass a huge old Douglas-fir as you make your way upstream. Not long after this, the path arrives at some old stone ruins beside a junction with the Wildwood Trail.

To do the recommended loop, turn sharply right just in front of the ruins and gradually climb the Wildwood Trail on a mostly open hillside. One of the most common plants here is English ivy. This plant looks attractive as it spreads out on the forest floor and climbs the trees trunks, but it is actually an unwelcome introduced species that crowds out native vegetation. Park officials and volunteers wage a never-ending battle to rid the park of this menace.

You intersect closed Holman Lane just above a small meadow, and go straight on the hiker-only Wildwood Trail. This path quickly demonstrates its characteristic pattern, rarely gaining or losing much elevation, opting instead to zig into small forested gullies and zag out to equally heavily wooded ridges. Here in southern Forest Park the trees are nearly all conifers, mostly Douglas-firs, with a few western hemlocks and Pacific yews.

You keep left at an intersection with the Aspen Trail, after which the Wildwood Trail makes one of its few noticeable climbs. In the next 0.5 mile you gain approximately 300 feet in

Falls on Balch Creek, Forest Park, Portland, Oregon

four short switchbacks, then make a straightforward ascent of a sword-fern-covered slope. After this you level off and resume the pattern of zigzag level hiking. There is an abundance of birds in these woods, so bring binoculars to enjoy black-capped chickadees, rufous-sided towhees, dark-eyed juncos, hairy woodpeckers, American robins, winter wrens, and others.

Go straight at a junction with the Birch Trail and, about 0.3 mile later, meet the Wild Cherry Trail. To close the loop, turn sharply right and lazily descend a woodsy hillside to N.W. Leif Erikson Drive, which is closed to vehicles but teeming with joggers and bicyclists. You turn right on this road and soon arrive at a gate and small parking area.

To finish off the loop, follow the sidewalk beside N.W. Thurman Street as it goes gently downhill through a quiet neighborhood with lovely homes and colorful gardens. After about 0.7 mile, you cross Balch Creek Canyon on a tall bridge, at the far end of which are a staircase and a trail dropping to the parking area and your car.

Trip 6

Balch Creek to Pittock Mansion

(Map Area P-4, Map 2)

Distance	Elevation Gain	Hiking Time	Optional Map	Difficulty
4.4 miles	1000'	2.5 hours	None needed	**

Usually Open	All year
Best Times	Late March to mid-April
Agency	Portland Parks Bureau

Historic Pittock Mansion, with its carefully manicured lawns, exquisite gardens, and popularity with car-bound visitors, hardly qualifies as a wilderness destination. But its setting on a scenic highpoint in Portland's woodsy West Hills, with views that extend to five volcanic peaks, hardly makes it seem like a typical spot for city sightseeing either.

It's well worth anyone's time to tour the beautiful old house and stroll through the grounds—whether you arrive by car or by trail. But it is the trail that qualifies this hike as sufficiently wild for inclusion in this book. Following almost the entire length of wild Balch Creek, then ascending a hillside of stately conifers, this trail retains its wilderness character for all but the last couple of hundred yards. So this trip gives you the best of both world's—God's wild forests on the way, and a stunning man-made attraction at the end.

Stone ruins along Balch Creek, Macleay Park

Directions: From Interstate 405 in downtown Portland, take exit 3 for U.S. Highway 30 toward the town of St. Helens. From this off ramp you immediately exit onto N.W. Vaughn Street, which you follow for 0.3 mile to the traffic light at N.W. 26th Street. Turn left, then right in less than a block, onto N.W. Upshur Street. Follow this road for 0.5 mile to its end at a small parking lot and turnaround, directly beneath a tall suspension bridge on N.W. Thurman Street.

Begin the adventure by ascending the gorgeous trail up the canyon of Balch Creek, as described in Trip 5. This trip diverges from that one after 0.9 mile, at the stone ruins where you meet the Wildwood Trail. This time, instead of turning right, you go straight on the path beside Balch Creek and for the next 0.4 mile remain close to the north bank of this creek as it tumbles through a scenic woodsy canyon. Every foot of the trail is a joy, as you travel through the lush creekside vegetation. You finally cross the creek on a bridge and reluctantly leave the stream. Three switchbacks help you climb out of the canyon to a crossing of busy N.W. Cornell Road, the source of those traffic sounds you've been hearing for the last 0.2 mile.

The Wildwood Trail crosses N.W. Cornell Road at a grassy trailhead and reenters a lovely forest traveling a short distance to a junction with the Upper Macleay Trail. Either trail will get you to Pittock Mansion, and you are encouraged to combine the two paths into an enjoyable loop. For now, veer left on the Wildwood Trail and wander along at a nearly level grade on the hillside above N.W. Cornell Road. After about 0.5 mile, you bear right at a junction with Cumberland Trail and begin the 500-foot climb to Pittock Mansion. The sweat is offset by the joy of traveling through extremely attractive woods, with lots of beautiful old Douglas-firs and lush greenery on the forest floor. About 0.1 mile from the last junction, you come to a four-way junction with the Upper Macleay Trail, the end of the semi-loop mentioned above. To finish your climb to Pittock Mansion, go straight and ascend five well-graded switchbacks before the uphill rather abruptly ends and you arrive at a large parking lot for visitors to Pittock Mansion. Be sure to allow some time to explore the gardens, enjoy the view, and, if it's open, tour the old mansion. Tours of this 16,000-square-foot brick palace, built between 1909 to 1914, run daily from 1:00 P.M. to 5:00 P.M. and require a small entry fee.

Continuing south from Pittock Mansion, the Wildwood Trail drops to cross very busy W. Burnside Road, then wanders through the man-made plantings of Hoyt Arboretum and the manicured lawns in Washington Park. Both of these locations are worth visiting, but they aren't wild enough to be included in this book.

Trip 7

Audubon Sanctuary Loop Trails

(Map Area P-4, Map 2)

Distance	Elevation Gain	Hiking Time	Optional Map	Difficulty
1 to 5 miles	100 to 600'	1 to 3 hours	Trail brochure available from Nature Center	*

Usually Open	All year
Best Times	April and May
Agency	Portland Audubon Society

Although relatively small in size, the 160-acre Portland Audubon Wildlife Sanctuary is perhaps the nicest single sampling of Portland's West Hills. In addition to the usual attractive forests, you can enjoy Balch Creek, a lovely urban stream, and sit beside a quiet, lily-pad-filled pond. Concentrated throughout the preserve are lots of wildflowers and wildlife. The trails are open to the public year-round from dawn to dusk, but dogs are prohibited.

Directions: From northwest Portland, drive west on N.W. Lovejoy. This road bears to the right after crossing N.W. 25th, where it becomes N.W. Cornell Road. Continue on N.W. Cornell Road for 1.5 miles through two tunnels to the Audubon Sanctuary. There is a small parking lot in front of the bookstore, nature center, and wildlife rehabilitation buildings on the north side of the road. Additional parking is available in the gravel overflow lot on the south side of the road. If you are coming from the west, the Audubon Sanctuary is 1.5 miles east of the junction of N.W. Cornell Road and N.W. Skyline Boulevard.

Pond and gazebo in the Audubon Sanctuary

There are trails on both sides of N.W. Cornell Road, but if you have time for only a short stroll, stick with the trails to the north, as they are more interesting. A good gravel path begins from the east side of the parking lot, next to the wildlife care building, and drops quickly to a bridge over Balch Creek. This lovely urban stream drains a 2000-acre watershed, most of which is protected in either wild city parks or the Audubon Sanctuary itself, so the water remains reasonably clear.

On the other side of the bridge is the first of many junctions with trails that split off in many directions, all of them marked by names on wooden signs. Not surprisingly in an Audubon Society sanctuary, the trail names tend to have an avian theme—Woodpecker, Wren, and Jay—in addition to the Creek Trail along Balch Creek.

For now, go left at two successive junctions to quickly arrive at a small, lily-pad-filled pond. A wooden gazebo here provides an ideal viewing platform to look at the many rough-skinned newts that laze about in the water. After enjoying the pond, you have a choice of trails. For a 1.1-mile circuit of the preserve, a loop follows the pleasant Jay Trail through the trees and near the surrounding fences, roads, and homes that ring the sanctuary grounds.

The dense native vegetation along this route features a canopy of western hemlock, western red cedar, bigleaf maple, and a wide variety of wildflowers. In April and May, you can expect to see trillium, candyflower, twisted stalk, wood violet, star-flowered smilacina, and false solomon seal, among many others. Also in these spring months you will be treated to an unusual abundance of songbirds. This area is a favorite of local birders in search of migrating warblers, grosbeaks, sparrows, and other feathered songsters. The loop ends at the junction near the bridged crossing of Balch Creek.

For more exercise, it is possible to connect with the Forest Park trail system by taking a short path that parallels N.W. Cornell Road, to a head in a grassy area about 100 yards east of the Audubon buildings (see Trip 6). For an even closer option, simply cross N.W. Cornell Road and pick up the trails that explore the densely wooded hills south of the Audubon preserve. The Founders and Collins trails both make pleasant loops through these forests, gaining a fair amount of elevation as they wind up and down through the predominantly Douglas-fir woods. With no creek or pond, and less varied vegetation, these paths provide less interesting scenery than you find north of N.W. Cornell Road, but they are longer and give you a better workout. The loops connect and both eventually take you back to the parking lot and your car.

Portland and the Willamette Valley

Area P-5: Other Portland Area Parks

Even though their city is surrounded by wild country, most Portlanders find value in having some wild areas right within their midst. Over the years, city residents have consistently funded efforts to set aside parks and green spaces throughout the city and its adjacent suburbs. Obviously, the largest and most outstanding of these areas is Forest Park (see Area P-4), but there are dozens of other examples of the farsighted attitudes of Portland's outdoor lovers.

The network of parks and wildlife preserves includes extensive wetlands, such as north Portland's Smith and Bybee lakes, Beaverton's Fanno Creek Greenway, and southwest Portland's Council Crest, the highest point in the city. Most of these green spaces have at least some trails that are worth exploring, but they lack any true wilderness. A few of the parks, however, are both large enough and wild enough to give the hiker the feeling of being well away from the city's noise and crowds.

Two prime examples are Powell Butte Nature Park and Tryon Creek State Park. Hiking the scenic trails here will increase your appreciation of earlier Portlanders as well as the hard work of those who look after the parks today. If you'd like to get involved with the laudable organizations that protect the wild character of these preserves, you can find their addresses and phone numbers in Appendix B.

Trip 1

Marquam Nature Park Loop

(Map Area P-5, Map 1)

Distance	Elevation Gain	Hiking Time	Optional Map	Difficulty
1.3 to 8 miles	300 to 1500'	1 to 4 hours	None needed	* to **

Usually Open	All year
Best Times	Late March to mid-April / Early November
Agency	Portland Parks Bureau

For proof of the claim that Portland is a city that includes wilderness within its borders, you need look no further than Marquam Nature Park. Downtown office workers looking to withdraw temporarily from the rat race can literally walk to this unspoiled gem on their lunch hour for a healthy dose of the medicine that only wilderness provides. This little park protects an amazingly wild canyon of dense forests. It's hard to believe that it is only a few blocks away from the world of skyscrapers and traffic.

Directions: From downtown Portland, simply follow S.W. 6th Avenue south to the overpass at Interstate 405 and the traffic light just to the south. Stay on S.W. 6th Avenue, following signs to Oregon Health Sciences University (OHSU), and travel 0.3 mile to a traffic light where S.W. Terwilliger Boulevard goes left. Go straight on S.W. Sam Jackson Road and continue 0.2 mile to where the road makes a hairpin turn to the left. You turn to the right and immediately arrive at the tiny parking lot next to the Marquam Nature Park Shelter. All of this can be done as an easy half-hour walk from downtown or by taking the regular Tri-Met bus service to either OHSU or the S.W. Terwilliger Boulevard turnoff. If you are driving, note that there is a two-hour limit on parking.

A network of trails radiates from this trailhead, giving you a wide variety of destinations and choices. The easiest alternative, a loop in the lower forested canyons, is also the wildest. Longer trails head off for more distant locales and connect with trail systems in other parts of the West Hills. Immediately above the open-sided shelter, the wide, gravel trail splits at the start of the loop. Either direction is fine, but for a clockwise loop turn left on the Terwilliger Trail and hop over a low chain across the path.

This gravelly old road is now just a wide trail that climbs fairly steeply up a densely wooded canyon. Wooden catch basins trap the water in the gully beside you, eliminating what once was a pretty little creek. The trail itself is often wetter than the gully leading to several muddy spots, so don't wear your best shoes. After 0.3 mile you come to a junction where the old road continues straight on its way to S.W. Marquam Hill Road and S.W. Terwilliger

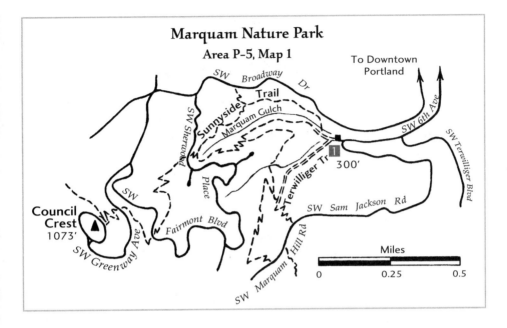

Marquam Nature Park
Area P-5, Map 1

Boulevard. For the short loop, turn sharply right on a narrow foot trail that traverses back along the forested hillside and, after just 50 yards, comes to another junction.

For the recommended loop, stay straight on the lower trail and soon hop over a tiny, splashing creek. After this, the trail very gradually gains elevation, then contours as it curves left into the next canyon. The forests in this remarkably wild canyon are a mix of Douglas-fir, western hemlock, western red cedar, and bigleaf maple. Below these big trees are lots of shrubs, especially red elderberry, vine maple, and thimbleberry. English ivy is incredibly abundant, and while it looks attractive, the dense mat covering the forest floor has effectively crowded out most of the native plants and flowers.

When you come to the next junction you have a choice. The quickest way to return to your car is to veer right and drop directly back down to the shelter. For a longer trip, bear left and climb several gently graded switchbacks to the next junction. If you want a long hike with a good view as a payoff, turn left and follow this trail for 1 mile as it switchbacks uphill, crosses three neighborhood roads, and tops out on Council Crest, the highest point in the city of Portland. There are sweeping views here, which makes this spot well worth visiting, but it isn't really a wilderness destination, since it has paved road access, manicured lawns, and a radio tower.

To stay on the wilder lower loop, bear right at the junction and hike on the Sunnyside Trail as it zigzags downhill and comes to a junction with a trail going left to S.W. Broadway Drive. You close the loop by going straight and losing elevation for another 0.3 mile. The last part of this descent is through a brushy area with blackberry brambles and a grassy meadow. The trail ends at a junction about 50 yards above the Marquam Nature Park Shelter.

Trip 2

Tryon Creek State Park Loop

(Map Area P-5, Map 2)

Distance	Elevation Gain	Hiking Time	Optional Map	Difficulty
1 to 7 miles (depending on route)	100 to 400'	0.5 to 3 hours	*Tryon Creek State Natural Area brochure*	*

Usually Open	All year
Best Times	Early April
Agency	Oregon State Parks—Portland Metro region

Tryon Creek State Park is a tiny wilderness treasure. Although surrounded by busy roads and housing developments, the park's forested canyon effectively isolates the visitor in a cocoon of wilderness where the sounds of birds and babbling creeks overwhelm the distant hum of traffic and trains. The 645-acre park is a treat at any time of year, but is most enjoyable in the first week of April when the preserve's signature flower, the white-blooming trillium, is on full display. This is also when other flowers, such as skunk cabbage, salmonberry, and wood violet, are most prominent. In addition, the red alder trees have yet to grow their summer leaves, so the forest feels more open and inviting. Despite these ideal conditions, in midweek the trails are lonesome, most of the visitors being school children on field trips.

The park is laced with a confusing network of trails. Some paths are specifically designed for bicyclists, others for equestrians, and still others for hikers. It is very easy to take a wrong turn when faced with so many junctions and choices. Fortunately, the park is relatively small, so it's impossible to get too far off course. You can easily create your own itinerary amid the maze of footpaths. The route described here is only one suggestion.

Directions: From downtown Portland, go south on Interstate 5, then take S.W. Terwilliger Boulevard exit 297. Drive south on S.W. Terwilliger Boulevard 2.2 miles, through several traffic lights and junctions. Turn right into the main parking area for Tryon Creek State Park.

From the north end of the parking area follow the Maple Ridge Trail for a short distance to Jackson Shelter where it turns right. This gentle path wanders downhill amid a forest of western red cedar, western hemlock, Douglas-fir, and red alder, with common understory species like Oregon grape, sword fern, and licorice fern keeping everything green. The path is covered with gravel, so mud is at a minimum, which does *not* hold true for most trails in the park.

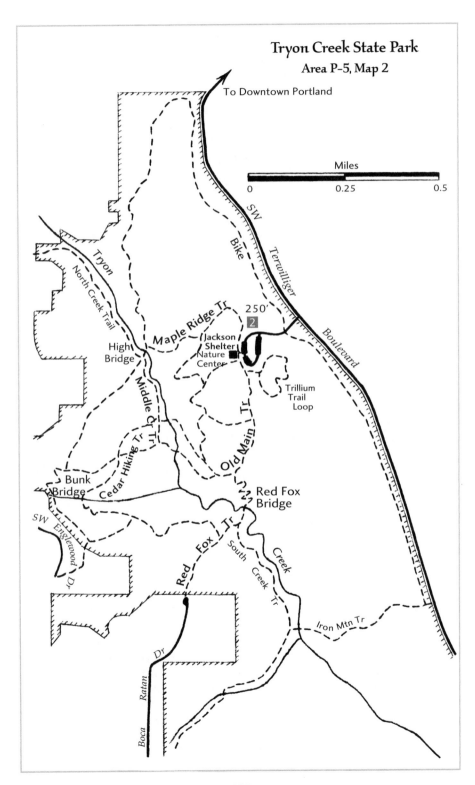

Tryon Creek State Park
Area P–5, Map 2

To Downtown Portland

Miles

0   0.25   0.5

SW Bike

SW Terwilliger

Tryon

North Creek Trail

Maple Ridge Tr.

250'
2

Jackson Shelter
Nature Center

Boulevard

Trillium Trail Loop

High Bridge

Middle Cr Tr

Old Main Tr

Cedar Hiking Tr

Bunk Bridge

Red Fox Tr

Red Fox Bridge

SW Englewood Dr

South Creek Tr

Creek

Iron Mtn Tr

Red Fox Dr

Boca Ratan Dr

You remain on the Maple Ridge Trail all the way down to High Bridge over Tryon Creek, which you cross, then turn left onto the Middle Creek Trail. This creekside route goes downstream 0.2 mile—part of it across a boardwalk that provides dry access over a skunk-cabbage bog—to a junction. Turn right onto the Cedar Hiking Trail and make a short, brisk climb past some excellent trillium displays to the canyon rim. Listen in this area for the calls of screech owls in the trees, especially in the early morning and around dusk. You keep going straight at a four-way junction with the West Equestrian Loop, following signs for Red Fox Bridge, then go up and down a bit to Bunk Bridge, which spans a trickling side creek.

From this bridge, walk a short distance further to a junction with the Hemlock Trail, a short spur route that leads to S.W. Englewood Drive. You go straight for about 0.4 mile, then turn left at the intersection with the Red Fox Trail, where you turn left. This path descends to a junction with the South Creek Trail, where you go straight, then cross Red Fox Bridge. To return to your car, climb four short switchbacks to a junction with Old Main Trail, and turn right. The final section of your tour follows a nearly level route past the Nature Center and back to the parking lot.

Trip 3

Powell Butte Loop

(Map Area P-5, Map 3)

Distance	Elevation Gain	Hiking Time	Optional Map	Difficulty
3.5 miles (with many other options)	300'	1 to 4 hours	Use trailhead brochure (still inadequate)	*

Usually Open	All year
Best Times	Late March to May
Agency	Portland Parks Bureau

Powell Butte Nature Park is a surprisingly wild 570-acre urban oasis that protects the slopes of an extinct volcano between Portland and Gresham. Most of the rolling peak is covered by a rare, low-elevation, grassy meadow, while the northern and western slopes host beautiful forests more typical of our region. You'll never realize it as you hike, but underneath the trail is a 50-million-gallon reservoir used by the Portland Water Bureau as the apex of its distribution system to more than 700,000 users in the Portland area. The park's 9 miles of official trails are a recreational haven for all types of outdoor lovers, in part because off-road vehicles are prohibited. Keep in mind that, except for the wild coyotes and foxes, all dogs are required to be on leash.

Directions: Follow S.E. Powell Boulevard (U.S. Highway 26) 3.4 miles east from its junction with Interstate 205, then turn right (south) at the light for S.E. 162nd Avenue. This road goes up a hill and in just 0.5 mile dead-ends at a large gravel parking lot, just inside Powell Butte Nature Park.

A wild confusion of trails goes off in all directions from the parking lot and, for that matter, all over the mountain. Most of these are unsigned and are not part of the official trail inventory, but they are indistinguishable from the official paths. Although the park makes a point of stressing the need for visitors to stay on established trails, this becomes very difficult, since there are no signs identifying trails that are not part of the established system. Do your best, but you should expect to make at least a few wrong turns. Fortunately, it is impossible to get really lost, and since all the trails are equally attractive, you can't go wrong.

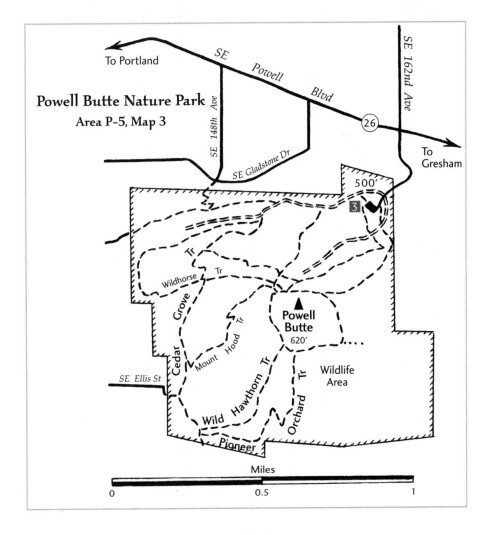

Old walnut orchard atop Powell Butte

For a trip that includes all of the park's major environments, try taking a large circle on the trails around the perimeter. Start by following the paved wheelchair-accessible trail that leaves from the northwest end of the parking lot and goes southeast, climbing gradually for 0.6 mile, in one long switchback to the rolling meadows atop Powell Butte. As you ascend, you will pass several unsigned trails and cross a service road, but it's best to stick with the paved path. In the spring, expect to see lots of woolly bear caterpillars doing their best slinky-toy impersonations across the pavement in front of you. Be careful not to step on these colorful and cuddly native residents.

At the top of your climb, the paved route ends at a junction with a dirt trail. For the outer loop of the park, turn left and walk along the scenic ridge-line of Powell Butte, past a few inviting picnic tables in an old walnut orchard. Also here is a useful "mountain finder," where railroad ties in the ground point towards distant snow peaks and lesser nearby summits. Bear right at an unsigned junction just past the mountain finder, then cross a shallow depression to come to another unsigned junction.

For the recommended route, turn right here and walk beside a designated wildlife area on your left that is closed to public access. The wildlife seems to appreciate this concern, as you are likely to spot rabbits, sometimes deer, and lots of songbirds, especially various warblers, towhees, and sparrows, all taking advantage of the people-free environment.

At the next signed junction, turn left onto the Pioneer Orchard Trail, which drops below the meadowlands and enters some exceptionally attractive woods. Western red cedar, Douglas-fir, and red alder are dominant here, while the forest floor hosts many woodland wildflowers, such as yellow violets, candyflower, fairy bells, and twisted stalk. From here, the path descends steadily to cross a gully with a seasonal trickle of water, then curves to the west and drops some more. You may see a house or two through the foliage or hear the distant sounds of traffic on Foster Road to the south, but in general the hike stays wonderfully wild.

Eventually you come to a junction at the southwest corner of the park, where you turn right and, just 10 yards later, bear left at a junction with the Wild Hawthorn horse trail. You are now on the Cedar Grove Trail. You ascend slowly through deep forest, then go straight through at a junction with a spur trail, which goes left to a trailhead on nearby S.E. Ellis Street. A little while later, you go straight again where the Mt. Hood Trail leads off to the right. Climb up the woodsy canyon of a seasonal creek, passing some enormous old Douglas-firs and lots of western red cedars, with their distinctive sinewy bark. When you reach a confusing four-way junction with the Wildhorse Trail, you make a short jog to the left to cross the tiny creek, then turn right and resume travel on the Cedar Grove Trail.

After climbing a bit, you top a low ridge and come to a series of very confusing unsigned junctions. The "proper" route is as much a matter of opinion as anything else, but generally try to avoid any major turns to the left and you will soon break out of the forest and enter the extensive meadows on Powell Butte. From here, simply follow any of several trails and old service roads that all tend to head generally northeast and converge on their way back to the parking lot and your car.

Portland and the Willamette Valley

Area P-6: Sandy River

Fed by melting snow and glaciers on Mt. Hood, the Sandy River is a major tributary of the Columbia, adding its waters to that great river about 12 miles east of Portland. As one of the few rivers in the area whose main branch is free of dams, the Sandy still supports significant runs of salmon and other anadromous fish. In fact, in late September this is one of the best places in the area to watch these dauntless fish struggle upriver to spawn.

Even when the fish aren't running, it's fun to explore the river's canyon, since it is home to abundant wildlife and impressive old-growth forests. The canyon is also very scenic, as the river has carved a 700-foot-deep gorge into the foothills of the Cascade Mountains. There are three attractive preserves along the river's final 10 miles, all of which have good trails for hikers to enjoy.

Trip 1

Sandy River Delta

(Map Area P-6, Map 1)

Distance	Elevation Gain	Hiking Time	Optional Map	Difficulty
4.2 miles	100'	2 hours	None are adequate	**

Usually Open	All year (may be flooded in winter)
Best Times	All year
Agency	Lewis & Clark State Park

North of Interstate 84, on the east side of the Sandy River, is an undeveloped area of state parkland that protects a flood-prone region of meadows, cottonwood bottomlands, and backwater sloughs. Although there are no signed trails, the entire region is open to hikers and it is laced with a network of unofficial trails and old roads. There isn't any real destination, but the walking is easy and enjoyable, with diverse wildlife and nice views of the surrounding mountains, in a surprisingly quiet and wild setting. The area is especially popular with dog lovers, who come here to exercise their pets in an unrestricted environment. The hike described here visits the park's most noteworthy feature, the confluence of the Columbia and Sandy rivers.

Directions: Leave Interstate 84 eastbound at exit 18 for Lewis & Clark State Park. The exit road makes a clover-leaf loop and comes to a road junction, where you turn right, go under the freeway, and 0.2 mile later park at a gated road on the left. Be sure not to block access to this road when you park.

The road splits immediately on the other side of the gate. The road that continues straight runs too close to Interstate 84 to be enjoyable. You turn left and follow the northbound road atop an old dike, which goes through a black-cottonwood forest. Lining the route are lots of blackberries, which ripen in August, providing a delicious diversion for hikers. Although several unsigned side paths drop to the left, on their way to fishing spots on the Sandy River, the main road always goes straight, taking you to a meadow where you bear to the right off the dike.

As you travel north, the sounds of the freeway fade away and are gradually replaced by the songs of rufous-sided towhees, American robins, and song sparrows. The road passes numerous unsigned paths that invite further exploration, but the route of the main road is evident at all intersections, and it is your best choice for this hike. In winter, there is lots of standing water on the road, and even more on the side routes, so wear boots that keep your feet dry. In the mud surrounding these puddles, look for tracks of raccoon and deer.

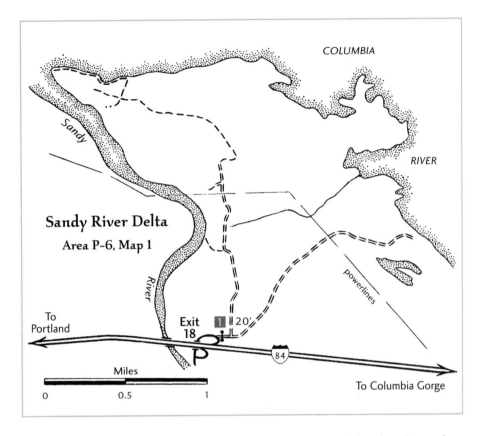

The road crosses a sandy backwater slough of the Columbia River, then goes through a gate and passes under two sets of powerlines in a large grassy area. To the east and southeast, you will see Mt. Hood and the distinctive profile of Larch Mountain, among other landmarks. Bring binoculars to get a closer look at the deer in this area that bound away at the sight of hikers. Also look for red-tailed hawks circling overhead in search of a meal.

Keep going straight where the road splits again beneath the second powerline, and follow an overgrown grassy track. Not far past the powerlines, you come to a fence line that curves in front of the road. Turn right, go through the dilapidated fence, and climb to an old dike on the other side of a low grassy vale. To reach the Columbia River—the closest thing to an identifiable destination in this area—turn left on a trail that slowly curves to the west. After about 0.6 mile you'll reach a four-way junction. Turn right and in about 400 yards you should reach the sandy shore of the Columbia River beside a large sign warning river dredges of an underground pipeline. The two industrial towns across from you, in Washington, are Camas and Washougal.

To check out the confluence of the Sandy and Columbia rivers, walk west for about 0.2 mile along the beach to the meeting of the waters. This is a fine place to take a leisurely lunch while you watch the gulls and bald eagles usually found here. Return the way you came, or take the time to explore some of the many side routes, if you are looking for more exercise.

Trip 2

Oxbow County Park Loop

(Map Area P-6, Map 2)

Distance	Elevation Gain	Hiking Time	Optional Map	Difficulty
2.0 to 5.5 miles	100 to 500'	1 to 4 hours	None are adequate	**

Usually Open	All year
Best Times	All year / late September
Agency	Oxbow County Park

Oxbow County Park is a justifiably popular preserve that provides the perfect mix of natural and man-made attractions. In addition to manicured campsites and picnic areas, complete with all the amenities, there are wild forests, quiet ridges, lots of wildlife, and dozens of tranquil riverside locations perfect for relaxing. An intricate network of trails gives you access to the entire park, with every foot of every path providing very pleasant scenery. In late September and early October, the river comes alive with spawning salmon, making this one of the best and most popular places to observe these magnificent fish struggling to complete their life cycle. Pets are not allowed in the park.

Directions: Leave Interstate 84 at exit 17 in Troutdale. The exit road parallels the freeway for about 0.5 mile to a junction with S.W. 257th Drive. Turn right on this road, signed MOUNT HOOD COMMUNITY COLLEGE, and drive 2.8 miles. Then turn left onto N.E. Division Street. Follow Division (which becomes S.E. Oxbow Road) for 4.4 miles through a couple of intersections. Bear left at a fork to stay on the main road. In 0.7 mile you arrive at a four-way junction where the main road turns 90 degrees to the right. You turn left, following signs to Oxbow Park, and drive 1.5 miles on Hosner Road to the park entrance station, where you must obtain a day-use pass. After paying the entry fee, drive the park road past several pullouts and picnic areas. There are numerous places to start hiking, but the recommended one is at Group Area A, at a large gravel pullout on the left.

From Group Area A, you begin hiking by crossing the park access road and picking up a gravel service road that climbs Alder Ridge. In about 200 yards you come to a junction with a trail that goes off to the left. The park's main loop route follows this trail, but for a highly recommended and enjoyable side trip, stay on the service road. This road continues climbing through areas of lush, wet vegetation, with maiden-hair ferns and horsetails especially abundant. In about 0.2 mile, a trail crosses the route, just before the road tops a ridge. Before taking this trail, continue on the road for another 50 yards to see a large, scenic meadow, rimmed by tall flowers like foxglove and cow parsnip.

To make the pleasant loop in the trees around this meadow, retrace the 50 yards back to the trail junction and turn either way. This horse trail wanders through open red-alder and bigleaf-maple forests, along an almost perfectly level course. The trails on Alder Ridge are the quietest in the park, providing a welcome change from the popular routes closer to the river and road. But beware of the overhanging stinging nettles, which grow abundantly along the trail. Avoid touching this plant, because contact with exposed skin causes a temporary but very painful stinging sensation. The deer don't seem to mind, however, as they frequently use this path, and in muddy areas you are likely to see deer tracks, and perhaps some of the hoofed creatures themselves. On the far side of the meadow, you pass several nice clifftop viewpoints some 300 feet above the rushing Sandy River. If you feel the need for some extra exercise, take a side trip off the loop on a trail that climbs a heavily wooded ridge to the southwest. This path climbs a dozen short switchbacks in coniferous woods to a trailhead at the end of a residential road. **Note:** Don't try to *start* your hike here as there is no legal parking.

After completing the loop around the meadow, walk back down the gravel service road to the trail junction mentioned earlier, and turn right (downhill) on a narrow trail that descends to the valley floor. This takes you to a tiny opening and a wooden fence near the campground, then through a lovely woodland, with dense thickets of sword fern under a canopy of old-growth Douglas-fir and bigleaf maple. You pass a couple of junctions with unmarked side trails, then come to a fork in the trail marked by a signpost saying simply "J". Bear right here, looping gradually around the end of Alder Ridge, and eventually reach a junction with the riverside trail beside the Sandy River.

The trail to the right dead-ends, so turn left and follow the river downstream. Several side trails lead down to the water, and you'll want to check out as many as time allows, because the scenery and wildlife viewing are excellent. Birdwatchers will delight in watching the swallows zip over the water in search of insects and the fast-flying merganser ducks zooming upstream, just above the surface of the water. You might also want to join the human anglers trying their luck in the river, but be prepared to share the action with such natural anglers as river otter, great blue heron, osprey, and an occasional bald eagle. Using much less sophisticated methods, these creatures seem to fare just as well as those of us using expensive poles and tackle. Another tempting activity, especially on hot summer days, is to take a dip in the water. Stick to wading in the shallows, however, as the river is dangerously swift and the water is very cold, so swimming isn't recommended.

The trail passes a rustic picnic shelter, then slowly curves around the looping bend in the river that gave Oxbow Park its name. Along the way, you may be confused by several side trails to the left and by a few places where flooding has washed out the main trail, requiring detours. Stay on the main loop trail at all junctions, and the route will eventually lead you to a boat

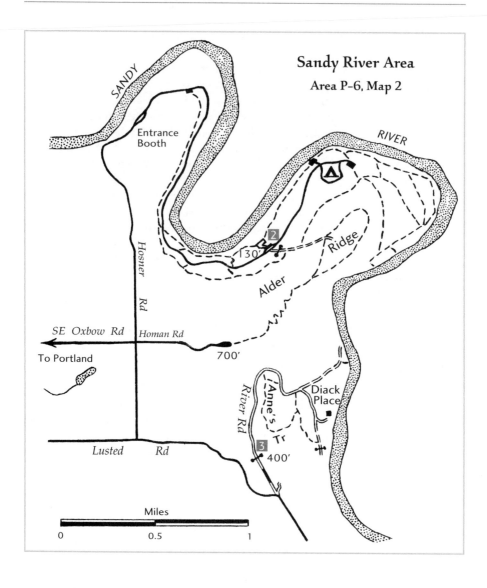

Sandy River Area

Area P-6, Map 2

ramp. You cross the parking lot here, then climb a bit to follow the loop trail on a bench above the river. On your left, you will be very close to the well-kept picnic areas and horseshoe pits of the park, but despite these unnatural intrusions, the trail retains a remarkably wild character, especially on week-days. On these quiet days, you may see rabbits hopping away from you into the brush or, in spring and early summer, you may even be visited by a spotted fawn tentatively coming out of the woods to have a look. About 0.3 mile from the boat ramp, you reach Group Area A and your car.

Trip 3

Sandy River Gorge Loop

(Map Area P-6, Map 2)

Distance	Elevation Gain	Hiking Time	Optional Map	Difficulty
2.6 miles	500'	2 hours	None are adequate	**

Usually Open	All year
Best Times	All year
Agency	The Nature Conservancy

Immediately upstream from popular Oxbow County Park is a much quieter area owned by the Nature Conservancy, a private nonprofit group that works to protect biodiversity. The Sandy River Gorge Preserve is a 436-acre parcel of land set in a 700-foot-deep gorge with fine examples of old-growth Douglas-fir and western red cedar. The Nature Conservancy manages the land for its educational and scientific attributes, and to this end they prohibit visitors from camping or building campfires. You also are not allowed to travel by motorcycle, bicycle, or horse, and dogs are prohibited. Groups of 10 or more people need a special use permit, which you can obtain by contacting the Nature Conservancy at (503) 230-1221.

The Diack brothers owned part of the property and worked hard for its preservation. Their noteworthy accomplishments in conservation included tireless and successful efforts to get the Sandy River officially protected in both the Oregon and the federal scenic rivers systems. In addition to their conservation work, these two doctors were important community leaders. Dr. Arch Diack, a surgeon, invented the heart defibrillator, while his brother, Sam, is the father of the Oregon Museum of Science and Industry (OMSI).

Directions: Leave Interstate 84 at exit 17 in Troutdale. The exit road parallels the freeway for about 0.5 mile to a junction with S.W. 257th Drive. Turn right on this road, signed MOUNT HOOD COMMUNITY COLLEGE, and drive 2.8 miles, then turn left onto N.E. Division Street. Follow Division (which becomes S.E. Oxbow Road) for 4.4 miles through a couple of intersections, then bear right on Altman Road and go 0.4 mile to a four-way junction. Here you turn left onto Lusted Road and follow this rural route 1.7 miles to the bottom of a steep downhill section. Immediately at the bottom of this downhill, turn left on unsigned River Road, in front of some farm buildings. Follow this gravel road 0.3 mile to a gate. Be sure not to block this gate when you park.

The hike begins when you go around the gate and immediately come to a large sign on your left. Here you will learn about the area's natural history, as well as the history of its preservation.

Unfortunately, the trail map shown on this sign is incomplete and inaccurate, so don't rely on it.

River Road descends across private property, passes below and to the left of a farmhouse, then enters wilder, forested terrain. The woods are composed mostly of lovely western red cedar and moss-draped bigleaf maple, mixed with some western hemlock, Douglas-fir, and Pacific yew. The most abundant understory species are sword fern, holly, and blackberry. As you descend, salmonberry becomes more common, and the impressive old-growth trees get larger, with some specimens up to 500 years old. Shortly after the road completes a sweeping turn to the right, you arrive at a junction with the rather faint Anne's Trail.

To do the loop, turn right on Anne's Trail and 150 yards later bear right at an unmarked junction. Despite being a bit muddy and overgrown, this route is enjoyable to hike, as it drops to a seasonal creek, then works around an open meadow frequented by a small band of elk. The sunny borders of the meadow are crowded with 3-foot-tall bracken ferns, which are liberally fertilized with piles of elk droppings. Watch your step.

Just past the meadow, the trail comes to a small grassy opening and a junction. Anne's Trail goes left and soon returns to River Road. To explore more forest, turn right and follow a good trail that winds around in the trees to meet a small road. Turn left here to reach a junction with River Road. About 200 yards to the right are the buildings of the Diack Place.

To reach an even better riverside location, go left on River Road 0.2 mile to a road junction. Then go right on a jeep road 0.3 mile to a nice lunch spot on the rocky banks of the river. Nicely rounded by countless years of moving water, the rocks here make comfortable seats. There is also a good view downstream to the yellowish sandstone bluffs in Oxbow Park. To return to your car, go back to River Road and follow it past two junctions with Anne's Trail, then up the woodsy hillside to the trailhead.

Sandy River, Nature Conservancy Preserve, Oregon

Upper Butte Creek Falls, near Scotts Mills, Oregon

Portland and the Willamette Valley

Area P-7: Willamette Valley Foothills

The Willamette Valley's rich farmland and mild climate have attracted people for at least 150 years, when this valley was the original goal of pioneers on the Oregon Trail. They arrived here eager to settle on this fertile land of rolling meadows, forests, and wetlands, in hope of building a better life. Their eagerness ensured that almost every acre of the original wilderness would become farmland or cities, so virtually no wild land remains today.

Only a few scattered places like Champoeg and Willamette Mission state parks are publicly owned and, while these are worth visiting, they hold too little wild land for their trails to be recommended in this book. However, at Baskett Slough National Wildlife Refuge, northwest of Salem, you can still find a remnant of the original Willamette Valley, making the trails here well worth a visit.

Even in the foothills of the Cascades, on the eastern border of the valley, most of the land has been logged over so many times that it has effectively become just one big tree farm, like a more extensive version of the Christmas Tree farms commonly found in these hills. The Santiam State Forest is one such place, but two little-known waterfalls on Abiqua and Butte creeks remain very wild despite the nearby clearcuts. Still, for truly overwhelming scenery, you can't top Silver Falls State Park. This forested canyon and its ten major waterfalls were too spectacular for even the old-time loggers to despoil, and the state set Silver Falls aside as what would turn out to be the crown jewel of arguably the best system of state parks in the nation. Every Oregonian must visit Silver Creek Falls at least once, and most will find that once is not enough.

135

Willamette Valley

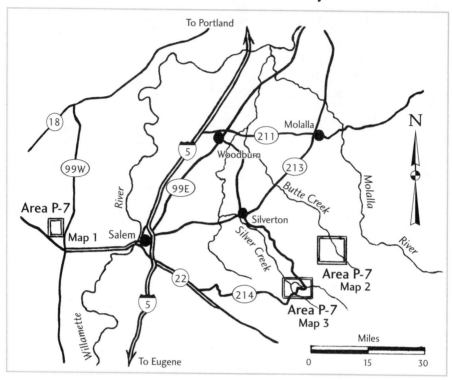

Tiny falls above Abiqua Falls, near Scotts Mills, Oregon

Trip 1

Mount Baldy & Baskett Slough Loop

(Map Area P-7, Map 1)

Distance	Elevation Gain	Hiking Time	Optional Map	Difficulty
1.5 to 4.2 miles	300′	1 to 2 hours	None needed	*

Usually Open	All year (for Mt. Baldy Loop); May 1 to September 30 for rest of hike
Best Times	May
Agency	Baskett Slough National Wildlife Refuge

In the mid-1960s, concern about the declining numbers of the dusky Canada goose led to the establishment of three national wildlife refuges in the Willamette Valley, the winter home of the goose. Thanks in part to these preserves, the goose's numbers have stabilized and even grown.

Hikers have also benefited from the refuges, which give them a chance to see what the Willamette Valley looked like before the land was largely transformed into farms. Baskett Slough, the most northerly of these refuges, has much to offer the outdoor lover. Here you will discover rolling hills covered with grasses and Oregon white oak trees, extensive lowland marshes, and lots of wildlife in addition to the geese. A handful of trails provide access to some of the best parts of the 2492-acre refuge.

Directions: Take U.S. Highway 99W south from Tigard and stay on this highway for 30 miles through Newberg to a junction with State Highway 18 south of McMinnville. Turn south, staying on Highway 99W toward Corvallis, and drive for 17 miles to a junction just shy of milepost 56. Turn right on gravel Coville Road and drive 1.5 miles, then turn into the signed trailhead parking lot on the right.

You begin by climbing a grassy old road up a pleasant hillside covered with native vegetation including grasses, scattered Oregon white oak, blackberry, serviceberry, wild rose, and black hawthorn. In May, flowers like buttercup and a few camas add color to the scene. Thickets of head-high poison oak proliferate in almost every open area, so rule out any thoughts you might have of going off trail.

After 0.2 mile, you come to an unsigned fork where you bear left and ascend to a ridgeline junction in a grassy saddle. You turn left here and wander up to the nearby summit of Mt. Baldy, with its oval-shaped wooden viewing platform. From here you'll enjoy a fine view of the distant Coast Range and the surrounding farmlands, as well as the wildlife-rich, shallow marshes nearby to the south.

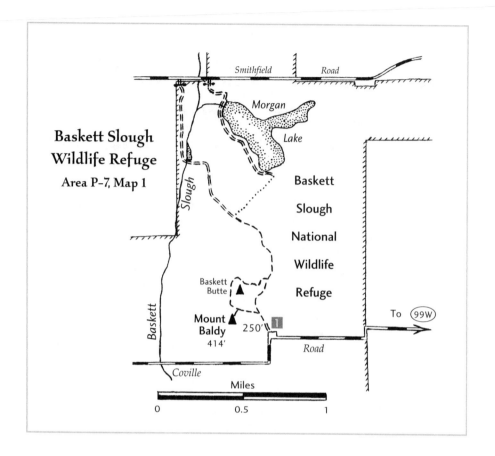

As this is a wildlife refuge, there are, of course, lots of animals. You will probably hear the honking of geese on the marshes or flying overhead. Red-tailed hawks and American kestrels patrol the skies, while four-legged predators like coyotes and bobcats prowl the hillsides in search of a meal. Deer bound away from hikers, and many species of songbird nest in the oaks and shrubs. To help protect all of this wildlife, the refuge prohibits dogs from the trail.

From the viewing platform, return to the grassy saddle and bear left on an unsigned but obvious footpath, which departs from the open meadow and meanders through a surprisingly dense deciduous forest of Oregon white oak, bigleaf maple, and Oregon ash. Growing in the dappled sunshine of the forest floor are sword ferns, prairie star flowers, and an abundance of poison oak. Oak woodlands like this have become rare ecosystems in the Willamette Valley, so this hidden treasure is a treat.

The trail's circuitous route across the slopes of Baskett Butte ends at a T-junction. To keep the trip short, you can turn right here and return to your car in just 0.5 mile. If you are visiting between October 1st and April 30th, you will *have* to take this route, because the rest of the refuge is closed to protect

138

the wintering waterfowl. If you are visiting in late spring or summer, however, you can turn left and explore more of the refuge's diversity.

For the longer trip, follow the path as it goes through a grassy swale, then curves to the left descending an oak-studded hillside to a lower area of fields and marshes. At the bottom of the hill, you meet the end of a quiet gravel service road and follow it as it goes north and west through several fields and past cattail marshes, to a dike across sluggish Baskett Slough.

In the marshy lakes on either side of the road, you will probably see and hear red-winged blackbirds, raspy-voiced marsh wrens, swooping northern harriers, and flocks of western sandpipers, who zip past in search of mudflats where they can feed. Killdeer nest in the drier open fields, and the adults are known to lead you away from their eggs and young by feigning a broken wing. From the marsh, the road continues north along a fence line on the border of the refuge, all the way to a gate at Smithfield Road.

Years ago, it was possible to return to Baskett Butte by way of a service road and a mowed trail that led past Morgan Lake. The trail portion of this route is no longer signed or maintained, but you can still follow its course. To do so, walk east on Smithfield Road to just past a large barn on the left, then turn back into the refuge on the closed service road.

This road curves over to Morgan Lake, then crosses the dam forming the lake, where you will probably see geese and ducks on the water or spot a nutria sunning itself on the shore. To close out the loop, follow the overgrown road around the west side of Morgan Lake to a hedgerow near the lake's seasonal inlet creek. From here you wander southwest across a grassy field about 0.5 mile, back to the end of the quiet gravel service road below Baskett Butte.

Trip 2

Abiqua & Butte Creek Falls

(Map Area P-7, Map 2)

Distance	Elevation Gain	Hiking Time	Optional Map	Difficulty
2.0 miles (combined)	400' (combined)	1.5 to 2 hours (combined)	USGS—Elk Prairie (trails not shown)	**

Usually Open	Mid-March to early December
Best Time	Mid-May / Late October to early November
Agency	Santiam State Forest

Hidden in the hills east of Silverton, Abiqua and Butte Creek falls are among the state's most spectacular waterfalls. Given their beauty, it is a shame that only a handful of Oregonians have ever heard of them. This lack of publicity is due entirely to the unmarked trail access, rather than any deficiency

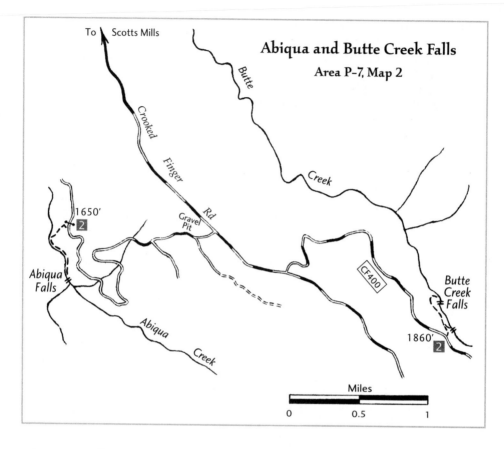

in scenery. The same geologic conditions that created nearby Silver Falls State Park—basalt cliffs bisected by rushing streams—also created these natural wonders. And while the scenery isn't as concentrated as it is at Silver Creek Falls, the solitude more than compensates for the extra drive and effort.

Directions: For both destinations, begin by driving to the small community of Scotts Mills, reached by a well-signed road going east off State Highway 213 between Silverton and Molalla. From the southeast side of the bridge over Butte Creek, in the middle of town, turn south on Crooked Finger Road and climb this rural route 9.5 miles to the end of pavement. Exactly 1.5 miles past the end of the pavement is a junction with an unmarked gravel road on the right.

Abiqua Falls

To reach Abiqua Falls, turn right at the unmarked junction and drive 0.1 mile to a small gravel pit, where you go straight and pass through a gate. (**Note:** This gate is usually open, but if not, you can just park here and walk. This adds 4.8 miles and 1000 feet of elevation to the round-trip hike.) Past the gate, you drive downhill and go straight at another junction 0.3 mile beyond the gravel pit. About 2.1 miles from this last junction the sometimes rough road comes to a locked gate just inside a clearcut. Park on the side of the road about 50 yards back from the gate.

To find the unsigned trail to the base of Abiqua Falls, leave the road about 100 yards before the gate and walk downhill on a small skid road. Follow it 100 yards and, just before entering a recently logged area, turn left on an obvious foot trail. This steep route drops 0.2 mile to the banks of lovely Abiqua Creek, where you turn upstream.

From here the going is sometimes tricky, as you scramble over rocks and follow portions of a rough trail for 0.3 mile to the basalt amphitheater at the base of the falls. Birdwatchers will enjoy the sight of dippers zipping past and singing amidst the roar of the falling water, while photographers will delight in the excellent picture opportunities featuring foregrounds of the creek, mossy rocks, and overhanging trees. This is just the kind of lonesome spot that adventurous explorers love to discover.

With a bit of detective work, you can find a rough scramble trail that goes to the top of Abiqua Falls. The unsigned route leaves the access road at a small pullout about 0.3 mile before you reach the last gate. After about 150 yards the path splits. The steep trail to the right leads to a rather scary and dangerous overlook of Abiqua Falls, while the rugged and slippery path going straight leads to the top. Only confident and experienced hikers should contemplate taking either of these routes.

Butte Creek Falls

From the turnoff for the road to Abiqua Falls, continue on Crooked Finger Road another 0.6 mile, then turn left on possibly unsigned Road CF 400. Drive exactly 1.9 miles, then pull into a small parking area on the left that is lined with large logs. The unsigned but well-beaten trail that leaves the parking area has received some welcome maintenance in recent years, with gravel added to the wet spots and boardwalks over the dampest areas.

After just 0.2 mile, you come to a junction with a short spur trail that goes to the right and leads to the 20-foot-high upper falls, a broad spread of falling water that is well worth a visit. From this turnoff, the main trail continues downstream along the canyon wall another 0.3 mile to a rocky viewpoint of much-more-attractive Butte Creek Falls. The mossy forest setting, the 80-foot-high twisting cataract, and the rocky gorge combine to make this an ideal lunch spot. Don't forget your camera and plenty of film, as the fall demands to be captured from many different viewpoints.

Trip 3

Silver Falls State Park Loop

(Map Area P-7, Map 3)

Distance	Elevation Gain	Hiking Time	Optional Map	Difficulty
7.8 miles	700'	4 hours	Use park brochure	**

Usually Open	All year (except during winter storms)
Best Times	All year
Agency	Silver Falls State Park

Don't come to Silver Creek Falls in search of mountain views; the depths of this forested canyon don't offer any. Don't come to Silver Creek Falls in search of flowers; it has its share of forest wildflowers, but no standout displays. And definitely don't come to Silver Creek Falls in search of solitude; the place is overrun with your fellow *Homo sapiens* practically every day of the year. But despite all that, absolutely **DO** come to Silver Creek Falls. With ten spectacular falls tightly packed into a verdant canyon, including five over 100 feet tall, the park is a waterfall lover's paradise.

If this park were located in almost any other state, it would be a national park and probably world famous. But in Oregon, with that state's embarrassment of outdoor riches, the park is well known only to residents of the Beaver State.

The hike is glorious in the spring, when water flows are high, and the sounds of falling water thunder out of the canyons. It is also a joy in summer, when the shades of green are positively overwhelming. Fall is nice too, when bigleaf-maple leaves turn yellow and cover the trails in a crinkly bed of foliage. Even winter is spectacular, especially during a cold spell, when the falls become ice castles, and occasional snowfalls make for stunning photographs. The best plan is to visit in all seasons, so you won't miss any of the park's faces and moods.

Directions: If you are coming from the Portland area, drive south on Interstate 5 and take Woodburn exit 271. Turn east on State Highway 214 and follow this pleasant rural road for about 30 miles, through the charming city of Silverton and up to Silver Falls State Park.

You can start this hike at either of two trailheads. By far the more crowded one is South Falls, where a huge parking area also services a very popular picnic area. Much less crowded is the North Falls parking lot, on the north side of the bridge over North Fork Silver Creek. There is also a small parking lot at the trailhead above Winter Falls, but

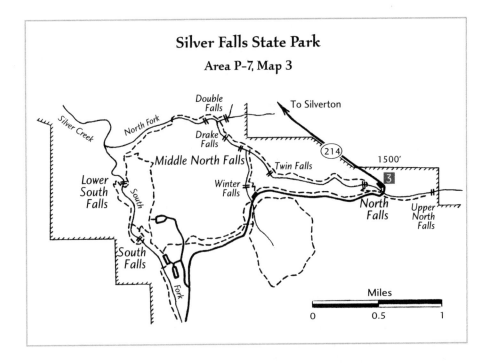

Silver Falls State Park
Area P-7, Map 3

Silver Creek

North Fork

Double Falls

To Silverton

Drake Falls

Middle North Falls

214

1500'

Twin Falls

Lower South Falls

South

Winter Falls

3

North Falls

Upper North Falls

South Fork

South Falls

Fork

Miles

0   0.5   1

parking here is restricted to just two hours, which does not allow you enough time to complete the hike. Regardless of where you start, the park charges a day-use fee, and you must display a permit on your dashboard when parked in any of the lots. Permits are available either at the entrance station at South Falls or at the automatic pay station at North Falls.

If you start from the less crowded North Falls lot, you immediately drop to a footbridge over North Fork Silver Creek and come to a junction. For an excellent side trip, turn right here and loop under the highway bridge. Follow this route upstream for 0.2 mile to beautiful Upper North Falls, which by itself would make this trip worthwhile, but it is only a small sampling of the glories to come in this park.

Returning to the junction below the North Falls trailhead, hike west and you soon come to a second junction, which is the start of the loop. To save the best scenery for last, go left on the path toward South Falls and traverse steep slopes covered with dense Douglas-fir and western-hemlock forests. On the rim of the canyon just above you is Highway 214, but the traffic sounds are never too intrusive. Most of the route is viewless, but at one point you come to a break in the trees and can look back up the canyon to towering North Falls.

Just short of 1 mile from the trailhead, you come to the small roadside parking lot for Winter Falls. If you want to visit this falls, turn right at the trail junction here, then switchback downhill beside this tall waterfall. If you want a short 2.9-mile loop, you can continue down the trail below Winter Falls to a bridge over Silver Creek, where you turn right and return to your car at North Falls.

For the complete loop, continue hiking on the trail paralleling the road, and you will soon come to a junction with a paved bike trail. You can follow either the hiker's trail or the bike route, as both wind through attractive forests for about 1.5 miles to the area around busy South Falls. There are several roads and trails in this area, not all of them very well-signed, but you really can't get lost if you just keep going west.

From the north end of the main parking area, you pick up the paved trail that follows a fence line guarding the steep drop-off of the rim beside 177-foot-high South Falls. To pick up the loop trail, simply follow the crowds going north and drop down into the huge bowl holding this classic falls. Snapping photographs all the way, you follow the paved trail as it takes you under the lip of a basalt cliff and into a huge, dry cavern behind the wall of water. This cavern, like the others you will find along the loop trail, was formed over millions of years as the falling water eroded the soft soils under a hard layer of basalt on the lip of the falls.

After this exciting walk, you come to a junction with a trail to the right, which goes over a bridge and returns most tourists to their cars at the South Falls parking lot. For the hiking loop, you go straight and leave the paved trail in favor of a quieter dirt path in the deep woods. The canyon is densely forested with Douglas-fir, western hemlock, western red cedar, bigleaf maple, and lots of ferns. Trillium and other small wildflowers carpet the forest floor. The beautiful South Fork Silver Creek on your right is always a joy and provides many chances to observe cheerful dippers searching for food in the clear waters.

The next highlight is Lower South Falls, a 93-foot waterfall in another cliff-walled bowl. To reach this falls, the trail switchbacks several times and travels down a series of stairs, which may be dangerously icy in winter. At the bottom of the steps, the trail contours behind this impressive sheet of water, then climbs a bit to a junction. Go straight and walk slightly downhill to a bridge over North Fork Silver Creek, which flows through a moss- and fern-lined slot canyon. The bridge here was washed out by floods in 1996, but the new one looks pretty sturdy.

The canyon walls become a little less steep, but no less beautiful, as the trail closely follows the cascading creek. At a bend in the stream, Lower North Falls makes a sloping 30-foot drop over a small cliff into a deep pool. Just past this falls is a junction with a 120-yard trail that goes up a side creek to tall and delicate Double Falls, an outstanding side trip.

The main trail travels above Drake Falls, which is difficult to see in a deep canyon on your right, then works its way up to the much more attractive Middle North Falls. A side trail contours around and curves behind this gorgeous falls, in yet another eroded cavern.

A short distance past Middle North Falls is a junction with the trail up to Winter Falls. You go straight and continue up the lush canyon to Twin Falls, which anywhere else would draw rave reviews, but here seems rather prosaic. Finally, as the slopes get progressively steeper, you approach the loud drop of awe-inspiring North Falls. This 136-foot-tall waterfall bursts out of a narrow chute on the lip of a basalt cliff and arcs down into the enormous bowl below. Photographers will love it. The trail goes through a cavern behind this fall, then switchbacks up the steep south side of the bowl, back up to the junction just a few hundred yards from your car.

Base of Double Falls in Silver Falls State Park, Oregon

The Columbia River Gorge

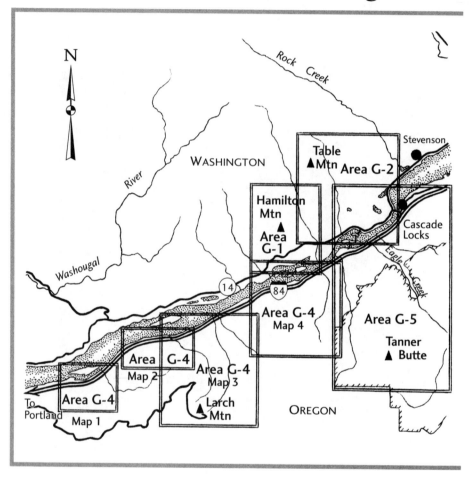

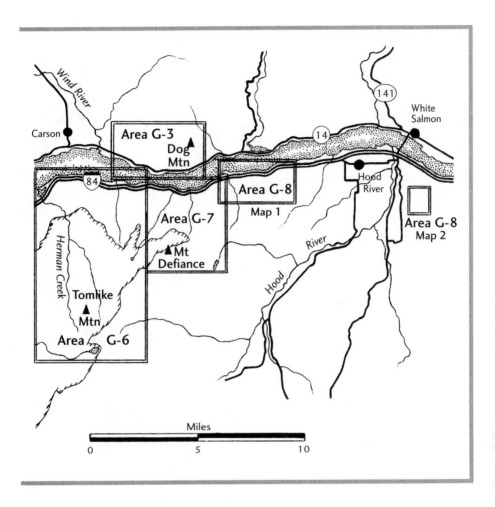

Lower section of Multnomah Falls, Oregon

# The Columbia
River Gorge

Area G-1: Beacon Rock State Park

ALTHOUGH WASHINGTON ORIGINALLY HAD TO BE SHAMED INTO MAKING
IT A STATE PARK, BEACON ROCK HAS SINCE BECOME A CROWN JEWEL IN
THE STATE'S SUPERB PARK SYSTEM. In 1935, when the Biddle family
offered the property to the state for use as a park, the Washington legislature
initially declined the gift. Embarrassment forced them to change their minds
when the state of Oregon offered to take the land and make it an *Oregon* park.
Today, every Washington resident, as well as visitors from other states, can
enjoy the result of this fortuitous decision.

Beacon Rock is the core of an ancient volcano, and its boosters claim it is
the second largest free-standing rock monolith in the world, surpassed only
by the Rock of Gibraltar. When you stand at its base, you are not inclined to
dispute this claim. The massive, 848-foot-tall basalt block rises in columns
directly above the Columbia River, and it is truly an awe-inspiring sight.

But this 4650-acre park protects much more than just this celebrated pinnacle. The preserve stretches back into the hills to the north and provides protection for an extensive range of creek canyons, forested hills, and soaring
mountains. More importantly from a hiker's standpoint, the park encompass-

es over 20 miles of trails and old roads that explore this backcountry—all off-limits to the plague of all-terrain vehicles.

Note: Beginning in 2003, a day-use parking fee of $5 ($50 for an annual pass) is required at Beacon Rock State Park. The pass is good at all Washington state parks.

Trip 1

Beacon Rock

(Map Area G-1)

Distance	Elevation Gain	Hiking Time	Optional Map	Difficulty
1.8 miles	600'	1 hour	*Green Trails–Bridal Veil*	*

Usually Open	All year (except during winter storms)
Best Times	March to November
Agency	Beacon Rock State Park

By far the most recognizable landmark in the Columbia River Gorge is Beacon Rock, rising above the river in one enormous basalt monolith. Back on October 31, 1805, William Clark, co-captain of the Lewis and Clark expedition, wrote of a "remarkable high detached rock" that was "about 800 feet high, [which] we called Beacon Rock." Thanks to a feat of engineering almost as remarkable as the rock itself, visitors today can do something that Lewis and Clark could not: walk a good trail to the top.

Directions: Drive east from Vancouver on State Highway 14 for about 34 miles to the unmistakable rock on the south side of the road. Park in the paved lot beside the restrooms just below the rock's eastern cliffs. The trail begins about 50 yards west of the parking lot.

You begin with a gentle climb through a typical Gorge forest of Douglas-fir, western hemlock, and bigleaf maple. In late April it also features splashes of the large, white blossoms of Pacific dogwood trees. The trail gradually works its way around the west side of Beacon Rock, first in forest, then above a talus slope, and finally onto the sheer basalt cliffs of the rock itself.

You are bound to be awed by the engineering of the trail, especially when you come to a plaque informing you that the trail was built from 1915 to 1918 by just two men, Henry J. Biddle and his assistant, Chas Johnson. Most of the path is blasted out of the rock face with wooden catwalks across the airiest places. Dozens of tiny switchbacks are carved into the rock, some across places that are so steep the trail has to loop around on top of itself to make its way upward. Metal handrails line the entire length of the route to provide a

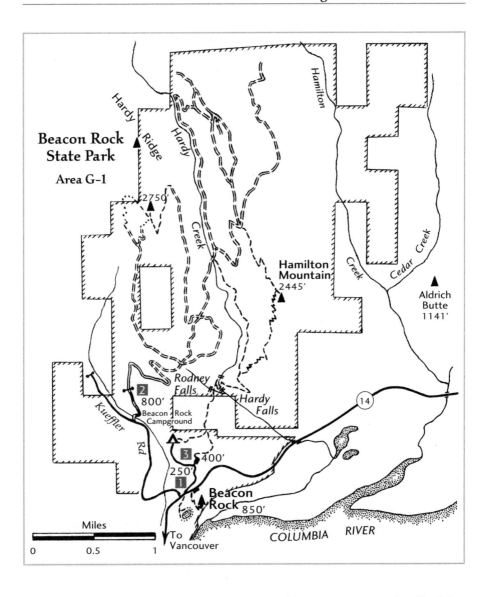

Beacon Rock
State Park

Area G-1

level of safety and comfort for those afraid of heights. Amazingly, all of this
was accomplished while still keeping the uphill grade quite gentle. If this trail
were planned for construction today, it would cost millions of dollars. Indeed,
it probably wouldn't be permitted at all, being considered too dangerous to
build.

The trail, which is definitely *not* for acrophobics, goes through a metal
gate, which is closed in winter if the trail is too icy, then begins a series of
switchbacks up the west and south sides of the rock. The views improve as
you ascend, but most of the route is open to the afternoon sun, so it can be
uncomfortably hot on summer days. Eventually, the path rounds a ridge with
fine views to the south and west, then works its way to the summit through

open forests on the southeast side of the rock. As you might expect, the views from the top are superb, although some directions are blocked by small trees. You cannot expect to be alone, however, as the trail is very popular and the summit area quite small.

Hikers who are up for a bit of bushwhacking can extend this outing by taking a much quieter, 0.8-mile, unsigned nature trail that leaves from a parking area about 75 yards west of the Beacon Rock trailhead. This path drops through the forest beside Highway 14 to a marshy pond, then loops around this pool. There are some good views of Beacon Rock from the south shore of the pond, which also has a wealth of frogs, ducks, beavers, and other interesting wildlife. Much of the route around the pond, however, is badly overgrown with blackberry brambles and stinging nettles, so most people will want to skip this adventure.

Trip 2

Hardy Ridge Loop

(Map Area G-1)

Distance	Elevation Gain	Hiking Time	Optional Map	Difficulty
6.7 miles	2100′	3.5 hours	*Green Trails–Bridal Veil* (part of trail not shown)	***

Usually Open	March to November
Best Times	Mid-April to June
Agency	Beacon Rock State Park

There are thousands of miles of old logging roads winding through the forests of the Pacific Northwest. Hikers have not traditionally looked at them as a recreational resource, but that may be a mistake. Some of these old roads lead to very worthwhile locations, and they can serve effectively as wide, well-maintained trails with relatively easy grades.

This outing in a little-visited corner of Beacon Rock State Park is an excellent example. The old jeep routes here are intended now to be a playground for mountain bikers and equestrian visitors, but hikers are also welcome and none of the routes are crowded.

Directions: Drive east from Vancouver on State Highway 14 about 34 miles to Beacon Rock, a huge basalt monolith just south of the road. Turn left on Kueffler Road just west of the park headquarters building, and drive uphill on this paved route. After 1.0 mile, turn right on a gravel side road signed for the equestrian trailhead. Drive this route 0.4 mile to the developed turnaround, complete with parking, pit toilets, picnic tables, and horse ramps.

The route from the trailhead begins as a closed gravel road and gradually winds up long switchbacks on a hillside covered with red alder and Douglas-fir. About 0.5 mile after the road switches from gravel to rough dirt, you come to a four-way junction. The jeep road to the right makes a 1-mile loop. The roads going straight and to the left form the ends of the recommended longer loop. The loop is easier to follow if done counterclockwise, so go straight and gradually climb for about 0.4 mile to a second four-way junction.

You turn left at this junction and follow an old road overgrown with grasses that makes its way up the east side of a ridge. There are some decent views of Hamilton Mountain to the east, but most of the route is in the trees as you climb for 1.6 miles to where the old road simply ends. Continue the ascent on a good trail that curves off to the left climbing steadily in a dense second-growth, western-hemlock forest.

After a long uphill traverse, you make a switchback and emerge from the trees on an open rocky ridgeline where the views are superb, amply compensating for the long climb. Only the view to the north is blocked by trees, so take some time to look west down the length of the Gorge toward Vancouver, south to the rugged Oregon side of the river, and, best of all, southeast to Hamilton Mountain and down to Bonneville Dam.

The trail continues uphill along the narrow ridge, passing numerous exceptional viewpoints from moss-covered rock outcroppings. Completing the loop gets a little tricky, as the official trail ends here and the footpath beyond this point becomes indistinct and very easy to lose. Navigation is made even more difficult by the numerous game trails that crisscross your route. Hikers who are not experienced route-finders should simply turn around and return the way they came. Others can try the very sketchy route that briefly follows the ridge to a minor saddle, then drops down the west side and makes a switchback to meet the far end of the old road you saw at the beginning of the loop.

To close the loop, follow this road as it crosses a mix of open rocky slopes and forested areas, taking a scenic sidehill course. The road passes a junction with a jeep route going up to the left and continues descending with downhill segments interrupted by long level stretches. From April to June, the brushy areas beside the trail are alive with the songs of rufous-sided towhees, dark-eyed juncos, and winter wrens. After 1.6 miles, you return to the main road at the first four-way junction mentioned above and turn right to return to your car.

Trip 3

Hamilton Mountain Loop

(Map Area G-1)

Distance	Elevation Gain	Hiking Time	Optional Map	Difficulty
7.6 miles	2000'	4 to 5 hours	*Green Trails—Bridal Veil*	***

Usually Open	March to November
Best Times	April
Agency	Beacon Rock State Park

While its signature basalt monolith is Beacon Rock State Park's primary highlight, the view from atop Hamilton Mountain is a close second. The wildflower-spangled slopes of this peak provide some of the most memorable views in the entire Columbia River Gorge. The trail described here provides a varied and scenic approach to the summit views—visiting waterfalls, skirting impressive cliffs, and passing through meadows that in April are covered with terrific wildflower displays.

Directions: Drive east from Vancouver on State Highway 14 about 34 miles to Beacon Rock, a huge basalt monolith just south of the road. To reach the Hamilton Mountain trailhead, bear left on the campground access road and drive 0.3 mile, then turn right into the marked trailhead parking lot. **Note:** This access road opens for the season on about April 1, so if you are visiting out of season, you will have to park at the lot beside Beacon Rock and walk up the gated road.

The trail starts in front of the restrooms at the northeast corner of the parking lot. You begin by walking past a sign board, then loop around the back side of the restroom building on a woodsy hillside. The wide path steadily gains elevation for about 0.5 mile, before the forest cover breaks and you cross beneath a set of powerlines. From here you'll obtain a decent view of Hamilton Mountain, although the scene is somewhat despoiled by the powerlines. At the far end of the clearing, go straight at an unsigned, but obvious, junction with a trail going back toward the park's campground. Soon after this you reenter the forest, as the trail begins to level off. In early-to-mid April, the forest sprouts many woodland wildflowers, chief among them being bleeding heart, trillium, wood violet, and twinflower.

The trail crosses a small side creek on a quaint wooden bridge, then contours to a second tributary creek, below a large waterfall. Just past this, you reach much larger Hardy Creek, which cascades in a series of impressive falls, both above and below the main trail.

Before the route crosses the creek, a short side trail drops off to the right to a mediocre viewpoint of Hardy Falls below the trail. A short distance past this turnoff, a second dead-end trail goes left to visit Pool of Winds, where you'll be blasted by the spray of Rodney Falls—a refreshing experience in summer, but uncomfortably cold in winter. These waterfalls are a good low-elevation destination for winter visitors or hikers with children.

The main trail loses about 50 feet of elevation to reach a wooden bridge over rushing Hardy Creek, then begins to go uphill. The next 0.5 mile formerly climbed steeply up a series of short switchbacks, but in late 2001 the path was rerouted. It now ascends gradually in a long switchback with an easier grade and better views to a possibly unsigned junction with the return route of this loop. For the most direct route to the summit, turn right and switchback 23 times through increasingly open and attractive terrain. The switchbacks end temporarily at a major highlight of the trip, where a short side trail goes out to a dizzying viewpoint atop a rock outcropping. From here, there are first-rate views of Beacon Rock, which looks surprisingly small from up here. The view also takes in highpoints on the opposite side of the Gorge, such as Tanner Butte and Nesmith Point. Circling in the air both above and below you are violet-green swallows and graceful turkey vultures, effortlessly soaring on the thermals. If you are getting tired, you can turn around here, already amply rewarded for your efforts so far.

From this viewpoint the trail traverses a partly forested hillside with nice views to the northwest of the alder-choked valley containing Hardy Creek. You pass a great view of the lichen-covered cliffs below the summit of Hamilton Mountain, then make a final push up a couple of dozen often very short switchbacks to a junction on the windy summit ridge. To the right, there is a short dead-end trail to a brushy viewpoint, but that view is no better than the one you already enjoy. The best part of this view is looking east to Table Mountain and Aldrich Butte.

You can make a loop on a trail that has a more gradual descent and is easier on the knees than the one you just completed. Turn left (north) at the ridgetop junction and follow the path along the top of the view-packed but breezy ridge. After 0.2 mile, the trail drops down the west side of the ridge on two long switchbacks, then traverses a forested hillside and comes to an open, wind-whipped saddle. At this saddle you meet a road that is closed to cars, except for the occasional park maintenance vehicle. The road forks at the saddle. To return to your car, follow the leftmost branch and hike downhill, as the road uses two long switchbacks to make its way down into the canyon of Hardy Creek. Just above the creek at a final switchback is a junction where you turn left (downstream) and soon come to a tiny meadow, where a road culvert crosses the stream.

To complete the loop, leave the road just before it crosses the culvert and pick up a trail paralleling the creek. This virtually level route contours for 1.1 miles along the alder-covered hillside above the creek, then rejoins the Hamilton Mountain Trail at the junction 0.5 mile above Hardy and Rodney Falls.

The Columbia River Gorge

Area: G-2: Table Mountain Area

Table Mountain is the flat-topped monument of the central Columbia River Gorge. The sheer basalt cliffs of this massive landmark rise dramatically above the river, in an impressive display of the region's fascinating geology. Like most of the rock in the Gorge, Table Mountain is a remnant of a series of massive lava floods that buried over 50,000 square miles of eastern Washington and Oregon between 17 and 10 million years ago. Over the intervening millennia, the rock was uplifted and tilted to the south; the Columbia River kept pace with the uplifting, carving downward to create the Gorge.

The steepness of the cliffs you see today, however, is due to more recent geologic events. As recently as 13,000 years ago, Ice Age glaciers in Montana and Idaho backed up massive lakes. When the ice dams broke, they released floods of biblical proportions. Water inundated virtually all of eastern Washington, and its only outlet to the sea was through the narrow Columbia River Gorge. These floods scoured out rock and debris at the bottom of the Gorge, leaving behind the sheer cliffs that the waterfalls tumble over today.

Then, about 700 years ago, a massive landslide fell from the slopes of Table and Greenleaf mountains and left behind the cliffs near their summits and a jumbled mass of debris below. All of this history is visible to the trained eye when looking at the exposed rock on Table Mountain, but even amateurs can add to their enjoyment of the scenery by knowing at least a little about the geologic timeline.

The Pacific Crest Trail provides the best hiker's access to the cliffs and viewpoints on Table Mountain, more so since the trail was rerouted to take you high up on the peak's slopes. It also gives you ready access to other nearby destinations, which will bring you back time and again for outstanding outdoor adventures.

Table Mountain, Columbia River Gorge, Washington

Trip 1

Table Mountain

(Map Area G-2)

Distance	Elevation Gain	Hiking Time	Optional Map	Difficulty
15.4 miles	3600'	8 to 9 hours	*Green Trails–Bonneville Dam*	****

Usually Open	Late March to November
Best Times	May to June
Agency	Columbia River Gorge National Scenic Area

The climb to the top of Table Mountain, one of the most distinctive landmarks in the Columbia River Gorge, is not for the faint of heart (or of legs or lungs, for that matter). The elevation gain and the distance are both significant, making this a challenge for hikers no matter what their ability level. Adding to the difficulties is that fully half the elevation gain is concentrated in just the last 1.2 miles, making for a *very* steep stretch, which must be tackled *after* you complete the long approach.

Because it opens early in the year, mountain climbers often use this route to get in shape for the climbing season. For ordinary hikers, the prize for this tough hike is the outstanding view from the flat top of the peak, one of the most far-ranging anywhere in the Columbia River Gorge.

Directions: The quickest way to reach this trailhead is to take Interstate 84 east from Portland to Cascade Locks exit 44. Follow the exit road for about 0.3 mile, then turn right on a clover leaf that takes you up to Bridge of the Gods. After paying the toll, you cross the bridge and come to a junction with State Highway 14. Turn left and drive 2.0 miles to the spacious Bonneville Trailhead parking lot on your right.

Note: There is a much shorter approach to the Table Mountain area that starts from Greenleaf Slough to the south. This unsigned path deserves mention because it has been popular for years and still receives fairly heavy use. This approach, however, crosses private property that is signed NO TRESPASSING. It is, therefore, not recommended to the general public.

Your trail's first few feet follow a gated road to a sign identifying the Tamanous Trail. This footpath climbs in an open Douglas-fir forest to a decent view across the river from a low ridgeline. This scene is pleasant but gives only a faint hint of what is to come. The connector trail finishes its 0.6-mile route at a junction with the Pacific Crest Trail, where you turn left.

The next 1.6 miles are a little boring, as the trail takes a circuitous course through the boulders and hummocks of an ancient landslide. There is a fair

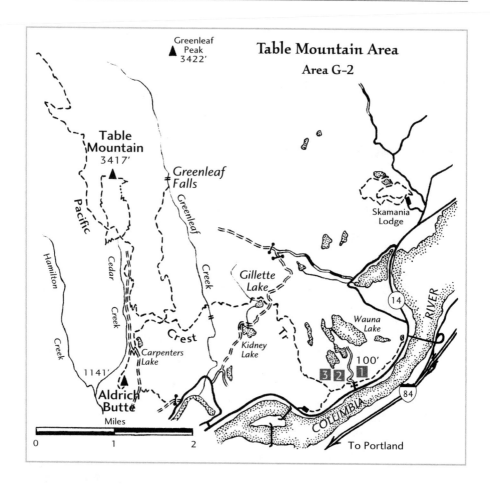

amount of up and down in this section, and forests block any views, so the going is a bit tedious until you reach an unexpected gravel road. (Unfortunately, this road has no legal public access, so you can't shorten the trip by starting here.)

The trail crosses this road and follows an abandoned jeep road under a set of powerlines, then loops around to the northeast shore of Gillette Lake. The lake's warm swimming waters and decent camps are reached by a short side trail. Beyond the lake, the PCT crosses the inlet creek and begins a gradual, forested climb to the bridged crossing of Greenleaf Creek. This clear stream is the last reliable water on the trip, so you may want to stop here for a rest.

The trail climbs a few short switchbacks, then makes a woodsy traverse to the first really worthwhile view of this hike at Greenleaf Viewpoint. The vista is a bit restricted by trees, but you can still see Bonneville Dam and its related developments, as well as the imposing cliffs and forested ridges on the Oregon side of the Gorge. About 0.2 mile later, you cross a gully with a small creeklet and continue to a four-way junction with an unofficial trail that is usually marked with an orange survey ribbon tied to a tree. This trail is the turn-off point for the shorter hike options of Greenleaf Falls (Trip 2) and Aldrich Butte (Trip 3).

For Table Mountain, go straight on the PCT, staying on the level as it crosses a second tiny creek, then ascends six quick switchbacks to the top of a small ridge just above a jeep road. The trail turns right, following the ridge-crest, and continues to climb northward. The route crosses the paralleling jeep road twice, then comes to a four-way junction, marked by homemade signs.

The trail to the right is the wickedly steep east side of the loop to the top of Table Mountain. It's usually better to take this trail on the way back, so continue straight on the PCT, cross a dry gully and contour to a second four-way junction on a ridgeline.

The PCT goes straight, but to reach the summit and its grand views, turn right and begin climbing. Actually, *climbing* is hardly an adequate word for what you are doing, because the uphill is so steep. In the next 1.1 miles, you ascend fully 1700 feet and, since much of the way is exposed to the sun, you'll pour out gallons of sweat on a hot day. The route is rocky, but if you take it slow, which the steepness forces you to do in any event, it's not overly dangerous. At the frequent rest stops demanded by the grade, you enjoy ever-improving views, so at least your effort is continuously well compensated.

Once you reach the flat summit of Table Mountain, turn right (east) and wander on a boot path along the partly forested top to any of several outstanding viewpoints. Directly below you, the Gorge extends both west and east in all of its awesome beauty.

Rising majestically over the hills on the Oregon side is pointed Mt. Hood, covered by its permanent mantle of snow. If you take the trail all the way to its end, you will look down from dizzying cliffs on Table Mountain's precipitous eastern face and see the entire route of your hike. Bring a windbreaker for protection against the almost constant winds. You will also want a lunch to replace some of those calories you just burned up and a camera with plenty of film.

To complete the loop, turn south off the summit about 150 yards from the eastern end, then pick up a sometimes sketchy boot path. The route drops steeply through some brushy and rocky areas, but can easily be followed by experienced hikers. As you descend, you pass to the left of two imposing rock pinnacles, Sacaquawea and Papoose rocks, which frame dramatic photos of Bonneville Dam, Mt. Hood, and the Gorge. Eventually, the downhill trail enters denser forest and returns to the PCT at the first of the four-way junctions mentioned above.

Trip 2

Greenleaf Falls

(Map Area G-2)

Distance	Elevation Gain	Hiking Time	Optional Map	Difficulty
12.2 miles	1500'	6 hours	*Green Trails–Bonneville Dam*	***

Usually Open	All year (except during winter storms)
Best Times	April
Agency	Columbia River Gorge National Scenic Area

If you are in the Table Mountain area, and find that the weather has turned gloomy, skip the viewpoint destinations at Aldrich Butte and Table Mountain, and head instead for Greenleaf Falls. The trip is even better in the sunshine, of course, but the pleasant forests, together with the little-known twisting cascade at trail's end, are equally impressive under a layer of clouds. Really adventurous hikers can combine this destination with a trip to Aldrich Butte for the best of both worlds.

Directions: The quickest way to reach this trailhead is to take Interstate 84 east from Portland to Cascade Locks exit 44. Follow the exit road for about 0.3 mile, then turn right on a clover leaf that takes you up to Bridge of the Gods. After paying the toll, you cross the bridge and come to a junction with State Highway 14. Turn left and drive 2.0 miles to the spacious Bonneville Trailhead parking lot on your right.

Follow the 0.6-mile connector trail to its junction with the Pacific Crest Trail. Turn left and hike the PCT as described in Trip 1 for 3.9 miles, all the way past Gillette Lake and over the bridge spanning Greenleaf Creek. About 0.6 mile past this bridge, you hop over a small, seasonal creek and climb for another 200 yards to a junction with an unofficial trail that is marked only with an orange survey ribbon tied to a tree.

Turn right at this junction and follow a route that used to be a logging road, but, since it has been closed for so many decades, is now barely a trail. The path soon skirts the right side of a tiny marsh, where there are tantalizing views of Table Mountain's impressive cliffs and the pointed pinnacles called Sacaquawea and Papoose rocks. The route now heads north and climbs steadily, but never too steeply, through pleasant second-growth forests. The trail tops a minor ridge with rather disappointing views, then loses elevation for about 0.2 mile and makes two short, rounded switchbacks, before resuming its very gradual ascent.

Greenleaf Falls near Table Mountain, Washington

The next major highlight is about 0.8 mile past the switchbacks, where you cross a large, moss-covered talus slope. The opening here is directly beneath the cliffs of Table Mountain, a neck-craning 1800 feet above you. The sheer cliffs are the result of a massive landslide that fell away from Table Mountain about 700 years ago. The debris from this slide, over which you have been hiking for the entire trip, changed the course of the Columbia River and even temporarily blocked the stream. Many scholars believe that this is the source of the Native American legend about a natural "Bridge of the Gods" over the Columbia River. If you can tear your eyes away from the close-up views, try shifting your gaze southward to the top third of Mt. Hood, poking over Tanner Ridge on the Oregon side of the Gorge.

From the talus slope you should be able to hear the sound of multi-tiered Greenleaf Falls just a short distance northeast. This cataract is actually several smaller waterfalls that are formed where good-sized Greenleaf Creek tumbles down a series of twisting cascades. It is hard to get a good view of the entire falls, but the two-pronged cataract right above the trail is worth the hike all by itself. Really athletic hikers may be tempted to scramble up the slopes beside the falls, hoping to get a better look. This effort is not only dangerous, it doesn't result in any improvement in the view, so don't take it.

Trip 3

Aldrich Butte

(Map Area G-2)

Distance	Elevation Gain	Hiking Time	Optional Map	Difficulty
12.4 miles	1500'	6 to 7 hours	*Green Trails–Bonneville Dam*	***

Usually Open	All year (except during winter storms)
Best Times	April
Agency	Columbia River Gorge National Scenic Area

Aldrich Butte is an easier alternate destination, for hikers who don't want to tackle the difficult trip to the top of Table Mountain (Trip 1). Aldrich is neither as high as its neighbor to the north, nor is its view as expansive, but you'll still find it well worth a visit, especially in early spring when other trails are still covered by snow.

Directions: The quickest way to reach this trailhead is to take Interstate 84 east from Portland to Cascade Locks exit 44. Follow the exit road for about 0.3 mile, then turn right on a clover leaf that takes you up to Bridge of the Gods. After paying the toll, you cross the bridge and come to a junction with State Highway 14. Turn left and drive 2.0 miles to the spacious Bonneville Trailhead parking lot on your right.

Follow the 0.6-mile connector trail to its junction with the Pacific Crest Trail. Turn left and hike the PCT as described in Trip 1 for 3.9 miles, all the way past Gillette Lake and over the bridge spanning Greenleaf Creek. About 0.6 mile past this bridge, you hop over a small, seasonal creek and climb for another 200 yards to a junction with an unofficial trail that is marked only with an orange survey ribbon tied to a tree.

For Aldrich Butte, you turn left on a sometimes overgrown, but obvious, old road that descends very gradually through mostly deciduous woods on a muddy tread. Based on the footprints visible in the mud, this route is more popular with cloven-hoofed residents than with boot-wearing visitors. The route crosses two seasonal creeks, the second of which requires a short detour where the old road has been washed out. After the second creek, the path skirts the west side of frog-filled Carpenters Lake to a junction at the lake's south end. You turn right here on a closed jeep road and make two quick switchbacks to an unsigned junction with a jeep route.

Turn left on the jeep route and climb steadily but moderately around the west side of Aldrich Butte to a flat turnaround just below the summit. From the top, there are fine views of the Columbia River, the town of North Bonneville, highpoints on the Oregon side of the Gorge, and nearby Table and

Hamilton mountains. In addition to the views, there are usually violet-green swallows and ravens circling overhead. In the first half of April, colorful purple grass widows grace the open south-facing slopes below the top. There are some nice picnic spots at the summit, the old concrete foundations of a building providing welcome stools.

The Columbia River Gorge

Area G-3: Dog Mountain Area

The eastern end of the Columbia River Gorge enjoys a lot more sunshine than areas to the west. On those all-too-common days of low clouds or light rain in the western Gorge, the clouds usually dissipate near Dog Mountain, giving way to blue skies and real, rather than *liquid*, sunshine. This drier climate brings with it a (very) few rattlesnakes, but there are positive consequences as well. Chief among these are the expansive meadows covering the south side of Dog Mountain, which in mid-to-late May put on the best wildflower displays in the region. For generations, hikers have made the pilgrimage up the long, steep trail here to view the acres of arrowleaf balsamroot, lomatium, lupine, larkspur, paintbrush, and other colorful blossoms. Mid-week trips allow you to enjoy the show in relative peace. For more solitude try the path up nearby Wind Mountain, a prominent highpoint just west of much taller Dog Mountain but missing the flowers. The trail here isn't signed or shown on any map, so the human population is very low.

Trip 1

Wind Mountain

(Map Area G-3)

Distance	Elevation Gain	Hiking Time	Optional Map	Difficulty
2.7 miles	1100'	2 hours	*Green Trails-Bonneville Dam & Hood River* (trail not shown)	**

Usually Open	All year (except during winter storms)
Best Times	All year
Agency	Columbia River Gorge National Scenic Area

Almost any high point in the Columbia River Gorge could accurately be named "Wind Mountain." This prominent landmark is no more windy than

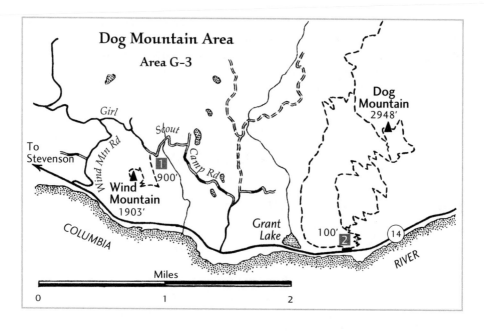

neighboring peaks, but a windbreaker is still mandatory, especially if you want to spend some time at the top taking in the view. The well-graded path up Wind Mountain is not on any map but, rest assured, it's there. The trail is neither as spectacular nor as crowded as the one up adjacent Dog Mountain, but this hike does include some interesting Native American history, which the trip up Dog Mountain does not.

Good trail manners are always important, but that is especially true for hiking on Wind Mountain. A short section of the lower trail crosses private land, and while the owners have not traditionally barred public access, it is important that visitors not abuse this privilege. In addition, the sensitive archeological site at the summit necessitates that hikers exercise the greatest care not to disturb the resource.

Directions: Drive east on State Highway 14 from the town of Stevenson to milepost 50.7 about 1 mile beyond the bridge over the Wind River. Turn left (north) on Wind Mountain Road and after 1.0 mile turn right at the junction with Home Valley Road. Just 0.4 mile later, turn right on Girl Scout Camp Road and in 0.3 mile come to the end of the pavement, where you'll find ample parking space at a rocky saddle. To reach the trailhead, walk 0.1 mile down the rough dirt road that runs downhill from the other side of the pass, then look for the unsigned footpath going off to the right.

The path ascends steadily, but not terribly steeply, on a hillside covered with the usual Douglas-fir forests; salal, sword fern, and Oregon grape populate the understory. The ever-present Gorge breezes whistle through the tree tops, but they rarely bother the hiker, who is protected by the surrounding big trees. The path rounds a ridge and follows the ridgeline for 0.1 mile, before bearing off to the left and climbing another hillside. Three quick switchbacks take you higher still, and as you approach the summit, you cross two rockslides with good views east to Augspurger and Dog mountains.

Just before the top of the mountain is a large sign explaining the Wind Mountain Vision Quest Site. Here you learn that Native Americans used this site for as many as 1000 years in a traditional, religious rite-of-passage for young men. The youngsters came here in solitude to fast and seek guidance from their animal gods. Some tribal members still come here for this purpose. To protect this important archeological and cultural site, it is crucial that hikers not stray *even one foot* from the trail so as not to disturb any of the rock pits built by Native Americans. Restrain your pets and children too.

The view from the top is partly obstructed by trees, but it is still excellent. The best views are to the west toward the town of Carson, Table Mountain, and distant Silver Star Mountain. To the south are the cliffs and peaks on the Oregon side of the Gorge, Mt. Defiance being the tallest of many highpoints.

Trip 2

Dog Mountain Loop

(Map Area G-3)

Distance	Elevation Gain	Hiking Time	Optional Map	Difficulty
7.2 miles	2900'	3 to 5 hours	*Green Trails–Hood River*	***

Usually Open	Late February to December
Best Times	Mid-to-late May
Agency	Columbia River Gorge National Scenic Area

The secret of Dog Mountain's charms got out generations ago, because it was a secret that would be impossible to keep. The bulky mountain is prominently in view to tens of thousands of drivers zipping back and forth on Interstate 84 and Washington State Highway 14. For hikers, the huge, open meadows covering the mountain's upper slopes are an irresistible attraction, because they hold a promise of both views and flowers. Once you actually hike the trail, that promise is spectacularly fulfilled with some of the Gorge's most stunning views and the best flower displays in the scope of this book.

Directions: Cross the Columbia River on the Bridge of the Gods at Cascade Locks and drive east on State Highway 14 for 12 miles to the huge lot for the Dog Mountain Trail on your left.

From the trailhead parking lot, you are faced with an immediate decision. Your choice of trails will be dictated primarily by which is stronger, your knees or your lungs. If your lungs and cardiovascular system are strong, then opt for the much steeper old trail that begins from the east side of the lot. If your lungs aren't up for this tiring ascent, but your knees are strong enough to handle the steep descent when you return on the old trail, then climb the longer, gentler, new trail that takes off from the west end of the lot. Photographers will want to select the steeper route to get to those fam-ous meadows as quickly as possible, because the best pictures are looking west down the Gorge in the early morning.

If the steeper old trail is your choice, you will begin on an abandoned road. After just 100 yards, leave the road on a foot trail that goes left. You'll have no real opportunity to celebrate this change to wilder country, however, because you immediately face a series of steep switchbacks. In the first 0.5 mile you gain almost 700 feet under a canopy of big old Douglas-firs and Oregon white oaks. The most common lower-growing plant is poison oak; in the heat of late spring and summer, careful hikers are kept on their toes as poison oak teams up with rattlesnakes to create a dual hazard.

At a fork in the trail after 0.5 mile, the older, less scenic trail veers left. You'll want to turn right, a choice made easy in spring by the appeal of a sign saying TO THE FLOWERING INFERNO, which is both a charming name and an accurate description. This path is more gradual than what you've already endured, but there are still lots of switchbacks and few breaks in the relentless ascent. After about 1 mile, the trail leaves the trees in favor of an open, grassy viewpoint. Flowers here give a taste of what is to come, lupine, paintbrush, and balsamroot being the star attractions. The only disappointing thing about this view is how far you still must look up to see the higher meadows and viewpoints near the top of Dog Mountain.

Filled with the hope of great scenery and a determination not to give up, you trudge uphill away from this viewpoint, foregoing switchbacks in favor of a straightforward woodsy ascent. About 0.5 mile later, you go right at a junction with the old trail and continue climbing, now at a wickedly steep grade. Just 0.5 mile (and several rest stops) later, you are rewarded with the start of the summit meadows. Some of the most photogenic views and best flowers are near the lower edge of the meadows. Looking west down the Gorge is especially appealing, as distinctive Wind Mountain makes for an impressive landmark, with the large, yellow blossoms of arrowleaf balsamroot providing colorful foregrounds for photographs. While the uphill is not over yet, from now on the scenery is so good you will hardly notice the exertion. Something you probably *will* notice is that like most Gorge hikes, chilly winds often sweep across these meadows, so bring a windbreaker.

At an open ridgecrest is a possibly unsigned junction with two trails that form a 1.1-mile loop around the summit of Dog Mountain. The easier, but much less scenic, route goes straight from this junction and loops mostly through forests. The shorter, steeper, more spectacular route goes left and crawls up the view-packed ridgeline.

A little before the more scenic route reaches the summit, the return trail of this hike veers off to the left. After absorbing all of the views up and down the Gorge that you can handle, turn onto this path and hike north, staying in the gorgeous sloping meadows for another 0.7 mile, before you reach a junction. To return to your car, turn left and make five long, downhill switchbacks in open forests and meadows. Views to the west aren't comparable to those from the top of Dog Mountain, but they are still very good. After the switchbacks end, you make a long, gradual descent across the woodsy western slopes of Dog Mountain. Occasional views through the trees allow you to see lots of wild country near Wind Mountain as well as a rural road,

View west from slopes of Dog Mountain, Washington

some homes, and a Girl Scout camp. Eventually, the trail curves slowly to the left (east) above Grant Lake and finishes its descent on a hillside above Highway 14.

The Columbia River Gorge

Area G-4: Multnomah Falls Area

The western end of the Columbia River Gorge is the easiest part of that wonderful area to reach for hikers from Portland. Fortunately, it also has some of the Gorge's best scenery. The region's tallest waterfalls, highest cliffs, most luxuriant forests, and deepest canyons are all concentrated in the compact, 14-mile-long section between Crown Point and Tanner Creek on the Oregon side of the Gorge.

Right in the middle of this spectacular stretch of scenery is world-famous Multnomah Falls. Hundreds of thousands of people visit this awe-inspiring site every year, making it the most popular tourist destination in the state. This wide fame is well deserved, but it will also give you headaches, if you don't like crowds. However, there is a wide variety of nearby trails, some crowded, others lonesome, where you can get away from the tourist hordes. From rugged scrambles up jagged ridges to easy strolls to secluded waterfalls, all hikers can find something to meet their preferences. And it's all close enough to the city that you can take off for a few hours in the afternoon, get some exercise, and be back in time for dinner. Life just doesn't get much better than that.

Trip 1

Latourell Falls Loop & Bridal Veil Falls

(Map Area G-4, Map 1)

Distance	Elevation Gain	Hiking Time	Optional Map	Difficulty
3.4 miles (combined)	700 feet (combined)	2.5 hours (combined)	*Green Trails–Bridal Veil*	**

Usually Open	All year (except during winter storms)
Best Times	April and May
Agency	Guy W. Talbot & Bridal Veil Falls State parks

The Columbia River Gorge is justifiably famous for its waterfalls. From the west, the first major waterfall you encounter is Lower Latourell Falls, and it provides one whale of an introduction! Plunging 249 feet in a single sheer drop, this falls is a very impressive sight. The awe-inspiring scene is far from private, however, since there is a developed viewpoint just 150 yards from the road.

For more privacy, hikers can make a highly enjoyable loop to beautiful Upper Latourell Falls, a great place to quietly enjoy the Gorge's two best attributes—waterfalls and lush vegetation. The trails in nearby Bridal Veil Falls State Park are too short to be included separately in this book, but they are also too spectacular to be entirely overlooked. Since the loop to Latourell Falls is relatively short, you'll probably have some extra time and energy, and Bridal Veil Falls is the perfect place to expend that extra energy.

Directions: Take Interstate 84 east from Portland to Bridal Veil exit 28, then follow the 0.4-mile access road to the Old Columbia River Highway. You turn right (west) and drive 0.9 mile to reach Bridal Veil Falls State Park and its large

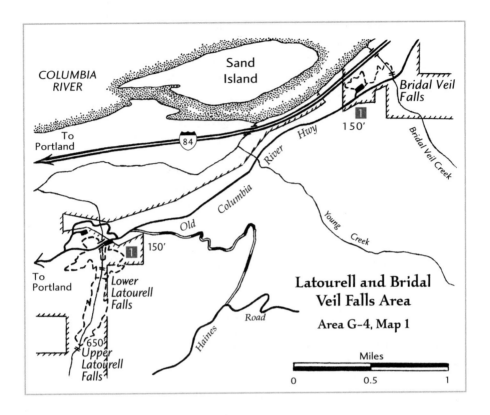

COLUMBIA
RIVER

Sand
Island

To
Portland

84

River

Hwy

150'

Bridal Veil
Falls

Bridal Veil Creek

Columbia

Old

Young

Creek

To
Portland

1

150'

Lower
Latourell
Falls

Road

Haines

**Latourell and Bridal
Veil Falls Area**

Area G-4, Map 1

650'
Upper
Latourell
Falls

Miles

0   0.5   1

parking lot on the right. For Latourell Falls, continue another 2.0 miles west to the good-sized parking area on the left.

From the Latourell Falls parking lot, a wide, paved trail goes rather steeply uphill to a smashing view of Lower Latourell Falls. The spot is so photogenic that countless travelers have gone back to their cars for additional film. To escape the tourist hordes, you bear left, away from the developed viewpoint, and immediately leave the paved trail behind. The footpath ascends a lush, green hillside, especially appealing in April and May when it bursts with spring greenery, and in early November, when the bigleaf-maple leaves turn bright yellow. The path splits just after you climb to a less photogenic viewpoint at the top of Lower Latourell Falls.

For a short loop that skips the upper falls, turn right, but for the rewards of the full loop trip, go left. This trail goes upstream 0.5 mile in a lovely woodsy canyon, crossing several quaint wooden footbridges on its way to a bridge just below twisting Upper Latourell Falls. The last fall of this cascade is short, but perfectly suited for great pictures; the scenic bridge and over-hanging tree limbs create an excellent foreground.

The downstream return route follows the path on the west side of the creek, back to the junction with the shortcut trail mentioned above. You go left here and make two quick switchbacks, gaining about 150 feet, to an attractive pair of viewpoints looking up and down the Columbia River. From here, you make a lazy descent back to the road, which you cross, then go down some stairs on the north side of the road. The trail goes through a picnic area, then turns right and travels under a tall, arcing highway bridge. You cross the creek one last time and emerge at the base of Lower Latourell Falls. Schedule plenty of time for gawking here, not only at the falls, but at the almost perfect displays of columnar basalt in the surrounding amphitheater. A wide-angle lens is essential to do the scene justice with your camera. The last couple of hundred yards of trail back to the parking lot are gently uphill.

If you want to include a visit to Bridal Veil Falls, park in the lot for Bridal Veil Falls State Park. The trail to the falls starts at the east end of the parking lot and wanders under a shady canopy of bigleaf maple and Douglas-fir. On either side of the wide gravel path are masses of tall thimbleberry, vine maple, and other shrubs. The 0.3-mile trail drops in one long switchback to a bridge over Bridal Veil Creek. You turn right here and climb a flight of stairs to a stunning overlook of two-tiered Bridal Veil Falls. The scene is most impressive when the creek is running high after spring rains.

If you are up for still more exploring, take the Overlook Trail Loop, which heads north from the restroom building near the parking lot. True to its name, this paved nature trail passes several good viewpoints. It is especially attractive in late April and early May, when the meadows along the way are carpeted with the beautiful blue blossoms of camas. This small state park, in fact, has Oregon's largest surviving camas fields in the Columbia River Gorge. Please stay on the trails, because these plants are very sensitive and cannot survive being trampled. After 0.4 mile, the trail returns you to the west end of the parking lot.

Trip 2

Angels Rest

(Map Area G-4, Map 2)

Distance	Elevation Gain	Hiking Time	Optional Map	Difficulty
4.6 to 7 miles	1500 to 2000'	2.5 to 4 hours	*Green Trails–Bridal Veil*	***

Usually Open	February to December
Best Times	Mid-April to June
Agency	Columbia River Gorge National Scenic Area

Like some ancient castle battlement, the rocky fortress of Angels Rest rises dramatically above the forested ridges of the western Columbia River Gorge. The trail to the top is justifiably one of the most popular in the Gorge, because it has a classic mix of good exercise, easy access, and outstanding

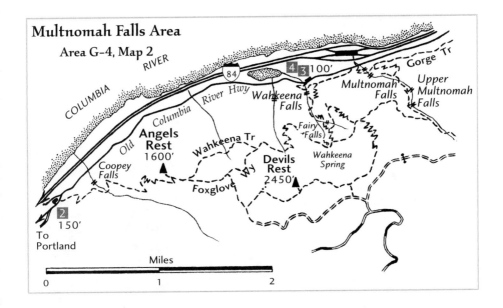

Multnomah Falls Area
Area G-4, Map 2

COLUMBIA RIVER

Columbia River Hwy

Old Columbia

Angels
Rest
1600'

Coopey
Falls

Wahkeena Tr

Foxglove

Wahkeena
Falls

Fairy
Falls

Devils
Rest
2450'

Wahkeena
Spring

Multnomah
Falls

Upper
Multnomah
Falls

Gorge Tr

2
150'
To
Portland

Miles
0   1   2

scenery. In mid-April, the forests along the trail support some of the finest displays of beautiful white trillium in the region.

Directions: Take Interstate 84 east from Portland to Bridal Veil exit 28, then drive the exit road 0.4 mile to the junction with the Old Columbia River Highway. The large parking lot for the Angels Rest Trail is on your right.

The trail leaves from the south side of the road, then goes uphill through a lovely Douglas-fir forest. If you are visiting in mid-April, expect to be delighted by thousands of trillium filling the forest with their spectacular three-petaled white flowers. The trail goes up a couple of switchbacks, then traverses to a mediocre viewpoint before moving into a creek canyon. You'll get only a partial look at Coopey Falls below you on the left, but when you come to the bridged creek crossing, there is a good view of a smaller, but attractive, 30-foot waterfall.

After the creek, the uphill begins in earnest, as you traverse a hillside covered with bigleaf maples and red alders whose mossy trunks sprout licorice ferns by the hundred. On the forest floor are bracken and sword fern, as well as some poison oak, especially in the rocky areas. A series of short switchbacks takes you through forests and finally up a rocky slope to a ridgetop junction with the side trail that leads out to imposing Angels Rest. Turn left on this rather rugged trail and follow it out to the end of the flat-topped rock formation, where a confusion of side trails leads to stunning viewpoints up and down the Gorge.

This entire area was burned in a 1991 wildfire, leaving behind weathered snags both on the summit and on many of the surrounding hillsides. It is interesting to observe how some stands of trees were left untouched by the flames, while others were totally obliterated, and how the flowers and shrubs

Angels Rest, Columbia River Gorge

have benefited from the increase in available light. Near the summit, you can expect to see pink wild rose, blue iris, white carrot, yarrow, daisy, yellow wallflower, red columbine, and tall blue larkspur—all taking advantage of the nearly treeless slopes. Peak flower time is usually in May.

Angels Rest is a very exposed location, which makes it particularly susceptible to the famous Gorge winds. It is not uncommon for the winds to be blowing so strongly that you are literally unable to stand up at the summit. If the howling gales are such that you can't eat your lunch in comfort, or if you just want more exercise, you might consider extending this hike to include a nice loop into the more protected forests nearby. To take this loop, return to the main trail and follow it up the ridge for 0.1 mile to a junction. Go left on the trail toward Wahkeena Falls and travel nearly on the level into a shady forest. Here the ground is covered with white-blooming plants like vanilla leaf, star-flowered smilacina, and false lily-of-the-valley. After about 0.4 mile, you will reach a small creek and a nice site for a picnic or camp that is protected from wind by big Douglas-firs and western hemlocks.

To complete the loop, climb briefly away from the creek and cross a burn area where tall pink fireweed and blue larkspur crowd the trail. Just before you leave the burn area, look for a small sign for Foxglove Way, going sharply back to the right. Turn right onto this path and climb out of the burn area back into deep woods. The trail gets wider as it joins a barely recognizable old jeep track and comes to a junction. You turn right and contour through a forest where the trail often travels under the spreading limbs of vine maples, then goes down a ridgeline back to the junction a little above Angels Rest.

Trip 3

Devils Rest Loop

(Map Area G-4, Map 2)

Distance	Elevation Gain	Hiking Time	Optional Map	Difficulty
9.0 miles	2500'	4 to 6 hours	*Green Trails–Bridal Veil* (part of route not shown)	***

Usually Open	Late March to December
Best Times	April to June
Agency	Columbia River Gorge National Scenic Area

Other than a similar name, Devils Rest shares little in common with its better known neighbor, Angels Rest. While the latter is a dramatic viewpoint on a towering rock abutment, the former is an unassuming forested knoll, with little in the way of views. While the trail to Angels Rest ascends a burned-over hillside, the path up Devils Rest climbs a densely forested realm of waterfalls and lush vegetation. The two locations can be combined into one hike, but it is better to do them on separate trips tailored to enjoying their individual charms and attributes. The author usually selects his destination based on the weather. If the skies are clear and promise outstanding views, head for Angels Rest. If the clouds are low and threatening, then Devils Rest is the better choice, because the forests and waterfalls on this trail are just as impressive under overcast skies as sunny ones.

Directions: Take Interstate 84 east from Portland to Bridal Veil exit 28, then drive the exit road 0.4 mile to the junction with the Old Columbia River Highway. Go left (east) on the old highway and drive 2.6 miles to the roadside parking lot for Wahkeena Falls.

The initially paved trail starts at the bridge over cascading Wahkeena Creek and climbs in one long switchback to an upper bridge, right in the spray of the falls. From here, you climb a hillside covered with luxuriant gorge vegetation on a switchbacking gravel trail to a ridgecrest where a 30-yard side trail leads to a good viewpoint. The main trail goes steeply upstream beside loudly cascading Wahkeena Creek until it crosses a tributary creek beside Fairy Falls. From here, you climb a series of short switchbacks to a junction.

Either route from this junction will work as the first part of this loop, but the views are better if you take the one to the left and hike out to a ridgecrest, where another short spur trail leads to a good viewpoint. From this junction, the route ascends seven quick switchbacks to another ridgetop junction, this one with the alternate route from Fairy Falls. Turn left and in 50 feet bear right (uphill) on a possibly unsigned, but obvious, trail that makes a series of evenly spaced and moderately graded switchbacks up a woodsy hillside. At the top of the climb, the trail curves to the right to follow the edge of a ridgeline. Although it stays close to a steep drop-off, the trail is surprisingly gentle with only very gradual uphill sections. The forest floor along this high ridge is dominated by common flowering plants like bunchberry, false solomon seal, twisted stalk, anemone, wild iris, and yellow wood violet.

As you make your way south and west along the ridge, ignore an unsigned path to the left leading to an unseen forest road, but do take advantage of two short side trails to the right, which lead to nice viewpoints. After a final climb, you come to a junction just a few yards below the top of Devils Rest. The forested summit has lots of large, moss-covered boulders and is quite lovely despite its ominous name.

To continue the loop trip, go back to the junction with the path just below the summit, then turn west onto the trail signed FOXGLOVE WAY. This boot path is not shown on any official maps and isn't maintained by the Forest Service, but it's easy to follow as it descends steeply through dense, head-high shrubbery to an unsigned junction. Bear left and walk gradually uphill for 0.2 mile on a wide trail that obviously used to be a jeep road. At another unsigned junction with an abandoned jeep track, you turn right and go downhill at a gentle grade to a switchback and a signed junction.

The path to the left goes down to Angels Rest (see Trip 2), but to close out this loop, turn right on a narrow trail that winds through the trees, then goes down through a burned area to a junction. Turn right on a well-maintained path that immediately leaves the burned area and descends a series of switchbacks. This trail drops from the top of a rocky slope, then down a forested hillside, where the vegetation tells a story about the benefits of natural fire. A huge fire swept through this forest in 1991, and evidence of this blaze can still be seen, in the form of several burned snags and lots of charred bark on the living trees. But this fire had benefits as well, as you can see from the dense ground vegetation, which has taken advantage of the increased sunshine to produce a profusion of greenery. The most conspicuous of the sun-loving plants here is a spectacular and unusual 4-foot-tall species of larkspur that boasts striking blue flowers in early June.

At the bottom of the switchbacks, the trail does an up-and-down traverse of a hillside to reach a camp beside large Wahkeena Spring, where a full stream gushes directly out of the ground. Just 100 yards beyond the spring is a trail junction. Turn left and descend a series of switchbacks that in 0.4 mile takes you back to the junction above Fairy Falls.

Trip 4

Multnomah – Wahkeena Falls Loop

(Map Area G-4, Map 2)

Distance	Elevation Gain	Hiking Time	Optional Map	Difficulty
5.4 miles	1700'	2.5 to 4 hours	*Green Trails–Bridal Veil*	**

☁

Usually Open	All year
Best Times	April to June
Agency	Columbia River Gorge National Scenic Area

Even without the waterfalls, this magnificent loop trip would be worthwhile. The western Columbia River Gorge is famous for its lush greenery, and probably the most beautiful forests of all are found in the canyons and hillsides near Multnomah Falls. The dense forest canopy and the luxuriant tangle of ferns, mosses, and other plants make for a verdant rainforest of stunning beauty. But despite the lovely forests, it is the waterfalls that are the star attraction of any hike in this area.

In addition to famous Multnomah Falls, which at 542 feet is one of the highest falls in North America, the loop trip includes visits to at least half a dozen other falls on upper Multnomah Creek and neighboring Wahkeena Creek. The downside of hiking here is crowds. With its wide fame, enormous parking lot, and even its own exit off a busy interstate freeway, Multnomah Falls is said to be the most visited tourist attraction in the entire state of Oregon. For crowd control purposes, especially on weekends, it is probably best to start this loop at quieter Wahkeena Falls.

Directions: Take Interstate 84 east from Portland to Bridal Veil exit 28, then drive the exit road 0.4 mile to the junction with the Old Columbia River Highway. Go left (east) on the old highway and drive 2.6 miles to the roadside parking lot for Wahkeena Falls.

The trail starts at the bridge over loudly cascading Wahkeena Creek, where you can look straight up at 242-foot-high Wahkeena Falls, a twisting cascade of water in a narrow chute. The paved trail makes one switchback, then comes to a bridge over Wahkeena Creek, in a grotto beside the falling water. You can expect to get showered with spray when making this crossing, which will be welcome on hot summer days and bone-chilling in the winter months.

After the bridge, the trail turns to gravel and comes to a second switchback, where a wire gate blocks access to the closed Perdition Trail. Past this junction, your trail keeps climbing, often beside mossy rock walls, up a hill-

Upper Multnomah Falls

side covered with luxuriant vegetation, including thimbleberry, goatsbeard, cow parsnip, maiden-hair fern, columbine, beardtongue, and poison oak. Ten uphill switchbacks weed out most of the tourists and take you up to a ridge just above the top of Wahkeena Falls. From this ridge, a short dead-end side trail to your right leads to a fine viewpoint.

The main trail goes upstream steeply, climbing beside loudly cascading Wahkeena Creek, then crossing the flow twice on wooden plank bridges. With dense thickets of lady and maiden-hair fern covering the canyon walls, and a shady canopy of western red cedar and western hemlock, this area has a jungle-like feel. Past the second bridge, a few short, steep switchbacks take you to a split in the creek and up to the base of lacy Fairy Falls. A wooden bench here allows hikers to relax and enjoy the sight and sound of falling water. Five more short switchbacks lead up to a junction with the Vista Point Trail. You can turn either right or left here, as the trails meet again in about 0.5 mile. The left route goes by a nice viewpoint and switchbacks up a ridge to the junction where the two trails reunite. The route to the right goes through lush greenery to a junction near Wahkeena Spring, where you turn left and climb a wooded hillside to the same ridgetop junction.

From this point, you turn east on the Wahkeena Trail and immediately pass an unsigned trail that goes to the right up to Devils Rest (Trip 3). Go straight on the Wahkeena Trail, which takes you over tiny Shady Creek and contours across a heavily wooded north-facing slope, before descending into the canyon of Multnomah Creek. You turn left (downstream) at the junction with the Multnomah Creek Trail and closely follow this beautiful stream to a switchback which takes you down to the base of Upper Multnomah Falls. This almost perfect falls is neither as tall nor as famous as its lower namesake, but still commands the attention of hikers and their cameras.

Continue downstream 0.5 mile, past a succession of waterfalls of various heights, to a junction with the other end of the closed Perdition Trail and a huge culvert over Multnomah Creek. Just past this crossing, you meet a very popular side trail that bears left and leads to the viewpoint at the top of Multnomah Falls. Don't expect to be alone here, as virtually all the occupants of the hundreds of cars you can see parked below seem to make this spot their hiking goal. From here, you descend a series of switchbacks on a paved trail that has been pounded by countless thousands of pairs of tennis shoes, to a much photographed bridge between the two tiers of Multnomah Falls. You then follow this busy trail downhill, partly on stone steps, to the historic lodge at the base of the falls.

To return to your car, you can either walk west on the Old Columbia River Highway or follow the parallel, poison-oak-lined Gorge Trail, which starts a few hundred feet west of the lodge. It is only 0.8 mile by either route to Wahkeena Creek.

Trip 5

Larch Mountain Upper Loop

(Map Area G-4, Map 3)

Distance	Elevation Gain	Hiking Time	Optional Map	Difficulty
6.0 miles	1300'	2.5 to 4 hours	*Green Trails–Bridal Veil*	**

Usually Open	Late May to October
Best Times	June
Agency	Columbia River Gorge National Scenic Area

Except for the major volcanic snow peaks, Larch Mountain is probably the most recognizable landmark on the Portland skyline. This hike allows you the opportunity to get a close look at the features that give this mountain its distinctive profile, especially the high rock outcropping called Sherrard Point, right at the summit. And while this relatively easy outing won't give you the same sense of accomplishment you get from climbing to the summit from Multnomah Falls (Trip 6), it also won't give you the sore muscles and blisters that come with the longer hike.

Directions: From Interstate 84, take Corbett exit 22 and drive 1.4 miles up the steep access road to the south. Turn left on the Old Columbia River Highway and after 1.9 miles bear right at a fork onto E. Larch Mountain Road. Follow

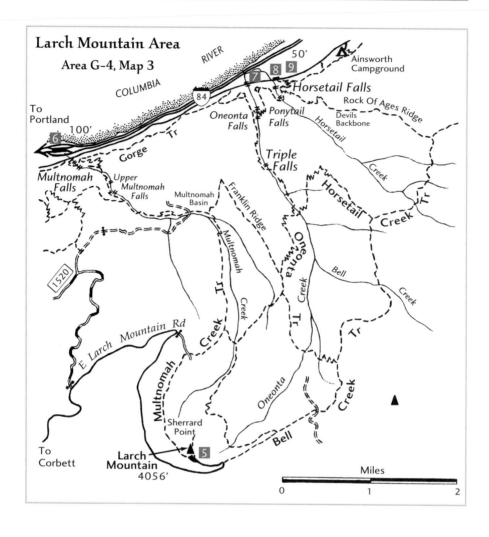

Larch Mountain Area

Area G-4, Map 3

COLUMBIA RIVER

50'

Ainsworth Campground

84

Horsetail Falls

Rock Of Ages Ridge

To Portland

100'

6

Oneonta Falls

Ponytail Falls

Devils Backbone

Horsetail

Gorge Tr

Multnomah Falls

Upper Multnomah Falls

Multnomah Basin

Triple Falls

Horsetail Creek

Creek

Tr

Franklin Ridge

Multnomah Tr

Multnomah Creek

Oneonta Creek Tr

Bell Creek

Creek

1520

E. Larch Mountain Rd

Multnomah Creek Tr

Oneonta Tr

Bell Creek Tr

Sherrard Point

Oneonta Creek

To Corbett

Larch Mountain 4056'

5

Bell

Miles

0   1   2

this good paved road for 14.5 miles to the large parking lot and turnaround just below the summit of Larch Mountain.

The Multnomah Creek Trail leaves from the southwest corner of the parking lot and follows a gravel path past several widely spaced picnic tables. After 0.1 mile, you go left at an unsigned junction, and gradually descend through a cool, shady forest of Pacific silver fir and western hemlock. Initially, there is virtually no ground cover, only a few scattered huckleberry bushes and beargrass plants, but as you descend these are joined by increasing numbers of oxalis, star-flowered smilacina, trillium, vanilla leaf, and bunchberry. The gently graded trail gradually loses elevation, following a wide but viewless ridge, on a trail covered with needles and soft dirt that provide excellent cushioning for every footfall.

After 1.5 miles, you cross a closed dirt road and immediately thereafter pass a good, but waterless, campsite. Below this, the trail loses elevation more quickly on a gravel path for 0.5 mile to a junction. The main trail goes straight, but for this loop you turn right and wind downhill for 0.2 mile to an excellent camp and a log bridge over the softly trickling headwaters of Multnomah Creek.

You are now at the bottom of a basin that 4 million years ago was part of a fiery volcano and, more recently, was carved out by Ice-Age glaciers. Both fire and ice are long gone now, but they have been replaced by equally impressive old-growth forests. The trees here may not be quite as big as those at lower elevations, but they are splendid nonetheless.

On the other side of the log bridge is a junction, where you turn right, climb past some massive old-growth trees, then skirt the left side of a lovely meadow that features great views up to craggy Sherrard Point. This meadow used to be a lake sitting in a glacial cirque. Over thousands of years, the lake gradually filled with sediment, becoming a meadow. In time, the meadow too will disappear, to be replaced by forest. For now, this marshy paradise is home to lots of water-loving wildflowers, especially marsh marigold and shooting star. Mosquitoes also like this habitat, so be sure to bring repellent.

Beyond the meadow, the trail climbs in fits and starts through dense forest. As you climb, take a break from time to time to appreciate the birds. You may see or hear winter wrens, dark-eyed juncos, or either of two types of thrush. The varied thrush looks like a slimmed down robin that got all dressed up with an extra orange eye stripe and a black breast band. The hermit thrush looks rather drab, but has a fascinating, almost metallic, buzzlike call. If the birds don't interest you, try examining the vegetation. The old-growth forests here have lots of Pacific silver and grand fir, Douglas-fir, and western hemlock. Many of the oldest trees have fallen and now serve as nurse logs for young trees. Beneath the shade of these big trees grow ground-cover species, like queens cup, false lily-of-the-valley, and a high concentration of deer fern.

The trail turns left and keeps wandering uphill. You go over an indistinct ridge, then join an ancient roadbed that is noticeable only because it allows you to travel at a perfectly level grade for the next mile. During this time, you cross several tiny trickles forming the headwaters of Oneonta Creek, then make a long traverse to meet the Oneonta Trail on a wooded ridgeline. You turn right here and follow the trail up a gently sloping ridge 0.8 mile, meeting the E. Larch Mountain Road at a switchback that is just 0.3 mile below the parking lot. Simply walk the road shoulder from here up to your car.

Before leaving for the day, be sure to take the easy but crowded 0.2-mile trail that goes to the top of Sherrard Point. The paved path leaves from the northwest corner of the parking lot and traverses a heavily wooded hillside, before climbing a series of steps to the rocky overlook. From this exceptional grandstand you can see five towering volcanic snow peaks (Mounts Rainier, St. Helens, Adams, Jefferson, and, of course, nearby Hood), as well as countless lower summits that you could spend hours identifying.

Trip 6

Larch Mountain from Multnomah Falls Loop

(Map Area G-4, Map 3)

Distance	Elevation Gain	Hiking Time	Optional Map	Difficulty
16.3 miles	4300'	9 to 12 hours	*Green Trails–Bridal Veil*	****

Usually Open	Late May to October
Best Times	June
Agency	Columbia River Gorge National Scenic Area

With good paved roads providing access to both ends of this hike, it's not surprising that both Multnomah Falls and Larch Mountain are very crowded. The trails connecting these two locations, however, are amazingly quiet. Well, perhaps it isn't all that amazing, when you consider that it takes a lot of sweat to get from one to the other. Although not overly steep, it is a very long way up, from nearly sea level at the base of Multnomah Falls to over 4000 feet at the top of Larch Mountain. If you can arrange a car shuttle, the best plan is to start from the top and hike downhill, but starting from the bottom, it's best to plan on doing a long, scenic loop. From a crowd-control standpoint, one advantage of this approach is that, in order to complete this hike in one day, you have to start out very early in the morning, which means that few tourists will be around to distract from the views of Multnomah Falls at the trailhead.

Directions: From Interstate 84, take Multnomah Falls exit 31 and park in the enormous lot built to accommodate the millions of tourists who come to visit this famous falls.

Follow the crowds through the tunnel under the eastbound lanes of Interstate 84 and to the historic log Multnomah Falls Lodge. After elbowing aside your fellow visitors and snapping a few pictures from the stonework viewing area at the bottom of the falls, turn right on the wide trail that heads uphill on stone stairs.

This paved trail climbs in a long switchback up to the much-photographed bridge that spans the flow below the tall upper part of Multnomah Falls and above the shorter lower cascade. You cross the bridge, making sure to smile for the dozens of photographers snapping pictures from below, and climb a bit more to a junction with the Gorge Trail. You stay on the main paved route and ascend a series of switchbacks all the way to the short side trail that goes to the viewing platform at the top of the 542-foot falls.

After admiring the view, you leave the tourist hordes behind and begin hiking up the Multnomah Creek Trail. You quickly cross the creek on a huge culvert and come to a junction with the closed Perdition Trail. Keep left and climb beside the cascading stream, in a wet canyon of lush vegetation. On your left, the creek drops over a series of hard-to-view falls of varying heights. A little after crossing under a massive rock overhang that will often shower you with water, you come to photogenic Upper Multnomah Falls, then switch-back away from this lovely falls and traverse to a junction with the Wahkeena Trail (see Trip 4).

Keep straight on the main trail and about 0.2 mile later cross Multnomah Creek on a bridge, then go lazily uphill along the banks of the creek about 0.3 mile to a trail split. To the left is a short but rugged high-water route that bypasses a creekside section of trail that is usually flooded during spring snow melt. If the lower route is feasible, take that one, as it is both easier and more attractive. After a few hundred yards, the two routes reunite and soon come to an old dirt road and a possible camp. You cross the road and continue upstream about 0.2 mile to a junction.

The shortest route to Larch Mountain goes straight on the Multnomah Creek Trail, but for a longer, more scenic route, turn left on the Franklin Ridge Trail. This path goes over a low ridge, then gradually climbs a forested hillside to an open clearing on top of Franklin Ridge. The best views are to the east, over the depths of Oneonta Creek Canyon, and west, over Multnomah Basin.

The trail turns right here and goes back into the trees on the ridgecrest. For the next mile or so, the trail goes up in stair-step fashion, with some steep uphill pitches and some relatively level sections. Most of the way, you are among the trees, but there are also frequent breaks that provide excellent views to the east. When you reach a junction with the Oneonta Trail, which drops steeply to the left, you go straight and lose some elevation, through an area of extensive blowdown. After just 0.3 mile, you come to the next junction, where you turn left on the Oneonta Trail.

Walk through attractive mid-elevation forests, up a sloping ridge, then lose some elevation and make an easy crossing of Oneonta Creek, which should get your feet wet only during high water. Then go over a low ridge and splash through an even smaller creek before climbing rather steeply up a half dozen short switchbacks to a junction with the Bell Creek Trail. You turn right and travel mostly on the level to the south and west.

The trail comes to a dirt jeep road, where you walk a short distance to your right to pick up the continuation of the trail. After another 0.4 mile, go straight at a final junction and climb 0.8 mile up a gently sloping ridge to where the trail ends at a switchback on paved E. Larch Mountain Road. To reach the top of the mountain, you veer right and walk the shoulder of the road 0.3 mile to the parking lot just below the summit.

Having come this far, you won't want to miss the opportunity to take in the view from Sherrard Point. To reach it, take a crowded, 0.2-mile paved trail from the northwest corner of the parking area up to the developed viewpoint. Signs point you to the five major volcanic peaks you can see from the summit

(Mounts Rainier, Adams, St. Helens, Hood, and Jefferson), but you will have to rely on either experience or a good map to pick out the hundreds of lower summits visible in every direction.

To return to Multnomah Falls, pick up the Multnomah Creek Trail from the southwest corner of the parking lot and walk through a cool forest, past a dispersed picnic area. The trail gradually descends a sloping ridgeline for 1.5 miles, then crosses a closed dirt road. You walk downward for another 0.5 mile and go straight at a junction, staying on the main Multnomah Creek Trail. This path descends at a steady grade on a wooded hillside, then crosses a scree slope and makes a short switchback down to Multnomah Creek. After crossing the main creek, you go downstream for 0.3 mile, make a couple of more very short switchbacks, and cross a tributary creek. A short distance past this ford is the junction with the Franklin Ridge Trail.

Trip 7

Oneonta Gorge

(Map Area G-4, Map 3)

Distance	Elevation Gain	Hiking Time	Optional Map	Difficulty
1.2 miles	50'	1 to 2 hours	USFS–Trails of the Columbia Gorge	**

Usually Open	July to September
Best Times	August and September
Agency	Columbia River Gorge National Scenic Area

This trip is only for adventurous souls who don't mind getting wet. There is no trail up Oneonta Gorge, although the route is never in doubt. In lieu of a trail, you simply wade up the bed of Oneonta Creek, through a spectacular slot canyon. It is best to wait until late summer to do this outing, because the water level will be lower then and, with the hot temperatures, you will actually welcome getting soaked. The standard hiking clothing doesn't apply to this adventure. Your best options are ratty old tennis shoes with good tread for wading, and either shorts or a swimsuit. It is also advised that you have a dry change of clothes in the car for when you return.

Directions: Drive Interstate 84 east from Portland and take Bridal Veil exit 28. At the end of the 0.4-mile exit road, turn east on the Old Columbia River Highway. After 3.1 miles, slow down to pass the crowds at Multnomah Falls Lodge and, 2.0 miles later, park in any of the small lots near the bridge over Oneonta Creek.

A short trail leads down to the water beside a large sign on the east side of the bridge. This sign informs you that Oneonta Gorge is a special botanical area, with a unique ecosystem of delicate ferns and mosses. In deference to this special status, visitors must be extremely careful to avoid disturbing the plant life.

With this in mind, you make your way upstream, sometimes walking on rocks and sometimes simply wading up the creek itself. The canyon narrows very quickly, so within just a few short yards you are already squeezing into the 15-to-20-foot-wide slot canyon. You'll need to crane your neck to see up the 200 or so feet of vertical walls rising to the top of the canyon. The walls are covered with an array of ferns,

Oneonta Gorge

giving this cool grotto a jungle-like feeling. In the mid-1990s floods washed down this canyon and temporarily blocked the route with a massive log jam. If the logs are still there, or have been replaced with new ones, you must be extremely careful crawling over them. The route may be closed to travel, if the Forest Service feels it is too dangerous. Call ahead for the latest conditions. Even without the special hazard of logs, hikers must still watch where they put their feet, because it is easy to turn an ankle on the slippery rocks.

In places the creek bends and you can walk on gravel bars, but the creek also has some deep pools that you must wade into or try to scramble around. Some of these pools can be waist deep, depending on the water level in the creek. After about 0.6 mile, you arrive at the head of the gorge, where spectacular 100-foot Oneonta Falls drops over a sheer cliff.

There is very little light in this slot canyon, so photographers must use a tripod and fast film to get pictures. They also will want to protect their gear in plastic bags as they hike, to avoid getting everything wet should they slip on a rock while wading. The vertical canyon walls are impressive, but they absolutely preclude any exit other than going back the way you came.

Trip 8

Horsetail Falls to Triple Falls

(Map Area G-4, Map 3)

Distance	Elevation Gain	Hiking Time	Optional Map	Difficulty
4.5 miles	700'	2 hours	USFS–Trails of the Columbia Gorge	**

Usually Open	All year (except during winter storms)
Best Times	April to June / Late October to early November
Agency	Columbia River Gorge National Scenic Area

Everything that makes the Columbia River Gorge so special is on spectacular display on this easy hike. There are lush forests, fern-lined grottos, deep slot canyons, excellent viewpoints, and, of course, lots of impressive waterfalls. Not surprisingly, all of these features have made this hike extremely popular. The large parking lot at Horsetail Falls overflows on summer weekends, so try to arrive early in the day or visit on a weekday.

Directions: Drive Interstate 84 east from Portland and take Bridal Veil exit 28. At the end of the 0.4-mile exit road, turn east on the Old Columbia River Highway. After 3.1 miles, slow down to pass the crowds at Multnomah Falls Lodge and, 2.5 miles later, turn left into the large parking lot on the north side of the highway, directly across from Horsetail Falls.

The well-signed trailhead is just a few yards east of 176-foot Horsetail Falls, a beautiful, twisting, roadside cataract that is as far as most car-bound tourists ever get. Hikers can take the wide, well-graded, gravel path, as it slowly switchbacks up a densely vegetated slope, with lots of bleeding heart and maiden-hair fern growing under some impressive examples of bigleaf maple and Douglas-fir. At the fourth switchback is a junction with the Gorge Trail.

Turn sharply right and take two more switchbacks before making a level traverse at the base of a basalt cliff curving to the left into the canyon above Horsetail Falls. Immediately in front of you is an impressive falls that is officially given the rather prosaic name of Upper Horsetail Falls, but for decades hikers have given it the more colorful moniker of Ponytail Falls. In deference to this tradition, some Forest Service trail signs even use this name.

Not that you will need any encouragement, but take some time to admire this falls as it plunges down a slot in a basalt cliff and shoots out over an overhanging ledge. The trail goes behind the falls, taking advantage of the dry grotto under the ledge to give visitors a unique perspective of standing under a wild waterfall.

After leaving the amphitheater holding Ponytail Falls, the trail contours across a steep hillside with several mossy rockslides. Just as the trail begins to curve left into the canyon of Oneonta Creek, two unsigned trails go right to visit dramatic viewpoints. The best views are to the east, to such landmarks as Nesmith Point, Beacon Rock, Aldrich Butte, and Hamilton Mountain. Back on the main trail, you walk south, staying on the level past a dripping overhanging rock, then begin a series of six downhill switchbacks. At the second switchback, there is a signed viewpoint where you can look directly down into the depths of Oneonta Gorge. This amazing, fern-lined slot

Horsetail Falls

canyon is only about 20 feet wide, and often has fallen trees spanning the chasm as much as 200 feet above the creek at the bottom.

At the bottom of the switchbacks a metal bridge spans Oneonta Creek just below a lovely 60-foot falls. Just downstream, and out of sight, is the even more impressive, 100-foot Oneonta Falls, where the creek drops into the slot canyon. Once across the bridge, you climb two switchbacks and come to a junction. If you only want a short trip, bear right. But if you want to visit one of the finest waterfalls in the Columbia River Gorge (or anywhere else, for that matter), then turn sharply left and make a long gradual uphill traverse on the cliffs above the deep canyon of Oneonta Creek. After about 0.2 mile, you make two uphill switchbacks, then walk on the level across almost vertical slopes, before dropping slightly to an unsigned junction. Bear left and drop 50 feet to a dramatic viewpoint of Triple Falls.

This magnificent falls is especially appealing because the creek splits into three almost perfectly even parts each of which cascades over the cliff in twisting falls. Individually, these falls are works of art, but together they are a masterpiece. A visit here is worthwhile during any season, but one of the nicest times to visit is in the autumn when the bigleaf maples turn yellow and sprinkle the canyon with color.

To close out the trip, return along the Oneonta Trail to the junction above the bridge. Instead of going back the way you came, go straight at this junction and climb gradually to a junction with a spur trail to the right, which leads to some fine viewpoints. The main trail curves to the left, going across a rockslide with an abundant population of pikas that like to peep at passing hikers. From here, you descend gradually through dense forests to a junction at a switchback.

The Gorge Trail goes straight, but you turn right and descend in a long traverse to the Old Columbia River Highway. To return to your car, simply walk along this road for 0.5 mile, past the bottom of Oneonta Gorge and back to Horsetail Falls. There is no sidewalk, and almost no shoulder, so be very alert for traffic on this narrow road.

Trip 9

Rock of Ages – Horsetail Creek Loop

(Map Area G-4, Map 3)

Distance	Elevation Gain	Hiking Time	Optional Map	Difficulty
9.4 miles	3300'	5 to 7 hours	USFS–Trails of the Columbia Gorge	****

Usually Open	Mid-April to October
Best Times	Mid-April to June
Agency	Columbia River Gorge National Scenic Area

The hike up Rock of Ages Ridge is not for the faint of heart. Every time I take this route, I envision mountain goats getting together around the campfire to tell horror stories about how steep it is. There are compensations, however. Chief among these are the terrific views from a rocky ridge called the Devils Backbone, together with the fun loops this route accesses on rarely hiked trails in the backcountry of the Gorge. One of the best of those loops follows the quiet Horsetail Creek Trail down to Oneonta Creek and past great waterfalls back to your car.

Directions: Drive Interstate 84 east from Portland and take Bridal Veil exit 28. At the end of the 0.4-mile exit road, turn east on the Old Columbia River Highway. After 3.1 miles, slow down to pass the crowds at Multnomah Falls Lodge and, 2.5 miles later, turn left into the large parking lot on the north side of the highway, directly across from Horsetail Falls. This trailhead gets very busy on summer weekends, so arrive as early as possible.

This popular trail starts just east of Horsetail Falls and climbs four switchbacks to a junction with the Gorge Trail. You turn sharply right and climb two more switchbacks, then make a short traverse to where the trail curves to the left into the canyon holding Ponytail Falls.

Just 20 yards after turning this corner, look for an unsigned use path veering uphill to the left over the roots of a large Douglas-fir tree. You turn onto this trail and in a few yards pass one of those small, ominous signs you see from time to time in the Gorge saying TRAIL NOT MAINTAINED, which always means that the path will be steep and difficult. True to this rule, the ridiculously steep trail crawls over roots and rocks and charges up slopes where the trail is quite slippery when wet. A sturdy hiking pole will help to keep you steady, and you'll feel better from time to time using your hands to help pull yourself up. Adding to the difficulties are lots of poison oak plants, although they are usually easy to avoid.

In order to go around trees and rocks, the path makes lots of small dips and turns, but it is always very steep as you ascend the slopes east of Ponytail Falls. After about 0.4 mile, there is a split in the trail. The path to the left looks like the main route, but it actually dead-ends after about 75 yards at a good viewpoint on a rocky overlook. The main trail goes to the right and contours for 100 yards across a steep, mostly open hillside with lots of oak trees, before climbing steeply once again. The trail makes several twists and turns before curving left and reaching a narrow slot in the ridgecrest. You turn right here and keep climbing at an extremely steep grade up to a grassy ledge perched on the spine of the ridge.

This narrow rock crest is called the Devils Backbone, and the trail goes right along its spine. Sometimes this spine is only a few inches wide, and it drops off very steeply on both sides, so be very careful. For acrophobics, a safer but less spectacular path skirts around the left side of Devils Backbone. If your shaky nerves allow you the luxury of looking around, you will be delighted with the terrific views of the forested ridges to the south, as well as across the river all the way to Mt. Adams. Flowers abound, especially yarrow, yellow daisy, stonecrop, buckwheat, blue bellflower, and onion.

Once past this dramatic section, the trail becomes somewhat easier, as you climb at a more moderate grade in deep woods, always on or near the ridgecrest. There are still some very steep sections, but the trail here is not as rugged or as difficult as it was below. You will get occasional glimpses through the trees on the left of the towering rock buttress called Rock of Ages, for which this ridge was named, but mostly you stay in viewless forests. A little past a short section where you actually lose some elevation, the steep climbing begins again on a final push to the top of the rim. You will know when you reach the top, because the ridge widens rather abruptly, and the trail's grade becomes remarkably gentle. The forests here feature lots of perky little wildflowers, like starflower, star-flowered smilacina, and pipsissewa, whose cute little pink blossoms turn downward. Once on top of the rim, the path gently winds along for about 1 mile, staying near a steep drop-off on your left, before coming to a junction with the Horsetail Creek Trail.

To make the loop, turn right (downhill) on the quiet Horsetail Creek Trail and very quickly come to a tiny splashing tributary of Horsetail Creek, amid dense riparian vegetation that is dominated by devils club, salmonberry, lady fern, and baneberry. Over the next mile, you will cross three larger branches of the creek, each separated by a rounded woodsy ridge. None of the crossings have bridges, but the creeks can all be crossed with simple rock hops. After the final crossing, you gradually climb for about 0.5 mile to a junction with the rarely traveled Bell Creek Trail, where you turn right.

It's pretty much all downhill from here, but most of it is gradual. First, you go down a gentle wooded slope, then, just as the slope ends at a steep drop-off, you switchback to the left on what is only the first of 15 remarkably well-graded switchbacks. After six switchbacks, look for a 50-foot spur trail to the left that goes to a small rocky overlook with nice views of Sherrard Point on Larch Mountain, peeking over Franklin Ridge.

After the last of the 15 switchbacks, you make a long descending traverse to the south, crossing two tiny tributaries of Oneonta Creek along the way, then make six short, but quite steep, downhill switchbacks to an unbridged crossing of Oneonta Creek. There are lots of boulders in the creek that appear to invite a dry-footed crossing. But these smooth rocks are dangerously slippery, so it is much safer either to search for a log crossing or simply ford the creek. It is an easy ford, and your feet will appreciate the cool water.

A short distance up the opposite bank is an excellent campsite and a junction with the Oneonta Trail. You turn right and drop quickly to another crossing of Oneonta Creek, this time on a nice, safe log bridge. From here, you descend along the east bank of the stream, as the trail drops rapidly to keep pace with the cascading creek. This section of trail is very attractive because the forest is dense, mossy, and elegant, and the creek is a constant joy for both visiting humans and the resident dippers, who dive under the water in search of food.

After about 0.7 mile, you cross the creek on a wide plank bridge and, just downstream, come to a short side trail on the right that leads to an overlook of gorgeous Triple Falls. This is the usual turnaround point for hikers coming up Oneonta Creek, so from here on the trail is very crowded.

You follow the Oneonta Trail as it works along the steep slopes above the deep canyon of Oneonta Creek for 0.9 mile, then turn sharply right at a junction. You drop to a crossing of the creek just above one waterfall and just below another before climbing a set of six switchbacks past a dramatic view of Oneonta Gorge. From here, you contour around a ridge and finally return to Ponytail Falls, closing the loop.

Trip 10

Nesmith Point

(Map Area G-4, Map 4)

Distance	Elevation Gain	Hiking Time	Optional Map	Difficulty
9.8 miles	3800′	5 to 6 hours	*Green Trails–Bonneville Dam & Bridal Veil*	****

Usually Open Late April to early November
Best Times Mid-May to mid-June
Agency Columbia River Gorge National Scenic Area

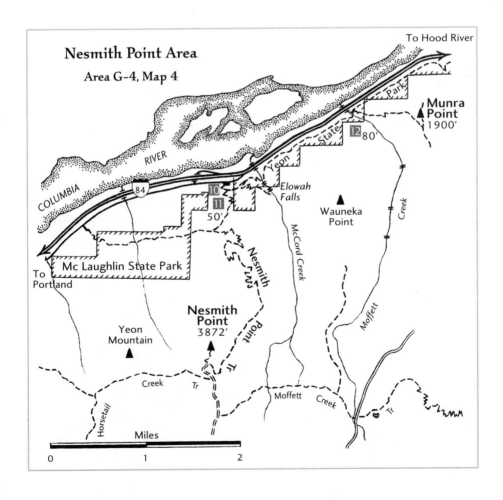

When hikers new to our region drive Interstate 84 through the Columbia River Gorge, they often crane their necks to see the tops of the towering cliffs and think, "Wow, the view up there must be great, but, man, it looks like a long way up!" Well, they're right on both counts, and Nesmith Point is the place to prove it. As one of the highest points directly overlooking the river, Nesmith Point provides excellent, if partially obstructed, views over much of the scenic masterpiece that is the Gorge. Be prepared to pay a stiff physical admission fee to enjoy the show. Just as it appears from the bottom, it *is* a long way up to Nesmith Point, so be prepared.

Directions: Coming from the west on Interstate 84, take Ainsworth Park exit 35 and turn left, following signs for Dodson. After just 150 feet, turn right on Frontage Road and drive 2.2 miles to the large parking lot on the right for Yeon State Park.

The trail starts at the west end of the parking lot and makes one quick switchback past a leaky wooden water tank to a junction. You turn right and walk gradually uphill for 0.9 mile, through dense forests to a junction with the Gorge Trail, just before a rocky slope and gully. Turn left here and you soon begin the promised long, hard climb. There is no shortage of switchbacks, far too many to count, but they don't prevent the route from being relentlessly steep. At first, you make your way out to a small ridgecrest viewpoint, then climb up a gully, with switchbacks taking you back and forth across the usually waterless bottom. There is lush vegetation here beneath the trees: ferns, false solomon seal, thimbleberry, and other species crowd the gully.

View of Mt. Adams as seen from the Nesmith Point Trail

The route leaves the gully and traverses a nearly vertical slope to round a ridge, then makes several short switchbacks up the ridge's west side, where you can expect to crawl around logs and washouts. The trail recrosses the ridge, then crosses the slopes of a large basin. Here you will get your first good views of the nearby cliffs and, across the river, of Beacon Rock and Mt. Adams in Washington. You make your way over to the head of the basin, before once again switchbacking back and forth across a cedar-filled gully, then finally reach a narrow ridgeline, where you can look down into McCord Creek Canyon to the east. You meet your first beargrass and huckleberry plants here too, which, as usual in the Gorge, means that the worst of the climb is over.

The trail turns up the ridge, staying on its east side, to pass through lovely mid-elevation woods of Douglas-fir, Pacific silver fir, and hemlock. The grade is considerably less severe than it was below, but still ascends steadily uphill, as the trail curves to the right and gently climbs a final section to a junction with an abandoned road.

To reach the summit, turn right and follow this curving road for 0.3 mile to the old lookout site atop Nesmith Point. Views here are excellent to the west, but trees block every other direction. For better vistas, continue past the high point and drop about 200 yards to a larger opening, where you can look not only west, but also north to Beacon Rock, Hamilton Mountain, and Mt. Adams, and even straight down to the area near the trailhead.

The trail to the top of Nesmith Point is about as much as any reasonable dayhiker can handle, but backpackers can use this trail as the jump-off point for longer trips. The most logical options are west to Oneonta Creek via the Horsetail Creek Trail and east to Tanner Creek on the recently reopened Moffett Creek Trail. Car shuttles to the trailheads at Horsetail Falls or Tanner Creek make these long trips more manageable.

Trip 11

Elowah Falls

(Map Area G-4, Map 4)

Distance	Elevation Gain	Hiking Time	Optional Map	Difficulty
3.0 miles	600'	1.5 to 2 hours	Green Trails–Bonneville Dam	*

Usually Open	February to December
Best Times	Mid-April to June
Agency	John B. Yeon State Park

Several factors come together to ensure that Elowah Falls is an exceptional waterfall, even in an area with so many to choose from. First it's *tall*, plunging 289 feet in a single shooting fall. Second, the setting is incredibly dramatic: a circular amphitheater of basalt cliffs, sprinkled with green mosses and lichens. Third, you get two falls for the price of one, with a second impressive drop of water tucked away above the famous lower falls. Finally, the two trails exploring the falls are both spectacular and of very different character. The higher trail is perched on a rock ledge blasted out of the cliffs beside the falls, while the lower trail explores the mossy canyon at the falls' base.

Directions: Coming from the west on Interstate 84, take Ainsworth Park exit 35 and turn left, following signs for Dodson. After just 150 feet, turn right on Frontage Road and drive 2.2 miles to the large parking lot on the right for Yeon State Park.

The trail leaves from the west side of the lot and climbs in one switchback past a leaky water tank, to a junction with the trail to Nesmith Point. Stay on the wide main trail to the left, walking through lovely woods, first of bigleaf maple then of Douglas-fir, to a junction of the two trails that explore the falls. The upper trail goes sharply right and climbs moderately, on five increasingly short switchbacks, up a mostly open slope with lots of wildflowers. Look for stonecrop, tiger lily, columbine, penstemon, and a host of others amid the rocks and mosses. You pass the remains of an old water diversion pipe, then travel a dramatic section of trail that has been blasted out of the sheer basalt cliffs. Metal guard rails have been installed here to help acrophobics feel safe. Views from this airy perch are very good, featuring distant looks at Table Mountain and Mt. Adams in Washington, but these are quickly forgotten as you round the corner to be confronted with the magnificent sheer drop of Elowah Falls in a huge, cliff-walled basin below you. Photographers should note that this steep, north-facing cliff gets very little sunlight, so you may need fast film and a tripod to take pictures in the low light. Stop to gawk as long as you like, then snap a few dozen pictures and walk the level trail up to the canyon above the falls, to where pleasant McCord Creek Falls hides. For most of the year, this waterfall is actually a pair of side-by-side flows. In high water, it is a three-part cascade. The trail ends at the creek just above this falls.

To explore the lower trail, retrace your steps to the junction and turn east on a trail that goes past a rockslide, then drops in six quick switchbacks to a bridge over McCord Creek, in a bouldery glen below the towering lower falls. Late October to early November is the ideal time to visit because the bigleaf maple trees will be bright yellow, adding a distinct autumnal ambiance to the scene. From the bridge, the trail continues east to Munra Point and Wahclella Falls, as part of the low-elevation Gorge Trail. Although noisy and not very wild, due to the proximity of Interstate 84, this is a pleasant walk for those seeking additional exercise.

Trip 12

Munra Point

(Map Area G-4, Map 4)

Distance	Elevation Gain	Hiking Time	Optional Map	Difficulty
2.8 miles	1800'	2 to 4 hours	*Green Trails–Bonneville Dam*	***

Usually Open	April to November
Best Times	May to June
Agency	Columbia River Gorge National Scenic Area

Munra Point is one of the most recognizable landmarks in the western Columbia River Gorge. The narrow, bald-topped ridge, with its distinctive pointed top, is an irresistible destination for adventurous hikers. But, to get there, you'd better be *really* adventurous! The trail, using that term loosely, is definitely not for everyone. It is so steep in places that you will have to use your hands to grab onto roots and limbs, to help pull yourself up. On the lower part of the hike, the poison oak is so abundant it's practically impossible to avoid. Finally, when the tread is wet, it can be dangerously slippery, so try to save this hike for a dry spell. The great views and abundant wildflowers at the summit are worth the effort, but don't be misled by the short distance.

Directions: The only parking near the trailhead is along the westbound lanes of Interstate 84, so if you are coming from Portland, drive the freeway to Bonneville Dam exit 40 and circle around to the westbound lanes. Drive 1.1 miles and park in an unsigned gravel lot on the right.

Walk west along the freeway shoulder 0.1 mile until just before the bridge over Moffett Creek. From here, look for and follow a faint path, going south through a small grassy area, that leads you under the tall highway bridge for the *eastbound* lanes of Interstate 84. You then go up a brushy little slope for about 50 feet and intersect the Gorge Trail. Turn left and walk about 70 yards to an unsigned junction with an obvious boot path going up to the right. You turn onto this path and, a few yards later, pass a small sign tacked to a tree that states simply TRAIL NOT MAINTAINED—an understatement worthy of some kind of award.

The first 0.1 mile is moderately steep, but this will soon seem tame, as the path gets quite rocky and climbs rapidly through woods. You work your way up the south side of a steep ridge, then turn to the left and climb very steeply for about 0.2 mile, before reaching a ridgetop junction with a short downhill spur trail to a viewpoint. This makes a good excuse for a stop, but really the views are better at the top. Above the viewpoint, you generally stay close to the narrow crest, crawling over rock outcroppings, pulling yourself up beside trees and bushes, and dodging poison oak. Although steep and rugged, the path is reasonably obvious and easy to follow. Nonetheless, it is wise to look back from time to time, especially at any confusing spots, to ensure you can find the proper route to get back down.

The trail becomes increasingly exposed, with fewer trees and better views, as you climb. It levels off eventually, before curving to the right on an open, grassy slope. The most notable of the many flowers here is the wild onion, which carpets the area in early spring. Another notable feature is the wind, which often blows very hard at this exposed location. The path tops out at a junction at the crest of the open ridge. The old trail to the right just dead ends in the woods, so for the best views, turn left. This trail briefly follows the rocky ridge, then traverses the open slopes for about 0.3 mile, where it ends at a terrific overlook. The best views are straight down to Bonneville Dam and Tanner Creek, but you can also see Mt. Adams, Table Mountain, Hamilton Mountain, and, rather surprisingly, a snippet of Mt. Rainier. Stay as long as you want to enjoy the view. You've earned it.

The Columbia River Gorge

Area G-5: Eagle Creek Area

Eagle Creek is the largest tributary stream in the western Columbia River Gorge, but that is only the first of countless superlatives that apply to this creek. It also has the deepest and most spectacular canyon in the region, the most waterfalls, the highest cliffs, and some of the most outstanding forests.

Long ago, people recognized the charms of this stunningly beautiful stream and came here to enjoy the area. Ever since the Columbia River Highway was opened in 1915, the creek has been a favorite stopping place. The trail up the canyon, which was built at the same time, was one of the first to be built specifically for recreation in the Pacific Northwest. Campers came here too, and it is no exaggeration to say that the tradition of family camping in our national forests began at Eagle Creek. This was the first Forest Service campground built in the United States, and it has been popular with families since the early part of the twentieth century.

Outdoor lovers continue to flock here, attracted by the same spectacular scenery that their great-grandparents discovered almost 100 years ago. You too should come to Eagle Creek. In spite of its popularity, the scenery remains as it always has been: simply too good to miss. Fortunately for hikers who crave a bit of solitude, there are dozens of nearby trails where you can enjoy almost perfect wilderness solitude, even on busy summer weekends.

Trip 1

Wahclella Falls

(Map Area G-5)

Distance	Elevation Gain	Hiking Time	Optional Map	Difficulty
1.8 miles	300'	1 hour	Green Trails–Bonneville Dam	*

Usually Open	February to December
Best Times	Mid-April to June
Agency	Columbia River Gorge National Scenic Area

With such a wealth of waterfalls in the Columbia River Gorge, it strains an author's vocabulary to find enough different superlatives to cover each one. If any of the dozens of towering falls here were moved almost anywhere else in the country, it would draw millions of admirers. But here, with such an embarrassment of riches, people become a bit blasé. Still, no matter how jaded you may be, you won't want to miss this short trail to spectacular, two-tiered Wahclella Falls. The name, which rolls so nicely off the tongue, was suggested in 1915 by the Mazamas, a Portland hiking and climbing club, to honor the Native American name for a locality near Beacon Rock. For a while, the name was changed to the rather prosaic "Tanner Creek Falls," but in an unusual display of governmental good sense, the original name was restored and is now firmly established.

Directions: Leave Interstate 84 at exit 40 and turn right (south) at the bottom of the exit ramp. You immediately come to a T-junction and bear right, staying on the pavement, for about 100 yards to reach the parking lot for the Wahclella Falls Trail.

The first 0.2 mile of this hike follows an old gravel road beside the splashing waters of Tanner Creek, to a small concrete dam that diverts water for a fish hatchery downstream. Just past this dam, the footpath crosses a side creek right below a waterfall, where you might get a bit of a shower during high water. The well-constructed route then climbs gradually away from the creek, up a series of steps, for about 0.5 mile, to a fork in the trail that is the starting point of a small loop. Bear right and descend to a bridged crossing of the creek, then follow the west bank upstream to another bridge just below impressive Wahclella Falls. Near this spot, you may be intrigued by the enormous boulders that litter the bottom of the canyon. These came from a massive 1973 landslide that fell from the steep west wall of the canyon, temporarily damming the creek's flow. Today, the

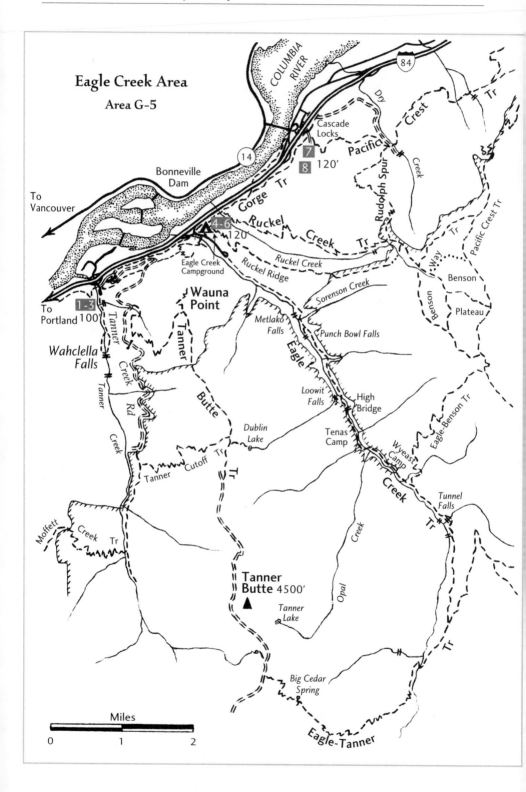

Eagle Creek Area

Area G-5

boulders are covered with mosses and ferns, and they make interesting fore-grounds for pictures of the falls.

The falls is made up of two parts—a long, wispy stream of water from the east side of the canyon, and a shorter, but more boisterous, 60-foot horsetail falls that shoots out of the slot canyon at the bottom. You'll need at least half an hour to snap pictures and just soak in the scene. Once you've had your fill of the view, climb a couple of tiny switchbacks and return along the loop trail on the east side of the canyon, back to the trail split.

Trip 2

Wauna Point

(Map Area G-5)

Distance	Elevation Gain	Hiking Time	Optional Map	Difficulty
10.4 miles	3200'	5 to 6 hours	*Green Trails–Bonneville Dam*	***

Usually Open	Late March to November
Best Times	Mid-April to early June
Agency	Columbia River Gorge National Scenic Area

Until recently, the trail to the excellent viewpoint at Wauna Point was a straightforward, not-too-difficult, 6-mile round-trip, starting from the quiet Tanner Creek Road. That hike has now been made into a much longer and more strenuous adventure, because the Tanner Creek Road is now closed to motor vehicles, adding 4.4 miles and over 1000 feet of elevation gain and loss to the round-trip hike. The advantage of this closure is that it significantly increases the chances of solitude for those hikers willing to make the extra effort. And Wauna Point is worth the effort. With a mountain bike, you can shorten the walking distance by riding the closed Tanner Creek Road to the old trailhead.

Directions: Leave Interstate 84 at exit 40 and turn right (south) at the bottom of the exit ramp. You immediately come to a T-junction and bear right, staying on the pavement, for about 100 yards to reach the parking lot for the Wahclella Falls Trail.

Pick up the eastbound Gorge Trail at a sign directly opposite the T-junction, and follow it up a switchback. You then traverse a forested hillside, where the sounds of traffic on Interstate 84 disturb the natural quiet, but at least the forest is attractive. You make two short switchbacks, then a long traverse to a junction with a powerline access road, about 0.8 mile from the trailhead. Follow this route for 0.2 mile to a junction with the closed Tanner Creek Road, where you turn right and walk uphill as the road rounds a ridge and enters the canyon of Tanner Creek. The signed Tanner Butte Trail leaves from the left side of the road, just before you cross a small creek in a side canyon.

Having reached a true foot trail, you follow the rocky Tanner Butte Trail as it climbs beside a splashing creek that tumbles over a series of small but attractive waterfalls. Water-loving plants, like maiden-hair fern, monkey-flower, and bleeding heart thrive in this environment. Overhead, drooping western hemlock and western red cedar are the dominant tree species. The fairly steep trail crosses two branches of the creek, traverses a hillside, then twice passes under a set of powerlines in forest openings that provide excellent views, both north toward Table Mountain and west to Munra Point.

After crossing a rocky powerline access road at a diagonal, you slowly climb a hillside above the powerline, in a Douglas-fir forest that comes alive in May with the white blossoms of Pacific dogwood trees. From here, six long switchbacks steadily, but not too steeply, lead you uphill. Five more short, steep switchbacks take you up to a viewpoint spur trail. The open area at this viewpoint provides good views to the west. A few hardy wildflowers, like larkspur, columbine, and onion, brighten the foreground.

After this viewpoint, you make a fairly long uphill traverse to the northeast on a heavily wooded slope. Along the way you cross a tiny seeping trickle of water, continuing to the point where the main trail turns sharply right, at a possibly unsigned junction.

For Wauna Point, you turn left, soon passing a sign that says TRAIL NOT MAINTAINED. The path descends gradually at first, then much more steeply, as it winds down the rocky spine of Wauna Point. After a series of very short switchbacks, you crawl carefully down a dangerously narrow rocky ridge to a small flat spot just above a steep drop-off. From here, you can enjoy a terrific view of steep-sided Eagle Creek Canyon to the east, Table Mountain to the north, Beacon Rock downriver to the west, and Bonneville Dam and the mighty Columbia River almost directly below you.

Daredevil hikers sometimes look at the map and see that Wauna Viewpoint (Trip 4) is directly below Wauna Point, and they dream of somehow connecting the two into a loop trip. Forget it! There is no trail, not even a remotely reasonable cross-country route, between the two. Trying it is a recipe for disaster. Go back the way you came.

Trip 3

Tanner Butte

(Map Area G-5)

Distance	Elevation Gain	Hiking Time	Optional Map	Difficulty
20.8 miles	4700'	10 to 12 hours	Green Trails–Bonneville Dam	****

Usually Open	Late May to October
Best Times	June
Agency	Columbia River Gorge National Scenic Area

The rounded summit of Tanner Butte, with its gouged-out eastern face, is a well-known landmark in the central Columbia River Gorge, visible from viewpoints more than 50 miles away. Since the line of sight goes in both directions, you might deduce that the views from Tanner Butte are also mighty impressive. And you'd be correct.

The view alone would be worth the hike, but in addition, the area around the mountain features wide, sloping wildflower meadows and scenic talus slopes, which are delightful even without the view. It's no wonder that hardy hikers have long enjoyed this outing, some making it a treasured annual trip.

That annual trip, however, must be rethought or at least planned differently now. Although it was never an easy hike, the trip to Tanner Butte was made even more difficult recently when the old Tanner Creek Road was closed to motor vehicles, making the hike a challenge that is probably best left to backpackers. But a handful of the most athletic dayhikers can still visit this classic destination. If you have a mountain bike, you can shorten the round-trip walking distance by 4.4 miles, which makes things a little more reasonable.

Directions: Leave Interstate 84 at exit 40 and turn right (south) at the bottom of the exit ramp. You immediately come to a T-junction and bear right, staying on the pavement, for about 100 yards to reach the parking lot for the Wahclella Falls Trail.

Follow the eastbound Gorge Trail that starts opposite the T-junction, then climb in switchbacks and traverses on a forested hillside. After about 0.8 mile, the trail follows a powerline access road for 0.2 mile to a junction with the closed Tanner Creek Road, where you turn right. Walk this road uphill as it rounds a ridge and enters the canyon of Tanner Creek. The signed Tanner Butte Trail leaves from the left side of the road, just before you cross a small creek in a side canyon.

The footpath goes up a lush little canyon with several small waterfalls, crossing two branches of the creek before climbing and twice going under a powerline. You cross the powerline access road at a diagonal and go up a series of six long and five short switchbacks on a heavily forested hillside. After the switchbacks, you make a long traverse to a ridgecrest junction where the unofficial Wauna Point Trail goes off to the left.

You turn right, staying on the Tanner Butte Trail, and begin a long, moderately graded ascent of a wide ridge. There are no views along the way, but the hiking is never tedious, as the forest is open and attractive. As you gain elevation, the forests gradually change to typical higher-elevation woods, dominated by Douglas-fir and Pacific silver fir, with lots of beargrass and huckleberries on the forest floor.

After 2.1 miles of climbing, you hit a possibly unsigned junction with the Tanner Cutoff Trail, heading downhill to the right. Go straight and, about 150 yards later, reach the junction with the 0.4-mile spur trail to Dublin Lake. If you are backpacking, this is a logical place to spend the night. The trail to the lake begins gently, but after 100 yards it drops quite steeply to the northwest corner of this small, forest-rimmed pool. The best place to set up your tent is at a camp on the southwest shore.

Back on the Tanner Butte Trail, you walk a short distance before dropping to an old jeep road. Look carefully here to note where you meet the road, as the trail turnoff is poorly signed on the way back. Walk south on this overgrown road 1.0 mile, staying on the west side of the wooded ridgeline, then descend slightly to a little saddle where the forest breaks up and the scenery abruptly improves. To the east, you can look down into the green depths of Eagle Creek Canyon, while due south is the steep northeast face of massive Tanner Butte. All around your feet are lots of colorful wildflowers, especially beargrass, lupine, paintbrush, and larkspur. The road is overgrown with huckleberries and foot-tripping beargrass, but the scenery is so good you won't have any complaints.

Still on the old road, continue south through increasingly open and attractive meadows and rocky slopes. Then go over a view-packed

Tanner Butte (from near Tanner Lake)

knoll and down to a wide saddle on the north side of Tanner Butte. The road works uphill from here and curves around the brushy west slopes of the butte, but if you want to reach the top of Tanner Butte, leave the road at the saddle and scramble cross-country up the northwest side of the peak. Try not to get too close to the steep drop-off on your left, as the rocks can be unstable. The first few hundred yards are rather difficult, as you have to fight through some brush, but then the going improves as the country opens up. From the top, those promised views extend to Mounts St. Helens, Adams, and Rainier in Washington, as well as Mt. Hood in Oregon. Hikers familiar with the area can also pick out shorter but no less attractive landmarks, like Washington's Silver Star Mountain, and Oregon's Larch and Chinidere mountains.

Backpackers can enjoy this view at leisure and have the time to take in some additional nearby scenery. One option is to scramble east from a saddle just south of Tanner Butte to the cirque basin which holds scenic little Tanner Lake. You can also walk cross-country, out a small ridge southeast of Tanner Butte, for some dramatic photos of the scenic butte, with snowy Mt. Adams in the distance.

Finally, if you want to make a grand three-day loop, you can descend into the Eagle Creek drainage on the rarely-used Eagle-Tanner Trail, past Big Cedar Spring (another possible campsite), then hike down the Eagle Creek Trail (Trip 5) back to civilization. A 3.0-mile section of the Gorge Trail connects the Eagle Creek trailhead with the Wahclella Falls trailhead to close out this magnificent 28-mile loop.

Trip 4

Wauna Viewpoint

(Map Area G-5)

Distance	Elevation Gain	Hiking Time	Optional Map	Difficulty
3.6 miles	950'	2 hours	*Green Trails–Bonneville Dam*	**

Usually Open	February to December
Best Times	Mid-April to May
Agency	Columbia River Gorge National Scenic Area

The Gorge Trail is a relatively new hiking option in our region. It manages to remain open practically all winter by keeping to low elevations near the Columbia River. It is also useful in other seasons for creating loop trips out of longer hikes in the backcountry of the Gorge. Taken separately, however, most sections of the route are so close to either the Old Columbia River Highway or Interstate 84 that they are just too noisy to be considered "wild," and therefore do not qualify for inclusion in this book. But where the trail follows older routes further away from the traffic, there are some very scenic hiking opportunities. One such segment is the trail up to Wauna Viewpoint, a little west of Eagle Creek.

Directions: Leave the eastbound lanes of Interstate 84 at Eagle Creek Recreation Area exit 41. At the bottom of the exit road, turn right and drive about 0.1 mile, then park in the small lot on the left, across from a prominent hiker's bridge over Eagle Creek. Parking is very limited here on summer weekends, so arrive early in the morning.

You begin by going west across the impressive hiker's bridge over Eagle Creek. This arcing wooden structure is supported by cables and sways a bit as you walk across, but it provides a nice look down at the creek's clear waters. Immediately on the other side of the bridge are a wooden bench and a junction. Turn right on the wide, gently graded trail, which climbs two short switchbacks under the shade of tall fir and hemlock trees, then traverses a wet hillside with lots of mossy overhangs that support an abundance of maiden-hair and lady ferns. The traverse ends at a fenced overlook, about 200 feet above Interstate 84 and Bonneville Dam.

The trail switchbacks to the left at this overlook and takes you uphill to three more switchbacks. These lead to a brushy opening with lots of thimbleberry, whose bright red berries look and taste like strong, tart raspberries and ripen in midsummer. Before eating too many berries, however, consider that the fruit will stain your skin, so you are likely to get caught literally red-handed.

Still climbing gradually, you come to a junction marked with one of the old stone signs still occasionally found in the western Gorge. These markers were permanently cemented into the rock at trail intersections, with destinations and distances chiseled into the stone. Changes to the trails over the decades have made the mileages suspect, but the signs still have a quaintly historical appeal.

To reach Wauna Viewpoint, you turn sharply left and climb six long switchbacks in a relatively open forest. One reason the forest is so open is that a fire burned through here in the 1990s, killing many smaller trees and leaving singed bark on the bigger ones that survived the blaze. One plant that has grown back abundantly is poison oak. Fortunately, unlike so many other trails in the Gorge, this path is wide enough to make it easy to avoid the plant.

The trail ends at a spectacular rocky overlook beside a powerline tower. To the west, you can see Munra Point, Beacon Rock, and long distances down the Columbia River. To the east are Bridge of the Gods, Cascade Locks, and the cliffs of Ruckel Ridge, across the canyon of Eagle Creek. Most impressive is the view directly across the river, to flat-topped Table Mountain and down to Bonneville Dam.

The name *Wauna*, which is used for several features in this area, is believed to be a Klickitat Indian word for a mythological being who represents the Columbia River.

Trip 5

Eagle Creek Trail

(Map Area G-5)

Distance	Elevation Gain	Hiking Time	Optional Map	Difficulty
4.2 to 12 miles	400 to 1200'	2 to 7 hours	Green Trails– Bonneville Dam	* to ***

Usually Open	March to December
Best Times	Mid-April to June
Agency	Columbia River Gorge National Scenic Area

The famous Eagle Creek Trail has been a favorite of local hikers since it was first built in 1915. The trail opened at the same time as the Old Columbia River Scenic Highway, providing a spectacular hiking destination for visitors just discovering the area. Today, it remains one of the most spectacular trails in our region. It leads hikers through a verdant canyon, beside waterfalls in every shape and size, along a creek that is almost unbelievably beautiful. Of course, lots of other people think this is a great hike too, so don't expect to be alone. To protect the resource, the Forest Service requires that backpackers camp only in designated sites, and they ask that you leave your dog at home.

Directions: Leave the eastbound lanes of Interstate 84 at Eagle Creek Recreation Area exit 41. At the bottom of the exit road, turn right and drive about 0.6 mile on a narrow paved road to the roadend parking lot. Parking is very limited here on summer weekends, so arrive early in the morning.

The trail is paved for the first 0.3 mile, as it wanders gradually uphill along the wooded hillsides, above the cascading stream. The path eventually climbs to some very steep slopes a few hundred feet above the creek, with nice views down into the canyon, and crosses several small, unnamed side creeks along the way, which add variety to the lush forest scenery. Poison oak is part of that lush vegetation, but the wide, heavily used trail makes avoiding the plant easy.

After 1.5 miles, you come to the first waterfall. A short side trail to the right makes a loop past a fenced overlook, where you can look up a narrow canyon to the impressive drop of Metlako Falls. Not long after this marvelous taste of things to come, you cross Sorenson Creek on a bridge and come to a junction with the side trail to the bottom of Punch Bowl Falls. Don't miss the chance to visit this spot as the trail drops to a world-famous view of this short, but spectacular, falls. For decades, calendars have featured this outstanding scene of a glassy creek, winding through a fern-lined grotto, with a perfect bowl-shaped falls that drops to a pool at the head of the canyon. This is a rewarding turnaround point for those who want an easy hike.

Back on the main trail, you traverse heavily wooded slopes to a viewpoint directly above Punch Bowl Falls, giving you a different perspective on this classic cascade. Above this point, the scenery grows even more dramatic, as you are forced to cross vertical basalt cliffs where the trail has simply been blasted into the side of the rock. The trail is wide enough so those afraid of heights shouldn't have a problem, but parents will want to keep a close eye on their children. In fact, young children probably shouldn't take this trail at all.

Along one of these steep slopes you get a terrific view of wispy Loowit Falls, on a side creek across the canyon. Shortly after this, you cross appropriately named High Bridge, which spans a slot canyon about 90 feet above the clear waters of Eagle Creek.

After the bridge, the slopes are less steep and are covered with dense forests. At Tenas Camp, the first allowable campsite along the creek, you may want to take a side trip to the creek to visit a lovely two-stage waterfall, which has very nice pools that invite a cold dip in the water. Above Tenas Camp, you recross the creek on a much shorter bridge, then work your way upstream to Wy'East Camp.

A short distance past this camp is a junction with the little-used Eagle-Benson Trail. If you are up for a steep side trip, follow this narrow trail for about 0.5 mile to an open, rocky overlook, with a perspective on Eagle Creek Canyon not available from the lower trail.

Resuming the main trail, you travel gradually uphill in partial forest, past Blue Grouse Camp, then traverse through forests and over talus slopes well above the creek. A steep side trail drops down one of these talus slopes, visiting an impressive waterfall on the creek, but most people skip this attraction and head straight for Tunnel Falls, in the side canyon just ahead. This colossal 120-foot-high falls on East Fork Eagle Creek drops over a sheer cliff in a shady side canyon. To get past this falls, the trail doesn't go *around* it, but goes *behind* it, in a manmade tunnel that was dynamited out of the cliff about halfway up the falls. You can still expect to get wet, but it's an exhilarating walk. Just past the falls, you round a ridge where the trail once again takes an exposed course blasted out of vertical basalt cliffs, right beside another tall falls, on the main branch of the creek. Metal cables here give acrophobic hikers something to hang onto and a greater sense of security. There is a terrific lunch spot on the flat creekside rocks, just above this falls.

The trail continues past this point all the way to Wahtum Lake. Unlike the route so far, the trail ahead gains a great deal of elevation and lacks the compensation of waterfalls. Most hikers have already had their fill of great scenery, and they turn back near Tunnel Falls.

Trip 6

Ruckel Ridge – Ruckel Creek Loop

(Map Area G-5)

Distance	Elevation Gain	Hiking Time	Optional Map	Difficulty
9.6 miles	3700'	5 to 7 hours	Green Trails–Bonneville Dam (part of route not shown)	****

Usually Open	Late April to early November
Best Times	Late April to May
Agency	Columbia River Gorge National Scenic Area

This classic but demanding loop features some of the best views and wildflower displays in the Columbia River Gorge. The views are outstanding, especially those of the deep canyon of Eagle Creek, while the wildflower displays in the meadows partway down the Ruckel Creek Trail are exceptional. But, you have to work very hard if you want to enjoy these attributes. The unofficial route up Ruckel Ridge is often extremely steep and should be attempted only by confident hikers in top condition. Even on the downhill, you will pay a hefty price in abused knees and jammed toes, so come prepared for both the good and the bad offered by this hike.

Directions: Leave the eastbound lanes of Interstate 84 at Eagle Creek Recreation Area exit 41 and turn right at the bottom of the exit road. You can either park in the lot immediately on your left or drive about 0.1 mile, then park in the small lot on the left, across from a prominent hiker's bridge over Eagle Creek. Parking is very limited on summer weekends, so arrive early in the morning.

From the lot next to the hiker's bridge, turn east and walk through a comfortable little picnic area, up the campground access road about 200 yards, to a large sign on your right that identifies the Gorge Trail. Turn onto this route and climb gradually through lush vegetation of skunk cabbage, ferns, and some menacing stinging nettles that hang over the trail. You go straight at an unsigned four-way junction after just 80 yards, then wind up to a fence line that keeps hikers back from a drop-off above Interstate 84. Walk east along the fence line, past campsites in Eagle Creek Campground. Just as the trail begins to go downhill, you turn right to pick up the campground loop road. When you reach camp #5, you will see a large sign for the Buck Point Trail.

This trail ascends six well-graded switchbacks, then comes to an unsigned junction. The official Buck Point Trail goes straight, but you turn left and soon pass a small sign saying TRAIL NOT MAINTAINED. You are now on the *unofficial* Ruckel Ridge Trail, and the difficult character of this route soon becomes apparent.

The first hazard, which will be with you for the first mile or so, is poison oak. It is quite prevalent beside the trail, so be sure to wear long pants. The really substantial obstacle of this hike, however, is the steep, rugged grade.

At first things are deceptively easy. You ascend six short switchbacks to a viewpoint beneath some powerlines. Then you wander on a gentle, forested path to a rocky area that features hardy wildflowers and a population of pikas who squeak loudly at passing hikers. From here, the trail switchbacks to the left and crawls over an area of boulders and sloping rocks to an open spot on the ridgeline. The route now gets a lot more difficult, as it turns right and climbs the crest of the ridge, making occasional detours to avoid cliffs and rock outcroppings.

Much of this very steep route keeps exactly to the spine of the ridge, often on a rocky tread that is only a foot or two wide, so acrophobics won't enjoy it much, but those who like exhilarating views will love it. A little over halfway up the ridge is a particularly narrow and dangerous section called the Catwalk. You can skirt it by way of a rough scramble path on the right-hand side. About 0.1 mile later, traverse the right side of a very steep, open, rocky slope, then go back into the forest and descend to a small saddle.

From the saddle, you again crawl up the spine of the ridge, with one detour to the left before the final, very steep push to the rim of Benson Plateau. You know you have reached the plateau when the uphill grade abruptly ends and you enter deep woods. The correct route becomes indistinct from here, but you generally go east, carefully looking out for cut logs, old blazes, or survey tapes tied to tree limbs to help with navigation. The path leads you to a rockhop or log crossing of Ruckel Creek, then goes on about 100 yards to an unsigned junction with the Ruckel Creek Trail.

To do the loop, you turn left on the Ruckel Creek Trail, as it descends very steeply from the lip of Benson Plateau—although not as steeply as the Ruckel Ridge Trail ascended it. Nearby, Ruckel Creek remains out of sight, but not out of sound, as it rollicks along in one long, cascade. The trail can be slick when wet, and hard on the knees at any time, so hiking poles are recommended. Just as you encounter the first bushes of poison oak, the downhill abates, and you contour across a series of large, sloping meadows that are separated by stands of Douglas-fir.

From late April to mid-May, these meadows are ablaze with color from the yellows of monkeyflower, lomatium, and groundsel, to the purples of cluster lilies and onion, the blue of lupine, the white of yarrow, and numerous other species. It is truly a spectacle you won't want to miss. There are also good views from the meadows, especially looking west to Ruckel and Tanner ridges.

The steep downhill resumes after the meadows end, as you descend 14 quick switchbacks. At the fifth, you hit a terrific clifftop overlook, where you can see Bonneville Dam and the Bridge of the Gods, as well as Wauna Lake and Table Mountain in Washington.

Native American rock pits along Ruckel Creek Trail

The rest of the way down is a mix of short switchbacks, traverses, and ridgecrest walking, which eventually takes you down to a moss-covered rockslide, where you will notice rock pits built by Native Americans for ceremonial purposes. As always, it is important that hikers respect the integrity of this site and not disturb even one rock. From here, you pass beneath a set of powerlines, then drop to the lovely banks of cascading Ruckel Creek and a junction with a paved bike trail.

Turn left and walk about 0.3 mile on this bike route to a junction with the Gorge Trail, bearing uphill and to the left. You can stay on the bike path, which soon takes you back to the lower parking area, or you can hike the Gorge Trail, past the campground, to the upper parking area near the hiker's bridge.

Trip 7

Dry Creek Falls

(Map Area G-5)

Distance	Elevation Gain	Hiking Time	Optional Map	Difficulty
4.2 miles	600'	2 to 3 hours	*Green Trails–Bonneville Dam*	**

Usually Open	All year (except during winter storms)
Best Times	April and May
Agency	Columbia River Gorge National Scenic Area

The Columbia River Gorge is a waterfall lover's paradise. There are hundreds, perhaps thousands of falls, ranging from towering cataracts right beside the freeway to hidden cascades miles from the nearest trail. Somewhere between these two extremes are the countless waterfalls reachable along the Gorge's hundreds of miles of trails.

One of the most attractive, but least visited, of this middle group is Dry Creek Falls. Perhaps this falls' scant popularity is due to the fact that no signs direct hikers to it. Or it may be the result of hikers wrongly assuming, from the creek's name, that it has no water. Whatever the reason, Dry Creek Falls remains on the list of falls enjoyed by only a small group of hikers who are "in the know," a group that now includes you!

Directions: From Interstate 84 east of Portland, take Cascade Locks exit 44. Follow the exit road for about 0.3 mile, then turn right on a clover leaf that takes you up toward Bridge of the Gods. Park in the Pacific Crest Trail parking lot, on your right in the middle of the clover leaf. This trailhead is closed throughout the winter and early spring. During these months you will have to leave your car in front of the concrete blocks that bar access to the parking lot.

The Pacific Crest Trail starts on the south side of the bridge-access road, then goes up the wooded roadside bank. After a short traverse you hook up briefly with a paved road that runs under the freeway, then bear right onto a narrow gravel road. Follow this road for 75 yards to a trail junction where you turn left onto a pleasant section of the PCT that gradually climbs through lush forests, dominated at first by bigleaf and vine maple and later by Douglas-fir. The forest floor is equally green with sword, bracken, and maiden-hair fern, vanilla leaf, twisted stalk, fringecup, and northern inside-out flower, among many others. In May and June, one of the most showy inhabitants of this forest is the tiger lily, with its tall stalks and gorgeous orange flowers.

After about 0.6 mile of gradual uphill, the trail joins a jeep road for about 50 yards, crosses under a powerline, then veers left back onto a true footpath. The PCT then crosses a series of steep hillsides and benches, with lots of impressively straight and tall Douglas-firs. Despite the uneven terrain, the trail remains remarkably level all the way to a jeep road, just before a crossing of Dry Creek. There is a camp here and a bridge over the creek—something that would obviously not be necessary if the creek were indeed dry.

To visit Dry Creek Falls, you turn right (uphill) on the jeep road and follow it for 0.2 mile to the base of the falls. There are a concrete dam and catch basin just below the falls, but they do nothing to diminish the beauty of this waterfall, a narrow chute of water that drops some 50 feet over a basalt cliff. The scene is exceptionally photogenic, so don't forget your camera.

If you want more exercise, continue east on the PCT for about 1.3 miles to visit a pair of interesting rock pinnacles on the north side of the trail (see Area G-6, Trip 1).

Trip 8

Rudolph Spur Way Trail

(Map Area G-5)

Distance	Elevation Gain	Hiking Time	Optional Map	Difficulty
10.4 miles	4000'	7 to 10 hours	Green Trails–Bonneville Dam	****

Usually Open	May to November
Best Times	May to early June
Agency	Columbia River Gorge National Scenic Area

Many trails reach the top of Benson Plateau, and since they all involve an elevation gain of 3800 feet or more, none of them are easy. Among that group of challenging outings, the most strenuous is the unmaintained route up Rudolph Spur. The trip is difficult, not only because it is one heck of a long way up, but also because it is very steep, and it requires scrambling over several downed logs. It also challenges you mentally, as this unofficial trail is often sketchy and requires some route-finding ability. In short, this trip is strictly for that group of hard-core hikers who relish exploring little-known routes and who don't mind paying the physical price that these trails demand.

Directions: From Interstate 84 east of Portland, take Cascade Locks exit 44. Follow the exit road for about 0.3 mile, then turn right on a clover leaf that takes you up toward Bridge of the Gods. Park in the Pacific Crest Trail parking lot, on your right in the middle of the clover leaf.

Follow the Pacific Crest Trail from the south side of the bridge-access road, as it crosses a forested hillside, then links up with a paved road to travel under the freeway. From here you veer right on a gravel road for 75 yards, turn left on the PCT, and walk this pleasant route for another 1.5 miles to the crossing of misnamed Dry Creek.

About 12 feet before you meet the jeep road that parallels the west bank of Dry Creek, look carefully for the unsigned Rudolph Spur way trail that veers south. Hikers should wear long pants on this rather overgrown route, as it climbs steeply on a densely forested hillside, gradually working away from the sound of cascading water in Dry Creek. Try not to step on the banana slugs that live here in incredible abundance, both for their sake and your own, as the squishing sensation rates very high on the disgusting scale. More pleasant are the loud staccato calls of pileated woodpeckers, the rattle of their smaller hairy woodpecker cousins, or the imitation of red-tailed hawks performed by Steller's jays.

The trail climbs quite steeply—this trail does *everything* steeply—to the top of a forested gully, then traverses a bit before rapidly losing about 100 feet of elevation. The trail then goes straight across a small talus slope, whose mossy rocks support lots of yellow stonecrop, as well as a population of pikas. Shortly after reentering the trees, this rugged hike significantly increases its challenge as the trail charges almost directly up a super-steep slope. Adding to the difficulties is the fact that you need to dodge sprigs of bothersome poison oak. Fortunately, the rewards increase, as you climb past forest openings with increasingly good views of Table Mountain and Wauna Lake in Washington, the Columbia River, and the Bridge of the Gods at Cascade Locks.

The path comes to the top of a minor ridge, then turns onto the spine of this ridge and goes very steeply uphill. The route is often sketchy, so route-finding skills are helpful, but the main requirements for hiking this section are strong thighs and determination. You will probably lose the route from time to time, but red survey tapes that have been tied to some of the rocks and trees provide excellent guidance. Lacking these, you can usually relocate the proper route just by sticking to the crest of the ridge.

You will eventually come to a perfect rest stop, in a good-sized opening on the ridge, with fine views and lots of wildflowers, like yellow daisies, lupine, lomatium, and stonecrop. This spot also tends to catch the constant Gorge breezes, which are welcome on this long climb.

The unrelentingly steep ascent continues as you come to a rocky meadow, with outstanding views down to Cascade Locks, and lots of higher-elevation flowers, like wallflower, phlox, and cliff penstemon. Just above this meadow is a second open area, with reddish rocks and almost no vegetation. The trail disappears briefly here, but you can find it easily enough by looking for the point where it heads into the trees on the left, about 50 feet after you start the climb up the reddish rocks.

Beyond this point, the trail improves considerably; the route is generally well defined and no longer as steep. This is also where you begin to encounter tufts of beargrass—a sure sign that most of the climbing is over. The trail now makes a long, gradual up-and-down traverse to the east, on a steep hillside. The biggest obstacle along this section is having to crawl over lots of small downed trees on this unmaintained trail.

After about 0.5 mile, you begin a series of six fairly steep switchbacks, then traverse below a ridge. Just as the trail curves around a minor ridgeline, it turns sharply uphill to the right. The trail here is rather indistinct, but you are aided by occasional yellow paint spots on the trees marking the trail. It is often a good idea to look behind you from time to time, to ensure that the paint spots mark the route in that direction as well. The final 0.1 mile crosses a corner of Benson Plateau and is basically flat until the trail ends at an unsigned junction with the well-maintained Ruckel Creek Trail.

You could return the way you came, but it is easier on the knees if you make a loop out of this hike by following the Ruckel Creek Trail on the way down. For this option, turn right and descend steeply from the lip of Benson Plateau, down to a series of spectacular, hanging meadows. Once the meadows end, you switchback down to an outstanding clifftop viewpoint, then continue through more fairly steep switchbacks to a set of powerlines and a junction with a paved bike path.

To close out the loop, you turn right on the 12-foot-wide bike path and walk through a tunnel of trees, following the route of the historic Old Columbia River Highway. The walk is pleasant, except for the overwhelming noise pollution from Interstate 84 just a few yards to your left. After 0.7 mile, the bike route passes under the freeway through a tunnel, while the Gorge Trail for hikers veers off to the right, staying on the south side of the divided highway. By either route, it is 1.2 miles back to your car.

The Columbia River Gorge

Area G-6: Herman Creek – Wyeth Area

Relatively little-known Herman Creek hides amid the steep, forested ridges and canyons east of Cascade Locks. This wild and beautiful stream drains an impressively deep canyon, with ridges rising thousands of feet on either side providing athletic hikers with enticing goals for high viewpoints. But there are plenty of options here for easier hikes as well.

The lower trails lead to quiet forests, splashing creeks, and rocky pinnacles—all the wonderful scenery that is common in the Columbia River Gorge. Waterfalls are relatively rare, but that is the only typical Gorge feature that Herman Creek lacks. In addition to scenery, Herman Creek's more easterly location affords a partial rain shadow, so the weather here is slightly better than in the locations farther west. While the added sunshine is a bonus, the area still gets enough rain to ensure that the forests are lush and enchanting. There's a lot to admire here and, with fewer fellow admirers, you can enjoy it all in blessed peace and quiet.

Trip 1

Herman Creek Pinnacles

(Map Area G-6)

Distance	Elevation Gain	Hiking Time	Optional Map	Difficulty
6.0 miles	950'	3 hours	*Green Trails–Bonneville Dam*	**

Usually Open	All year (except during winter storms)
Best Times	Mid-March to June
Agency	Columbia River Gorge National Scenic Area

This is the easiest of several possible destinations radiating from the Herman Creek trailhead. Happily, it may also be the most interesting option, combining rich greenery with visits to lovely Herman Creek, a wispy waterfall, and a pair of fascinating rock spires. Add the good possibility of solitude, and this hike qualifies as one of the author's favorites.

Pinnacle on Pacific Crest Trail near Herman Creek

Directions: Leave Interstate 84 at Cascade Locks exit 44 and drive the main road (Wa Na Pa Street) through town. At the east end of town turn left on Forest Lane, following signs for the airport. Drive this road 2.0 miles to an overpass over the freeway. Turn left after the overpass and, 0.3 mile later, turn right at a sign for Herman Creek Campground. This narrow paved road climbs a short distance to a junction with the marked spur road to the trailhead on the right.

The path starts out in a shady forest of stately Douglas-fir and bigleaf maple, whose limbs and trunks sprout the usual growth of moss and licor-

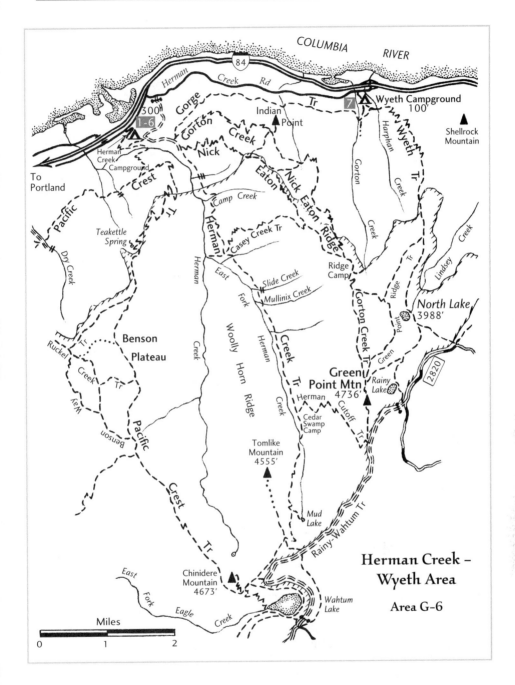

COLUMBIA RIVER

84

Herman Creek Rd

Gorge Tr

7

Wyeth Campground
100'

Shellrock
Mountain

300'
1-6

Indian
Point

Gorton Creek

Nick Creek

Harphan Creek

Gorton

Herman
Creek
Campground

To
Portland

Crest Tr

Nick Eaton Ridge

Wyeth Tr

Pacific

Teakettle
Spring

Camp Creek

Casey Creek Tr

Slide Creek

Mullinix Creek

Ridge
Camp

Point Ridge Tr

Lindsey Creek

North Lake
3988'

Dry Creek

Herman

East Fork

Herman Creek

Herman Creek

Gorton Creek Tr

Green Tr

2820

Benson
Plateau

Ruckel Creek

Tr

Tr

Woolly Horn Ridge

Green Point Mtn
4736'

Rainy
Lake

Wey

Benson

Pacific

Herman Cutoff Tr

Cedar
Swamp
Camp

Tomlike
Mountain
4555'

Crest Tr

Mud
Lake

Rainy-Wahtum Tr

Herman Creek –
Wyeth Area

Area G-6

East Fork Eagle Creek

Chinidere
Mountain
4673'

Wahtum
Lake

Miles

0   1   2

ice fern. The lazy route switchbacks uphill to cross a powerline access road, then curves into the canyon of Herman Creek and makes two more switchbacks, before coming to a trail fork. The main Herman Creek Trail goes left, but you bear right for this trip and make a pleasant descent on a semi-open hillside to a metal bridge spanning Herman Creek.

From the rushing creek, the path climbs a hillside with a nice mix of forest and talus slopes, where you may hear or see pikas. This charming species, which looks like a diminutive small-eared rabbit, normally prefers the rocky slopes of the high mountains, but it also finds surprisingly good habitat at low elevations throughout the Columbia River Gorge. About 0.9 mile from Herman Creek, you meet the Pacific Crest Trail and bear right on this famous path, which goes initially through woods, then across two large rocky areas. You splash through a small creek at the base of a wispy waterfall and, about 250 yards later, come to a pair of crumbly rock spires on your right.

A short side trail takes you to the base of these free-standing landmarks, but photographers will be frustrated by the pinnacles, because they are difficult to capture on film. One reason is that, for most of the year, their location beneath the north-facing cliffs of the Gorge ensures that they receive virtually no sunshine. Those who want some additional exercise can continue hiking west on the PCT for about 1.3 miles to Dry Creek, then make the short side trip upstream to spectacular Dry Creek Falls.

Trip 2

Benson Plateau via Pacific Crest Trail

(Map Area G-6)

Distance	Elevation Gain	Hiking Time	Optional Map	Difficulty
14.0 miles	4000'	7 to 9 hours	*Green Trails–Bonneville Dam*	****

Usually Open	May to October
Best Times	June
Agency	Columbia River Gorge National Scenic Area

No matter how you get there, Benson Plateau is a worthwhile goal. The flowers, especially beargrass, are abundant, the views are superb, and there are nice camps for backpackers to make this an overnight adventure. Unfortunately, there is no easy route to the top. Among the many difficult routes to choose from, the well-graded Pacific Crest Trail is probably the least demanding. It is also the least scenic, however, so you have to make a choice between exhaustion and exhilaration.

Directions: Leave Interstate 84 at Cascade Locks exit 44 and drive the main road (Wa Na Pa Street) through town. At the east end of town turn left on Forest Lane, following signs for the airport. Drive this road 2.0 miles to an overpass over the freeway. Turn left after the overpass and, 0.3 mile later, turn right at a sign for Herman Creek Campground. This narrow paved road climbs a short distance to a junction with the marked spur road to the trailhead on the right.

The path starts in a shady forest of stately Douglas-fir and bigleaf maple, whose limbs and trunks sprout the usual growth of moss and licorice fern. The lazy route switchbacks uphill to cross a powerline access road, then curves into the canyon of Herman Creek and makes two more switchbacks before coming to a trail fork. The main Herman Creek Trail goes left, but you bear right for this trip and make a pleasant descent of a semi-open hillside, to a metal bridge spanning Herman Creek. Once across the bridge, the path climbs a hillside with a nice mix of forest and talus slopes for 0.9 mile to a junction with the Pacific Crest Trail.

Turn left and travel southbound on the PCT as it gently traverses a scree slope where pikas scurry about and squeak at passing hikers. Then you enter forests of Douglas-fir and western hemlock, which will block the view almost all the way to the top of Benson Plateau. Between here and there, however, are dozens of irregularly spaced switchbacks and traverses that take you back and forth across a ridgeline, on a steady, moderate, uphill grade. Although never especially steep, it is still an awfully *long* way up, so take plenty of rest stops as you climb. There is no water available, so carry an extra quart or two, especially on hot days.

About 3 miles up the ridge, you reach a decent viewpoint at a small helispot, where you can rest and enjoy views of Herman Creek Canyon, Nick Eaton Ridge, and the area around Cascade Locks. It is also near this point that the vegetation changes, from low-elevation Douglas-fir and western hemlock, to high-elevation Pacific silver and noble fir, and western white pine. You will also see plenty of beargrass, always a good sign in the Gorge that you are nearing the top of your climb. In June of favorable years, the 3-foot-tall stalks of beargrass, with its clustered white flowers, put on a terrific show. After two more long switchbacks, look for a short, usually unsigned, side path to Tea-kettle Spring on your right. This little seepage is your only source of water after Herman Creek.

Several more switchbacks take you up to the edge of Benson Plateau, where the climb becomes much easier, and the scenery improves. You walk past a waterless camp and along a wide forested crest that extends northeast from the main Benson Plateau, to reach a junction with the Benson Way Trail. For the best views, stay left on the PCT as it travels along the eastern edge of the plateau, past several small meadows carpeted with wildflowers. Here, you will have outstanding views of the rugged Columbia River Gorge and distant Mt. Hood.

About 1.2 mile past the Benson Way junction is a junction with the Ruckel Creek Trail. The best view in the area is 100 yards straight ahead on the PCT. From this grandstand, you can look southeast to Woolly Horn Ridge, bald-topped Tomlike Mountain, pointed Chinidere Mountain, and distant Mt. Hood. Backpackers should know that the best camp on the plateau is about 0.3 mile west on the Ruckel Creek Trail, although it is popular with equestrians, so you may be sharing the camp with horses.

In the wildly contorted, up-and-down landscape of the Columbia River Gorge, the flatness of Benson Plateau is something of an oddity. This surface is the top layer of the ancient lava flows that buried the entire area between 10 and 17 million years ago. Since then, the Columbia River and its many tributaries have eroded the hard basalt rock by almost 4000 feet. So this flat remnant gives you some perspective both on the extent of the original lava flows and on the almost unbelievable amount of erosion that has diminished them over time.

Trip 3

Herman Creek Trail

(Map Area G-6)

Distance	Elevation Gain	Hiking Time	Optional Map	Difficulty
4.8 to 15 miles	900' to 2700'	2 to 8 hours	*Green Trails– Bonneville Dam*	** to ***

Usually Open	March to November
Best Times	Late March to June
Agency	Columbia River Gorge National Scenic Area

Herman Creek is one of the major streams of the Columbia River Gorge, and the trail up its canyon is an important artery for longer trips into the backcountry. However, the trail is also fine for shorter outings to more modest destinations. Unlike the trail up better-known Eagle Creek, the Herman Creek Trail stays above the stream on woodsy hillsides, where the only evidence of the creek is the sound of its cascading water. That's not to say that the trail is dull. Quite the contrary, there may be no major waterfalls to enjoy on the main creek, but there are plenty of delicate, wispy falls on side creeks. In addition, the forests here are some of the loveliest in the Gorge. And finally, unlike the extremely popular trail up Eagle Creek, on this trail it is possible to stop and enjoy the scenery, without the fear of being trampled by armies of fellow hikers.

Falls along lower Herman Creek Trail

Directions: Leave Interstate 84 at Cascade Locks exit 44 and drive the main road (Wa Na Pa Street) through town. At the east end of town turn left on Forest Lane, following signs for the airport. Drive this road 2.0 miles to an overpass over the freeway. Turn left after the overpass and, 0.3

mile later, turn right at a sign for Herman Creek Campground. This narrow paved road climbs a short distance to a junction with the marked spur road to the trailhead on the right.

The trail begins by winding uphill through a forest of stately bigleaf maple and Douglas-fir. Were it not for all the traffic sounds from Interstate 84, the forest would be quiet, but that adjective certainly doesn't apply now. The wide path ascends, passes under a set of powerlines, then continues gradually uphill through attractive, open forests, with lots of spring and early summer wildflowers, such as twisted stalk, inside-out flower, and tiger lily. The traffic sounds fade away as you turn the corner of a minor ridge and enter the canyon of Herman Creek. Two uphill switchbacks take you up to a fork in the trail, where you go left (uphill), staying on the Herman Creek Trail.

In a few hundred yards you arrive at a potentially confusing junction with a closed jeep road. Go straight—ignoring the unsigned routes that head downhill to the right and sharply back to the left—and walk 50 feet to a switchback, where you bear right (uphill) and climb slowly up the west side of a slope. Once at the top of the ridge, you walk on the level about 0.2 mile to long-abandoned Herman Camp, where several trail junctions are found. Go straight on the old road, now just a wide trail, and walk another 250 yards to a junction with the Nick Eaton Trail, where you go straight again and amble lazily along, mostly on the level or slightly downhill, until the old road ends and the route becomes an actual foot trail.

A little less than 1 mile from Herman Camp, you come to a tall, lacy waterfall, just above the trail on an unnamed side creek. After this, you climb a bit to an opening in the forest where picturesque oak trees frame good views of Herman Creek Canyon and heavily-forested Woolly Horn Ridge. This is a good turnaround point, if you want an easy hike.

Shortly after the viewpoint, you enter the Mark O. Hatfield Wilderness Area, then make a mostly level detour into and out of the side canyon holding Camp Creek, which has an easy rockhop crossing. Still wandering along at a gentle grade, and carefully watching your step to avoid the trailside poison oak, you make some minor ups and downs for the next 1.5 miles to a good campsite beside a junction with the Casey Creek Trail. For an interesting side trip, turn right, walk through the camp, and veer right on a sometimes steep 0.3-mile trail that drops to the confluence of Herman Creek and East Fork Herman Creek. There is an inviting campsite here, or you can simply eat your lunch, enjoying the cascading stream, mossy rocks, cavorting dippers, and dense, overhanging vegetation.

This spot is another good turnaround point, but if you're still going strong, then get back on the Herman Creek Trail and begin a long, gradual climb for the next 3.3 miles. Along the way, you cross a half dozen or more splashing side creeks, not all of which have names or flow all year. The second one, Slide Creek, feeds a tall, wispy waterfall that drops over a scenic cliff just above the trail.

None of the creeks has a bridge, but only Mullinix Creek cannot be easily crossed with dry feet. Here, you can either make a simple ford or scramble a few yards upstream to cross on a log. All of this water provides habitat for dense riparian vegetation, dominated by devils club, with its enormous, foot-wide leaves that hide rows of nasty thorns underneath.

The long climb eventually takes you to a junction with the Herman Cutoff Trail, which goes off to the left just before a tiny creek near Cedar Swamp Camp. The trail shelter that used to stand here is gone, but it is still a pleasant place to spend the night or eat your lunch beneath big, old-growth western hemlocks and western red cedars. For dayhikers this is the last logical turnaround point, unless you are really athletic and plan to make a long loop via Green Point Mountain (See Trip 5).

Trip 4

Gorton Creek – Nick Eaton Ridge Loop

(Map Area G-6)

Distance	Elevation Gain	Hiking Time	Optional Map	Difficulty
8.0 miles	2600'	4.5 hours	*Green Trails–Bonneville Dam*	***

Usually Open	April to early November
Best Times	May
Agency	Columbia River Gorge National Scenic Area

This excellent loop trip provides a nice sampling of what makes ridge walks in the Columbia River Gorge so nice. In most hiking areas, you are satisfied if the trail includes a single major highlight, such as a mountain lake, a high viewpoint, or a flower-covered meadow. But Gorge hikes always manage to come up with several highlights in the same package. On this trip, for example, you can enjoy lush forests, a spectacular rocky overlook, and brightly-colored wildflower meadows—all in one compact trip. The only typical Gorge feature lacking is a waterfall, but let's not be greedy.

Directions: Leave Interstate 84 at Cascade Locks exit 44 and drive the main road (Wa Na Pa Street) through town. At the east end of town turn left on Forest Lane, following signs for the airport. Drive this road 2.0 miles to an overpass over the freeway. Turn left after the overpass and, 0.3 mile later, turn right at a sign for Herman Creek Campground. This narrow paved road climbs a short distance to a junction with the marked spur road to the trailhead on the right.

The trail begins by winding uphill through a forest of bigleaf maple and Douglas-fir with lots of ferns and poison oak crowding the tread. The path passes under a set of powerlines, then continues gradually uphill through attractive woods. You round a small ridge to enter the canyon of Herman Creek, then follow two uphill switchbacks to a fork in the trail, where you bear left (uphill).

In a few hundred yards, you arrive at a potentially confusing junction with a closed jeep road. Go straight—ignoring unsigned routes that head downhill to the right and sharply back to the left—and walk 50 feet to a road switchback, where you bear right (uphill) and climb slowly on a road up the west side of a slope.

The dense forest canopy here provides lots of shade, and it keeps the forest floor remarkably free of ground-cover plants. Shortly after the route levels off, you arrive at long-abandoned Herman Camp and a confusing set of junctions.

The main jeep track goes straight, but you turn left to enter the old camp area and pick up the Gorton Creek Trail at a small sign to the southeast. Follow this hiker-only trail as it ascends a lovely open forest, without a hint of the claustrophobic feeling often associated with trails in the Gorge. In early May, white-blooming forest wildflowers brighten the forest floor—baneberry, vanilla leaf, star-flowered smilacina, false solomon seal, twisted stalk, valerian, and white anemone. You may hear the occasional train whistle, but freeway sounds are only a distant murmur. Wind in the trees and bird songs are a pleasure for your ears.

You continue at a moderate uphill grade for 2.6 miles, including six short switchbacks, to a junction with the Ridge Cutoff Trail. So far, there have been only occasional small breaks in the tree cover, limited to partially obstructed views. Now, you can satisfy your hankering for broader vistas by making a superb side trip to nearby Indian Point. To reach it, go straight at the junction and walk about 50 yards, then turn left on an unsigned side trail that goes steeply downhill. In about 0.1 mile, this trail leads to the dramatic views

Indian Point, Oregon

from Indian Point, a rocky outcropping on the side of a cliff. Adventurous hikers can scramble over the rocks to the top of the point, where they can spot Mounts Adams and St. Helens, and enjoy fine views up and down the Columbia River.

To complete the main loop, return to the junction with the Ridge Cutoff Trail and turn south. The trail climbs steeply at first, then levels off and comes to an area with an abundance of May wildflowers. Look for red-flowering currant, blue anemone, red paintbrush, yellow wood violet, and thick patches of yellow glacier lilys. The almost constant Gorge winds whistle pleasantly through the trees, and help to cool off sweaty hikers.

The path tops out at a junction with the Nick Eaton Trail, where you turn right and descend in forest 0.4 mile, before enjoying the trip's next highlight, a series of open meadows with some of the best flower gardens in the Columbia River Gorge. There are plenty of lomatium, prairie star, strawberry, larkspur, ballhead waterleaf, paintbrush, stonecrop, serviceberry, and enough other species to blanket the hillside with a rainbow of colors. The views are also good, especially of the gaping canyon of Herman Creek, Woolly Horn Ridge, and Benson Plateau, with fine vistas to the west, down the Columbia River. The dozens of steep downhill switchbacks that wind through the meadows can be tough on your knees, but amid such scenery, who can complain? The meadows are frequently broken by forested sections that add shade and variety to the hike.

Sadly, the meadows are with you for only about 0.5 mile before you reenter forest and drop through several dozen more switchbacks. The trees get larger as you descend, eventually including really grand old specimens of Douglas-fir and western hemlock. The woodsy path bottoms out at a junction with the wide Herman Creek Trail. To close the loop, simply turn right and, in about 200 yards, reach the trail junction at Herman Camp.

Trip 5

Green Point Mountain Loop

(Map Area G-6)

Distance	Elevation Gain	Hiking Time	Optional Map	Difficulty
19.6 miles	4300'	9 to 12 hours	*Green Trails—Bonneville Dam*	****

Usually Open	Late May to early November
Best Times	June
Agency	Columbia River Gorge National Scenic Area

Green Point Mountain over Rainy Lake

This book includes dayhikes of all lengths and difficulty levels, so hikers of all abilities have a range of options to meet their needs. Near the high end of the difficulty range is this loop over Green Point Mountain. At nearly 20 miles, this hike is a major challenge, but for those ready for that challenge, it is well worth the effort. The view from atop Green Point Mountain is the equal of any in our region, and before you even get there, you'll pass by waterfalls along the Herman Creek Trail and travel through miles of some of the finest forests in the Columbia River Gorge. Backpackers can make this into a pleasant weekend trip, with a night at Cedar Swamp Camp.

Directions: Leave Interstate 84 at Cascade Locks exit 44 and drive the main road (Wa Na Pa Street) through town. At the east end of town turn left on Forest Lane, following signs for the airport. Drive this road 2.0 miles to an overpass over the freeway. Turn left after the overpass and, 0.3 mile later, turn right at a sign for Herman Creek Campground. This narrow paved road climbs a short distance to a junction with the marked spur road to the trailhead on the right.

The trail begins by winding uphill through a forest of bigleaf maple and Douglas-fir, then passes under a set of powerlines. From there, you continue gradually uphill around a small ridge and make two uphill switchbacks to a fork in the trail. Bear left (uphill) and, in a few hundred yards you arrive at a potentially confusing junction with a closed jeep road. Go straight—ignoring unsigned routes that head downhill to the right and sharply back to the left—and walk 50 feet to a road switchback, where you bear right (uphill) and climb slowly on the road up the west side of a wooded slope. Once at the top of the ridge, you walk on the level for about 0.2 mile to long-abandoned Herman Camp, where several trail junctions are found.

Go straight on the old road, now just a wide trail, and walk another 250 yards to a junction with the Nick Eaton Trail. You go straight again to continue on the gently-graded Herman Creek Trail for 1 mile to a tall waterfall on an unnamed side creek. Then you pass a good viewpoint and move in and out of side canyons to a campsite next to a junction with the Casey Creek Trail. This is the beginning of the loop trip.

After this campsite, the formerly gentle Herman Creek Trail steepens, continuing south, and steadily gains elevation for the next 3.3 miles. Along the way, you cross half a dozen splashing side creeks, skirt another tall waterfall, and move through dense forests. The long climb eventually takes you to a junction with the Herman Cutoff Trail, which goes to the left, just before Cedar Swamp Camp. If you are making this into a two-day backpacking trip, this comfortable site is the most logical place to spend the night.

To reach Green Point Mountain, turn east on the Herman Cutoff Trail, cross a sluggish little creek, and begin a steady climb. In the next 2.3 miles, you make nine long switchbacks up a heavily wooded hillside. The switchbacks keep the grade from becoming overly steep, but it is still tiring. Finally, you come to a small abandoned building at a junction with an old jeep road.

Turn left here and, almost immediately, leave the road in favor of the Gorton Creek Trail, which runs uphill along a ridgeline. In a little less than 1 mile, you come to the open summit of Green Point Mountain, where you can sit down and enjoy the view. From here, you can see all the major volcanic snow peaks in our region, as well as most of the recognizable high points in the Columbia River Gorge, all the way west to Larch Mountain. The most impressive sight, however, is looking east down to Rainy Lake, and northeast to the bald, rocky summit of Mt. Defiance.

Reshoulder your pack and drop down the trail on the north side of Green Point Mountain to a junction. Bear left here and make a very gradual descent in open forests for 1.5 miles to the next junction, where you bear left again and descend a series of short, rather steep, switchbacks. At the bottom of these switchbacks is a saddle and a sign identifying Ridge Camp. A smaller sign directs you to the nearest water, at the end of a 0.2-mile spur trail to the east.

To close the loop, you contour across open slopes, on the east side of Nick Eaton Ridge for a short distance, then come to a junction with the Nick Eaton Trail. Bear left and walk near the crest of the ridge, savoring some excellent views from several openings along the way. At the next saddle, you come to another junction, where you turn left on the Casey Creek Trail. This is where you lose all of the elevation you gained before. The trail is rather narrow and quite steep as it loses 2500 feet in 2.1 miles, which explains why you don't want to make this loop in the opposite direction. As compensation for jammed toes, you are treated to some good views and abundant wildflowers in a steep meadow about halfway down. Eventually, you get back to the junction near the campsite on the Herman Creek Trail, turn right, and return to your car.

Trip 6

Gorge Trail – Herman Creek to Wyeth Campground

(Map Area G-6)

Distance	Elevation Gain	Hiking Time	Optional Map	Difficulty
5.3 miles (one way)	800 feet (one way)	2.5 hours (one way)	USFS–Trails of the Columbia Gorge	**

☁

Usually Open	All year
Best Times	April to May / Late October
Agency	Columbia River Gorge National Scenic Area

This rarely-traveled trail was constructed in the late 1990s as a section of the low-elevation Gorge Trail. Most hikers are unaware of its existence, as no other guidebooks include this trip. Those who discover this route find it to be a welcome link in the interconnected trail system of the central Gorge, because it makes some excellent loop trips possible. Backpackers and sturdy dayhikers looking to visit Herman Creek and North Lake can use this trail to visit both areas, without having to retrace their steps.

The leisurely route is also a pleasant dayhike in its own right, providing a quiet stroll through forests and over talus slopes, with nice views of the Columbia River and surrounding cliffs. The route is open all year (except during winter storms) and is easy enough for hikers of virtually any ability level, especially when it is done as a one-way trip with a short car shuttle. As on most low-elevation routes in the Gorge, poison oak is common here. Learn to recognize and avoid it. The hike is described from west to east.

Directions: Leave Interstate 84 at Cascade Locks exit 44 and drive the main road (Wa Na Pa Street) through town. At the east end of town turn left on Forest Lane, following signs for the airport. Drive this road 2.0 miles to an overpass over the freeway. Turn left after the overpass and, 0.3 mile later, turn right at a sign for Herman Creek Campground. This narrow paved road climbs a short distance to a junction with the marked spur road to the trailhead on the right.

To leave a second car at the Wyeth trailhead, go east on Interstate 84 to Wyeth exit 51. Turn right at the end of the exit road and, almost immediately, turn right again on Herman Creek Road. After 0.1 mile, turn left into Wyeth Campground and drive through this comfortable and attractive area, keeping right at all intersections, to the signed trailhead parking lot.

View west from Gorge Trail #400 near Wyeth

The trail begins by winding uphill through a stately forest of bigleaf maple and Douglas-fir, with lots of ferns and poison oak crowding the tread. The path passes under a set of powerlines, then continues gradually uphill through attractive woods. You round a small ridge to enter the canyon of Herman Creek, then follow two uphill switchbacks to a fork in the trail, where you veer left (uphill). In a few hundred yards you arrive at a potentially confusing junction with a closed jeep road.

Go straight—ignoring unsigned routes that head downhill to the right and sharply back to the left—and walk 50 feet to a road switchback. Bear right (uphill) and slowly climb up the west side of a wooded slope. Shortly after the route levels off, you arrive at long-abandoned Herman Camp and a confusing set of junctions. The poorly-signed Gorge Trail begins at the northeast corner of the camp area on your left.

The path sets a leisurely course through the dappled sunshine of an open forest, with lots of vine maple and bracken fern forming an understory. The eastbound trail goes along at a level or very slight downhill grade, in and out of little canyons, most of which have no water. The scenery doesn't change much as you hike, but it's never dull, because of the mixed forests and lush greenery. An abundance of vine maple make this quiet hike enjoyable in late October, although by then almost no sunshine reaches these north-facing slopes.

About 1 mile from Herman Camp, you cross a steep, narrow skid road and continue your nearly level traverse. As you continue east, you pass the base of some moss-covered scree slopes, where you can catch glimpses of the towering cliffs of Nick Eaton Ridge on your right. Three types of ferns, as well as Oregon grape and thimbleberry, compete for dominance on the forest floor, while Douglas-fir, western red cedar, and western hemlock vie with deciduous species, such as Pacific dogwood and bigleaf maple, for dominance above.

The trail comes close to, and briefly follows, a parallel set of powerlines, then crosses a large rocky slope with good views of the Columbia River. Conveniently, busy Interstate 84 is hidden from view by trees, making for more attractive photographs. On this rocky slope, listen for the peeping sounds of pikas, cute little guinea-pig-like creatures, who find good habitat among the rockslides in the Gorge. The next landmark is the easy crossing of two branches of splashing Grays Creek, followed by another scree slope with disappointing river views, but excellent looks up to the cliffs and rocky pinnacles to the south. This nicely varied mix of forest and occasional scree slopes continues as you slowly descend, gradually approaching the powerlines and freeway on your left. The path bottoms out as it detours briefly inland to a wooden bridge over rushing Gorton Creek, then immediately thereafter hits a junction with the Wyeth Trail. To close your hike, turn left and soon arrive at the Wyeth Campground and trailhead.

Trip 7

Wyeth Trail to North Lake

(Map Area G-6)

Distance	Elevation Gain	Hiking Time	Optional Map	Difficulty
11.4 miles	3800'	6 to 7 hours	*Green Trails–Bonneville Dam*	****

Usually Open	Mid-May to November
Best Times	June
Agency	Columbia River Gorge National Scenic Area

Like many other Gorge hikes, the Wyeth Trail will provide you with a *really* good workout. It's a long way up from the Columbia River, near sea level, to North Lake at the top. In fact, mountain climbers often use this path as a conditioning hike in the spring. Fortunately, the climb is well shaded by trees, and the woods are always attractive, so there are compensations for all the sweat.

Directions: Take exit 51 off Interstate 84 east of Cascade Locks and turn right at the end of the exit road. You immediately turn right again on Herman Creek Road and, after 0.1 mile, turn left into Wyeth Campground. Keep right at all intersections in this comfortable and attractive campground to reach the signed trailhead parking lot.

The wide trail follows an old road for about 150 yards to a signed junction. To the right, the Gorge Trail heads west to Herman Creek, while straight ahead is an old trail that is no longer used. You turn left and cross a hillside above the parking lot, before coming to an unsigned junction with a spur trail that heads sharply left, back to the campground. You go straight and cross an open area under a set of powerlines, then go back into the trees.

Next, you hop across the clear waters of 6-foot-wide Harphan Creek and turn uphill. Up to this point, you have done only some modest ups and downs, from here on, however, the downgrades disappear, and steady uphill is all you get.

Very quickly, the trees make a transition from mostly bigleaf maple to mostly Douglas-fir, while sword fern and Oregon grape cover the forest floor. Before long, you reach the first of what will be many switchbacks. The first 10 are rather long and well graded, following a recently realigned route. At the end of these, you cross a tiny but reliable creek, where you can splash your head with water and take a short rest.

Above this, you make a series of much shorter and somewhat steeper switchbacks, before you break out of the woods and reach a small but welcome rocky clearing, above the steep slopes of Harphan Creek Canyon. There is a nice variety of wildflowers here, and fine vistas to the Carson area in Washington. Both make good excuses to stop climbing for a while and take another needed rest stop.

For the next mile, you alternate between trees and open rocky areas, affording you a pleasant variety of scenery. The uphill grade is sometimes steep, sometimes only moderate, but it never ceases.

Finally, after the last open clearing, you make eight more switchbacks and come to a junction with the Green Point Ridge Trail, a possible loop option for athletic hikers. More importantly, you have now completed virtually all of the uphill.

To reach North Lake, bear left at the junction and travel through a higher-elevation forest of Pacific silver fir and western white pine. The trail now loses a bit of elevation, as you cross a marshy area and an open slope with nice views east to distinctive Mt. Defiance, the highest landmark on the Oregon side of the Columbia River Gorge. Cross a couple of tiny creeks, then make a final uphill push to North Lake, which you reach by taking a short side trail to the right.

After all that effort you might be a bit disappointed with North Lake. It is formed by an earthen dam and has lots of dead snags around its shores, so it's not the most aesthetically pleasing pool in our region. It does, however, boast several decent campsites on its south shore and a good view of the talus slopes of Green Point Mountain, to the southwest.

If you have enough energy to visit a somewhat prettier pool, and to make a loop with great views, then bear left around North Lake and soon come to a junction. You bear right here and walk very gradually uphill in forest to a second junction. If you want to visit Rainy Lake, go left and come to this attractive mountain lake in about 0.5 mile. Like North Lake, Rainy Lake has some snags, but it also has a first-rate view of Green Point Mountain and very nice camps for backpackers. This lake is also accessible by a very short trail that connects with a nearby logging road, so you should expect some company.

If you want to make the loop, turn right at the junction before Rainy Lake and climb a mix of woodsy slopes and open rocky areas for 0.6 mile to a four-way junction on top of a ridge. To return to the Wyeth Trail, go north at this junction and follow the Green Point Ridge Trail, which closely follows the edge of the ridge above North Lake. After 1.5 miles, you bear right at a junction and continue downhill another 1.2 miles, back to the junction with the Wyeth Trail mentioned earlier. This optional loop adds a total of 2.3 miles and 800 feet of elevation gain to your hike.

The Columbia River Gorge

Area G-7: Starvation Creek Area

In the winter of 1884, a blizzard trapped two trains in the Columbia River Gorge, west of Hood River. The trains had almost no food on board, and since the people were stranded for several days, there was concern for their survival. Skiers brought in supplies by making the difficult 8-mile trek from Hood River. So, despite the bleak-sounding name that resulted from this incident, no one actually starved. Fortunately, traveling conditions have significantly improved in the century since Starvation Creek got its name. Today the cliffs, waterfalls, and viewpoints in this area are accessible right off an interstate freeway, yet they still manage to retain most of their original wild character.

The scenic trails that explore the Starvation Creek area have a split personality. The lower sections travel past towering waterfalls, then climb a short distance to excellent viewpoints from wildflower-covered, rocky overlooks. These low paths are relatively easy, are open virtually all year, and provide some of the most scenic early-spring hiking in this book. By contrast, the trails to higher destinations climb to the loftiest elevations in the Columbia River Gorge. As a result, they are long and arduous, and they are the last hiking options in the Gorge to be free of snow each year.

There isn't much in the way of middle ground between these two options. So come to Starvation Creek early in the spring and return in early summer. During the months in between, however, it would be wise to head elsewhere. As with all areas in the eastern Gorge, poison oak is abundant along the lower trails, so watch your step.

Trip 1

Shellrock Mountain

(Map Area G-7)

Distance	Elevation Gain	Hiking Time	Optional Map	Difficulty
2.8 miles	1300'	2.5 hours	*Green Trails–Hood River* (trail not shown)	**

Usually Open	All year (except during winter storms)
Best Times	All year
Agency	Columbia River Gorge National Scenic Area

Not maintained by any land agency, and not shown on any map, the trail partway up Shellrock Mountain joins a long list of such overlooked routes lacing the isolated parts of the Columbia River Gorge. Built to access a United States Geological Survey station, this little-known and rarely-traveled path features very convenient access, excellent views, and some interesting history. The route is a real gem, but it is not good for hikers with children due to some exposed sections and a rather steep grade. Although not necessary on every trail, high-topped boots are essential on this hike because the very uneven and rocky trail seems designed to give you a sprained ankle, especially when the rocks are wet, and you are traveling downhill. Since the trail is not maintained, please do your part to keep it up by removing any deadfall and helping to rebuild obliterated sections.

Directions: Drive Interstate 84 east from Portland to a spot 0.7 miles beyond milepost 52 and pull off the freeway into a small unmarked gravel area just off the right shoulder. There is a guardrail here with a small white sign stating PROPERTY OF DEPT. OF TRANSPORTATION - HIGHWAY DIVISION. In order to return to Portland after your hike, you will have to get back on the eastbound lanes of Interstate 84 and drive to Exit 56 at Viento State Park, where you can turn back west. Be very careful when you get back on the freeway as there is no merge lane.

Hop over the guardrail and walk east on a section of the old scenic highway, through a tunnel of trees. Traffic zips by on the busy freeway just a few yards to your left, and poison oak crowds the route, but the hiking is easy and the forest is attractive. After less than 100 yards, look for a small path on the right and turn onto it.

This well-graded trail ascends a slope of moss-covered rocks in five evenly-spaced switchbacks, to a junction with a section of a historic wagon road. Much of the stonework used to build this old route is still visible and interest-

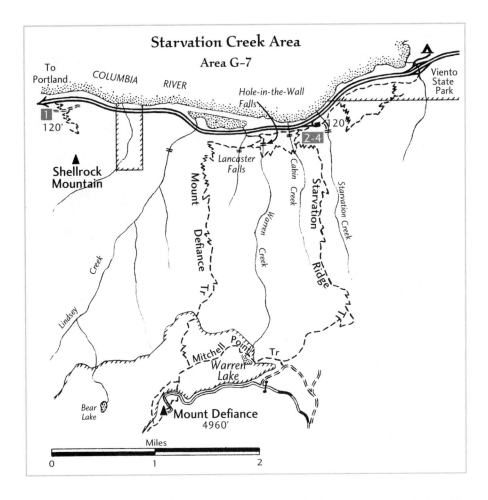

Starvation Creek Area

Area G-7

Bear left (uphill) on the old wagon road and follow it for about 80 yards to where the road starts to curve into the trees. Turn sharply right here on an obvious trail and resume switchbacking up the rocky slope. Even though you never quite escape the sounds of big rigs barreling along Interstate 84, the trail is otherwise remarkably wild and attractive. It climbs steadily and rather steeply in 10 switchbacks all the way to the top of the rocky slope. The view from here is especially good looking east down the Gorge to Mitchell Point and north to Dog and Augsberger mountains.

You may want to call it quits here, as the trail beyond this point becomes less distinct and much more rugged and overgrown. There is also a lot more poison oak to deal with, so you must be careful where you step. If you decide to trudge on, follow the sketchy up-and-down route into the trees and make a series of five switchbacks and short but difficult traverses, before you eventually emerge from the trees at an old wooden overlook and survey site. From here, you can enjoy a quiet lunch while taking in the nice view.

View of Wind Mountain from Shellrock Mountain

There is no trail beyond this point to the actual summit of Shellrock Mountain, about 1 mile away and 800 feet higher. The bushwhack to the top is extremely difficult, and the view is almost entirely blocked by trees, so it's just not worth the effort.

Trip 2

Mount Defiance Trail

(Map Area G-7)

Distance	Elevation Gain	Hiking Time	Optional Map	Difficulty
11.9 miles	4800'	8 to 12 hours	*Green Trails–Hood River*	****

Usually Open	Late May to October
Best Times	June
Agency	Columbia River Gorge National Scenic Area

At 4960 feet, Mt. Defiance is the highest point directly overlooking the Columbia River Gorge. The loftiness of this spot ensures that visitors enjoy an exceptional view, extending from the familiar Cascade snow peaks, to the agricultural Hood River Valley, to the mighty river far below. The height also ensures that since the hike starts at near sea level, it will be a difficult challenge. The elevation gain is truly daunting, so this hike should be left solely to the fittest athletes. Serious mountain climbers looking for a conditioning hike love this outing, but all others should think twice.

Directions: Drive east on Interstate 84 to Starvation Creek exit 54 and park in the small lot for Starvation Creek State Park. This exit is accessible only to eastbound traffic, so on your return you have to continue east to exit 56 at Viento State Park to get back on the westbound lanes.

The signed path begins from the west end of the lot and follows the highway shoulder, separated from the noisy traffic by a concrete barrier. The perfectly level trail slowly works away from the freeway, although the sounds of cars and trucks remain dominant as you wander through the woods. Much of the route follows the historic Old Columbia River Highway, which ensures an easy grade, but you'll need to watch your step to avoid poison oak, a very common plant in the eastern Gorge.

Just 0.3 mile from the trailhead, a tiny sign marks the steep Starvation Cutoff Trail, which goes up the slope on your left. Go straight and catch a glimpse of Cabin Creek Falls as you continue walking west to a much better view of Hole-in-the-Wall Falls on Warren Creek. This 100-foot falls isn't exactly manmade, because it always existed, but in 1938 highway engineers diverted the flow into a tunnel so drivers on the old highway could avoid a shower.

A little past the bridge over Warren Creek is a junction with the Starvation Ridge Trail, going back to the left. The Mount Defiance Trail goes straight and passes beside the rather short but lovely Lancaster Falls, a 20-foot-high spreading cascade of water.

Up to this point the trail has remained almost level, but since you know the hike gains 4800 feet, logic dictates that the uphill must begin soon, and it does. A little less than 0.5 mile from Lancaster Falls, the path cuts to the left and launches into the expected ascent, with two dozen short switchbacks. The grade isn't excessively steep, but it's consistently uphill, so your calves and Achilles tendons better be prepared. The ascent is also bone dry, so carry an extra quart of water in your pack for hydration.

The first switchbacks climb the east side of the heavily wooded ridge, while the later ones (and there are lots of later ones) cut back and forth near the crest of the ridge. While most of the route is in deep woods, a couple of grassy and rocky openings provide decent views of Lindsey Creek Canyon to the west and welcome excuses for rest stops.

The climbing doesn't end when the switchbacks do, because after an all-too-brief level stretch, you resume charging up the ridge. At about the 3200-foot level are the first beargrass plants. This is usually a welcome sign in the Gorge, indicating that your climb is almost over, but that isn't the case here. This is disappointing, but compensation comes in the form of views from openings in the trees near the edge of some rocky talus slopes.

You turn right at the junction with the Mitchell Point Trail, which goes east to Warren Lake, and resume climbing. About 0.2 mile later, look for a possibly unsigned trail to the right and turn onto this route as it gradually ascends a view-packed talus slope on the west side of Mt. Defiance's summit. On the south side of the peak you reach a junction, where you turn left and make the short final push to the top.

Even though you share the open summit with a jeep road and a microwave station, these only briefly detract from the view. There is lots to look at in every direction, so allow some time to take it all in. Below you to the west is sparkling Bear Lake, and spreading out from there are various recognizable high points like Tanner Butte, Tomlike Mountain, and Indian Mountain. To the northwest are Table Mountain, Silver Star Mountain, and decapitated Mt. St. Helens. Rising prominently to the north is snowy Mt. Adams. To the east are a part of the Columbia River, Hood River Mountain, and the distant wheat fields of the Columbia Plateau. Most striking is the view south to horn-shaped Mt. Hood. Hikers familiar with the region can spend hours picking out familiar places. Before spending those hours, however, keep in mind that you still face a long hike back down before the day ends, and while going down may sound easy, countless hikers who have suffered from bad knees and jammed toes after completing the descent would beg to differ.

For variety on the return trip, you can take a shorter but less scenic trail from the top that switchbacks down through woods and crosses the closed jeep road twice before getting back to a junction with the Mount Defiance Trail. Another return loop option is the long, steep Starvation Ridge Trail (see Trip 3), although this path serves better as the uphill leg of a loop returning via the Mount Defiance Trail.

Hikers who want to visit the summit of Mt. Defiance but who can't handle the rigors of the Mount Defiance Trail, have the option of taking a much easier route from Forest Road 2820 to the south that gains only 1500 feet in 2 miles. Although easier on the body, this trail is less scenic and requires an extra hour or more of driving on bumpy gravel roads.

Mt. Hood from Mt. Defiance

Trip 3

Starvation Ridge to Warren Lake

(Map Area G-7)

Distance	Elevation Gain	Hiking Time	Optional Map	Difficulty
8.6 miles	3800'	5 to 7 hours	*Green Trails–Hood River*	****

Usually Open	May to October
Best Times	June
Agency	Columbia River Gorge National Scenic Area

So you've looked at the distance and elevation gain totals for the Mount Defiance Trail (Trip 2) and decided that, even though you're in good shape, that trip is beyond your abilities. Before you give up on getting to the top of Mt. Defiance, consider the two other options that reach the same goal.

The first is a relatively easy back-door approach, from a logging road to the south. Although pleasant, this trail requires a drive of almost two hours, so it is beyond the range of this book.

Another option is to do the trip as a two-day backpacking loop. For this approach, hike up the Starvation Ridge Trail, spend the night at scenic Warren Lake, then return on the Mount Defiance Trail. It won't be much fun hauling your gear up to Warren Lake, but you'll have all day to do it, and you can cool off at day's end with an invigorating dip in a lovely mountain lake. The trip is also worth taking separately as a dayhike to Warren Lake, which is the trip described here.

Directions: Drive east on Interstate 84 to Starvation Creek exit 54 and park in the small lot for Starvation Creek State Park. This exit is accessible only to eastbound traffic, so on your return you have to continue east to exit 56 at Viento State Park to get back on the westbound lanes.

The signed path begins from the west end of the lot and follows the highway shoulder, separated from the noisy traffic by a concrete barrier. After 0.2 mile, you turn left on the sketchy Starvation Cutoff Trail and switchback steeply up through attractive Douglas-fir and bigleaf-maple forests for 0.5 mile to a junction with the Starvation Ridge Trail. You turn left here and make a series of 10 uphill switchbacks to a good viewpoint beneath a powerline tower.

From here, the trail turns right and ascends rather steeply up a narrow ridge, mostly under a canopy of big trees. You keep this up for 2 exhausting miles, never straying far from the ridgecrest, despite a few short switchbacks. There is one good viewpoint along the way, but little else to break up the steady climb. A break does come eventually, when the grade of the climb lessens a bit so you can cross a small rocky area, then contour across a brushy slope with decent views of distant Mt. Adams.

The trail then goes up a series of short switchbacks, crosses a scree slope, and comes to the edge of an old clearcut. This landmark may not be aesthetically pleasing, but it does provide you with the opportunity to congratulate yourself on completing most of the uphill.

The trail curves to the right, away from the logging scar and works gradually uphill in deep woods of smaller, high-elevation trees, like Pacific silver fir. Beargrass blossoms brighten the way in June. At the top of a couple of shorter switchbacks, you hit the end of another road and logged area. You skirt this spot and soon reenter deep woods, now traveling on a basically level trail. You pass a mediocre viewpoint and, 0.3 mile later, reach an unsigned junction with the Mitchell Point Trail.

The path to the left goes 50 yards to a closed logging road, but you turn right and descend slightly for 0.4 mile to Warren Lake. This lovely pool is backed by a scenic rockslide and provides good swimming for tired hikers. The shore has a fair amount of brush, but there are a couple of good campsites at either end of the lake. Mosquitoes can be bothersome in June and early July.

If you are continuing to Mt. Defiance, keep hiking on the Mitchell Point Trail as it rounds the northwest side of Warren Lake and climbs a scenic, mostly open slope with good views. The trail reenters woods and, 0.8 mile from Warren Lake, comes to a junction with the Mount Defiance Trail. To reach the summit, turn left and follow the trail uphill, as described in Trip 2. If you are doing this trip as a loop, it is marginally easier on the knees to go up the Starvation Ridge Trail and down the slightly better-graded Mount Defiance Trail.

View west from near Starvation Creek

Trip 4

Starvation Creek Explorations

(Map Area G-7)

Distance	Elevation Gain	Hiking Time	Optional Map	Difficulty
0.1 to 9.2 miles	50 to 2200'	0.5 to 5 hours	Green Trails–Hood River (some trails not shown)	**

Usually Open	All year (except during winter storms)
Best Times	April
Agency	Columbia River Gorge National Scenic Area

Most hikers who come to Starvation Creek are looking to tackle the long, rugged climbs of Mt. Defiance (Trip 2) or Starvation Ridge (Trip 3), but these trips have two big drawbacks. The first and most obvious is their difficulty, well beyond the ability level of most dayhikers. The second problem is that they climb to elevations that are snowbound several months of the year. Both of these problems can be avoided by spending your time on the lower trails around Starvation Creek. These scenic paths provide enough exercise for a decent workout, without making you feel like you just survived army basic training. They also remain open all year, so on a sunny early spring day you can check out some lovely country without having to strap on snowshoes.

Directions: Drive east on Interstate 84 to Starvation Creek exit 54 and park in the small lot for Starvation Creek State Park. This exit is accessible only to eastbound traffic, so on your return you have to continue east to exit 56 at Viento State Park to get back on the westbound lanes.

Start your explorations by walking the paved, 150-yard trail up to 186-foot Starvation Creek Falls. In recent years, this trail has been blocked off well back from the towering falls, so the view is no longer as good as old timers remember, but you will still want to spend some time gazing up in awe at the portion of the falls you can see.

If you're in the mood for history, rather than wilderness, then your next exploration should be the wide trail going east toward Viento State Park. This gently-graded, 1.1-mile segment of the historic Old Columbia River Highway has a paved surface, and it visits several good viewpoints just above Interstate 84. The trail stays near the busy and noisy freeway the entire way, so it's not terribly wild, but it is interesting, especially if you take the time to read the interpretive signs near the trailhead, which inform you of the history of this road.

A rugged option for hikers who aren't allergic to poison oak is to follow the old highway west for about 250 yards, then turn right on an unsigned and hard-to-find path that steeply climbs several irregular and overgrown switchbacks to the base of a powerline tower. From here, you turn left (east) and for 1 mile follow another rough use path past several more viewpoints and powerline towers. When you reach the top of a rocky slope, turn left on a path covered with loose rocks and descend this rough trail back down to the old highway. Although there are good views on this hike, the thickets of poison oak along this loop route are virtually impossible to avoid. Only experienced route-finders should try this trail, and then only in winter and early spring before the poison oak gets too frisky and its poisonous toxin isn't as virulent.

Probably the best of the explorations lead from the Mount Defiance Trail west of the parking lot. This path initially follows the freeway shoulder, with a concrete barrier separating you from the traffic, then veers away from the freeway onto segments of the old highway.

The woodsy path goes below wispy Cabin Creek Falls, which is hard to see from the trail, then past Hole-in-the-Wall Falls, whose natural flow was diverted in 1938 by highway workers, but is still impressive. After crossing Warren Creek on a bridge, the trail continues to a junction with the Starvation Ridge Trail. Before turning left on this path, take 15 minutes to go straight on the Mount Defiance Trail for 0.2 mile to visit 20-foot-high Lancaster Falls. After returning to the junction, turn onto the Starvation Ridge Trail and climb to a crossing of Warren Creek in the woods above Hole-in-the-Wall Falls, then ascend a grassy wildflower meadow to a dramatic clifftop overlook. From here, you can see the entire Starvation Creek area, as well as hulking Dog Mountain across the river in Washington.

The trail then switchbacks downhill, crosses Cabin Creek, and comes to a junction with the Starvation Cutoff Trail. Before taking this return leg of the loop, consider going straight on a worthwhile side trip up 10 short switchbacks under a set of powerlines to a final good viewpoint at the base of a powerline tower. To close this dramatic loop, return to the junction with the Starvation Cutoff Trail and descend this steep route for 0.5 mile back to the Mount Defiance Trail.

The Columbia River Gorge

Area G-8: Hood River Area

The farther east you go in the Columbia River Gorge, the drier the climate becomes. Although the elevation remains virtually unchanged, the surrounding Cascade Mountains sap most of the moisture out of the clouds. Taking advantage of this rain shadow effect are the lucky residents of Hood River, Oregon. Their little slice of paradise enjoys an almost perfect climate that is rarely too wet, too hot, or too cold. Once a quiet farming town catering to the fruit-growing industry, this community has recently become a busy recreational hot spot, with lots of shops catering to the thousands of windsurfers who flock here to enjoy the clean water, outstanding scenery, and reliable winds.

Hikers come here too, and not just for the better weather, but also for the scenic trails that go through open forests and expansive meadows alive with a mix of mountain, desert, and forest wildflowers. Most of the area's excellent trails are beyond a one-hour drive from Portland, but those west of town in the Gorge and on Hood River Mountain, just a few miles southeast of town, meet this criterion.

Just to the west of the city limits, two adjacent state parks protect the scenic forests and high points at the eastern edge of the Columbia River Gorge. Vinzenz Lausmann and Wygant state parks both feature quiet trails generally overlooked by Portland hikers, who rarely drive this far east. Even less well known is Hood River Mountain, at the north end of a long, north-south ridge that separates the fertile Hood River Valley from the desert country to the east. The spacious wildflower meadows atop this ridge provide some of the most outstanding vistas in our region.

Trip 1

Wygant Trail Loop

(Map Area G-8, Map 1)

Distance	Elevation Gain	Hiking Time	Optional Map	Difficulty
8.5 miles	2100'	4 to 5 hours	Green Trails–Hood River (part of trail not shown)	***

Usually Open	March to early December
Best Times	Late March through mid-May
Agency	Oregon State Parks-Columbia River Gorge region

This little-known route offers hikers a lot of variety in a relatively small package. It starts with a treat for history buffs by following a short section of the historic old Columbia River Highway, then visits a quiet creek canyon and a string of spectacular viewpoints that provide unusual perspectives of the eastern Columbia River Gorge. Before setting out on this adventure, however, be warned that poison oak is extremely abundant in this area. This leafy menace is probably more of a hazard along this trail than on any other hike described in this book. Hikers must watch their step, wear long pants, and wash all of their clothes immediately upon their return.

Directions: Drive Interstate 84 to Mitchell Point Overlook exit 58 and take the short exit road to a parking lot. Since exit 58 has access only to and from the eastbound lanes of Interstate 84, in order to return to Portland you will have to continue east to Hood River exit 62, then turn around to get on the westbound lanes.

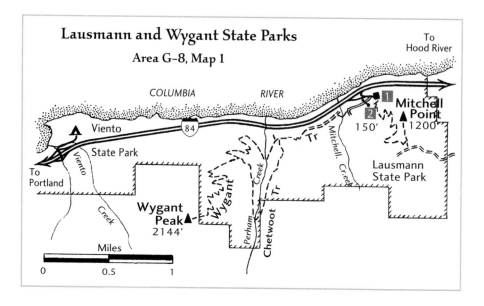

The signed Wygant Trail follows a closed road that goes west from the lower (northwest) end of the parking lot. Walk about 250 yards, then as the road turns left, take a signed footpath that veers right, into the trees. This trail takes you to a log bridge over small Mitchell Creek, then descends slightly to join a section of the Old Columbia River Highway.

After 0.3 mile, you leave this old road, now being invaded by mosses and poison oak, and walk up a little gully through open Douglas-fir forests. About 1 mile from the trailhead is a junction with the Chetwoot Trail, which is the return route of the recommended loop. You go straight and, a few yards later, pass a side trail to a viewpoint on your right. Only hikers who aren't allergic to poison oak should take this overgrown route, as the stuff is unavoidable.

You turn south and pass under a set of powerlines, then cross Perham Creek on a log bridge and turn north again, crossing back under the same powerlines. The next highlight is a spectacular little viewpoint in an open area just on your right. Almost 200 feet directly below this overlook is busy Interstate 84, but your attention will be drawn much more to the outstanding views of Mitchell Point to the east and Dog Mountain to the northwest. In April, a whole array of delicate wildflowers bloom on this open slope, providing colorful foregrounds for photographs.

This viewpoint makes a good turnaround point for hikers who don't want to do a lot of climbing. If you are up for a bit more exercise, however, follow the trail as it turns sharply south into the Douglas-fir woods and begins climbing. You cross under the powerlines yet again and make a series of short switchbacks, followed by a long traverse and one more switchback, to a junction with the Chetwoot Trail. If you want to visit higher viewpoints, turn right and make first a traverse, then a series of long switchbacks for 0.5 mile to an excellent higher viewpoint, at a clifftop break in the trees on a ridge. From here, you can even look over the hills on the Washington side of the Gorge to see a small part of Mt. Adams.

The trail above this point is not maintained very well, but experienced hikers can follow the narrow route as it ascends a series of 15 short switchbacks for the next 1.2 miles, mostly in dense forest, to the top of Wygant Peak. The view here is rather disappointing, but if you continue downhill through the trees to the northeast for about 200 yards, you will emerge at a nice, private meadow with excellent views to the west.

To resume the recommended loop, go back down the trail 1.7 miles to the Chetwoot Trail junction and hike that gently graded path as it makes a long downhill traverse into the canyon of Perham Creek. You cross that little stream, then turn north and traverse the oak-studded slopes east of the creek. The oaks here are mostly of the harmless Oregon white oak variety, but not-so-harmless poison oak is also common. You intersect the powerlines a final time, and come to the rough powerline access road. Jog to the right along this road for about 50 feet to reacquire the trail, then quickly return to the junction with the Wygant Trail.

Trip 2

Mitchell Point

(Map Area G-8, Map 1)

Distance	Elevation Gain	Hiking Time	Optional Map	Difficulty
2.4 miles	1200'	1.5 hours	Not really necessary	***

Usually Open	All year (except during winter storms)
Best Times	Late March through April
Agency	Oregon State Parks–Columbia River Gorge region

Although thousands of motorists drive past prominent Mitchell Point every day, few bother to stop at small Lausmann State Park at its base. Fewer still take the hike to the top of this rugged monolith to enjoy the terrific views and flowers there. One reason is that very few people even know that it is *possible* to hike to the summit. Even so-called "comprehensive" guidebooks on trails in the Columbia River Gorge overlook this fine route, despite easy highway access and big rewards at the end of a good trail. Here is your opportunity to correct this oversight.

Directions: Drive Interstate 84 to Mitchell Point Overlook exit 58 and take the short exit road to a parking lot. Since exit 58 has access only to and from the eastbound lanes of Interstate 84, in order to return to Portland you will have to continue east to Hood River exit 62, then turn around to get on the west-bound lanes.

The unsigned Mitchell Point Trail leaves from the upper (south-east) corner of the parking lot. The route follows a paved path heading toward the restroom building, but after about 75 feet you bear left onto an obvious, but unsigned, old gravel road. The gravel route loops to the right for about 100 yards, then you veer left on an obvious foot trail into the trees. This trail climbs moderately steeply in lush woods of Douglas-fir and bigleaf maple, above a trickling seasonal creek on your right, then it switchbacks to the left, away from the creek, and climbs steeply on a rocky path. The forest here is broken by open, rocky areas that are rimmed by twisted specimens of Oregon white oak, as well as the less welcome, shiny-leafed poison oak crowding the trail. You'll hear plenty of traffic sounds from the freeway below, but you'll also enjoy many spring wildflowers, such as lomatium, Oregon grape, larkspur, and prairie star.

Two more switchbacks take you up to and across a scree slope directly below the sheer cliffs of Mitchell Point. From this open, rocky area, you'll get your first good views across the Columbia River, to Dog and Wind mountains and large Drano Lake, which are cut off from the river by a bend in Washington State Highway 14. You briefly leave the scree in favor of woods, then switchback and recross the rocks at a higher elevation, with even wider vistas. Leaving the rocks a second and final time, the trail's grade gets less severe, as you continue through Douglas-fir forests, with lots of vine maple forming an understory, and common plants like vanilla leaf, Oregon grape, and various mosses on the forest floor.

Mitchell Point from trail just below summit, Oregon

As the freeway sounds fade away, you emerge from the trees in a brushy saddle south of Mitchell Point, then enter an open swath beneath a set of powerlines. The somewhat overgrown but easy-to-follow path now climbs a bit more to a trail junction. The trail to the right goes a short distance to a powerline access road, but your route turns left and follows the open spine of a ridge. Abundant late-April wildflowers here include arrowleaf balsamroot, lupine, onion, and fringecup. Twisted oak trees frame good pictures of the rocky summit of Mitchell Point directly ahead. Views up and down the Gorge are superb, and they improve with every step as you ascend to the usually windy summit.

The exposed top isn't recommended for acrophobics, but it allows you to look east to small farms near Hood River, north to a tiny bit of the top of Mt. Adams, northwest to Dog and Wind mountains, and west to such landmarks as Mt. Defiance and Table Mountain. At the base of the towering cliffs on the west side of Mitchell Point, you can see the freeway exit and the entire route of this hike. The jagged spine of Mitchell Point continues a short distance north from the high point, but the rocks are far too dangerous for exploration on foot.

Trip 3

Hood River Mountain

(Map Area G-8, Map 2)

Distance	Elevation Gain	Hiking Time	Optional Map	Difficulty
1.8 to 2.9 miles	600'	1 to 3 hours	None	*

Usually Open	March to November
Best Times	Late April to mid-May
Agency	Private property (SDS Lumber Company)

You won't find this leg-stretcher in any other guidebook—there isn't even a sign at the trailhead—but this lack of publicity is no reflection on the trail's worth. The stunning view from trail's end extends from a flower-covered hillside, down to the orchards of the Hood River Valley, and up to the horn-shaped spire of Mt. Hood. Few trails provide so much reward for so little effort. If you time your visit for late April or early May, the flower show alone is worth the trip.

This property is owned by the SDS Lumber Company in Bingen, Washington. The company prohibits motorized travel, but it is kind enough to allow public access for all other users. It is important that visitors not abuse

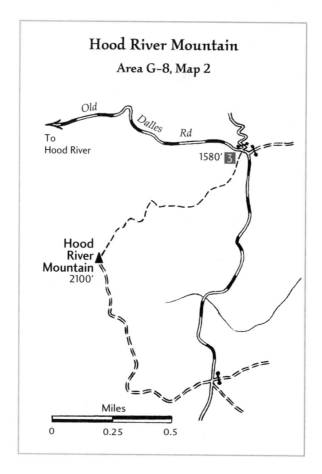

Hood River Mountain

Area G–8, Map 2

Old Dalles Rd

To
Hood River

1580' **3**

Hood
River
Mountain
2100'

Miles

0   0.25   0.5

this privilege, to ensure that respectful hikers and mountain bikers can continue to enjoy this area.

Directions: Take Hood River exit 64 off Interstate 84 and drive south on State Highway 35. After 0.4 mile, turn left on East Side Road and follow it 1.5 miles to the turnoff for Panorama Point County Park. Keep straight on East Side Road and, just 0.4 mile after the park turnoff, turn left on Old Dalles Road. Drive east on this initially paved, then bumpy gravel route for 2.1 miles to a saddle beneath a set of powerlines. Park on the side of the road, but be sure not to block access to the gated road going north from the pass.

The hike begins by going over a low berm on the south side of the road and following a wide mountainbike trail. The path is easy to follow as it goes through open woods of second-growth Douglas-fir, ponderosa pine, and Oregon white oak. In early May the trail is lined with numerous flowering shrubs, the most prominent of which are white-blooming serviceberry and red-flowering current. After about 0.5 mile, the path briefly levels out, then intermittently climbs for another 0.4 mile, before you rather suddenly emerge from the brush at the open, grassy summit of Hood River Mountain.

Sit back and enjoy! Gentle breezes blow over the summit, carrying butterflies to pollinate the many flowers that carpet the open slopes. The most abundant of those wildflowers are yellow balsamroot and lomatium, red paintbrush, and blue lupine and larkspur. Views are superb, with Mt. Adams and part of Mt. Rainier visible to the north, and a snippet of Mt. St. Helens to the northwest. Most spectacular of all, though, is the view of horn-shaped Mt. Hood over the orchards and farms of the Hood River Valley. Convenient flat-topped rocks provide nice "chairs" on which to sit and enjoy the view without trampling the flowers. For maximum enjoyment, bring a wildflower identification guide, a good friend, and a picnic lunch.

You could simply return the way you came, but for more exercise, consider making a loop out of this trip by continuing south along the summit ridge. The wildly scenic up-and-down path follows along the edge of a flower-covered meadow that provides great views as you hike. About 0.6 mile from the top, the route curves to the left, away from the summit ridge. You then drop through more meadows to another unsigned trailhead on a gravel road. To complete the loop, simply turn left and walk this little-traveled road 1.1 miles back to your car.

Salmon-Huckleberry Area

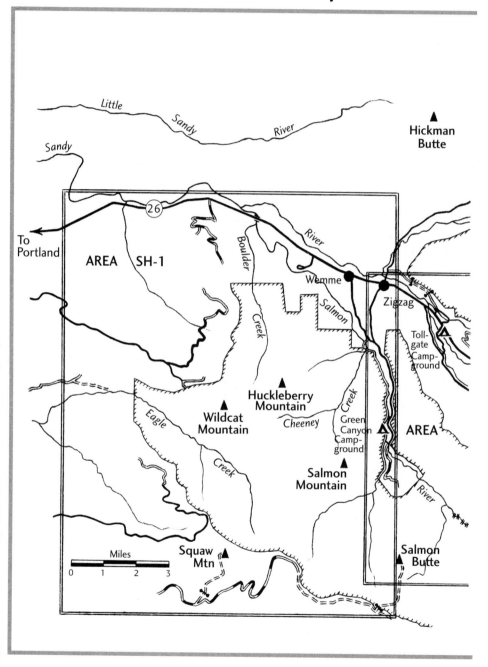

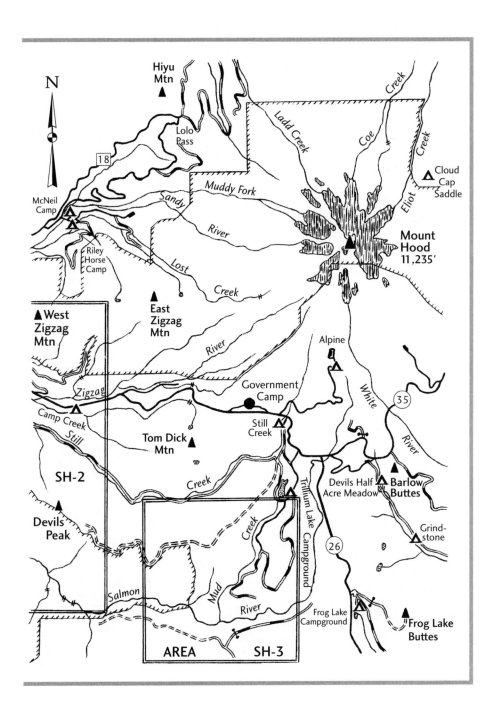

N

Hiyu
Mtn

Lolo
Pass

Ladd Creek

Coe Creek

Eliot Creek

Cloud
Cap
Saddle

18

Muddy Fork

Sandy

River

McNeil
Camp

Riley
Horse
Camp

Lost

Creek

Mount
Hood
11,235'

West
Zigzag
Mtn

East
Zigzag
Mtn

River

Alpine

Zigzag

River

Government
Camp

White

35

Camp Creek

Still

Tom Dick
Mtn

Still
Creek

SH-2

Creek

Devils Half
Acre Meadow

Barlow
Buttes

Devils
Peak

Creek

Grind-
stone

Mud

26

Trillium Lake Campground

Salmon

River

Frog Lake
Campground

Frog Lake
Buttes

AREA   SH-3

Salmon River near Green Canyon (the old Salmon River Trail, in Mt. Hood National Forest)

Salmon-Huckleberry Area

Area SH-1: Western Salmon-Huckleberry Wilderness

THE SALMON-HUCKLEBERRY WILDERNESS WAS ONE OF THE LARGEST AND MOST IMPORTANT AREAS PROTECTED IN THE LANDMARK OREGON WILDERNESS ACT OF 1984. Preserved in this relatively little-known wilderness are some 44,600 acres of rugged ridges and remote stream canyons in the hills southwest of Mt. Hood. The trails exploring this area provide a perfect complement to the busier paths in the adjacent Mount Hood Wilderness. Instead of a glacier-clad volcano and alpine meadows, this wilderness features view-packed ridges, waterfalls tucked into almost inaccessible canyons, and thousands of acres of quiet forests, ranging from low-elevation, old-growth groves to more open higher-elevation woodlands.

With fewer human disruptions, wildlife thrives in this area and is often encountered by quiet hikers. Salmon spawn in the clear streams, and black bears prowl the forests. Hikers are often startled by the sudden furious flapping of ruffed grouse, who seem to wait until the last possible moment to take flight from an approaching human. Fast-moving snowshoe hares scamper away into the brush, while slow-moving western toads plod along in the undergrowth. All of these things can be enjoyed on paths with a trail population that is a fraction of that on more famous routes just a few minutes' drive away.

The western part of this large wilderness is dominated by a series of interconnecting subalpine ridges, topped by occasional meadow openings. The views from these ridges are excellent, as are the displays of beargrass and Pacific rhododendron in the open forests during June and early July. Trails follow all of these ridges, providing miles of fun hiking and opportunities for dozens of outstanding wilderness adventures.

Trip 1

Eagle Creek

(Map Area SH-1)

Distance	Elevation Gain	Hiking Time	Optional Map	Difficulty
6.4 miles (with longer options)	900'	3 to 5 hours	*Green Trails–Cherryville*	**

Usually Open	March to December
Best Times	May to November
Agency	Zigzag Ranger District (Mt. Hood National Forest)

Some trails you hike because the trailhead is nearby and easy to reach. Others you hike because they provide spectacular views or great mountain scenery. The Eagle Creek Trail gives you neither of these, and that's probably why so few people hike it. On this trip, just finding the trailhead is something of an adventure, and the only views feature rather ugly cut-over slopes near the trailhead. So what's the attraction? The answer is a beautiful rainforest and solitude.

Directions: Take exit 12 off Interstate 205 and drive east on State Highway 224/212. Turn right (south) where these roads split, following Highway 224 and signs for Estacada. Near milepost 19, at a junction 1.1 miles past the intersection with State Highway 211, turn left at a sign for Eagle Fern Park and the Eagle Creek Fish Hatchery. After 0.2 mile, go straight at a stop sign, now traveling on S.E. Wildcat Mountain Drive. Exactly 1.8 miles later, bear right on S.E. Eagle Fern Road. Follow this paved route for 9.1 miles, staying straight at several minor intersections, then turn right on S.E. Harvey Road. This narrow road soon turns to rough gravel with lots of lurking potholes, each with its own sinister plan to ambush your car's suspension system, so take it slow. The road travels through ugly clearcuts and past several side roads, most of which are blocked by berms. The only questionable junctions are at 1.3 miles,

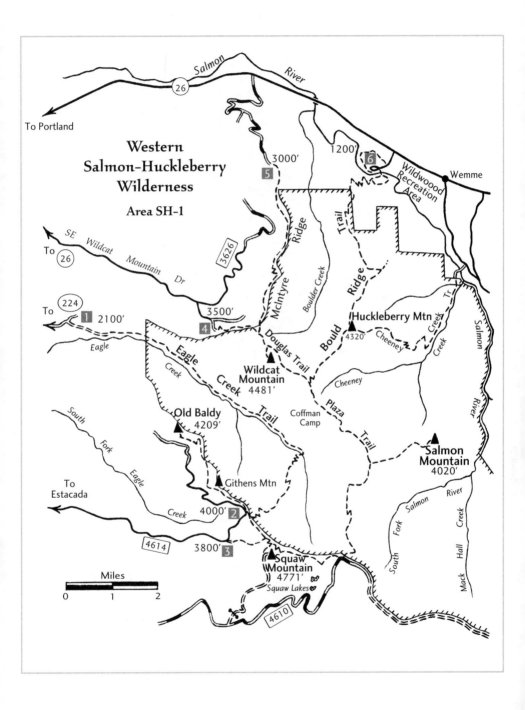

Western
Salmon-Huckleberry
Wilderness

Area SH-1

Carved wooden chair on the Eagle Creek Trail

where you bear left, and at 2.0 miles, where you go straight. Exactly 2.5 miles from the start of S.E. Harvey Road, park beside an unsigned jeep track angling down to the right. **Do not** try to drive down this "road." Your car will never forgive you.

Walk downhill on the jeep route for about 1 mile, through rather unattractive, partially cut-over woods, into the canyon of Eagle Creek. Eventually, the road narrows to a footpath, and you come to a signboard for the Eagle Creek Trail. Up to this point, you probably were wondering why anyone would consider this hike to be worthwhile, but now things dramatically improve.

From here on, you walk through an impressive old-growth rainforest, composed mostly of western hemlock and western red cedar, with hanging mosses draping from nearly every limb. Old snags and downed nurse logs provide space for young trees to grow and homes for wildlife. On the forest floor, brambles of salmonberry show off their dark pink blossoms in the spring and edible salmon-colored berries in late summer. In open areas, the ground is carpeted in May with oxalis, with its shamrock-shaped leaves and five-petaled white blossoms. On the often muddy trail, you will probably see few boot prints, but lots of dainty, crescent-shaped hoofprints of deer and the more substantial oval tracks of elk. From the forest, you will hear the raspy calls of chestnut-backed chickadees and the loud rollicking songs of winter wrens, who possess a decibel-to-body-weight ratio that would make an air horn jealous. A more soothing and constant sound comes from unseen Eagle Creek on your right. Overall, this is one of the nicest cathedral forests in our area.

The easy path makes several gentle ups and downs but never works too hard, as it wanders slowly up the canyon. Just before you reach a wooden sign announcing your entry into the Salmon-Huckleberry Wilderness, you encounter the first of many nice campsites along this trail. You splash across a dozen or so little side creeks, but never come close to Eagle Creek itself until about 3.2 miles from your car when the trail forks. The smaller path to the right goes 80 yards to a spacious creekside camp. The strikingly beautiful waters of Eagle Creek flow right past the camp as they rush over boulders and under logs spanning the flow.

This makes a very attractive and satisfactory goal, but to enjoy additional awe-inspiring forest scenery, simply go upstream as far as time and energy allow. You will discover more splashing tributary creeks, lots of big trees, a small marshy meadow, and plenty of places for quiet contemplation. Eventually, the muddy, overgrown trail crosses the creek and charges up steep, sketchy switchbacks on the ridge to the south. That part of the trail gets only spotty maintenance, however, and has few compensations for your efforts, so it can't be recommended.

Trip 2

Old Baldy

(Map Area SH-1)

Distance	Elevation Gain	Hiking Time	Optional Map	Difficulty
7.6 miles	1200'	3 to 4 hours	Green Trails–Fish Creek Mtn & Cherryville	**

Usually Open	Mid-May to October
Best Times	June and July
Agency	Estacada Ranger District (Mt. Hood National Forest)

Although the view from Old Baldy is not as dramatic as that from nearby Squaw Mountain, this old lookout site is still well worth visiting because it provides a different perspective of Mt. Hood and a fine view of the green depths of Eagle Creek Canyon, which you can't see at all from Squaw Mountain. Another big advantage of Old Baldy is that, unlike on Squaw

Mountain, you won't have to deal with noisy motorcycles disturbing the peace and quiet of your hike.

Directions: Drive 1.5 miles southeast of Estacada on State Highway 224, then turn left on Surface Road and drive 1.2 miles to a junction. Turn right on S.E. Squaw Mountain Road and climb this paved, rural route for 13 miles to where the paved road narrows to a single lane, then continue another 1.6 miles to a small pullout on the right shortly after the road begins to go downhill. There is room for only two or three cars to park here.

Pick up the trail about 10 yards north of the road pullout and turn left (northwest) on the Old Baldy Trail. For a little less than 1 mile the trail steadily ascends a ridgeline heavily wooded with hemlocks and firs, then contours around the upper slopes of small Githens Mountain. Bear right at the unsigned junction with an abandoned trail in a small opening on the western shoulder of this peak, then contour over to a saddle on the rim overlooking Eagle Creek Canyon. Trees generally hide the view, but you can catch some nice looks into the canyon and north to the area around Wildcat Mountain. Closer to your feet are the moss-covered rock formations on the edge of the dropoff.

The trail travels up and down close to the rim all the way to a high point, just before the trail turns left. For the best viewpoint on the trip, leave the trail and head cross-country for about 15 yards to a clifftop opening visible through the trees on your right. From this dramatic location you can see over the deep, forested depths of Eagle Creek Canyon and up to Mt. Hood rising in the northeast, with part of Mt. Adams visible over a shoulder of the closer volcano. From this viewpoint, the trail makes two downhill switchbacks, then goes up and down on a wooded traverse, before climbing a final time to the summit of Old Baldy. The foundations of the old lookout site are still visible to the careful observer, but trees have grown to block most of the former views.

Trip 3

Squaw Mountain

(Map Area SH-1)

Distance	Elevation Gain	Hiking Time	Optional Map	Difficulty
3.2 miles	1000'	2 hours	Green Trails–Fish Creek Mountain	**

Usually Open	Mid-May to October
Best Times	June and July
Agency	Estacada Ranger District (Mt. Hood National Forest)

Squaw Mountain is the most dramatic destination in the southwest Salmon-Huckleberry Wilderness, with expansive views extending over the heavily clearcut slopes to the south and west, and the more natural hillsides in the adjoining wilderness area to the north. At the summit of this generally overlooked little peak, you can also see distant high points, from Olallie Butte and Mt. Jefferson to the towering landmark for all of northwest Oregon, Mt. Hood. The short trail to the summit is easy enough for almost any hiker, making this one of the best viewpoint trips in our area for hikers not ready for the long, difficult climbs to other viewpoint destinations.

Directions: Drive 1.5 miles southeast of Estacada on State Highway 224, then turn left on Surface Road and drive 1.2 miles to a junction. Turn right on S.E. Squaw Mountain Road and climb this paved, rural route for 13 miles to where the paved road narrows to a single lane. Continue another 0.7 mile to where the road makes a sweeping curve to the left. Turn right on a bumpy, unsigned road that goes about 250 yards to a gravel turnaround in a clearcut. The trail, marked only with a tiny wooden sign saying 505, goes up the roadbank about 100 feet before you get to the turnaround.

The trail slowly makes its way uphill in a mountain-hemlock and noble-fir forest beside a trickling creek. The lush riparian vegetation near the water is dominated by salmonberry, with its bland-tasting, orange-colored berries, and thimbleberry, which has a more powerful red fruit. There is also an unusually high concentration of baneberry, which in midsummer features delicate clusters of white flowers. As the trail veers away from the creek, it climbs more steeply, and in July the forest opens up with lots of beargrass and beardtongue blooming.

Just before the top of a forested ridge is a junction with the Old Baldy Trail, coming in from the left. You go straight and ascend at a steady, moderate grade for 0.5 mile in dense forest to a junction in the saddle of a spur ridge that goes to the south. To reach Squaw Mountain, bear right and hike along

Mt. Hood from Squaw Mountain

the scenic, partially forested ridge for 0.3 mile to where the trail ends at a closed jeep road. Turn left and walk 100 yards up this road to the summit.

The excellent view from the rocky summit of Squaw Mountain includes the marshy Squaw Lakes to the east, hundreds of square miles of forested ridges to the south and west, and, most prominently, snow-capped Mt. Hood, which rises beautifully over the ridge to the northeast. Motorcyclists often visit Squaw Mountain by riding the closed jeep road that connects with a logging road to the south, so you may have to share this view with some noisy machines.

Trip 4

Douglas Trail

(Map Area SH-1)

Distance	Elevation Gain	Hiking Time	Optional Map	Difficulty
13.6 miles	2800'	7 to 9 hours	*Green Trails–Cherryville*	**
(with many shorter options)			*& Government Camp*	

Usually Open	June to October
Best Times	Late June to mid-July
Agency	Zigzag Ranger District (Mt. Hood National Forest)

Although this hike starts in a manmade eyesore, it soon becomes a very pleasant up-and-down ridge walk in the western part of the Salmon-Huckleberry Wilderness. Using this higher-elevation "backdoor" trailhead allows you to let your car tackle most of the uphill, avoiding the long climbs required for other viewpoint trails in this wilderness. In addition, the trail has numerous possible destinations and opportunities for a shortened trip, so people of all hiking abilities can enjoy this route. Visitors are attracted not only to the easier trail and fine views, but also to the flowers, because in early July of favorable years, the open woods here come alive with the blossoms of pink rhododendrons and white beargrass.

Directions: Drive U.S. Highway 26 for 2 miles east of Sandy, then turn south (right) on S.E. Firwood Road, where the highway makes a sweeping curve to the east. Drive this road 3.4 miles, through two intersections, to a four-way junction. Turn left here on S.E. Wildcat Mountain Drive, and climb this paved road for 9.5 miles to where it enters National Forest land and becomes a one-lane paved road. Just 0.6 mile later, turn right on an unsigned paved route and continue another 0.8 mile to a junction. You bear right and, 0.2 mile later, park at the far end of an ugly and much abused old rock quarry, now the local playground for ATV enthusiasts and target shooters. To locate the unsigned trailhead, walk about 150 feet east to an upper gravel lot and pick up the obvious trail going east into the trees.

The Douglas Trail, as this foot-and-horse path is called, immediately enters a mountain-hemlock and Douglas-fir forest, with lots of bracken fern, beargrass, and rhododendrons in the understory. Only 250 yards from the quarry, you reach the first highlight, a fine clifftop view looking south to Old Baldy and the heavily forested Eagle Creek drainage. Pinemat manzanita and ground-hugging juniper add to the scenery from this open viewpoint, as do scattered wildflowers like stonecrop.

The trail soon reenters the woods and climbs, sometimes near a generally unseen logging road on your left, to a junction with the McIntyre Ridge Trail. The signpost here is often vandalized by target shooters, and may not be standing, but the junction is obvious. For an excellent short hike, turn left here and walk 0.4 mile to an open meadow with lots of beargrass and views of Mt. Hood.

To continue with the recommended hike, go straight at the junction and climb steadily 0.5 mile to a junction with the short spur trail up Wildcat Mountain, the area's highest point. This is another excellent short destination, although the views here are blocked by brush. Those seeking more exercise should go straight at the Wildcat Mountain turnoff and begin a long descent. Partway down this ridge, you pass through a scenic rocky area with superb vistas, both south to Mt. Jefferson and north all the way to Washington's Mt. Rainier. This spot is the best turnaround point for intermediate hikers.

If you decide to push on from here, about 1.2 miles from the Wildcat Mountain turnoff, you reach the junction with the Plaza Trail, which goes sharply back to the left on its way to Huckleberry Mountain. You may consider turning left here, as Huckleberry Mountain is yet another worthy goal. Those continuing on to the final destination of Salmon Mountain should go straight at the Plaza Trail junction and descend to a long, woodsy saddle at the east end of which is comfortable Coffman Camp. This campsite is a pleasant spot to spend a quiet night in the wilderness, with water available about 200 yards down a marked trail to the north, at a muddy but reliable spring.

To continue on to Salmon Mountain, hike east from Coffman Camp, going up then down in pleasant but viewless forest, which in late August supports lots of wild blueberries with unusually large and juicy fruit. More ups and downs lead you to a final junction. To reach Salmon Mountain, turn left and follow the increasingly rugged path 1.8 miles, around a series of rock formations, to the end of the trail at a high point in the Salmon Mountain ridge. There are outstanding views here of the Salmon River Canyon and Mt. Hood, making the long hike worthwhile.

Trip 5

McIntyre Ridge

(Map Area SH-1)

Distance	Elevation Gain	Hiking Time	Optional Map	Difficulty
8.2 miles	1400'	4 hours	*Green Trails–Cherryville*	**

Usually Open	May to early November
Best Times	Mid-June to mid-July
Agency	Zigzag Ranger District (Mt. Hood National Forest)

If you are forced to select a single ridge walk in the Salmon-Huckleberry Wilderness, this should be the one. All the ridges have fine views, most have good flowers, and many provide plenty of solitude, but McIntyre Ridge has arguably the best of all three. With a location on the western edge of the wilderness, this ridge allows you to see not only ever-present Mt. Hood, but also familiar features in the Willamette Valley that are not visible from the other ridges. The meadows here are better as well, with superior displays of beargrass that fill the meadows with tall white blossoms in favorable years. Since the trailhead is higher, it requires a lot less sweat to reach the highlights here than on most other trails. Despite all these attributes, relatively few Portland-area hikers take this trail, perhaps because the access road is a bit bumpy and poorly signed.

Directions: Take U.S. Highway 26 east from Sandy about 11 miles to milepost 36 and turn right (south) on E. Wildcat Creek Road. If it helps to have a landmark, this turnoff is right next to a large brown-and-white sign that says MT. HOOD RECREATIONAL AREA—WELCOME. Climb this narrow and sometimes rough gravel road 2.1 miles, past several unsigned junctions with blocked-off side roads, to a major junction. You go straight, staying on E. Wildcat Creek Road, and drive another 2 miles to a clearcut at roadend. There is no trail sign immediately in view, and parking is limited.

Several confusing ATV trails head off in various directions from the end of the road. To find the hiking trail, follow the motorcycle tracks to the southeast corner of the old clearcut, where you will see a sign for the McIntyre Ridge Trail in the uncut trees just beyond the clearing. Blessedly, the trail immediately enters wilderness land, so you quickly leave the noisy machines behind.

Since you are starting at a fairly high elevation, you skip the usual western-hemlock and western red-cedar forests, and start immediately in a forest dominated by mountain hemlock, noble fir, and, as always, Douglas-fir.

In June and July, these forests come alive with the pink blossoms of Pacific rhododendron.

The gently-graded trail does quite a bit of up and down, but manages to slowly gain elevation, staying mostly in the forests. After 1.5 miles, you ascend consistently for about 0.5 mile to reach the first of McIntyre Ridge's fine meadow viewpoints. The most memorable vista, as always, is looking east to Mt. Hood.

Although it is a worthwhile spot for a rest stop, don't turn around at this first viewpoint, because better rewards lie ahead. The trail moves inland a bit and climbs steadily, in a half dozen small switchbacks, to the edge of a much larger meadow, which is filled with the tough, grassy leaves and tall white blossoms of beargrass. Not every year is graced with good beargrass displays—because the individual plants bloom in two- and three-year cycles—but in off years, other flowers take up the slack, especially lavender cliff penstemon, yellow lomatium and stonecrop, and blue lupine and larkspur.

This meadow, which in addition to flowers has a first-rate view of Mt. Hood, is a worthwhile destination all by itself, but it's hard to stop here. To see more, your first challenge is to find the right trail. The meadow has a couple of confusing unsigned junctions that have obviously led many hikers astray. The proper route goes to the right on what is initially a rather faint path. Soon it gets more distinct and climbs through the trees to a final meadow that is the largest of all. Beargrass is even more abundant here, and the views are truly superb, featuring not just Mt. Hood, looming impressively over Huckleberry Mountain to the east, but also west to Portland and the farm country of the Willamette Valley. Bring a sack lunch to enjoy this spot in style.

Adventurous hikers can continue this hike another mile to a junction with the Douglas Trail (Trip 4). From here, you can turn left and climb to a junction with a short side trail that leads to the summit of Wildcat Mountain. The viewpoint here is higher than the one on McIntyre Ridge, but trees obscure most of it, so it's not really an improvement and is beneficial only for more exercise.

Trip 6

Huckleberry Mountain

(Map Area SH-1)

Distance	Elevation Gain	Hiking Time	Optional Map	Difficulty
10.5 miles	3100'	5 to 7 hours	*Green Trails–Government Camp*	***

Usually Open	Late May to October
Best Times	Mid-June to mid-July
Agency	Zigzag Ranger District (Mt. Hood National Forest)

Like most of the ridge walks in the Salmon-Huckleberry Wilderness, the long trail up Huckleberry Mountain provides both good exercise and fine views from the summit. From the small, rocky meadows at the top, you can take in a vista that includes not only snowpeaks like Mounts Jefferson, St. Helens, and nearby Hood, but also the rapidly growing developments around the towns of Wemme and Zigzag, and a whole array of ridges and lower summits spread out in every direction. Tiny wildflowers at your feet are a perfect small-scale complement to the large-scale views.

Directions: Drive U.S. Highway 26 east toward Mt. Hood and turn right, into the Wildwood Recreation Site, just past milepost 39. You must pay a day-use fee when you enter. Park in the lot for the picnic area after about 0.5 mile.

The trail begins on the north side of the restrooms and immediately crosses the rushing Salmon River on a long bridge. On the far side of the bridge is a fork with a nature-trail loop, where you turn right and follow the river downstream. The path wanders on the level through a shady forest of red alder and Douglas-fir, passes a junction with the upper portion of the nature-trail loop, then veers away from the river and begins to climb.

The first part of the climb is a series of switchbacks and traverses that combine to steadily, but not overly steeply, lead you up a forested hillside. The route levels off a bit after about 1.7 miles, where you briefly follow a long-abandoned logging road. Near the start of this section, you are treated to a good view of Mt. Hood and Hunchback Mountain. In June the forests host lots of Pacific rhododendron covered with pink blossoms. In early July, the open areas come alive with foxglove, daisy, beargrass, iris, and other wildflowers.

You enter the wilderness at the 2-mile point in your hike, shortly after which you make two quick switchbacks and climb to a ridgecrest saddle. A short side trail leads to a second good view that extends over the same scene as before, but it is improved by the added elevation. Now you work southeast, ascending along a narrow ridge. At one point you gain an excellent perspective to the west of Wildcat Mo untain, McIntyre Ridge, and trailless Boulder Creek Valley.

After more climbing, you leave the ridgetop and cross a north-facing slope with a small, trickling creek, before coming to another saddle and an unsigned junction. To the left, an unmaintained path leads down toward private property. Your route goes right and climbs a ridge overgrown with beargrass for a final 1 mile to the rocky meadows at the high point of Huckleberry Mountain.

There is another way up Huckleberry Mountain, which follows the Cheeney Creek Trail from an unsigned trailhead south of Welches. While this is a very interesting and attractive route, in order to take it, you have to park a mile or more away and walk in. The private landowners near the trailhead are in a dispute with the Forest Service about public access and are adamant about not allowing anyone to park nearby. They have even been known to enforce their view with tow trucks. An easier option, with no parking problems, is to use the Douglas Trail from the west (Trip 4). To reach Huckleberry Mountain, just turn north at a junction with the Plaza Trail a little after you pass Wildcat Mountain.

Salmon-Huckleberry Area

Area SH-2: Central Salmon-Huckleberry Wilderness

The central part of the Salmon-Huckleberry Wilderness is the most accessible and popular part of this large wild area, and it features the most dramatic canyon scenery. The centerpiece is the Salmon River Canyon, where the wilderness' namesake stream flows through a spectacular 3000-foot-deep forested chasm and tumbles over a series of waterfalls. These waterfalls are guarded by cliffs and rocky hillsides that make them virtually inaccessible to the average hiker, but the view from the trail is easily reward enough for making the hike. Less crowded trails explore a variety of environments around the central canyon, from high viewpoints at former lookout sites to quiet old-growth forests at low elevations. Best of all, every trail has easy road access on generally good paved roads.

Trip 1

Old Salmon River Trail

(Map Area SH-2)

Distance	Elevation Gain	Hiking Time	Optional Map	Difficulty
5.2 miles	150'	2.5 hours	*Green Trails–Government Camp*	*

Usually Open	All year
Best Times	April to November
Agency	Zigzag Ranger District (Mt. Hood National Forest)

Stately old-growth forests and a beautiful clear river are the highlights of this easy hike, which is suitable for children and usually open all year. Another nice feature is that there is no bad season for this stroll, as the scenery changes little from month to month. Anglers should note that this portion of the Salmon River is managed as a catch-and-release trout stream, and fishing for salmon or steelhead is prohibited.

Directions: Take U.S. Highway 26 to the town of Zigzag and turn south onto E. Salmon River Road, just west of the junction with the E. Lolo Pass Road. Follow this paved route for 2.7 miles to the marked lower trailhead for the Old Salmon River Trail, at a pullout on the right.

The trail wastes no time in plunging down through old-growth western-hemlock and western red-cedar forests. The dense forests provide plenty of shade, making this a pleasantly cool trip even on the hottest summer day. The canopy of magnificent old trees helps to make rainy winter days more comfortable as you hike beneath a natural umbrella.

In the darkness below the trees, the forest floor is covered with oxalis and sword fern, while mosses drape from every tree limb. As you travel upstream, the trail sometimes approaches the road, so you may see or hear cars, but the murmuring "river music" and the calls of dippers dominate throughout the hike. The gentle path never does much up or down, and it uses quaint little plank bridges to cross tiny tributary creeks.

You drop down to the banks of the rushing Salmon River, then turn south and begin the gentle upstream walk. Along the way, the trail passes several short side trails to the river that are all worth taking and often lead to excellent riverside campsites. Several short spur routes also go left up to the road if you want to shorten the hike. The forest and river scenery doesn't change much as you hike, but it is so pleasant you wouldn't really want it to. At the 1.5-mile point the trail intersects and follows the road shoulder for 200 yards

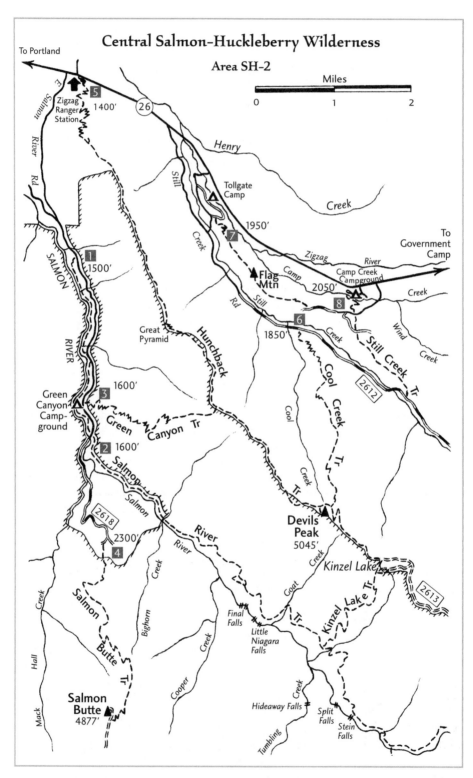

Central Salmon-Huckleberry Wilderness

Area SH-2

Miles

0   1   2

To Portland

E. Salmon River Rd.

⑤ 1400'
Zigzag Ranger Station

㉖

Henry Creek

Still Creek

Tollgate Camp △ 1950'

⑦

To Government Camp

Zigzag River

Camp Creek Campground ⚠

① 1500'

SALMON RIVER

Great Pyramid

Hunchback

Flag Mtn ▲ 2050'

⑧

Still Rd.

⑥ 1850'

Cool Creek

Still Creek Tr 2612

Wind Creek

③ 1600'

Green Canyon Campground △

Green Canyon Tr

Cool Creek Tr

② 1600'

Salmon

Salmon

2618

2300'

④

Salmon River

River

Bighorn Creek

Devils Peak 5045'

Cool Creek Tr

Goat Creek Tr

Kinzel Lake

Kinzel Lake Tr

2613

Salmon Butte Tr

Hall Creek

Mack Creek

Cooper Creek

Final Falls

Little Niagara Falls

Salmon Butte ▲ 4877'

Hideaway Falls

Tumbling Creek

Split Falls

Stein Falls

before returning to the riverside forests in a stand of bigleaf maple and red alder. Above this you enjoy more of the same river-and-forest scenery for the next 0.5 mile, until you come to Green Canyon Campground. Staying near the river, you skirt around the campground, then go 0.4 mile further to a reunion with the road, just below the large parking lot for the Salmon River Trail.

Trip 2

Salmon River Canyon

(Map Area SH-2)

Distance	Elevation Gain	Hiking Time	Optional Map	Difficulty
7.2 miles (to canyon viewpoint)	900'	3 to 4 hours	*Green Trails–Government Camp & High Rock*	**

Usually Open	March to December
Best Times	May
Agency	Zigzag Ranger District (Mt. Hood National Forest)

The Salmon River Canyon is the scenic highlight of the Salmon-Huckleberry Wilderness and has been a popular hiking destination for decades. The first couple of miles of this trail travel through one of the best old-growth forests in our region, staying close to the banks of the river.

After this, the trail traverses steep, forested slopes, well above a string of spectacular waterfalls that are inaccessible to all but the most daring adventurers equipped with ropes and, frankly, not much common sense. But, you don't have to be a risk taker to enjoy this hike, because even the main trail provides outstanding scenery, including sloping meadows that allow hikers plenty of great views and a memorable outdoor adventure.

Directions: Take U.S. Highway 26 to the town of Zigzag and turn south onto E. Salmon River Road, just west of the junction with the E. Lolo Pass Road. Follow this paved route for a 5.0 miles to a large gravel parking area on the left, just before a bridge over the Salmon River.

The trail begins beside a prominent sign on the east side of the road, then works its way upstream on the Douglas-fir-covered slopes above the water. After curving down to a viewpoint above a large, deep pool in the river, you wander lazily through an exceptionally impressive old-growth forest of massive Douglas-fir, western red cedar, and western hemlock. Moss hangs from the limbs and covers the trunks of these old giants, while ferns and new young trees grow up out of nurse logs, where some of the trees have succumbed to time and blown down onto the forest floor.

The forest continues to inspire awe as you keep working upstream, passing many glassy pools, small rapids, and quiet riffles in the clear waters of the river. After about 2 miles, you come to Rolling Riffle Camp, below the trail on the right, which is a popular spot for families on summer weekends. Please camp only in the designated sites, to avoid damaging the land.

Shortly after this camp, the trail pulls away from the water and climbs at a gentle but steady grade up the hillside north of the river. You cross several small tributary creeks along the way, allowing you to douse your head if the weather gets too hot for comfort. The trees are smaller now, as these slopes are less protected than the river-level flats, and are subject to periodic wind and fire.

Shortly after climbing out of a good-sized side canyon, the trail splits and a short, pebble-strewn loop path bears to the right, out to an open, meadowy slope with outstanding views up the canyon. Almost 600 feet below, the river cascades in the depths of the cliff-walled chasm. This is a rewarding turn-around spot that provides hikers with the best canyon view on the trip.

If you are continuing up the canyon, return to the main trail and look for several short scramble paths dropping to the right in the next few tenths of a mile. These routes lead to stunning overlooks of towering Final and Frustration falls on the main stem of the river, but the paths are *extremely* steep, and the small rocks on the tread make the route slippery and much too dangerous for anyone who isn't quite experienced and sure-footed. People have fallen off and died in accidents from these cliffs, so take these warnings seriously!

Most dayhikers turn around here, but really athletic types, and those making this into a backpacking adventure, can continue up the canyon. You traverse, generally on the level, to a camp at Goat Creek, then gradually ascend to a junction with the Kinzel Lake Trail. Here you have a choice. You can stick with the Salmon River Trail, which climbs gradually up this lovely, forested canyon all the way to the upper trailhead south of Trillium Lake, or you can turn left on the Kinzel Lake Trail.

The latter path climbs steeply for 2 miles to the primitive car campground at tiny Kinzel Lake, where you meet the Hunchback Trail. Turn west on this path and follow it past Devils Peak and down to a saddle where you meet the Green Canyon Trail. You can then descend on this trail to the E. Salmon River Road just 0.3 mile north of your car. The total length of this difficult loop trip is 15.7 miles.

Trip 3

Green Canyon Trail

(Map Area SH-2)

Distance	Elevation Gain	Hiking Time	Optional Map	Difficulty
5.6 miles (to highest viewpoint)	2200'	3 hours	*Green Trails–Government Camp*	***

☁

Usually Open	Mid-May to October
Best Times	June
Agency	Zigzag Ranger District (Mt. Hood National Forest)

Starting from the green depths of the Salmon River Canyon, the Green Canyon Trail climbs a woodsy hillside all the way up to the ridge between Hunchback Mountain and Devils Peak. The Forest Service reopened this old route in the mid-1980s, to give hikers access to long loop options on the Hunchback and Salmon River trails, but the path is worth hiking all by itself. The forests are just as enjoyable in cloudy weather as in the sun, but blue skies are preferable near the top, if you want to enjoy the fine view from there.

Directions: Take U.S. Highway 26 to the town of Zigzag and turn south onto E. Salmon River Road, just west of the junction with the E. Lolo Pass Road. Follow this paved route about 4.7 miles to Green Canyon Campground. Directly opposite the campground entrance road, look for a small brown sign for the Green Canyon Trail. Turn into the campground and immediately park in a small lot on the left side of the entrance road.

The trail starts by crossing a low-lying area of dense shrubbery, under a canopy of old-growth bigleaf maple, western red cedar, and western hemlock, with mosses hanging from nearly every limb. Relatively few birds live in the darkness of this dense forest. Two lively singers who do seem to thrive in this habitat are the winter wren and the chestnut-backed chickadee, which both fill the green depths with their rollicking songs.

The path gradually leaves the rainforest by curving off to the right, then switchbacking to the left, and making a long traverse up the hillside. Douglas-firs are added to the mix of trees as you climb, and the ground cover is now mostly vanilla leaf, sword fern, Oregon grape, and oxalis with its shamrock-shaped leaves.

The trail makes a series of 15 uphill switchbacks, mostly in forest, but with a couple of small, steep meadows that are home to flowers and some

Overlook near top of Green Canyon Trail

twisted oak trees. Because the uphill is fairly steep, and the tread quite narrow, it is not open to horses.

After this first set of switchbacks, you turn left and follow the top of a minor ridge, then traverse the steep left side of the ridge. When you come to a second ridge, there is a small opening with a nice view up to Devils Peak. From this viewpoint, you go up and down along the spine of this little ridge, then move to its left side and begin switchbacking again.

At the last of eight switchbacks that take you nearly to the top of the final ridge, there is a junction with an unsigned use path that goes straight for 50 yards to a small, rocky overlook. From this dramatic viewpoint, you can see Salmon Butte and other nearby forested ridges, but the best view is down into the green depths of the Salmon River Canyon, over 2000 feet below. The impressive scene is enhanced by the many flowers that live here, including lots of larkspur, paintbrush, and a particularly beautiful pink penstemon.

This viewpoint is the recommended stopping point, because it is a long way to the next highlight along this route. However, if you are interested in a long, rugged dayhike or backpacking loop, you can continue through open forest along a ridge for 0.6 mile to a junction with the Hunchback Trail. Turn right here and wander up and down (mostly up) for 2.4 miles to Devils Peak, then continue 1.6 miles to the isolated car campground at tiny Kinzel Lake. From here, you descend a rather steep, switchbacking trail, down to the Salmon River Trail, where you turn right and walk back on this popular path to the road just 0.3 mile from the Green Canyon trailhead.

Trip 4

Salmon Butte

(Map Area SH-2)

Distance	Elevation Gain	Hiking Time	Optional Map	Difficulty
8.6 miles	2800'	4 to 5 hours	*Green Trails–Government Camp*	***
			& High Rock	

Usually Open	June to late October
Best Times	Mid- to- late June
Agency	Zigzag Ranger District (Mt. Hood National Forest)

There are two types of hikes in the Salmon-Huckleberry Wilderness: canyon routes that follow cascading streams; and viewpoint excursions that start in deep woods and climb to ridgetop vistas. The Salmon Butte Trail is among the best of the latter type. This hike has one big advantage over other viewpoint options, because the trail is never steep and it follows an even, gentle grade throughout. That said, it's still a 2800-foot climb, so be prepared for some exercise.

Directions: Take U.S. Highway 26 to the town of Zigzag and turn south onto E. Salmon River Road just west of the junction with E. Lolo Pass Road. Follow this paved route 5 miles to a bridge over the Salmon River, then continue straight on a gravel road 1.7 miles to a small pullout on the left and an easily overlooked brown sign pointing to the Salmon Butte Trail.

Start by hiking 0.1 mile on an old road that is rapidly being encroached upon by young cedar, Douglas-fir, western hemlock, and vine maple. This road ends at an old parking area where the Salmon Butte Trail veers to the left and becomes a true footpath. The trail climbs through an old clearcut, now so overgrown it's hard to tell it ever was one, except for the universally young age of the trees. You'll know when you leave the old clearcut, because the trees get taller and the canopy thicker. The deep shade of this old-growth forest leaves the ground largely devoid of undergrowth, but there are lots of old downed trees that require a winding route to avoid.

The climb remains gradual as you go up a woodsy hillside. You round a ridge at a small rocky meadow, with decent views of the forested ridge of Salmon Mountain to the west. The undergrowth becomes thicker as you ascend another hillside that boasts a particular abundance of rhododendrons, which are covered with showy pink blossoms in mid-to-late June, the ideal time for this hike. A series of six moderately graded, but irregularly spaced, switchbacks takes you to a tantalizing ridgetop view, where you can see the top half of Mt. Hood.

Now you follow the ascending ridge through a tunnel of conifers, with beargrass lining the trail as you climb. Five more switchbacks take you to a junction with a long-abandoned jeep road. Turn right here and follow this rocky track another 0.3 mile to the open summit of Salmon Butte, a former lookout site that still sports the fine views typical of such locations. Mt. Hood, of course, dominates the skyline to the north-by-northeast, but you can also spot Mt. Adams in Washington, and look south to Olallie Butte and Mt. Jefferson. On very clear days you can even see the Three Sisters in the distance, to the south.

Trip 5

Hunchback Mountain

(Map Area SH-2)

Distance	Elevation Gain	Hiking Time	Optional Map	Difficulty
4 to 9 miles	1600 to 2900'	2 to 6 hours	*Green Trails–Government Camp*	***

Usually Open	Mid-May to October
Best Times	June
Agency	Zigzag Ranger District (Mt. Hood National Forest)

Forested Hunchback Mountain rises sharply from the lowlands around Zigzag and extends to the southeast like a 6-mile-long green finger. Along the way, several knuckles and warts rise up, providing high viewpoints for hikers on the Hunchback Trail. The long, generally lonesome trail has very easy road access and follows the entire length of this prominent ridge, providing hikers with both exercise and good views.

Directions: Drive U.S. Highway 26 to the east end of Zigzag and turn right into the Zigzag Ranger Station, almost exactly opposite the intersection with E. Lolo Pass Road. Park in the portion of the large lot just east of the ranger station that is specifically marked for trail users.

The trail starts in the lush Douglas-fir, western red-cedar, and western-hemlock forests that are so typical of our region. The forest floor is dominated by five different species of fern: ground-hugging deer fern; the delicate fronds of maiden-hair and lady fern; and 3-and 4-foot-tall bracken and sword fern. Almost immediately the trail begins climbing up to the first switchback, next to a rock wall that holds back the flow of an insignificant trickle of cool water. Beyond this rocky cistern, three more switchbacks take you to a short downhill section. You will need the respite this provides, as the next 14 switchbacks become increasingly steep.

During the first part of this climb, you hear the sounds of traffic speeding by on Highway 26. By the time you near the top of the ridge, these sounds are only a memory, and bird song and breezes are all that you will hear. The thinning soils and harsher environment gradually cause the forests to become more open. Rhododendron, beargrass, and salal are the dominant cover species. After finally topping the ridge and walking around the right side of a little knob, look for a side trail that heads left, back to a viewpoint atop the knob. This view of the Zigzag Valley and a tiny part of the top of Mt. Hood is enough for many hikers, who turn back here, fully satisfied.

To continue to higher viewpoints, stick with the Hunchback Trail as it becomes much more rugged, with lots of steep uphills and some downhills, always staying at or near the jagged, rocky ridgecrest. About 0.5 mile from the knob, you pass another possible turnaround point, at an excellent viewpoint on the spine of the ridge. This view features an unusually good perspective of the many ridges and highpoints in the Salmon-Huckleberry Wilderness to the south and west. Most notable are Huckleberry Mountain, the Cheeney Creek Valley, Salmon Butte, and Salmon Mountain. Colorful cliff penstemon, stonecrop, saxifrage, yarrow, and paintbrush grow amid the rocks.

Those who want still more views and exercise should push on, climbing steeply in forests to a signed 100-yard spur trail that goes to VIEWPOINT ROCKPILE. The name itself is an adequate description, although it is also worth mentioning that this particular pile of large rocks supports a population of pikas and provides the best views of Mt. Hood on this hike. Back on the main Hunchback Trail, you make a final short climb, then begin a long stretch of gentle hiking. For the next mile, the trail either stays level or makes a gentle ascent, passing through a dense forest with little or no ground cover. Views are blocked by trees, but the hiking is easy and pleasant. As the ridge begins to narrow again, you come to another signed, but sketchy, spur trail to VIEWPOINT HELISPOT 260. The views here are partly blocked by growing trees, but they are worth a look.

After this viewpoint junction, both the ridge and the trail get much narrower and rougher, with many short, steep ups and downs. The path stays mostly on the east side of the ridge, but for one extended stretch, it follows a 2-foot-wide rocky catwalk right along the spine. After a final steep climb, you reach a viewless highpoint and the trail turns right. If you go downhill on the main trail another 150 yards, you reach a final viewpoint spur trail, this one to Great Pyramid. This rocky viewpoint has trees blocking most directions, but it provides good vistas southeast to Devils Peak.

With a car shuttle you can make a long one-way adventure out of this hike. Just continue north over the steep ups and downs along Hunchback Ridge, then take either the Green Canyon Trail (Trip 3) or the Cool Creek Trail down from Devils Peak (Trip 6).

Mt. Hood from Cool Creek Trail below Devils Peak

Trip 6

Devils Peak

(Map Area SH-2)

Distance	Elevation Gain	Hiking Time	Optional Map	Difficulty
8.0 miles	3200'	4.5 to 6 hours	*Green Trails–Government Camp*	***

Usually Open	June to October
Best Times	June
Agency	Zigzag Ranger District (Mt. Hood National Forest)

The logic behind place names is sometimes hard to understand. Consider the Cool Creek Trail to the top of Devils Peak. Far from being evil, beautiful Devils Peak is the perfect sort of place to eat your lunch and marvel at God's handiwork. The Cool Creek Trail is another example. The long climb is anything but cool, and you never even get close to a creek. But, putting aside confusing names, this is a highly enjoyable hike, if you are up for the challenge of a substantial elevation gain.

Directions: Drive 1.4 miles east of Zigzag on U.S. Highway 26, then turn right on paved Still Creek Road. After 0.1 mile, you bear right at a confusing fork. Follow the single-lane paved road another 2.8 miles, to the end of pavement.

Almost 0.5 mile later, look carefully in the trees on the right for a small brown sign for the Cool Creek Trail. Park in a small pullout on the left, about 50 yards west of the trailhead.

The trail starts in a dense low-elevation forest of old-growth western hemlock and western red cedar, with lots of lush moss, deer fern, oxalis, delicate lady fern, and other ground-level species covering the forest floor. It is all very attractive, but a bit daunting, since you know that before the day is done you must climb from this low-elevation forest all the way up to a high-elevation environment. The path wastes no time in accomplishing this feat, foregoing a gentle warm-up in favor of an immediately steep ascent.

Not far from the trailhead, you pass through dense thickets of salal, which, surprisingly, is mixed with beargrass. Normally you don't encounter beargrass until much higher elevations, but on this shady, north-facing slope, the plant survives at elevations below 2000 feet.

After briefly following the spine of a minor ridge, you make an uphill traverse to the left and climb a series of short switchbacks to an opening in the forest. The sloping, open hillside looks like it has been selectively logged, which, in a way, it has. In this case, however, the selecting was done not by man but by natural avalanches and windstorms that toppled many of the trees. The result is a hillside with sparse forests, lots of June-blooming rhododendrons, and your first good views on the hike. From this slope, you can look north to the low, forested ridge of Flag Mountain, further north to higher Zigzag Mountain, and above them both to glacier-clad Mt. Hood.

After switchbacking up this slope, you traverse to the right and cross a seasonal trickle, which is your only chance to cool off by dousing your head.

Continuing uphill, the grade eases off somewhat as you enter a quiet, mid-elevation forest, with lots of 100-foot-high hemlocks, 8-foot-high rhododendrons, 3-foot-high huckleberries, and 6-inch-high bunchberries filling all the levels of this ecosystem.

The trail steadily, but no longer very steeply, ascends through these peaceful woods for about 0.5 mile, then climbs a few steep switchbacks. At the top of these switchbacks is a tiny cairn and an unsigned junction with an abandoned section of trail. Here you turn right and resume the gradual climb.

Lookout atop Devils Peak

The trees get smaller as you get higher. The dominant species are now mountain hemlock and Pacific silver and noble fir. The final 0.5 mile is up a slowly narrowing rocky ridge, with some excellent views of Mt. Hood. In addition to views, the rocky meadows support a good variety of wildflowers, including wallflower, paintbrush, lomatium, larkspur, phlox, and purple penstemon.

The climb ends at a junction with the Hunchback Trail, where you turn right. Walk about 100 yards on this trail, then turn left at a junction and walk a short spur trail to the top of Devils Peak.

The weather-beaten fire-lookout building at the summit is no longer used for fire detection, but it is kept open as a historic structure and a shelter for backpackers. Views are pretty good from the lookout building, but growing trees now obstruct many of the best vistas. Views of Mt. Hood are actually better from the ridge below. Perhaps the best views from the top are looking south to rounded Olallie Butte and pointy Mt. Jefferson.

Trip 7

Flag Mountain

(Map Area SH-2)

Distance	Elevation Gain	Hiking Time	Optional Map	Difficulty
4.4 miles	1200'	2 hours	*Green Trails–Government Camp*	**

Usually Open	Mid-March to November
Best Times	Mid-March to June
Agency	Zigzag Ranger District (Mt. Hood Nat Forest)

Although mostly a forest walk, the rarely-traveled Flag Mountain Trail includes at least one good viewpoint that is an ideal lunch spot. Another benefit of this trip is that the stiff climb in the first mile ensures that you'll get a good workout, despite this hike's short distance.

Directions: Drive U.S. Highway 26 east from Zigzag for 2 miles to the east end of the tiny town of Rhododendron. Turn right on poorly-signed Road 20, a narrow paved route that begins in a tunnel of large trees. Stay on this road for 1.7 miles, past several driveways to summer homes, then turn left on gravel Road 20-E. About 50 yards later, look on your right for a small sign for the Flag Mountain Trail. There is room for about three cars to park on the left side of the road.

This quiet path starts in a typical, low-elevation forest of western hemlock and western red cedar, with an abundance of sword fern, salal, and Oregon grape on the forest floor. You immediately pass two summer homes, then steeply ascend a woodsy hillside in four switchbacks. You'll hear the sounds of traffic on Highway 26 as you climb, but the cars are out of sight and not overly intrusive. When you top the ridge for the first time, solid forest breaks briefly at a tiny rock outcropping, providing decent views of Hunchback Mountain to the southwest.

Despite never escaping the sounds of Highway 26, the character of this trail remains very wild, as you make an often steep climb along the mountain's camelback ridge. The steep sections are mixed with welcome level bits, until you reach the top, at a fine viewpoint. Here, you get a good perspective of the deep-green Zigzag Valley, Enola Hill, West Zigzag Mountain, and snowy Mt. Hood, which towers over the green ridges. The shrubbery near the summit includes not only the salal and sword ferns from below, but a smattering of such mid-elevation favorites as manzanita and Pacific rhododendron.

This view is the highlight of the hike, but for more exercise you can continue east on the trail as it makes some gently graded ups and downs along the viewless ridge. The last 0.6 mile is nearly all downhill, and you lose about 300 feet in a straightforward descent, to a trailhead on an isolated gravel road.

Trip 8

Still Creek Trail

(Map Area SH-2)

Distance	Elevation Gain	Hiking Time	Optional Map	Difficulty
3.2 miles	300′	2 hours	*Green Trails–Government Camp*	*

Usually Open	March to December
Best Times	April
Agency	Zigzag Ranger District (Mt. Hood National Forest)

There is something very soothing about walking through an old-growth forest, and the Still Creek Trail amply demonstrates why. This classic and easy ramble takes you through a quiet cathedral forest with all the lush greenery, deep shade, and impressively large trees that make hiking in our area so good. This is a perfect choice for hikers who want an easy leg-stretcher on a day when the skies are gloomy or the higher Mt. Hood trails are still covered with snow.

Directions: Drive U.S. Highway 26 about 4.8 miles east of Zigzag and turn right into the Camp Creek Campground. After 0.1 mile, you turn right on the campground road and drive to the turnaround at the west end. There is room for two cars, directly across from a large pedestrian bridge over the creek.

You begin the hike by crossing the bridge and immediately turning left on the Still Creek Trail. From here, you wander upstream beside the clear water of rollicking Camp Creek, where you can look and listen for gray-colored dippers zipping above the water, and even diving into it, to feed on insect larvae and other prey. The creek's banks are overgrown with a beautiful mix of western hemlock, Douglas-fir, western red cedar, and Pacific yew, with long strands of moss hanging from every limb.

The path switchbacks away from the creek and takes you through more old-growth woods, whose shady canopy provides nice cool temperatures even on hot summer days. In April, the forest floor is brightened by the white blossoms of trillium. You cross an unobtrusive one-lane paved road, then wander at an uneven but mostly level grade through a forest of big old trees, to a crossing of a more primitive dirt road.

From here, you travel through denser woods, then slowly leave the big trees. You then cross a steeper hillside, where you will hear the splashing of Still Creek, below you on the right. The open forest here is home to perky chestnut-backed chickadees, which break the quiet with their raspy calls. One or two partial openings in the forest allow you to glimpse heavily wooded Hunchback Ridge to the southwest, but this remains basically a forest ramble. The last 0.2 mile drops about 150 feet to a poorly signed trailhead on gravelly Still Creek Road. For a good lunch spot, cross the road and drop to an unofficial car campsite beside lovely Still Creek. Return the way you came.

The author on the Still Creek Trail near Zigzag

Salmon-Huckleberry Area

Area SH-3: Eastern Salmon-Huckleberry Wilderness

The remote eastern edge of the Salmon-Huckleberry Wilderness hides some of the quietest trails in the Mt. Hood area. Just a few minutes drive from crowded Government Camp, these little-known paths explore open forests, pretty meadows, and clear streams. Those trails lack the spectacular appeal of nearby alpine hikes, but they are easy and fun to travel. Campers at busy Trillium Lake should consider these trails when they want to escape the lake's overcrowded shores and enjoy some of God's peace and quiet.

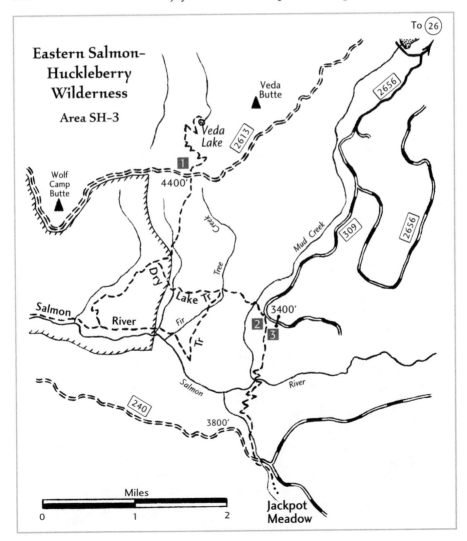

Trip 1

Veda Lake

(Map Area SH-3)

Distance	Elevation Gain	Hiking Time	Optional Map	Difficulty
2.8 miles	750'	1.5 to 2 hours	*Green Trails–Government Camp & High Rock*	**

Usually Open	Mid-June to October
Best Times	July / late August
Agency	Zigzag Ranger District (Mt. Hood National Forest)

In 1917, two locals named Vern Rogers and Dave Donaldson took it upon themselves to pack in a load of trout to a small, unnamed lake south of Government Camp, probably hoping to create a private fishing hole. Much to their surprise, their efforts garnered them a sort of immortality. To honor their achievement, the local forest ranger named the lake by combining the first two letters of each man's first name.

The offspring of the original fish can still be caught today. On their way to the lake's shores, visitors can also enjoy fine views of nearby Mt. Hood. All in all, this makes for a short but very satisfying little hike, well worth the lousy road access to the trailhead.

Directions: Take U.S. Highway 26 about 0.7 mile east of Government Camp, then turn south on the road to Still Creek Campground. Drive through the

Veda Lake

276

campground for another 0.7 mile, then keep straight at a junction where the campground loop road goes left. Following signs for Trillium Lake, you drive south on a pothole-filled gravel road for 0.4 mile to a junction where you turn right onto E. Chimney Rock Road.

This road goes past several private cabins for 0.4 mile to a four-way junction. You go straight on Forest Road 2613 and **slow down** because this soon becomes a miserably rutted and bumpy dirt road. After 3.7 carefully-negotiated miles, pull into a poorly marked parking area on the left, just opposite the trailhead.

The trail starts on the north side of the road next to a small brown sign, then climbs in a forest of Pacific silver fir and mountain hemlock. Tall red huckleberry bushes crowd the forest and provide a treat for the taste buds in late August. After gaining about 250 feet, you top a viewless ridge, then begin to gradually descend. About 200 yards later, you reach an excellent viewpoint of Mt. Hood, almost perfectly framed by the forested valley of Still Creek, with round Veda Lake sparkling in the basin directly below.

You switchback down past three more good viewpoints, at openings that provide sunshine for early-to-mid July wildflowers like lupine, paintbrush, beargrass, arnica, and showy Washington lily. The final descent is made on one long switchback down a partly forested hillside to the north shore of 3-acre Veda Lake. Ever since Vern and Dave stocked this lake, it has produced catchable brook trout. If fishing isn't your goal, the lake is also a good place to swim, camp, or just relax and enjoy a peaceful mountain setting.

Trip 2

Upper Salmon River Loop

(Map Area SH-3)

Distance	Elevation Gain	Hiking Time	Optional Map	Difficulty
5.9 miles	1200'	3 hours	*Green Trails–High Rock*	**

Usually Open	May to October
Best Times	May to October
Agency	Zigzag Ranger District (Mt. Hood National Forest)

Unlike the famous lower portion of the Salmon River Trail (Area SH-2, Trip 2) the upper part of this canyon has no waterfalls and no spectacular views, but it's also a lot less crowded. Solitude seekers come here not only for the quiet, but also to explore pretty side creeks and interesting, diverse forests that hikers on the lower trail miss.

Directions: Drive 1.8 miles east of Government Camp on U.S. Highway 26, then turn right (south) at the Trillium Lake junction. Follow paved Forest Road 2656 for 1.7 miles, passing the lake's campground and day-use area, to a junction near the southeast corner of the lake. You bear left, staying on Road 2656, and after 1.1 miles, you will come to a fork where you bear right. The pavement ends as you continue on a good gravel road for 0.7 mile to another fork. Bear right once again on Forest Road 309 and drive a final 2.0 miles to a trailhead sign. Park on the shoulder of the road about 20 yards past the sign.

 Two trails depart from this trailhead. For this loop, take the Salmon River Trail, which starts about 15 yards west of the parking area, off of a turnaround loop road.

This hiker-only trail descends through a relatively open forest to a log footbridge over misnamed Mud Creek, which is actually a lovely trout stream. After this, climb up and over a little ridge, hop across trickling Fir Tree Creek, and come to a junction at the start of the loop. Go straight on the Dry Lake Trail and traverse gradually uphill, before dropping slightly to cross yet another little creek, this one without a name.

The relatively dry slopes here support unusually high concentrations of western white pine, a lovely tree with soft, 3-inch-long needles and oversized cones. Also common here are chubby western toads, which resemble wart-covered rocks. They are very slow of foot, so be careful not to step on one.

After the creek crossing, you climb rather steeply to a sign marking your entry into the Salmon-Huckleberry Wilderness, then climb some more to a junction where you turn left and immediately start to lose elevation. For the next 1.6 miles, you gradually wind down into the Salmon River Canyon, generally staying in viewless but pleasant woods. Long before reaching the river, you hit a junction with the Salmon River Trail.

To the right, this long, scenic trail heads down toward the popular trailhead south of Zigzag. For this less-traveled loop, you turn left and gradually work your way upstream. Most of the way is in dense forests, but this scenery is twice broken by small side creeks, whose boggy areas support lots of skunk cabbage. The trail travels along the base of a large talus slope, before crossing two larger tributary creeks and climbing to a switchback. Still traveling uphill in open forests, the trail ascends steadily out of the main Salmon River Canyon and wanders up the smaller canyon of Fir Tree Creek. Shortly after hopping across this tiny creek, you return to the junction with the Dry Lake Trail, just 0.6 mile from your car.

Trip 3

Jackpot Meadow

(Map Area SH-3)

Distance	Elevation Gain	Hiking Time	Optional Map	Difficulty
5.8 miles	1200'	3 hours	*Green Trails–High Rock*	**

Usually Open	May to October
Best Times	June and July
Agency	Zigzag Ranger District (Mt. Hood National Forest)

This quiet trail is a good choice when you want to get away from the crowds. Even on the busiest summer weekends, this path remains lonesome, making it ideal for seekers of solitude. In addition to solitude, this trail provides hikers with a pleasant forest walk, visiting a beautiful spot along the upper reaches of the Salmon River, and giving you the chance to explore a lush mountain meadow. There may be no grand views, lakes, or any of the other attributes that tend to draw crowds, but the more subtle charms of the Oregon Cascades are nowhere on better display.

Directions: Drive 1.8 miles east of Government Camp on U.S. Highway 26, then turn right (south) at the Trillium Lake junction. Follow paved Forest Road 2656 for 1.7 miles, passing the lake's campground and day-use area, to a junction near the southeast corner of the lake. Bear left, staying on Road 2656, and after 1.1 miles, come to a fork where you bear right. The pavement ends as you continue on a good gravel road for 0.7 mile to another fork. Bear right once again on Forest Road 309, and drive a final 2.0 miles to a trailhead sign. Park on the shoulder of the road about 20 yards past the sign.

Two trails depart from this trailhead. You take the path to Jackpot Meadow, going downhill to the south, from just below the parking area. For the first mile, the easy trail gradually descends through an exceptionally interesting and diverse forest of western white pine, lodgepole pine, western hemlock, Alaska yellow cedar, Douglas-fir, and both Pacific silver and noble fir.

Once you reach the edge of the Salmon River Canyon, you descend two gentle switchbacks to a log footbridge over the clear, rushing stream. You'll probably have this spot all to yourself, so take some time to enjoy the waters and contemplate the subtle beauties of a mountain stream.

Once across the bridge, the trail goes upstream, past a small campsite, then switchbacks to the right and begins climbing moderately steeply away from the water. In three long then three short switchbacks to the south rim of the canyon, the trail ascends a forested hillside with unusually high concentrations of low-growing Pacific yew and slow-moving western toads. Now on a forested plateau, you gradually ascend to a small tributary creek, hop across the flow, then wander uphill to a trailhead on a dirt road.

To visit lovely Jackpot Meadow, with its little creek, grassy openings, scenic tree islands, and abundant wildflowers, you cross the road at a diagonal, then follow an unmaintained but obvious trail. This path crosses a sluggish creek, then travels around the east side of the meadow, just a few yards through the trees on the right. Take the time to go over to the meadow and explore. You will be rewarded with lots of wildflowers, especially camas, dandelion, shooting star, and aster. You may even be lucky enough to spot one of the sandhill cranes that occasionally nest here.

Jackpot Meadow

Log bridge over Salmon River, Jackpot Meadow Trail, Oregon

Mount Hood

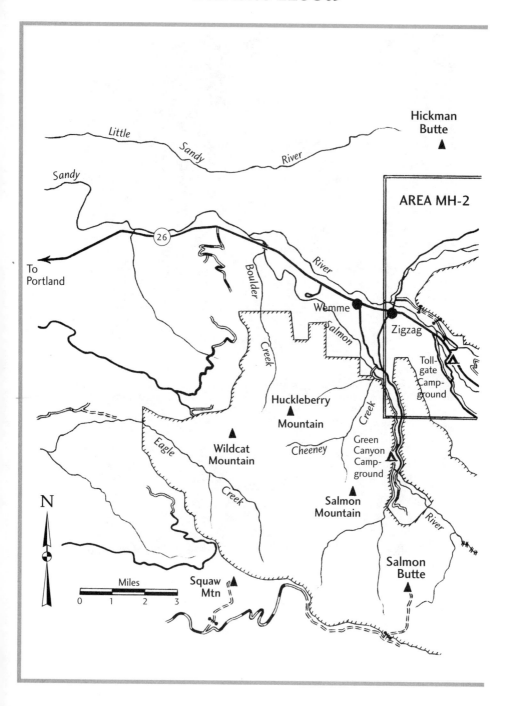

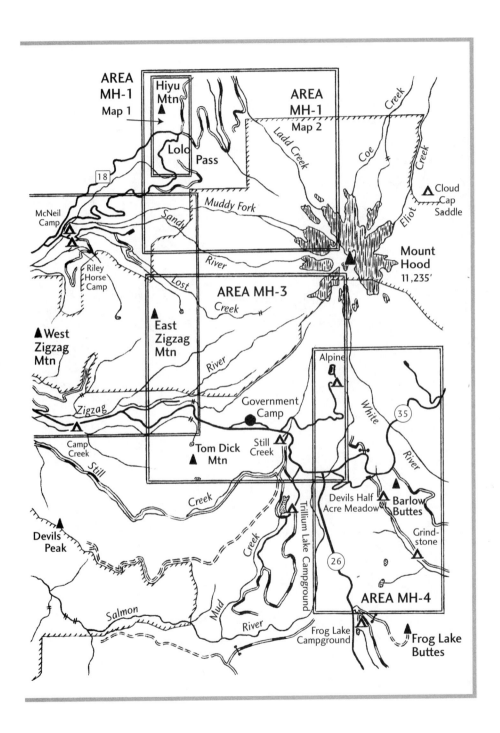

AREA
MH-1
Map 1

Hiyu
Mtn

AREA
MH-1
Map 2

Creek

Lolo Pass

Ladd Creek

Coe

Creek

Cloud
Cap
Saddle

Eliot

18

Muddy Fork

Sandy

McNeil
Camp

River

Lost

Riley
Horse
Camp

AREA MH-3

Creek

Mount
Hood
11,235′

East
Zigzag
Mtn

West
Zigzag
Mtn

River

Alpine

White

35

Zigzag

Government
Camp

Camp
Creek

Still

Still
Creek

Tom Dick
Mtn

River

Creek

Devils Half
Acre Meadow

Barlow
Buttes

Devils
Peak

Creek

Mud

Trillium Lake Campground

Grind-
stone

26

Creek

Salmon

River

AREA MH-4

Frog Lake
Campground

Frog Lake
Buttes

Mt. Hood from pond near Cairn Basin, Oregon

Mount Hood

Area MH-1: Lolo Pass Area

AT A LOW POINT NORTHWEST OF MT. HOOD, LOLO PASS IS PART OF THE WATERSHED DIVIDE BETWEEN THE SANDY RIVER, TO THE SOUTHWEST, AND THE HOOD RIVER, TO THE NORTHEAST. It is also a busy transportation corridor, with roads and powerlines using this pass as a convenient access through the Cascade divide.

Hikers find the pass to be a convenient place to reach the high country on the slopes of Mt. Hood. The trails here provide the easiest access to the spectacular alpine terrain on the north and west sides of the mountain, giving hikers the chance to get up-close-and-personal with the snowfields and ridges they see so often in the distance, from their homes in the Portland area. The scenery is everything your imagination thought it would be. For the few months each year that they are free of snow, the meadows carpeted with delicate alpine wildflowers, the cascading streams, the shimmering glaciers of jumbled ice, and the distant views, all add up to a hiker's paradise.

Trip 1

Buck Peak

(Map Area MH-1, Map 1)

Distance	Elevation Gain	Hiking Time	Optional Map	Difficulty
16.0 miles	2600'	7 to 9 hours	*Green Trails–Government Camp*	****

Usually Open	June to October
Best Times	Mid-June to mid-July / Mid-August to September
Agency	Zigzag Ranger District (Mt. Hood National Forest)

The Pacific Crest Trail runs 2650 miles from Mexico to Canada through the mountains of California, Oregon, and Washington. But you can tackle short segments close to home. One such segment is the route going north from Lolo Pass. Although the scenery doesn't compare to other trails higher on Mt. Hood, it is still very pleasant, and the view from Buck Peak provides ample compensation for your efforts. Additional compensation comes in the form of delicious huckleberries that ripen in late August.

Directions: Follow U.S. Highway 26 to Zigzag and turn north on the E. Lolo Pass Road. Climb this good paved road 10.6 miles to Lolo Pass, where the pavement ends and the Pacific Crest Trail crosses the road. The best parking is 100 feet down gravel Road 1810, which turns right from the pass.

Pick up the northbound Pacific Crest Trail and walk a short distance through a brushy area to a clearing beneath a set of powerlines. While far from natural, this opening provides good views of Mt. Hood, and plenty of sunshine for the abundant Pacific rhododendrons, which bloom from mid-June to mid-July. After the powerlines, you reenter a forest of lodgepole pine, Douglas-fir, Pacific silver fir, and mountain hemlock. Although there are only a few wildflowers on this slope, in late August and September the huckleberry bushes lining the trail provide an even better treat, or at least a tastier one.

The trail generally stays on the Hood River side of the watershed divide, but occasionally it passes onto the west side of the ridge and travels briefly in the Bull Run Watershed. This large basin provides the city of Portland with its famously clean drinking water. To protect this water quality, hikers are not allowed to travel off-trail, and camping is strictly prohibited. Keeping these restrictions in mind, you make a long, generally uphill traverse of the east side of a forested divide, then round a ridge on the northeast shoulder of Sentinel Peak.

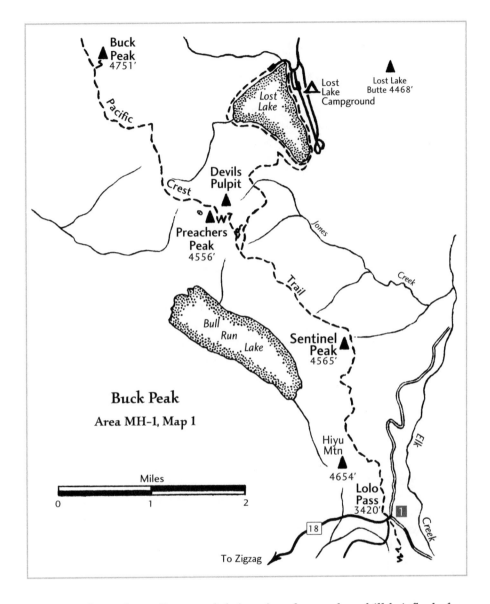

Buck Peak

Area MH-1, Map 1

From here, the trail curves left (west) and goes downhill briefly, before leveling off in a long wooded saddle. You then pass two more low, unnamed summits and come to a junction with trail 617, heading down to Lost Lake.

Go straight on the PCT, which travels uphill for about 250 yards, then passes a short side trail leading to a nice campsite beside Salvation Spring. Four uphill switchbacks now take you through an indistinct saddle between two minor high points titled Preacher's Peak and Devils Pulpit.

Continuing north, you stay in the forest on the huckleberry-lined trail as it drops to yet another saddle, northwest of Preacher's Peak, and regains the lost altitude by going over a rounded knoll. Going downhill once again, you drop to another pass, then climb to a junction.

To reach Buck Peak, turn right at this junction and ascend rather steeply for 0.4 mile to the summit. Views from the top are very good, although not of the 360-degree variety, as trees block several angles. Mt. Hood is the star attraction, but you will also enjoy looking east toward triangle-shaped Lost Lake and smooth-sided Lost Lake Butte.

Since you are now 8 miles from the trailhead, you've probably gotten enough exercise. If you want more exercise, however, just go back down to the PCT and keep walking north. You'll hit Canada eventually.

Trip 2

McNeil Point via McGee Creek

(Map Area MH-1, Map 2)

Distance	Elevation Gain	Hiking Time	Optional Map	Difficulty
8.9 miles	2700'	4.5 hours	Green Trails–Government Camp & Mount Hood	***

Usually Open	Mid-July to mid-October
Best Times	Late July to mid-August / early October
Agency	Hood River Ranger District (Mt. Hood National Forest)

For great scenery, you really can't go wrong on any trip near timberline on Mt. Hood. This wonderful outing doesn't disappoint, so bring plenty of film and a sense of awe—both are mandatory for maximum enjoyment. Another good item to bring along is an alpine wildflower guide. The number and variety of wildflowers here rival or surpass any other hike in this book. If you can visit on a weekday, you'll enjoy the views and wildflowers in relative solitude.

Directions: Follow U.S. Highway 26 to Zigzag and turn north on the E. Lolo Pass Road. Climb this good paved road for 10.6 miles to Lolo Pass, where the pavement ends and the Pacific Crest Trail crosses the road. Take the second right turn, onto gravel Forest Road 1810, and drive 1.5 miles, then turn sharply right at a small brown sign for the McGee Creek Trail. In just 0.2 mile, this narrow gravel road comes to the trailhead, at a pullout on the right.

 The trail, which is only intermittently maintained, follows a rocky old roadbed for 0.1 mile, then becomes a true footpath in a pretty forest of mountain hemlock, Douglas-fir, and Pacific silver

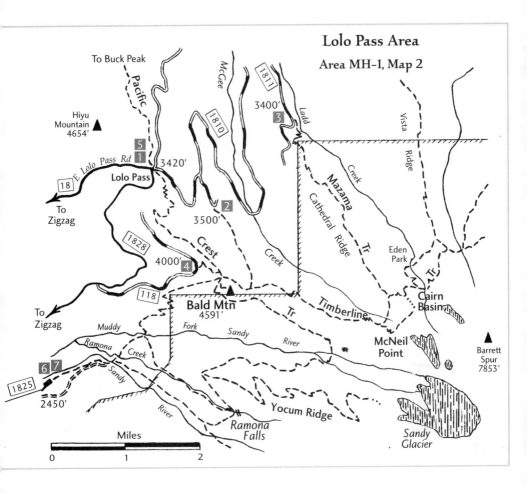

Lolo Pass Area

Area MH-1, Map 2

To Buck Peak

McGee

1811

Pacific

3400'

3

Ladd

Hiyu
Mountain
4654'

1810

Vista
Ridge

5
1

E Lolo Pass Rd   3420'

18   Lolo Pass

Mazama

Creek

To
Zigzag

2

3500'

Cathedral Ridge

Tr

Eden
Park

1828

Crest

4000'   4

Creek

Timberline

Cairn
Basin

118

Tr

To
Zigzag

Bald Mtn
4591'

Fork

Muddy

Sandy

River

McNeil
Point

Barrett
Spur
7853'

Ramona

Creek

Sandy

6 7

1825

2450'

River

Yocum Ridge

Sandy
Glacier

Ramona
Falls

Miles

0   1   2

fir. The first few miles of trail are lined with wild berries, especially blue-berries, which ripen in mid-to-late August. The uphill grade is moderately steep for the first 1.3 viewless miles. It leads to a junction with the Timberline Trail and a wilderness permit sign-in station.

You turn left at the junction and continue making a moderate ascent as the trees gradually get smaller at the higher altitudes. Finally, the uphill abates, and the path breaks out of the forest in two large ridgetop meadows, with terrific views of Muddy Fork Canyon and Yocum Ridge to the south, as well as Sandy Glacier, on the slopes of Mt. Hood, to the east. Lots of showy wildflowers in July and early August, especially beargrass and lupine, add to the scene. After some small ups and downs, the trail leaves the meadows, reenters forest, and makes four, short, uphill switchbacks. Just after the last of these is an unsigned, but obvious, fork in the trail, at a small clearing choked with early-August wildflowers.

For the direct route to McNeil Point, you turn right, onto an extremely steep and rugged trail. Please walk carefully, to avoid injuring yourself or tumbling rocks onto others below. It is also important that you stay on the trail to avoid damaging the flowers and trees, which have a hard enough time living in this harsh alpine environment.

The unofficial trail charges up a steep slope initially through a wildflower meadow that sports thousands of "old-man-of-the-mountains" (the midsummer incarnation of western pasque flower), paintbrush, lupine, bistort, valerian, aster, and groundsel, among other showy blossoms. After the meadow, you scramble uphill, sometimes having to use your hands to crawl over boulders and exposed roots. After 0.5 mile of this lung-and-thigh busting experience, you are rewarded with rather sudden relief at McNeil Point shelter. This old rock structure sits right at timberline, with only a few wind-whipped whitebark pines and mountain hemlocks in its vicinity. Camping here is discouraged, both to protect the fragile vegetation and to avoid the sometimes severe winds to which McNeil Point is exposed. It does make a magnificent lunch stop, however, and for that purpose, it is highly recommended. You can spend hours soaking in the view of Mt. Hood, the Portland area (all too often hidden under the haze of pollution), and three distant volcanoes in Washington state—Mounts Rainier, Adams, and St. Helens.

For a gentler return route and a chance to enjoy even more of this magnificent scenery, turn east from the shelter and follow a gently contouring footpath that crosses meadowy slopes and lingering snowfields. After about 0.6 mile, turn left and follow another boot path downhill, through a wide gully with lots of wildflowers. One especially abundant flower is spiraea, whose clusters of pink blossoms saturate the mountain air with a lovely perfume.

Where the use path hits the Timberline Trail, you turn left and quickly pass a junction with the newly reopened Mazama Trail, which goes to the right, down Cathedral Ridge (Trip 3). After this junction, you cross several small creeklets, then go up-and-down through wildflower meadows. Along the way, you pass two very photogenic snowmelt ponds, before getting back to the junction with the path up to McNeil Point shelter. From here, you simply return to your car the way you came.

A slightly shorter and *much* more crowded approach to this magnificent area is from the Top Spur trailhead (see Trip 4), but by starting from McGee Creek, you avoid most of the crowds.

Trip 3

Mazama Trail to Cairn Basin

(Map Area MH-1, Map 2)

Distance	Elevation Gain	Hiking Time	Optional Map	Difficulty
7.2 miles	2400'	3 to 4 hours	*Green Trails–Government Camp & Mount Hood*	***

Usually Open	Mid-July to October
Best Times	Late July to mid-August
Agency	Hood River Ranger District (Mt. Hood National Forest)

The old trail up Cathedral Ridge was abandoned by the Forest Service in the 1980s, after heavy blowdown made reopening and maintaining this scenic route too expensive. Taking matters into their own hands, members of the Mazamas, a Portland-based climbing and hiking club, used lots of hard work by volunteers to cut through logs and reroute the trail to allow hikers to once again enjoy this scenic path.

The new trail was dedicated in 1994 to commemorate the club's 100th anniversary, and it was officially renamed by the Forest Service in honor of the Mazamas. Local pedestrians owe a debt to the group, as the trail is very scenic and now provides the best-graded option of the several feeder trails on the mountain. Once you reach the famous Timberline Trail, there are all kinds of options for exploring an alpine wonderland that is the match of anything in the American West.

Directions: Follow U.S. Highway 26 to Zigzag and turn north on the E. Lolo Pass Road. Climb this good paved road for 10.6 miles to Lolo Pass, where the pavement ends and the Pacific Crest Trail crosses the road. Take the second right turn, onto gravel Forest Road 1810, and drive for 5.6 miles, then turn right on Forest Road 1811. Follow this narrow gravel route for 2.5 miles to the signed trailhead parking area on the left.

Start hiking in a recovering clearcut on a little ridge above loudly cascading Ladd Creek. When the clearcut ends, you enter forest and come to a wilderness permit and registration box, where you can obtain a free permit. Keep winding steadily uphill on this very well-built path, through a predominantly mountain-hemlock forest with a ground cover of almost solid bunchberry, a plant that features perky little four-petaled flowers in early summer and orange berries in late summer.

The trail switchbacks three times up a large talus slope, then enters a shady hemlock forest, with lots of head-high Pacific rhododendron blooming in late June. The trail then makes 14 short switchbacks, up to the top of Cathedral Ridge, where a sign marks your entry into the Mount Hood Wilder-

Mt. Hood from Cairn Basin

ness. From here, you climb more gradually, generally staying on the ridge's forested west side. As the snow melts in July, these forests come alive with thousands of beautiful, white avalanche lilies.

At the top of an extended steeper section, the forest cover breaks and you enter a gorgeous little ridgetop glade, with lots of pink heather blooming in July. Above this, you traverse a heavily forested hillside, then climb beside a small rockslide, through meadows, and past a shallow seasonal tarn. There are great views across this tarn directly ahead to Mt. Hood's rugged north face. Shortly after this is the signed junction with the Timberline Trail.

The possibilities for exploring are numerous and outstanding. The easiest choice is to turn left (east) and go about 0.5 mile over a low ridge and across several small creeks to Cairn Basin, which has excellent camps, lots of flowers, and partially obstructed views of Mt. Hood. From there, you can drop to the wildflower bonanza of Eden Park, or just keep going east on the Timberline Trail, to Elk Cove, Cloud Cap, and beyond. Another option is to follow unofficial trails up to the McNeil Point shelter (Trip 2). The most challenging option is to make the tough cross-country scramble up Barrett Spur, to where you can look down on either side to the deep crevasses of Ladd and Coe glaciers. No matter what you choose, it's all great, so enjoy!

Trip 4

Bald Mountain from Top Spur

(Map Area MH-1, Map 2)

Distance	Elevation Gain	Hiking Time	Optional Map	Difficulty
1.6 to 10.6 miles	500 to 1900'	1 to 4 hours	*Green Trails–Government Camp & Mount Hood*	* to **

Usually Open	Mid-June to October
Best Times	Mid-June to mid-July
Agency	Zigzag Ranger District (Mt. Hood National Forest)

It's almost sinfully easy to reach the great views of Mt. Hood from Bald Mountain. After a ridiculously short 0.8-mile amble, you hardly feel worthy of being able to sit back amid acres of wildflowers, looking up at a drop-dead-gorgeous view of Oregon's highest mountain. This is an ideal location to show out-of-shape visiting relatives why you rave so much about the beauties of the Pacific Northwest. Locals who feel guilty about how easy it all is, or who just want to get more exercise, can extend this hike past more great mountain scenery, either up to the alpine country around McNeil Point or on a long loop trip that explores the canyon of Muddy Fork Sandy River.

Directions: Drive U.S. Highway 26 to Zigzag and turn north on the E. Lolo Pass Road. After 4.3 miles, turn right on paved Forest Road 1825. In 0.7 mile, go straight on Forest Road 1828 and climb this narrow paved route for about 5.5 miles to a junction with gravel Forest Road 118. You bear right here, following signs to Top Spur Trailhead, then continue another 1.7 miles to the trailhead. Parking can be tight here on summer weekends.

The trail climbs away from the road in a shady, mid-elevation forest of Douglas-fir and western hemlock. In season, hikers in this forest can enjoy blooming bunchberries (June) or pick huckleberries (late August). Before you've even had a chance to break a sweat, you come to a junction with the Pacific Crest Trail, where you turn right. Just 50 yards later you find a confusing junction and a choice of trails.

To visit the summit of Bald Mountain, simply turn slightly to the right and walk south on the PCT for about 150 yards, then bear left on an unsigned trail. This path climbs for 0.2 mile to the summit, with its up-close-and-personal look at the west face of Mt. Hood. This will satisfy most people, but for an equally good view with much better flowers, return to the PCT and walk south, looping around to the south side of Bald Mountain. The trail breaks out of the trees and crosses steeply sloping meadows, with lots of flowers in June and July, and even better views of Mt. Hood than you had at the summit.

Hikers who want more exercise and are considering taking the long loop into Muddy Fork Canyon, need to take into account that that would require fording the Muddy Fork Sandy River. This ford can be a bit tricky in early summer, which is unfortunate, because that is when the flowers on Bald Mountain are at their best. The crossing can also be a problem on hot afternoons when meltwater from the snow and ice on Sandy Glacier swell the stream. If this doesn't deter you, follow the PCT gradually downhill, first across the open hillside, then back into the trees, where you lose the view of Mt. Hood. This well-graded path crosses several small creeklets, before coming to a campsite and the ford of Muddy Fork Sandy River. This glacial stream changes its course from time to time, but usually it has two or three main branches, spread out over about 0.4 mile. In the morning, you can probably hop across with dry feet, but wading, and a sturdy walking stick as a third leg, may be required in the afternoon.

Once across the flow, you pass more campsites and begin the winding traverse of the north side of Yocum Ridge. The route has some ups and downs, and crosses several small tributary creeks, but it isn't terribly strenuous. The trail is, however, subject to frequent washouts, which require expensive reconstruction efforts and closure of the route from time to time. Before you leave, call ahead to make sure the trail is open.

As usual on a north-facing slope, the cool, wet conditions support dense vegetation of thimbleberry, devils club, bracken fern, monkeyflower, and other greenery that overhangs the trail, which soak you to the bone when the plants are covered with either morning dew or water from a recent rain. The traverse ends by descending a little before you get to the ridgecrest, where you meet the Yocum Ridge Trail.

Go straight at this junction, staying on the PCT, and descend a drier south-facing hillside to a junction just before you reach Ramona Falls. You can get to this extremely popular spot by a much shorter trail (see Trip 6), but the crowds only slightly diminish your enjoyment of this classic cascade, which tumbles veil-like over a basalt cliff face. Backpackers must camp a minimum of 500 feet from the falls, preferably in the designated camping area south of the falls.

For the loop trip, you leave the PCT and travel west down the forested valley of Ramona Creek. Cross, then parallel this beautiful, clear creek for about 1 mile. Cross the creek again and bear to the right, away from the water. Turn right at a junction and almost immediately cross the rushing Muddy Fork Sandy River, this time, fortunately, on a bridge.

The most strenuous part of the trip now takes you up seven long and irregularly spaced switchbacks, on a forested hillside. The route is totally dry, so be sure to save enough water to quench your thirst on this final climb. You top out on a ridge, then climb at a more gentle pace back to the junction with the PCT near Bald Mountain.

If you don't want to deal with the ford of the Muddy Fork, a second alternative for a longer hike follows the Timberline Trail east from Bald Mountain. This path goes up along a wildly scenic ridge with lots of views and flowers, all the way to Cairn Basin and McNeil Point. For a complete description of this route, see Trip 2.

Trip 5

Bald Mountain from Lolo Pass

(Map Area MH-1, Map 2)

Distance	Elevation Gain	Hiking Time	Optional Map	Difficulty
6.8 miles	1600'	3 to 4 hours	Green Trails–Government Camp	**

Usually Open	June to October
Best Times	Mid-June to mid-July
Agency	Zigzag Ranger District (Mt. Hood National Forest)

The classic view of Mt. Hood from the meadowy slopes of Bald Mountain can be reached by a very short and easy stroll from the Top Spur trailhead (Trip 4). In some unexplainable way, however, the same view is better when you feel like you've "earned" it, by taking a longer approach. One such longer route follows the Pacific Crest Trail south from Lolo Pass. In addition to sharing the same famous view, this route has other attributes that you won't find on the shorter alternative.

First, you'll get more exercise, which is, after all, one of the reasons we go hiking. Second, the hike takes you through some very attractive woods that might be worth a visit all by themselves. Finally, even though the destination will probably be fairly crowded, you can at least approach it in relative solitude while you hike.

Directions: Follow U.S. Highway 26 to Zigzag and turn north on the E. Lolo Pass Road. Climb this good paved road 10.6 miles to Lolo Pass, where the pavement ends and the Pacific Crest Trail crosses the road. The best parking is 100 feet down gravel Road 1810, which turns right from the pass.

Start on the southbound PCT in an old clearcut next to the parking area. Trees are now up to 20 feet high here, but the old clearcut still has an open feeling, with lots of beargrass and Pacific rhododendron. In late June and early July, the display of color from these two species is a special treat.

After leaving the clearcut, the trail enters a hemlock-and-fir forest and climbs at a moderate grade. A dozen switchbacks lead you up a relatively dry hillside, before you switchback again and cross a wetter, more open slope, above a small puddle (calling it a 'pond' would be an overstatement). Shrubs like thimbleberry, rhododendron, devils club, and gooseberry have taken advantage of the extra sunshine here to grow in profusion.

After crossing the slope, you reenter forest and hit the top of a ridge where you get a nice view north down the valley of West Fork Hood River. From here, you turn up the ridge and contour around the south side of a forested knoll before returning to the ridgecrest. You then gradually lose elevation for about 0.4 mile to a junction with the shortcut from Top Spur. Go straight, and 50 yards later come to a confusing junction.

For the best views bear right, staying on the PCT, and walk about 150 yards to an unsigned junction. To go to the top of Bald Mountain, bear left and walk this use path 0.2 mile to the summit. The view east to Mt. Hood is very good but that's about all you can see, because trees block the vistas in all other directions.

For a more photogenic scene, go back to the PCT and loop around in the trees to the south side of Bald Mountain. Here, you enter the huge, steeply sloping meadows that gave Bald Mountain its name. These meadows sport lots of wildflowers and have terrific views of the Muddy Fork Valley and Mt. Hood to the east, and Yocum Ridge to the south. Photographs—and you'll kick yourself if you forgot to bring a camera—are best in the late afternoon when the lighting is most dramatic.

Trip 6

Ramona Falls Loop

(Map Area MH-1, Map 2)

Distance	Elevation Gain	Hiking Time	Optional Map	Difficulty
6.9 miles	1000'	3 to 4 hours	*Green Trails–Government Camp*	**

🔲

Usually Open	Late April to November
Best Times	Mid-May to July
Agency	Zigzag Ranger District (Mt. Hood National Forest)

The Ramona Falls Loop has long been the most popular dayhike on the west side of Mt. Hood. This is hardly surprising, as the 120-foot falls is a masterwork of nature, cascading beautifully over a moss-covered basalt cliff in a perfect fan shape. In addition to the falls, the hike allows you to enjoy some decent views of Mt. Hood, as well as a gorgeous walk along a quiet creek in a cool forest. Until recently, this fairly easy hike was even easier, because a rough dirt road took you to a trailhead 1.2 miles closer to the falls. The road was miserable to drive, and it forced people to choose between hiking an additional round-trip distance of 2.4 miles and putting their cars through the torture. Flood damage in 1996 closed the road.

Directions: Drive U.S. Highway 26 to Zigzag and turn north on the E. Lolo Pass Road. After 4.3 miles, turn right onto paved Forest Road 1825, which you follow for 1.2 miles, over a bridge, then go left at a fork, staying on Road 1825. About 1.5 miles later, you bear left at a junction and quickly arrive at the large parking area for the Ramona Falls Trail.

The trail leaves from the northeast end of the parking lot and travels up the wide valley of the Sandy River. The trail is sandy and rocky for much of the way, but it does go in and out of some lodgepole pines and hemlocks, providing at least some shade. After about 0.6 mile, the trail meets the closed road and parallels it all the way to the upper trailhead.

Once you reach the old trailhead, you cross the Sandy River on a metal bridge from which you can look up the canyon to Mt. Hood. About 100 yards later is a trail junction amid the short trees and brushy willows of this glacial flood plain. This is the start of the loop, so either fork will work, but it is slightly shorter going to the destination if you turn right.

This up-and-down path gradually works up the wide glacial valley of the Sandy River, sometimes near the unstable banks of the muddy stream, and sometimes in open forests struggling to survive this inhospitable environment. The area appears rather desolate and is completely dry, so it is better to hike this section in the cool of the morning, not the heat of the afternoon.

After 1.5 miles, you reach a junction with the Pacific Crest Trail, where you bear left onto it. You make two quick switchbacks, and wander through increasingly interesting and attractive woods for 0.5 mile, to a designated camping area. Backpackers should use this camp, as wilderness rules require that you camp at least 500 feet from the falls. The falls is a short distance ahead, and it immediately demonstrates why it was worth the hike.

The area near the base of this classic falls has been beaten to death by admirers, so what vegetation used to exist has been replaced by rocks and dirt, but the falls itself remains as charming as ever.

You cross a bridge at the base of the falls, then bear left at a junction and walk down a lush valley beside strikingly beautiful Ramona Creek. This clear stream tumbles over mossy rocks and flows beside water-loving plants as it makes its way down the gently sloping terrain. The contrast between the shady, green environment beside this stream and the virtual wasteland along the glacial flow of the Sandy River is striking. After the second crossing of the creek, veer right, away from the water.

At a junction near the Muddy Fork Sandy River, turn left (south) and walk a mostly level but very rocky and sandy trail over a low ridge. After crossing a bridge over Ramona Creek, the trail returns to the junction just before the bridge over the Sandy River.

Trip 7

Yocum Ridge

(Map Area MH-1, Map 2)

Distance	Elevation Gain	Hiking Time	Optional Map	Difficulty
17.4 miles	3800'	8 to 11 hours	*Green Trails—Government Camp & Mount Hood*	****

Usually Open	Mid-July to September
Best Times	Late July and August
Agency	Zigzag Ranger District (Mt. Hood National Forest)

Beyond the crowds at Ramona Falls, adventurous hikers can ascend a long ridge on the western spur of Mt. Hood to one of the most dramatic places in Oregon. The flowers, views, and close-up looks at the towering rocks and jagged glacial ice of Oregon's highest mountain are truly memorable.

The name of Yocum Ridge honors an important man in the history of this part of Oregon. Oliver C. Yocum was only a boy when he came to Oregon with the immigration of 1847. He made his mark on the state decades later as the developer of the Government Camp hotel and resort, still the most popular tourist area on Mt. Hood. As a long-time resident and climber, he probably guided more people to the top of Mt. Hood than has any other person. There is no better place to absorb the scenery and admire this early resident's exploits than atop the alpine ridge bearing his name.

Directions: Drive U.S. Highway 26 to Zigzag and turn north on the E. Lolo Pass Road. After 4.3 miles, turn right onto paved Forest Road 1825, which you follow for 1.2 miles, over a bridge, then go left at a fork, staying on Road 1825. About 1.5 miles later, you bear left at a junction and quickly arrive at the large parking area for the Ramona Falls Trail.

The sandy trail leaves from the northeast end of the parking lot and travels up the wide valley of the Sandy River. After about 0.6 mile, the trail meets a closed road and parallels it all the way to an old, upper trailhead. Now you cross the Sandy River on a metal bridge and, about 100 yards later, turn right at a junction. From here you walk an up-and-down path up the wide and rather desolate glacial valley of the Sandy River.

After 1.5 miles, you reach a junction with the Pacific Crest Trail, where you bear left onto it, make two quick switchbacks, and go 0.5 mile to Ramona Falls. You cross a bridge below this lovely cascade, then turn right onto the PCT at a junction, and go gradually up a hillside past dripping, moss- and fern-covered cliffs. At the top of the ridge, you meet the Yocum Ridge Trail and turn right.

Along Yocum Ridge

This path goes up the south side of the wooded ridge, often traveling through jungles of Pacific rhododendron, where spiders put up thousands of webs for the first hiker of the day to break through. You pass a rocky slope, then switchback up to the wide summit of the ridge. Another long switchback, with occasional steep sections, takes you up to a tiny shallow pond. Beyond the pond, the forest gradually becomes more open and the meadows more attractive, as you continue gaining elevation. In early summer, these openings come alive with masses of yellow glacier lilies and white avalanche lilies.

All around you now is some of the most beautiful country in Oregon. The trail passes through gorgeous sloping meadows, with scattered subalpine fir and mountain hemlock adding scenic contrast. Flowers abound, including bistort, columbine, beargrass, lupine, paintbrush, wallflower, larkspur, and so many others it would take pages to list them all. The most awe-inspiring scenery starts when you arrive at a stunning overlook above steep-walled Sandy River Canyon, where you can look up to the craggy ice sheet of Reid Glacier. An adjective like "dramatic" hardly seems adequate.

The main trail switchbacks to the left from this viewpoint, going up the ridge beneath some towering rock formations. When you top out on the ridge-crest, the trail turns to the right and climbs up the spine of the ridge. You soon climb above treeline and wander through alpine terrain that features unrestricted views, ranging from Mt. Rainier in the north to Mt. Jefferson to the south.

Finally, the diminishing trail comes to a rocky cliff, which athletic hikers can scale by steep, but not overly dangerous, routes up snowfields to a glorious alpine plateau. Follow this high ridge as far as you like, as it leads all the way to the base of Sandy and Reid glaciers, but just sitting back and enjoying the incredible views is more than enough for most hikers. On hot afternoons, hikers are often startled by loud cracking sounds coming from the moving ice of the glaciers.

Backpackers can haul their sleeping bags up to this paradise to enjoy gorgeous sunsets and the nighttime lights of the city of Portland. If you want to enjoy this experience, however, keep in mind that the area is extremely fragile, and that the only available water is obtained from the semi-permanent snowfields. If you are not backpacking, be sure to leave enough time to make the long walk back to your car.

Mount Hood

Area MH-2: Zigzag Mountain Area

The name *Zigzag*, which is applied to a number of features southwest of Mt. Hood, comes from something that hikers know intimately—the switchback. In October 1845, a man named Joel Palmer crossed the current Zigzag River Canyon high on the slopes of Mt. Hood. He described in his journal the method he employed to travel down the steep slopes:

> *The manner of descending is to turn directly to the right, go zigzag for about one hundred yards, then turn short round, and go zigzag until you come under the place where you started from; then to the right, and so on, until you reach the base.*

His description of what we now call a switchback led to the naming of the river and subsequently other nearby features.

Rather than being a single peak, Zigzag Mountain is actually a long ridge that extends southwest of Mt. Hood. The entire area is laced with trails that take you to high viewpoints and through open meadows that make enticing goals. But even without these destinations, the hiking would be a joy, because the entire ridge is a scenic marvel.

In addition to the great views of Mt. Hood and surrounding territory, two other features are particularly outstanding here. In July of favorable years, the displays of tall, white beargrass are consistently more impressive here than anywhere else in our region. A similar superlative description also applies to the area's abundant huckleberries. In late August, you can stuff yourself silly with the delicious blue fruit. Since you could never eat them all, the best plan is to bring something to transport the excess and take them home for making huckleberry pies and muffins—a Northwest delicacy that will make your memories of Zigzag Mountain last for a very long time.

Trip 1

Cast Lake & Ridge

(Map Area MH-2)

Distance	Elevation Gain	Hiking Time	Optional Map	Difficulty
11.2 miles	2500'	5.5 to 6 hours	*Green Trails–Government Camp*	***

Usually Open	Mid-June to October
Best Times	Mid-July / mid-to-late August
Agency	Zigzag Ranger District (Mt. Hood National Forest)

There are three big attractions in the Zigzag Mountain area: acres of blooming beargrass; fields of scrumptious huckleberries; and lots of outstanding views of Mt. Hood and beyond. Any one of these features would be more than enough to recommend a hike here.

The trail up Cast Ridge includes all three attractions, making for something close to hiking perfection. If you've come to see the beargrass in mid-July, keep in mind that beargrass plants bloom in two- and three-year cycles. As a result, in some years almost none bloom, but every six years, when the two- and three-year cycles coincide, the displays of tall white blossoms are breathtaking. Huckleberries are more consistent than beargrass. In the latter part of August these open ridges produce a tasty feast for both hikers and black bears. Most consistent of all, of course, is the view. On any clear day, Mt. Hood's snowy massif rises impressively to the northeast.

Directions: Follow U.S. Highway 26 to Zigzag and turn north on the E. Lolo Pass Road. After 4.3 miles, turn right onto paved Forest Road 1825 and drive 1.2 miles, over a bridge and to a junction. Turn right on Road 380, following signs to the Horseshoe Ridge Trail, and go 0.5 mile, passing Riley Horse Camp, to a small sign for the Cast Creek Trail on your left. Just past the trailhead is a small parking pullout on the right.

The dusty, horse-pounded route makes long, moderately steep traverses and switchbacks in a cool forest of western hemlock, Douglas-fir, and western red cedar. This used to be a rather steep footpath, until the Forest Service, largely for the benefit of equestrians, re-routed the trail and added several new switchbacks. The uphill grade is much more gentle now, but the trail is also 1.5 miles longer.

At the 13th switchback, you come to an obvious but viewless ridgeline. Here, the undergrowth abruptly changes to a distinctive mid-elevation mix of rhododendron, manzanita, and beargrass. From here, you stay on the level —even lose some elevation—for the next 0.5 mile, as you travel east along the ridgetop. After the climbing resumes, 10 gradual switchbacks lead to some

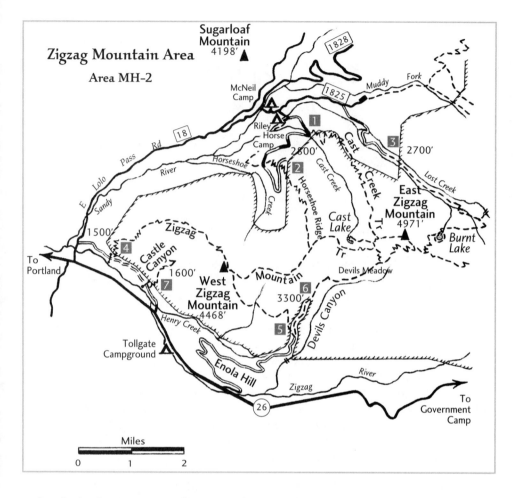

breaks in the trees, providing partial views of snowy Mt. Hood. By this time, the trees are smaller specimens, mostly western white pine and lodgepole pine. In July, it is also near here that you start to encounter more wildflowers and the first of the soon-to-be-abundant huckleberry bushes. The last 0.3 mile of the trail follows a view-packed, mostly open ridge.

At the junction with the Zigzag Mountain Trail, you have a choice of destinations. To the left, the best high viewpoint in the area, East Zigzag Mountain, is only 0.5 mile away. If you prefer a swim, turn right and go down-hill a few hundred yards to the Cast Lake Trail. You turn right here and hike 0.4 mile to this pleasant lake with its fair to good camps and fine swimming opportunities. Unfortunately, there is no good view of Mt. Hood from the lake, and the shore is brushy in spots. Nevertheless, this is the only reliable water in the area.

Backpackers spending the night at Cast Lake, or fit dayhikers making the loop connection to the Horseshoe Ridge Trail (Trip 2,) can explore beyond the Cast Lake turnoff. To do so, stick with the trail toward West Zigzag Mountain as it passes through a pretty little meadow with lots of pink spiraea in July and early August. Shortly after this meadow, you turn right at the junction with the Devils Cutoff Trail and climb, sometimes steeply, to some of the finest beargrass and huckleberry meadows in the state of Oregon. If you are continuing on to the Horseshoe Ridge Trail, you pass through many lovely meadows before reaching the trail junction, which is about 0.1 mile past an obvious highpoint in the ridge.

Trip 2

Horseshoe Ridge Trail

(Map Area MH-2)

Distance	Elevation Gain	Hiking Time	Optional Map	Difficulty
6.3 miles	2100′	6 hours	*Green Trails–Government Camp*	***

Usually Open	Mid-June to October
Best Times	Mid July / mid-to-late August
Agency	Zigzag Ranger District (Mt. Hood National Forest)

This pleasant hike has all the attractions of the neighboring Cast Creek Trail (Trip 1)—huckleberries, views, and beargrass—but it also has at least one big advantage over the other trail. This trail gets a lot less horse traffic, so it is less dusty and more pleasant for the hiker.

Directions: Follow U.S. Highway 26 to Zigzag and turn north on the E. Lolo Pass Road. After 4.3 miles, turn right onto paved Forest Road 1825 and drive 1.2 miles, over a bridge and to a junction. Turn right on Road 380, following signs for the Horseshoe Ridge Trail, and go 2.1 miles to a small sign for the Horseshoe Ridge Trail on your left. There is room for a few cars at a pullout near the trailhead.

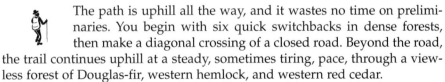 The path is uphill all the way, and it wastes no time on preliminaries. You begin with six quick switchbacks in dense forests, then make a diagonal crossing of a closed road. Beyond the road, the trail continues uphill at a steady, sometimes tiring, pace, through a viewless forest of Douglas-fir, western hemlock, and western red cedar.

This terrain is made for switchbacks, and the trail succumbs to this necessity with 16 sharp turns and several rounded curves that amount to long switchbacks. As you near the upper reaches of the ascent, the ground cover becomes a thick green mat dominated by oxalis the vanilla leaf, star-flowered smilacina, and other plants that provide variety.

After finally leaving the trees, you contour across the open southwest side of the ridge, through a meadow covered with huckleberries and various wildflowers. Look for beargrass, goldenrod, paintbrush, lupine, and fireweed.

Plan on spending plenty of extra time enjoying the flowers or picking huckleberries.

At the top of the ridge, there is a junction with the Zigzag Mountain Trail. To quickly reach the best viewpoint in the area, turn left for 0.1 mile, then scramble a few yards to the top of an obvious highpoint. This is a first-rate lunch spot, with an excellent view of bulky Mt. Hood, not far to the northeast. For details on a fine loop-trip possibility, see the description for the Cast Creek Trail (Trip 1).

Trip 3

Burnt Lake & East Zigzag Mountain
(Map Area MH-2)

Distance	Elevation Gain	Hiking Time	Optional Map	Difficulty
9.6 miles	2400′	4.5 to 6 hours	*Green Trails–Government Camp*	***

Usually Open	Late June to October
Best Times	July
Agency	Zigzag Ranger District (Mt. Hood National Forest)

Second only to Ramona Falls, Burnt Lake is the most popular hiking destination on the west side of Mt. Hood. This popularity is well deserved, and not just because this it is one of the few lakes in the Mount Hood Wilderness. The view across the swimmable waters of this 8-acre pool is picture-postcard perfect. The lake also has picnic and camp spots that are ideal for an easy backpacking trip or for eating lunch while contemplating the glories of the outdoors.

Just don't expect to be lonesome. People have flocked here for years in numbers that recently led the Forest Service to consider restrictions on the number of hikers allowed to visit the lake. For the time being, land managers are relying on volunteers to enforce wilderness regulations designed to protect the land. Please be a good outdoor citizen, and do your part to keep these voluntary rules from becoming mandatory limits on our hiking options. You can enjoy a bit more solitude as well as views that extend for hundreds of miles, by continuing your hike to East Zigzag Mountain.

Directions: Follow U.S. Highway 26 to Zigzag and turn north on the E. Lolo Pass Road. After 4.3 miles, turn right onto paved Forest Road 1825, which you follow for 1.2 miles, over a bridge. Go left at a fork, still staying on Road 1825, and about 1.5 miles later, bear right at a junction, where the road going left leads to Ramona Falls.

Stay on the right-hand road as it changes from pavement to rough gravel and climbs 1.6 miles to a road-end trailhead and parking area. **Note:** This road is very narrow and winds through many turns, so drive slowly and be on the lookout for oncoming traffic.

The first 1.8 miles of this hike are very gentle, as the trail gradually works its way up between two parallel creeks, on either side of a narrow valley. The heavy forest cover provides lots of welcome shade, while tiny forest wildflowers add some color. It's a very pleasant forest walk, despite the absence of views.

Just after crossing a small creek, you start on a newly rerouted section of trail, which is much better graded than the old switchbacking route. The gentle uphill takes you to a junction with a 100-yard spur trail, which goes left to a cascading waterfall on Lost Creek, then makes a switchback. From here, you make a long, steadily ascending traverse on a shady hillside covered with fir and hemlock, whose shade helps to keep tired hikers from becoming overheated.

For views, you get only occasional glimpses, but that soon changes, as you cross the clear outlet creek of Burnt Lake, and a few hundred yards later come to the northwest shore of the lake. A trail circles the lake, and several designated campsites are set back from the shore, if you want to spend the night. As always, avoid damaging the fragile shoreline vegetation by camping too close to the water. The most photogenic views of Mt. Hood are from the west and southwest shores.

To continue your hike to the viewpoint at East Zigzag Mountain, keep hiking on the main trail as it pulls away from the lake. The trail up to the ridgeline south of Burnt Lake has also been rerouted in recent years, changing what used to be a rather steep ascent into a longer but much more comfortable climb. The first part of the hike crosses relatively gentle terrain, with lots of forest openings. The final part of the climb switchbacks up a steep, north-facing hillside, whose dense forests provide shade for lingering snow patches early in the season.

Turn right at a junction on the ridgeline, then climb a bit further to a second junction. Go straight, and climb quite steeply for the next 0.3 mile, over increasingly rocky and open terrain, to the top of East Zigzag Mountain. Views extend in all directions, but the best is to the east, over the basin that holds Burnt Lake and up to shining Mt. Hood.

Beargrass above
Zigzag Mountain
Ridge, Oregon

Trip 4

West Zigzag Mountain from Zigzag

(Map Area MH-2)

Distance	Elevation Gain	Hiking Time	Optional Map	Difficulty
11.0 miles	3200'	6 to 7 hours	*Green Trails–Government Camp*	***

Usually Open	Late May to October
Best Times	June and July
Agency	Zigzag Ranger District (Mt. Hood National Forest)

The trail up to the old lookout site atop West Zigzag Mountain has a lot in common with other ridge walks southwest of Mt. Hood. Like the others, it's quite a long way to the top of West Zigzag Mountain, so this is a good choice for a conditioning hike. Also like the other ridge walks, this one features fine views from the top, with lots of wildflowers and plenty of tasty huckleberries to enjoy along the way. Unlike most of the other ridge walks, however, this trail is rarely steep. It makes its way gradually up a long series of switchbacks, rather than charging directly up the wooded slopes. Another advantage of this trail is that its southern exposure allows it to open for hiking two or three weeks before most of the others. Bring plenty of water, because none is available on the trail.

Directions: Drive U.S. Highway 26 to Zigzag and turn north on E. Lolo Pass Road. You cross a bridge over Zigzag River and, 0.3 mile from Highway 26, turn right on pothole-filled E. Mountain Drive. After 0.7 mile the road ends at a gate.

The trail starts right beside the gate and immediately begins the steady uphill pace that will prevail for the first 4 miles. The grade is deceptively gentle, so you may be tempted to start out at too fast a pace. Don't use up all your energy here, because the gentle grade is unrelenting, and it will eventually slow you down to a crawl if you don't conserve some energy.

The climb features no real highlights, as there aren't any good viewpoints, splashing creeks, or other reasons to make a stop. The entire route is heavily forested, a blessing for the welcome shade it provides on this long climb. To sustain your interest, you can just count switchbacks. More interesting is to study the subtle changes in vegetation that occur as you climb.

At the start are the usual forests of Douglas-fir, western hemlock, and western red cedar, with vine maple, sword fern, Oregon grape, and salal being the dominant species on the forest floor. Farther up the ridge, Pacific silver fir and western white pine are added to the mix, and Pacific rhododendron is now the most abundant shrub. In June, this latter species puts on a marvelous show of pink blossoms. Higher still on the ridge, you encounter Alaska yellow cedar, Engelmann spruce, and mountain hemlock, together with beargrass and tough-limbed manzanita bushes. Also in this zone are huckleberry bushes, which become increasingly common as you near the top. These vegetative milestones track your uphill progress, encouraging you to keep on trudging.

The first 16 switchbacks take you close to a ridgecrest, which you then follow on an uphill traverse to the east. After this, six more switchbacks draw you close to another ridgeline, which you ascend. By now, your thigh and calf muscles will recognize the pattern. Their complaints finally stop as you top out on the ridge, at a rather disappointing viewpoint near the high point of West Zigzag Mountain. Trees block most of the views, but you can peer through them to the east and northeast, to East Zigzag Mountain and Mt. Hood.

If you aren't exhausted from the climb, continue southeast, along the mountain's ridge, to a series of much more satisfying viewpoints. The trail here goes up and down, working its way past rocky outcroppings and cliff edges, where you trade the views of Mt. Hood on one side for views of the Zigzag River Valley on the other. A switchback and a narrow ridgecrest traverse take you to a final dramatic viewpoint, at the former site of the West Zigzag Lookout. Tiny alpine wildflowers, like phlox, stonecrop, and larkspur, cannot compete for your attention with the magnificence of the views.

Once you've soaked in all the scenery you and your camera can handle, brace your knees and return down all those switchbacks to your car.

Trip 5

West Zigzag Mountain from Enola Hill
(Map Area MH-2)

Distance	Elevation Gain	Hiking Time	Optional Map	Difficulty
5.0 miles	1300'	3 hours	Green Trails–Government Camp	**

Usually Open	June to October
Best Times	Mid-June to July
Agency	Zigzag Ranger District (Mt. Hood National Forest)

The Enola Hill Road provides a sneaky sort of back door approach to the Zigzag Mountain area, avoiding the long uphill hikes that other trips require. Here, your car does most of the work, so you might think that most hikers would opt for this alternative. The reason why relatively few do so, is that most hikers don't want to put their *cars* through the ordeal. The dirt road is passable for passenger cars, but it's a slow go, and not much fun to drive. Take this approach only if you think your car is in better shape than you are!

Directions: Drive 1.5 miles east of Rhododendron on U.S. Highway 26, and turn left (north) onto paved Forest Road 27. After 0.6 mile, this narrow road turns to rough gravel, switchbacks sharply to the left, and climbs a heavily wooded hillside. The road affords you little room to pass oncoming traffic, so take it slow, and be prepared to back up to the nearest pullout, if you meet a car coming down the hill. Actually, you won't be going very fast anyway, as the road is miserably rutted with rocks, potholes, and deep mud holes.

At a major switchback to the left, take the time to get out of your car and enjoy the view of a tall waterfall in Devils Canyon. The road ends 5.2 miles from the highway, at a small trailhead parking area.

Two trails leave from this trailhead. By far the more popular follows a long abandoned section of the Enola Hill Road heading northeast up Devils Canyon (see Trip 6). For the trail to West Zigzag Mountain, walk back down the road about 150 feet to a small sign for West Zigzag Trail #789. This trail is not maintained as regularly as most others in the Zigzag area, so you can expect to crawl over the occasional log. You can still easily follow the path, but it's a bit overgrown with grasses, ferns, shrubs, and herbs. After a rain, this wet, overhanging vegetation will get you soaked, so bring along rain pants and, possibly, gaiters in order to stay comfortable.

The path drops briefly to cross a seasonal creek, then begins climbing a long switchback to the top of a woodsy ridge. From here you descend about 200 feet to a small creek whose banks are crowded with lots of ferns, monkeyflower, bleeding heart, and other water-loving plants. One of those plants is stinging nettle, so be careful about what you brush up against. After hopping across the creek, you climb at an irregular pace on a trail that is often rocky, so watch your step. Beargrass and huckleberry become increasingly common as you approach a trail junction in a saddle on the top of the ridge forming Zigzag Mountain. To reach the dramatic viewpoint from the old lookout site on West Zigzag Mountain, you turn left and in just 0.2 mile reach the open viewpoint.

Hikers who want to tackle a long loop trip can turn right at the trail junction below West Zigzag Mountain and follow the increasingly open and spectacular ridgeline to the east. The up-and-down route passes massive wildflower meadows and lots of huckleberries as well as stunning views of Mt. Hood as you pass junctions with the Horseshoe Ridge Trail (Trip 2) and the Cast Creek Trail (Trip 1) before coming to the final high viewpoint at East Zigzag Mountain. From there you return on the route down Devils Canyon (Trip 6) back to your car.

Trip 6

East Zigzag Mountain from Enola Hill

(Map Area MH-2)

Distance	Elevation Gain	Hiking Time	Optional Map	Difficulty
8.0 miles	1700'	4 to 5 hours	*Green Trails–Government Camp*	**

Usually Open	Mid-June to October
Best Times	July
Agency	Zigzag Ranger District (Mt. Hood National Forest)

Just as the Enola Hill Road provides a shortcut to West Zigzag Mountain (Trip 5), it provides a much easier approach to East Zigzag Mountain. And while this trip misses Burnt Lake, it does have better meadows and more flowers than the approach from the north. That's a reasonable tradeoff, and ambitious hikers can still visit Burnt Lake if they want to by taking a side trip off the main trail.

Directions: Drive 1.5 miles east of Rhododendron on U.S. Highway 26, and turn left (north) onto paved Forest Road 27. After 0.6 mile, this narrow road turns to rough gravel, switchbacks sharply to the left, and climbs a heavily wooded hillside. The road affords you little room to pass oncoming traffic, so take it slow, and be prepared to back up to the nearest pullout, if you meet a car coming down the hill. Actually, you won't be going very fast anyway, as the road is miserably rutted with rocks, potholes, and deep mud holes.

The trail begins on a long-abandoned jeep route that was once the extension of the Enola Hill Road. While the width of this route identifies it as an old road, it has been so long since it was used by vehicles that it is now effectively an easy, gently graded trail. The vegetation along the route is lush and attractive, with lots of wildflowers, including some unusual varieties. Look for goatsbeard, beardtongue, devils club, tiger lily, goldenrod, and aster.

After about 0.7 mile, you enter the wilderness. Soon thereafter you will leave the forest and begin to travel through increasingly lush and attractive meadows. The old road stays generally level all the way to its end in Devils Meadow, where a close inspection may reveal evidence of an old car campground. If you'd rather inspect something more attractive, spend your time identifying the profusion of wildflowers. There are lupine and paintbrush, of course, but also larkspur, beargrass, arnica, spiraea, bistort, valerian, and other colorful species.

Now a true footpath, the route crosses a trickling creek and arrives at a junction with the Devils Tie Trail. This marks the end of a recommended loop trip you can take on your return from East Zigzag Mountain. For now, go straight at this junction and climb the open meadowy slopes covered with huckleberry bushes and a few scattered trees. In mid-to-late August, you will need to schedule extra time for feasting on huckleberries. Seven long switchbacks lead you up to a ridgetop junction, where you'll gain your first look at imposing Mt. Hood. If you want to visit Burnt Lake, turn right at this junction, then left at a second junction about 200 yards later. This switchbacking trail drops down a shady, north-facing slope to the shores of the popular lake.

To reach East Zigzag Mountain, the high point of the trip, turn left at the ridgeline junction and ascend a steep, rocky trail 0.3 mile to the summit. Views from here extend in all directions and include a look all the way south to distant Mt. Jefferson, but the main attraction is Mt. Hood. With binoculars you can even see the crevasses in Reid and Zigzag glaciers. Tiny alpine wildflowers such as lomatium, phlox, and cliff penstemon provide colorful foregrounds for pictures of the mountain.

To return by a different route, drop down the west side of the peak and come to a junction with the Cast Creek Trail, in a wooded saddle. You bear left at this junction and switchback down a bit more to a second junction, this time with the Cast Lake Trail. This lake is worth a visit, even though it doesn't have a view of Mt. Hood. To close out the loop, go straight at the junction and loop around a lovely little mountain meadow that is home to lots of spiraea, a small, pink-blooming shrub whose flowers have a wonderful aroma. Just past this meadow is a junction with the Devils Tie Trail. Turn left here and descend several short, steep switchbacks to the junction just above Devils Meadow.

Trip 7

Castle Canyon

(Map Area MH-2)

Distance	Elevation Gain	Hiking Time	Optional Map	Difficulty
1.8 miles	800'	1 hour	*Green Trails–Government Camp*	**

Usually Open	March to December
Best Times	April to June
Agency	Zigzag Ranger District (Mt. Hood National Forest)

This is a short but rewarding leg-stretcher, close to busy Highway 26, but a world away from the hustle and bustle of that traffic-plagued thoroughfare. Here you will enjoy a quiet forest, fascinating geology, and some reasonably good viewpoints. Another benefit is the good workout this short but rather strenuous path provides. It also will not take up too much of your time if you are on your way to more distant destinations.

Directions: For the shortest approach, drive U.S. Highway 26 for 1.8 miles east from Zigzag to Rhododendron. At the west end of town, turn sharply left (north) on E. Littlebrook Lane (which almost immediately becomes E. Arlie Mitchell Road), a narrow paved route that you should follow for 0.3 mile to a junction. Bear left here and follow signs for the BARLOW ROAD ROUTE. Drive 0.4 mile on a pothole-filled dirt road past driveways of summer homes to the Castle Canyon trailhead on the right. Since there is virtually no legal parking here (all of the driveways are conspicuously signed to keep out hiker's cars), you may be better off starting this hike 0.9 mile to the west, at the

View from end of Castle Canyon Trail near Zigzag

West Zigzag Mountain trailhead (see Trip 4). From that parking area you simply walk the washed out and permanently closed road between the two trailheads. The additional 1.8 miles of round-trip walking is pleasant and doesn't make the overall hike too long, considering the shortness of the path up Castle Canyon.

From the Castle Canyon trailhead, the trail climbs gradually in trees for a short distance to a wilderness permit station, then continues its gentle, woodsy ascent. A series of short switchbacks signals an increase in the grade, as you gain elevation rapidly up the spine of a little ridge. The slope is covered with trees but gradually provides a more open feeling with occasional glimpses of the steep sides of West Zigzag Mountain. The steep climb continues as you round the side of the rock pinnacles that give this trail its name. The ancient spires, part of an exposed volcanic dike, are covered with moss, ferns, and small shrubs that cling to the poor soil amid the rocks.

The trail ends with a final steep push to a rather disappointing overlook amid the rocks. Only very daring and sure-footed hikers should contemplate a further exploration down the knife-edge spine of the rocky ridge. The route is dangerous but leads to some nice viewpoints of the Zigzag area. Although it is difficult to get a decent view of the rock pinnacles themselves, the looks at the valley below and the distant ridges in the Salmon-Huckleberry Wilderness are ample compensation.

Mount Hood

Area MH-3: Southern Mount Hood

The south side of Mt. Hood around Government Camp and Timberline Lodge is the most accessible and popular area on the mountain. Thousands of visitors come throughout the year to take advantage of the ski areas and other developed attractions. Surprisingly, it is still possible to enjoy quiet trails amid all the tourist hordes. With a little inside knowledge, like that provided on the following pages, you can discover many hidden meadows, viewpoints, lakes, and forests just a short distance from all the hustle and bustle. The only really annoying aspect of hiking here is the difficulty in finding a place to park on summer weekends. Once you leave the parking lot, the trails are a joy.

Trip 1

Paradise Park Trail

(Map Area MH-3)

Distance	Elevation Gain	Hiking Time	Optional Map	Difficulty
12.4 miles	3100'	7 to 8 hours	*Green Trails–Government Camp & Mount Hood*	***

Usually Open	Mid-July to October
Best Times	Late July to early August
Agency	Zigzag Ranger District (Mt. Hood National Forest)

The Paradise Park Trail is a quiet, but tiring approach to the extremely popular Paradise Park area. There are relatively few highlights on this trail, but you will enjoy lots of solitude, especially compared to the extremely busy approach from Timberline Lodge (Trip 10). By connecting this trail with the Hidden Lake Trail (Trip 2), you can make a long, strenuous dayhike or very enjoyable weekend backpacking trip.

Directions: Drive east on U.S. Highway 26 from Zigzag to milepost 48.6, then bear left off the highway onto paved Forest Road 39. Drive 1.3 miles, then turn left on a dirt road with a sign for the Paradise Park Trail. This access road goes over a bridge and, about 100 yards later, comes to a parking and camping area beside the trailhead.

 The trail starts in a dense western-hemlock and western redcedar forest amid mossy rocks on a gently sloping bench above the rushing Zigzag River. The serious climbing doesn't begin

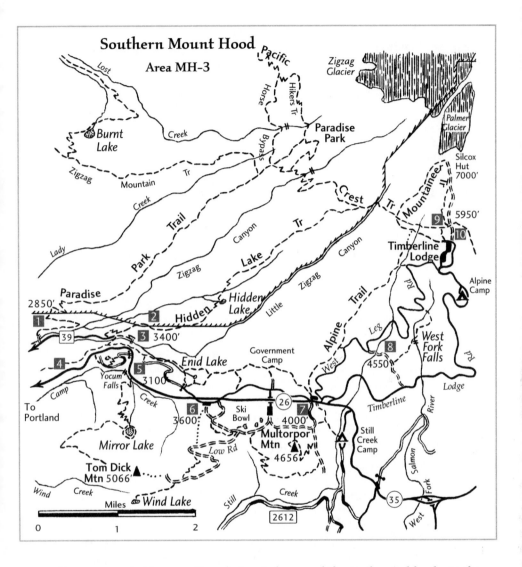

Southern Mount Hood
Area MH-3

until you come to the permit and sign-in box, and the trail switchbacks to the left. Six long, moderately ascending switchbacks take you up a viewless, woodsy slope, where July-blooming rhododendrons add some color to the scene. The trail then climbs above the traffic sounds of Highway 26, into the more soothing natural sounds of clicking juncos, rasping one-note red-breasted nuthatches, and the more varied songs of mountain chickadees. After the switchbacks end, the path comes to some open lodgepole-pine woods and goes along the edge of a precipitous cliff, with good views south to Tom Dick Mountain and Zigzag Canyon.

The grade of your climb picks up again as you enter thicker forests of noble and Pacific silver fir as well as Douglas-fir. On the forest floor, look for beargrass blooms in July and the downward-facing flowers of pipsissewa later in the summer. There are a few short switchbacks along this section but no real landmarks as the path climbs steadily, but not overly steeply, through the trees. Eventually you reach a junction with the Zigzag Mountain Trail coming in from the left. Go straight and almost immediately you will notice an improvement in the scenery. Most obvious are the abundant and colorful wildflowers, which peak in late July and include white valerian, blue lupine, green false hellebore, and yellow groundsel. Soon after you reach the junction a good view of the deeply eroded Zigzag Canyon and part of Mt. Hood appears.

Although the climbing isn't over yet, most of it is, and what little remains goes unnoticed because your attention will instead be turned to the scenery. Just 0.3 mile from the last junction, you go straight at a four-way junction with the equestrian bypass trail below Paradise Park. From here, you climb through increasingly open, flower-covered meadows to a junction with the Pacific Crest Trail.

The number and variety of flowers here are positively overwhelming. In addition to the previously mentioned species, you will enjoy bistort, Jacob's ladder, purple asters, pearly everlasting, and cat's ear. It's a riot of color in late July and early August—some of the best flower displays in the state of Oregon. If the summer has been cool and wet, then the flower show remains good all the way through Labor Day. The scattered trees at this altitude are mostly mountain hemlock and subalpine fir, which add to the magic of this alpine scene. It's probably impossible to resist the temptation to explore higher on the sloping meadows above the junction.

After satisfying your sense of adventure, return to the PCT and turn west for 0.3 mile to reach the many good camps and the dilapidated shelter at Paradise Park. Since this area is very popular, it is crucial that you camp only in official sites that have been used for years and can take the pounding—but don't build a fire.

To do the loop with the Hidden Lake Trail, turn east at the PCT junction and descend this route into Zigzag Canyon. Ford the stream a short distance below an impressive waterfall. Then climb long switchbacks out of the canyon to the junction with the Hidden Lake Trail. Turn right on this relatively little-used trail and descend, often fairly steeply, on a forested hillside. There are few flowers or other things of interest along this route, but the setting is tranquil and the trail is quiet, so the hiking is pleasant and the downhill miles go by quickly. The path goes through lots of huckleberries, but the shade here prohibits a bumper crop. About 0.2 mile after you hop over a splashing creek, the trail reaches tiny, marsh-rimmed Hidden Lake. This is a shallow pool with lots of bugs in July and little to recommend it other than solitude. The outlet creek does, however, have some impressive skunk cabbage with enormous leaves.

The path leaves Hidden Lake, climbs briefly, then descends through western-hemlock forests with lots of rhododendrons blooming in mid-July. The last mile of this trail is always within earshot of busy U.S. Highway 26 as it descends four steep switchbacks and arrives at Forest Road 39 at a gravel trailhead pullout. The Paradise Park trailhead is an easy 1.4-mile stroll down this road.

Trip 2

Hidden Lake

(Map Area MH-3)

Distance	Elevation Gain	Hiking Time	Optional Map	Difficulty
4.2 miles	700'	2 to 3 hours	*Green Trails–Government Camp*	**

Usually Open	May to early November
Best Times	June
Agency	Zigzag Ranger District (Mt. Hood National Forest)

People are always drawn to lakes. It doesn't really matter if the lake isn't very scenic, doesn't have many fish, or is too brushy and muddy to provide good swimming. All those unexciting qualities describe Hidden Lake, the small mountain pool that is the goal of this hike. But the hike is worth your time, in part because it is relatively easy, and in part because of the varied vegetation along the way, but mostly because at the destination you can lie back and enjoy the tranquillity of a forest-rimmed mountain pool with few other hikers around to disturb your sense of solitude.

Directions: Drive east on U.S. Highway 26 from Zigzag to milepost 48.6, then bear left off the highway onto paved Forest Road 39. Follow this route 2.7 miles and park in a gravel parking area on your left. If you reach the end of the road at the Little Zigzag Falls trailhead, you have driven about 0.3 mile too far.

The most difficult part of the hike is right at the beginning, as you wind up a series of four short switchbacks. The route is generally well graded, although there is a short rocky section that is quite steep. After coming to the top of the switchbacks, the path follows a partly open ridgeline with some decent views of Tom Dick Mountain and the Zigzag Valley. Unfortunately, the tranquillity of this scene is rudely broken by the sounds of traffic on busy Highway 26.

The trail gradually gains elevation as it winds through the trees and works away from the sounds of cars. The forests here support lots of rhododendrons, which fill the forest with pink blossoms from late June to mid-July. The trail eventually tops a low ridge, then goes briefly downhill to a crossing of a small creek, just downstream from Hidden Lake. A short spur trail goes through the brush to the shores of the lake, but it is also worth spending some time examining the outlet creek, which features an abundance of skunk cabbage. This plant loves wet environments and has enormous, shiny, green leaves. The large yellow flowers, which bloom in spring and early summer, are responsible for the unpleasant odor for which this plant is named.

The trail continues beyond Hidden Lake, crossing a splashing creek about 0.3 mile above the lake and climbing a rather monotonous, wooded ridge. The path has no real highlights, so it isn't really worth the hike on its own, but the often-steep path is sometimes used as the return route of a giant loop hike in combination with the Paradise Park Trail (see Trip 1).

Trip 3

Little Zigzag Falls & Enid Lake

(Map Area MH-3)

Distance	Elevation Gain	Hiking Time	Optional Map	Difficulty
4.0 miles	600'	2 hours	*Green Trails–Government Camp*	**

Usually Open	Late May to early November
Best Times	June / October
Agency	Zigzag Ranger District (Mt. Hood National Forest)

The 0.7-mile round-trip hike to Little Zigzag Falls is short for a full day-hike, but it makes an excellent leg stretcher for families with children. If you want a full day of hiking, you can add an enjoyable outing up the old Pioneer Bridle Trail to Enid Lake. Little Zigzag Falls is worth a visit because it is a pleasant cascade surrounded by deep woods. The setting makes the falls difficult to photograph, but that can't take away from the soothing tranquillity of the scene. Enid Lake is little more than a marshy pond, but it has a pretty setting and from it you can see the top one-third of Mt. Hood, so the scene is worth a look.

Directions: Drive east on U.S. Highway 26 from Zigzag to milepost 48.6, then bear left off the highway onto paved Forest Road 39. Follow this route for 3.0 miles to the roadend turnaround and parking area.

The trail to Little Zigzag Falls leaves from the east end of the parking area and follows the north bank of the clear, splashing Little Zigzag River. The easy path travels through a lush forest composed mostly of western red cedar and western hemlock, while beside the creek such water-loving plants as devils club, maiden-hair and other ferns, skunk cabbage, and false solomon seal crowd the bank.

After a little over 0.3 mile, the gentle uphill path comes to a small, open, bouldery slope and, immediately thereafter, a sturdy log bench at the base of Little Zigzag Falls, a twisting cataract that puts out a cool spray of water. This is a pleasant spot to eat lunch and enjoy the beauty of both falls and forest. From the bench, the path continues in two switchbacks to a disappointing overlook at the top of the falls, but this extra mileage is worthwhile only for the exercise.

The trail to Enid Lake leaves from the same trailhead and begins as a gated road taking off from the south side of the parking area. You cross the Little Zigzag River on a bridge, and climb the road on a partially forested hillside. After 0.1 mile, look for a trail tunnel going under the road, and drop down to it. You are now on the Pioneer Bridle Trail, which, as you might guess from the name, is an historic section of the old Barlow Wagon Road. Turn east on this wide trail and fol-

Little Zigzag Falls

low the shoulder of Highway 26 for a few dozen yards, then bear left back into the trees.

The trail soon leaves the traffic sounds behind and enters a quiet and lovely forest. The wide path is littered with the tiny needles and cones of hemlock trees and lined with huckleberry bushes that are laden with delicious fruit in late August. Much of the route is marked by blue diamonds on trees, which identify this as a cross-country ski route in winter. You go straight at an unsigned junction with a spur trail, which goes to the right to the end of a closed section of the old highway.

The quiet trail now very gradually gains elevation and eventually follows a lovely little mountain creek. The joyous sounds of bubbling water join with the sight of mossy rocks and lush riparian vegetation to make a magical scene. The streambed is choked with skunk cabbage, a plant with huge, shiny, green leaves and showy yellow flowers. The trail crosses the creek on a wooden footbridge, then veers away from it to a junction with the Enid Lake Ski Trail. Despite the name, this path does *not* visit Enid Lake, so bear right and stay on the Pioneer Bridle Trail to a junction right beside an upper trailhead on a barricaded section of the old highway. You turn left here on the Crosstown Trail and, after 0.1 mile, look for a 20-yard side trail to the left that leads to the shore of shallow Enid Lake. The best pictures are from the south shore.

Trip 4

Laurel Hill Chute Loop

(Map Area MH-3)

Distance	Elevation Gain	Hiking Time	Optional Map	Difficulty
1.3 miles	300'	1 hour	*Green Trails–Government Camp* (trail not shown)	*

Usually Open	Late April to November
Best Times	June
Agency	Zigzag Ranger District (Mt. Hood National Forest)

This is a convenient option for hikers who want to mix a bit of exercise with a dose of history. The view from trail's end is good, but the real attraction is standing above a rocky precipice and visualizing the exploits of pioneers who somehow managed to negotiate this ruggedly steep terrain in covered wagons.

Directions: Drive U.S. Highway 26 about 9 miles east of Zigzag and park in the small pullout on the right side of the road beside an historical marker.

The path begins by climbing a short flight of stone stairs to a junction with a section of old Highway 26. Turn right on this closed road. Then gradually climb past an interpretive sign and some openings that provide good views of Tom Dick Mountain and Zigzag Canyon. After about 150 yards, you bear left onto a signed footpath and slowly ascend five switchbacks through an open forest of Douglas-fir, western hemlock, and western red cedar. The forest floor is dominated by bracken fern, some salal, and two plants with showy June flowers—beargrass and Pacific rhododendron.

The climb tops a rounded hill, where there is an unsigned junction. You go straight and descend a bit to the viewpoint above Laurel Hill Chute. As you look down this very steep, rocky defile it is hard to envision how the early pioneers made it through here. They managed it by tying ropes around trees at the top of the gorge, and using muscle power to lower their wagons down the slope. This was an incredibly dangerous and difficult task, and your admiration of their achievement will increase when you realize that, even today, it is too dangerous for you to go down the chute of loose rocks on foot.

For a bit of variety on the return trip, make a loop by turning left at the unsigned junction mentioned earlier. This path follows what is believed to be the actual route of the old wagon road for 0.1 mile, then comes to a junction with an upper section of the old paved highway. You turn right on it, then walk down this route, which is gradually being taken over by encroaching willows and lodgepole-pine trees. You make one long, curving switchback before returning to the junction with the Laurel Hill Chute Trail and taking the stairs back to your car.

Trip 5

Mirror Lake & Tom Dick Mountain

(Map Area MH-3)

Distance	Elevation Gain	Hiking Time	Optional Map	Difficulty
3.2 to 6.4 miles	700' to 1500'	2 to 4 hours	Green Trails– Government Camp	**

Usually Open	June to October
Best Times	Late June and July
Agency	Zigzag Ranger District (Mt. Hood National Forest)

Mirror Lake has been a popular hiking destination for decades. With easy trail access and a classic view of Mt. Hood, it will likely remain popular for a long time. So don't come to Mirror Lake hoping for a quiet wilderness experience. On summer weekends hundreds of fellow admirers trek up this trail. It's best to visit on a weekday, although even then you should be prepared to meet plenty of people. By extending the hike up the western spur of Tom Dick Mountain, you can get more exercise and reach a nice viewpoint above most of the crowds.

Directions: Drive U.S. Highway 26 east toward Government Camp. A little before milepost 52, park in the large roadside pullout on the right side of the road. There is no trailhead sign here, but you can't miss the small trail bridge leaving from the parking area or the dozens of other cars already parked in the lot.

The trail starts by crossing a narrow bridge over Camp Creek a little upstream from unseen Yocum Falls. The wide, gently graded trail has been built to withstand the punishment of so many visitors. In places the Forest Service has installed wooden hand rails to keep people on the official trail. To protect the land, it is important that you never cut switchbacks and, even better, chastise anyone who does.

The trail traverses a short distance, then crosses a bridge over a tributary creek and returns to the forested hillside. The forests are relatively open, with lots of vine maple and Pacific rhododendron beneath a mix of evergreens, including Douglas-fir, western white pine, western hemlock, and western red cedar. You will make a long, gradual ascent to the base of a rockslide, before switchbacking to cross the slide higher on the slope. Look for pikas here busily gathering grasses to store for the long winter ahead.

Above the rockslide, the trail enters slightly wetter forest and makes a fairly long traverse. After this, you ascend three quick switchbacks and come to a junction just below the lake. The trail to the left immediately crosses the outlet creek, then loops around the lake's east and south shores. Much of the lakeshore is crowded with thick brush, mostly salmonberry, rose, willow, and slide alder. From the south shore, your eyes are irresistibly drawn to the stunning view of Mt. Hood, which is best seen by getting off the main trail and visiting any of several lakeshore picnic sites. The best photographs are usually taken during the afternoon. Windless days are preferable, because the water does indeed act like a mirror, although jumping fish often create circular ripples in the glassy stillness and temporarily disturb the reflecting properties that gave this lake its name. There is a fine meadow on the southwest shore of the lake, which in early summer has lots of blooming marsh marigolds and shooting stars. To protect these fragile meadows, please stay on the log planks marking the route of the trail. If you wish to camp at the lake, use the designated sites above the drier west shore.

To reach a quiet viewpoint, leave the lakeshore loop and climb a trail going southwest. The path travels through an open forest of lodgepole pine and mountain hemlock, then gradually climbs across an open hillside with lots of huckleberries and views to the town of Zigzag. When you reach a ridgeline, turn east, and slowly gain altitude. The trail becomes increasingly faint on this partly forested slope, but it is still easy to follow until it ends at an excellent viewpoint near a large cairn. From here you can look northeast to Mt. Hood and down on circular Mirror Lake, or spend your time picking out lesser landmarks tucked away in the Salmon-Huckleberry Wilderness to the south and west. In recent years, peregrine falcons have nested on the upper slopes of Tom Dick Mountain. To protect this endangered species, the Forest Service has restricted access beyond the viewpoint, so turn back here, well satisfied with what you have achieved.

Trip 6

Wind Lake

(Map Area MH-3)

Distance	Elevation Gain	Hiking Time	Optional Map	Difficulty
6.4 miles	1400'	3 to 4 hours	*Green Trails–Government Camp* (trail not shown)	**

Usually Open	Mid-June to October
Best Times	Late June and July / mid-August to September
Agency	Zigzag Ranger District (Mt. Hood National Forest)

Forest-rimmed Wind Lake hides in a quiet basin on the back side of Tom Dick Mountain. The lake seems to be a world away from the unsightly hustle and bustle of the ski area on the other side of the mountain. Surprisingly, few hikers take the time to visit this little gem, perhaps because there is no mountain view across its waters. But while Wind Lake will never be featured on calendars, it *is* a good place to enjoy the kind of solitude that is no longer possible at nearby Mirror Lake.

Directions: Take U.S. Highway 26 up to a little past milepost 52, near Government Camp, then turn right into the huge parking lot for Mount Hood Ski Bowl-West.

Begin by walking south past the main ski lodge buildings. When you come to the base of the ski lift and the alpine slide, bear left on a gravel and dirt road. This road climbs steeply for about 0.1 mile, then comes to a junction, where you turn left on Lake Road. About 75 yards later, turn right at a sign for South Trail and walk this pleasant footpath as it winds up and down through cedar and hemlock forests. The path parallels an unobtrusive dirt road for 0.5 mile, then meets and crosses that road. Instead of crossing, you turn right and walk on the road, under a ski lift, to a junction with a second jeep road signed LOW ROAD.

You turn sharply right on Low Road, which gradually climbs a hillside where the tree cover is occasionally broken by cleared ski runs. In late June and July, Pacific rhododendrons bloom here in profusion, helping to give the scene a wilder feeling. As you gain altitude, the open forests gradually change from mid-elevation species to higher-elevation varieties like lodgepole pine, Alaska yellow cedar, and mountain hemlock. After a little over 1 mile, the road hits the top of the main ski run above Ski Bowl-West and switchbacks to the left. Immediately after this switchback, you come to the warming hut for the ski area, where you will get terrific views of Mt. Hood.

Wind Lake south of Tom Dick Mountain

At this point, you have a choice of routes. The longer and gentler alternative is to stay on the gravel road as it climbs in one long switchback to the top of a ridge. The steeper and more direct route veers to the right at the hut and steeply climbs an open hillside. This mountain-bike trail uses a series of switchbacks to gain elevation and with every step provides increasingly far-ranging views. At the top of the ridge, you rejoin the road and turn right.

After just 100 yards, bear left onto a wide, but unsigned, footpath, which gently descends through an open forest of scraggly lodgepole pines for 0.5 mile to the shores of shallow Wind Lake. Although it lacks mountain views, this lake is quiet and very attractive. One of the nicest times to visit is in mid-to-late summer, when the shallow waters have warmed enough for a pleasant swim. During cold winters the lake may freeze, killing most of the brook trout that are planted here. As a result, fishing is only mediocre. Since very few anglers come here, however, it may be worthwhile to give it a try.

You can return the way you came, or, for variety, you could walk directly from the warming hut down ski slopes back to the lodge. Although quite steep, the route is obvious and the goal is always in sight.

Trip 7

Multorpor Mountain View & Loop

(Map Area MH-3)

Distance	Elevation Gain	Hiking Time	Optional Map	Difficulty
5.1 miles (combined)	1700' (combined)	3 hours (combined)	*Green Trails–Government Camp & Mount Hood* (trail not shown)	**

Usually Open	June to October
Best Times	Mid-June to Mid-July
Agency	Zigzag Ranger District (Mt. Hood National Forest)

The little-known summit of Multorpor Mountain provides a classic view of Mt. Hood and the busy ski town of Government Camp. The steep, unsigned trail to the top is rarely hiked, but it is well worth the effort for adventurous hikers who like good views. By combining this climb with the trail around the base of the mountain, you can enjoy a full day of scenic hiking.

Directions: Drive U.S. Highway 26 east to Government Camp and park in the lot for the Summit Rest Area on the north side of the highway. To reach the trailhead, you must walk across the highway, something that is easier said than done on summer weekends, when the traffic is very heavy.

For a bit of history, start by walking down a dirt road next to a gray post with an OREGON TRAIL marker. The road is about 80 yards east of the milepost 54 sign. This route immediately passes a cluster of wooden buildings near the highway, then comes to a trail-maintenance donation box and a trail sign. This sign, like most of the others along this route, is over 12 feet high in order to ensure that cross-country skiers can see it when traveling over deep snow. In summer, however, the average hiker needs to crane his neck, and possibly squint, to make out the small lettering on the lofty signs.

You bear left at the sign and follow the Barlow Trail, which immediately becomes either a very narrow abandoned jeep road or a very wide foot trail, depending on your point of view. You are now literally walking in the footsteps of pioneers, as this is a portion of the historic Barlow Wagon Road traveled by many of the early pioneers on the Oregon Trail. The surrounding forests are mostly mountain hemlocks, with a few firs and Alaska yellow cedars added for variety. The forest floor is sprinkled with beargrass, young evergreens, and huckleberry bushes.

A maze of cross-country ski trails and mountain-bike routes lace these forests, and they can get very confusing, so follow these directions carefully. About 0.1 mile from the highway, go straight at a signed junction with the

Barlow Trail and, a few hundred yards later, turn right at a sign saying TO SUM-MIT TRAIL. Follow this short footpath to a dirt road, which doubles as the Summit Trail, and turn left on the road. About 50 yards later, at an unsigned junction next to a small powerline, you turn left again, and climb a jeep track in the trees beneath the powerline.

Only 100 yards from the last junction, where the jeep route crests a small hill and begins to descend, look for an unsigned but obvious foot trail going up the steep hillside on your right. To visit the summit of Multorpor Mountain, turn right and follow this often-steep trail up a wooded hillside. In late June and July, lots of blooming Pacific rhododendron make for a nice visual treat. Even though it is obvious on the ground, this trail is not part of the Forest Service's trail inventory. Do your part to help maintain it, by removing any rocks, limbs, or debris that block the path. The 0.7-mile trail tops out at the rocky summit of Multorpor Mountain.

The view here is one of the best in the area. In addition to the main attraction of Mt. Hood, to your immediate north, you will also be able to pick out partially obstructed Mt. Jefferson, in the distance to the south, and Mt. St. Helens, peeking over a western spur ridge of Mt. Hood. Lesser summits include the talus slopes of Tom Dick Mountain, to the west, forested Eureka Peak, to the south, and rounded Barlow Butte, to the east. The woodsy valley of Still Creek curves away to the southwest.

To do the loop around Multorpor Mountain, go back down the steep trail to the jeep route and turn right. This rocky jeep track goes steeply downhill, then veers away from the powerline and meanders through the woods at a much more gentle grade. About 0.1 mile later, you turn right onto a trail that is marked with a sign stating that the path is open to hikers, mountain bikers, and skiers. This trail was constructed for the benefit of mountain bikers, so watch for two-wheeled travelers and let them pass unimpeded. This pleasant path alternates between dense woods and miniature forest openings, as it takes a circuitous route across the south side of Multorpor Mountain. Many different birds, including thrushes, warblers, kinglets, and flycatchers, provide treats for your ears, while a variety of wildflowers are a feast for the eyes.

The trail eventually descends about 200 feet, then curves right and regains that lost altitude (and more) by ascending a series of nicely graded switchbacks. At the top of this ascent, the trail makes an extended contour of a hillside covered with a very attractive forest. The path goes through a saddle, where you go straight at an unsigned junction, then almost immediately comes to a confusion of roads and ski runs in Mount Hood Ski Bowl. Your best bet is to go generally to the right staying on the lowest of several roads. From this road you should take the opportunity to bushwhack a few dozen feet through the trees and brush on your left, to visit the marshy Multorpor Ponds. These pools feature lovely reflections of Mt. Hood, but they also host abundant mosquitoes in late June and July.

To finish the loop, you need to find the dirt jeep road that serves as the Summit Trail. This is most easily done by simply making your way east, past a confusion of ski runs and maintenance sheds, to the Multorpor Restaurant

& Lounge at Ski Bowl-East. The signed Summit Trail takes off about 70 yards southeast of this building. Follow this quiet track for about 0.5 mile back to the Multorpor Mountain turnoff you passed earlier in the day. For variety on the way back, skip the connecting path to the Barlow Trail and simply stay on the main Summit Trail. This route takes you through open woods back to Highway 26 about 90 yards west of where you started. Carefully cross the highway to get back to your car.

Trip 8

West Fork Falls

(Map Area MH-3)

Distance	Elevation Gain	Hiking Time	Optional Map	Difficulty
2.8 miles	500'	1 to 2 hours	Green Trails–Mount Hood	**

Usually Open	Late June to October	
Best Times	July and August	
Agency	Zigzag Ranger District (Mt. Hood National Forest)	

This quiet forest hike is the perfect complement to the more spectacular mountain trails in the Mt. Hood area. Views aren't an issue on this hike, so if you are in Government Camp and the skies have turned cloudy, consider this little-known outing. The destination is a pretty little falls in a mossy canyon, but since the trail is unmarked, few people ever come to visit. Thus, in addition to a lovely setting, you will enjoy plenty of solitude.

Directions: Turn north off U.S. Highway 26, just east of Government Camp, onto the Timberline Lodge Road. After just 0.2 mile, turn left on a narrow, one-way road that goes west past some summer homes and lodges. Just 30 yards before this road rejoins Highway 26, turn right on unsigned West Leg Road. Follow this single-lane, paved road 1.6 miles to a sharp left-hand switchback, and look for a tall sign marking the East Leg Cross-Country Ski Trail. There is room for about three cars to park here.

Walk east on an old road through a cool forest mostly composed of mountain hemlock and lodgepole pine, with some Engelmann spruce and subalpine fir. Just 200 yards from the start, a road culvert takes you over splashing Still Creek, then you go very gradually downhill. About 0.8 mile from the trailhead, where the road makes a slow turn to the right, look carefully for an unsigned foot trail crossing the route. Turn left (uphill) and climb steadily, but not too steeply, on this trail, which is lined with beargrass and huckleberries that provide blossoms to enjoy in mid-July and fruit to eat in late August.

The trail goes about 0.6 mile, then it bears slightly to the right and drops gradually to a viewpoint on the slope beside West Fork Falls. The falls isn't a towering drop on the order of Multnomah Falls, but it has subtle charms, as it cascades about 40 feet over cliffs and rocks covered with bright green mosses, then tumbles into a shady canyon. The trail crosses the creek above the falls on slippery and unstable logs, then it follows the cascading creek upstream and eventually takes you back to West Leg Road. The falls is the main attraction, however, so most hikers simply turn around there.

Trip 9

Mountaineer Trail Loop

(Map Area MH-3)

Distance	Elevation Gain	Hiking Time	Optional Map	Difficulty
2.2 miles	1100'	1 to 2 hours	*Green Trails–Mount Hood*	**

Usually Open	Late July to late September
Best Times	August
Agency	Zigzag Ranger District (Mt. Hood National Forest)

The great diversity of landscapes that you can reach by just a short one-hour's drive from Portland is truly amazing. From the sea-level flats on Sauvie Island to the glaciers on Mt. Hood, this area has scenery to meet the preferences of any outdoor lover. This path, for example, climbs into the alpine zone, well above timberline, through a harsh land of permanent snowfields and rocks. Views extend for hundreds of miles, and tiny wildflowers brighten the rocky crevices.

Travel in this harsh environment involves some difficulties not encountered on most hikes. For one thing, the weather at these altitudes can be harsh and unpredictable. Blizzards can occur in any season, and there is nothing to slow the fierce winds. Save this trip for a clear, calm day. You might also notice that the air is slightly thinner up here—not enough to give you altitude sickness, perhaps, but enough to slow your progress while hiking. Finally, there is no shade above treeline, and at these altitudes it is very easy to get a sunburn. Put on sunscreen and wear a hat.

Directions: Turn north off U.S. Highway 26 just east of Government Camp onto the Timberline Lodge Road. Climb this winding, paved road 5.5 miles to the historic lodge with its acres of parking.

Walk west on the paved road past the south side of the lodge, then go under the start of the Magic Mile ski lift to a dirt road.

Turn left when the road splits, and walk about 50 yards to a sign for Mountaineer Trail 798. Walk west on this sandy path through an open forest of mountain hemlock and subalpine fir that struggle to survive at these high altitudes. Clark's nutcrackers, striking gray, black, and white birds who caw at you like small crows, are one of the few avian species that live at these altitudes. Flowers such as lupine, western pasque flower, phlox, lomatium, arnica, and partridge foot abound in the open forests and meadows, but they don't bloom until late summer.

The trail goes gradually up and down through this harsh environment, often crossing small gullies, which are usually filled with snow until mid-August. These openings also afford some terrific views to the south of Trillium Lake, Mt. Jefferson, and the Three Sisters. After about 0.4 mile, you go under a second ski lift, which, unlike the Magic Mile lift, is quiet because it is not used during the summer. The trail passes the marked site of the old Timberline cabin, then comes to a junction with the Pacific Crest Trail. You cross this route, staying on the Mountaineer Trail, and head steeply uphill. You soon enter a region where the subalpine firs cannot survive. They are replaced by hardier whitebark pines, which manage to survive in this windy environment because their branches are so flexible they can literally be tied in knots. As you climb, you might hear the distant rattle from the working Magic Mile lift, but otherwise things are amazingly quiet.

You reach the last of the ground-hugging trees and bleached snags about halfway up to your goal, the metal building at the top of the Magic Mile lift, and enter an area with unrestricted views. Towering above you is craggy Mt. Hood, with its glaciers shimmering in the summer sun. To the southeast are the semi-desert country of central Oregon and the dark, rounded forms of the distant Ochoco Mountains. To the west are the hazy lowlands of Portland and the Willamette Valley. Finally, to the south is the Ski Bowl development, Government Camp, Tom Dick Mountain, and a multitude of small, forest-covered peaks. Things get more crowded and busy as you approach the top of the Magic Mile lift, where you are treated to the peculiar sight in August of downhill skiers headed for the permanent snowfields on Palmer Glacier. Mt. Hood is the only place in North America, in fact, where it is possible to ski in a developed ski area for 12 months out of the year.

Once reaching the top of the lift, you make your way east over groomed snowfields for a short distance to the Silcox hut, an old stone building. To return to Timberline Lodge, pick up the old access road to this hut, which is now closed and serves as a wide, sandy trail, and follow it downhill. About halfway down this rather steep route, bear to the right onto an unsigned trail traveling above a snow-filled gully, which is often used as a summer ski run. Timberline Lodge and your car are always in sight as you reenter the zone of twisted trees and return to the parking lot. Watch your step as you approach the lodge, because the ground seems to come alive with chubby little golden-mantled ground squirrels. Sadly, these cute native residents now rely more on tourist handouts than their natural foods. Don't add to the problem by offering them anything.

Before heading home, take some time to tour the old lodge. It's worth taking the time to admire its magnificent architecture, massive stone fireplace, and wonderful wood carvings. Interpretive signs discuss the building's interesting history.

Trip 10

Timberline Lodge to Paradise Park

(Map Area MH-3)

Distance	Elevation Gain	Hiking Time	Optional Map	Difficulty
10.1 miles	2100'	5 hours	*Green Trails–Mount Hood*	***

Usually Open	Mid-July to October
Best Times	Late July to early August
Agency	Zigzag Ranger District (Mt. Hood National Forest)

Several trails converge on Paradise Park. Deciding which one is best for you depends on your preferences, your fitness level, and the time of year. The shortest, easiest, and most scenic approach follows the Pacific Crest Trail from Timberline Lodge. Not surprisingly, this is also the most crowded route. If you can get away on a weekday, or you don't mind sharing your outdoor experience with packs of out-of-state tourists, then this is the trail for you.

Directions: Turn north off U.S. Highway 26 just east of Government Camp onto the Timberline Lodge Road. Climb this winding paved road 5.5 miles to the historic lodge with its acres of parking.

From the back side of the lodge pick up a paved footpath marked with a small sign saying TIMBERLINE TRAIL. This route climbs briefly amid midsummer wildflowers to a junction with the Pacific Crest Trail. Turn left, go under a ski lift, then gradually wander at a slight downhill grade through open timberline meadows with good views south to Mt. Jefferson and the Three Sisters in the distant haze. You go straight at a four-way junction with the Mountaineer Trail, then soon reach the lip of the small canyon holding Little Zigzag River. The trail then drops to the "river" (nothing more than a small creek), crosses it on rocks, and climbs out of the little canyon. From here you travel in open subalpine forests to a junction with the little-used Hidden Lake Trail. Go straight on the PCT, then gradually lose elevation, first in the trees, then across open meadowy slopes where the soil is loose and sandy. After a couple of small zigs and zags, you reach the lip of, appropriately enough, Zigzag Canyon, where there is a stunning viewpoint.

Mt. Hood towers above the scene on your right, while directly below are the rocky and sandy canyon slopes and the rushing waters of the river.

The path briefly follows the edge of the canyon, then ducks into the trees and makes three long switchbacks down a cool, forested slope. There are several small creeks and springs on this segment that provide habitat for water-loving plants, including both yellow monkeyflower and pink Lewis' monkeyflower. At the bottom of the 1000-foot descent is a bridgeless crossing of Zigzag River. In early summer this ford can be wet and a bit tricky, but by mid-August it's a fairly simple rockhop. About 0.1 mile upstream from the crossing is an impressive waterfall, which is visible from the trail and can be reached by those willing to scramble over the loose rocks beside the stream. Once on the opposite bank, follow the PCT as it climbs in and out of a small tributary gully to a switchback and a junction with the equestrian bypass trail below Paradise Park.

The much-more-scenic hiker's trail turns back to the right and continues uphill as you regain all of the elevation you lost in reaching the Zigzag River. At first this route ascends through trees, then it crosses open slopes and switchbacks up a wide ravine with pleasant scenery but very little shade. Shortly after you finally reach the top of the canyon, there is a junction with the Paradise Park Trail (Trip 1). Explorations up the flower-covered meadow slopes to your right are highly recommended and very rewarding.

After doing some exploring, go west on the PCT to a crossing of Lost Creek, in a gully that positively bursts with wildflowers, and reach the camp area at Paradise Park just 0.3 miles from the last junction. Since this area is extremely popular, it is crucial that you camp only in official sites that have been used for years and can take the pounding—but don't build a fire.

It is hard to pass up the many additional explorations available in this area. The most rewarding one goes cross-country up and around a bluff northeast of Paradise Park and wanders up sloping meadows toward the rocks and glaciers on Mt. Hood's higher slopes. A somewhat easier option continues north on the PCT for 0.5 mile, to some great above-timberline meadows with lots of delicate heather and views of the wide bulk of Mt. Hood's southwest flank.

Mt. Hood over Zigzag Canyon on the PCT, Oregon

Mount Hood

Area MH-4: Barlow Pass Area

Samuel K. Barlow was a pioneer who brought his family to Oregon with the immigration of 1845. The horrendous difficulties the Barlow family encountered on their passage over the rugged Cascade Range convinced Samuel that he should build a road to accommodate future travelers who were finishing off their long journey to Oregon. The route that he developed became the first established road in the state.

The first people to travel this road were burdened with all of their worldly possessions and had to walk almost 2000 miles just to get here. As a result, they saw this country as nothing but a difficult obstacle. They probably never would have guessed that their descendants would return to these same mountains just for the fun of it! Part of that fun is the thrill of still being able to hike parts of the old road named for Samuel Barlow. But history is not the only attribute that draws modern-day travelers to this area. They also enjoy exploring quiet forests, climbing to grand viewpoints, and visiting forest-rimmed lakes. What the pioneers viewed as obstacles are now considered some of the most scenic features in the Mt. Hood area. What a difference 150 years can make!

Trip 1

Barlow Butte

(Map Area MH-4)

Distance	Elevation Gain	Hiking Time	Optional Map	Difficulty
3.7 miles	1100'	2 hours	*Green Trails—Mount Hood*	**

Usually Open	Mid-June to October
Best Times	July
Agency	Zigzag Ranger District (Mt. Hood National Forest)

This generally overlooked hike offers the outdoor lover two outstanding features. First, you start the trip literally in the ruts of the wagon route of the old Oregon Trail. History buffs will get a kick out of following the tracks of the old-time immigrants. Second, the hike ends with a superb view of Mt. Hood. Despite these attributes, even on busy summer weekends you are likely to have this trail all to yourself. Add to this the short distance and good workout, and this should be considered a "must do" hike for every Portland-area outdoor lover.

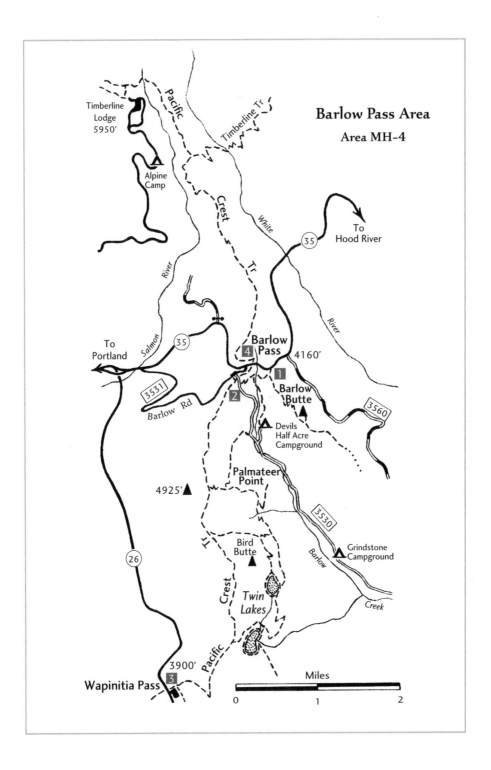

Timberline
Lodge
5950'

Pacific

Timberline Tr

Barlow Pass Area

Area MH-4

Alpine
Camp

Crest

White

To
Hood River

35

Tr

River

Salmon

To
Portland

35

Barlow Pass
4160'

4

1

River

Barlow
Butte

2

3531

Barlow Rd

3560

Devils
Half Acre
Campground

Palmateer
Point

4925' ▲

3530

Tr

Bird
Butte

Grindstone
Campground

26

Crest

Barlow

Twin
Lakes

Creek

Pacific

Miles

3900'

Wapinitia Pass   3

0   1   2

Directions: Drive U.S. Highway 26 a short distance east from Government Camp, then exit onto State Highway 35, following signs to Hood River. Just 2.7 miles later, you'll come to Barlow Pass. Turn right here, and drive 0.2 mile on single-lane, paved Barlow Road to the signed Pacific Crest trailhead.

From the north end of the parking lot, hike due east on the signed tracks of the Oregon Trail, then, after a few yards, cross the Pacific Crest Trail and go straight, staying on the historic wagon route. About 200 yards later, go diagonally across a dirt road and gradually lose elevation for 0.2 mile to a junction with the Barlow Creek Trail. You turn left, leaving the wagon road, and cross a tiny seasonal creek on a plank bridge. This trail climbs through a typical high-Cascades forest, mostly composed of Pacific silver fir and mountain hemlock. The sparse undergrowth, kept small by being smothered in snowdrifts for most of the year, is principally beargrass and huckleberry, with the white blooms of vanilla leaf, anemone, queens cup, and bunchberry adding their bright faces in July. Just before reaching a forested saddle, turn right at the marked junction with the Mineral Jane Ski Trail.

Now on a narrow footpath, you gradually ascend to the corner of a manmade clearing, where you can briefly glimpse the top half of Mt. Hood, before you return to the trees and climb. Your pace slows considerably as the trail angles sharply uphill and several short switchbacks guide you up a shady, north-facing slope. Eventually, you reach a ridgetop and an unsigned junction at a tiny opening in the trees. To the left, a sketchy track climbs for about 200 yards to the rocky summit of Barlow Butte. Unfortunately, the view of Mt. Hood from this highpoint is entirely blocked by trees.

To reach a more satisfying reward, turn right at the ridgetop junction and lose about 150 feet of elevation as you go through a scenic rock garden with lots of July blossoms. Look for stonecrop, lomatium, yarrow, groundsel, cats ear, penstemon, and many other species. You probably still won't be satisfied with the partially obstructed view of Mt. Hood though, so continue hiking through trees. Then climb for another 200 yards to a second open area with great views of towering Mt. Hood and the glacial outwash of the White River Valley to the north and the snowy landmark of Mt. Jefferson to the south. The best photos are from a rocky outcrop above the trail on the right.

The trail continues along the wooded ridge to the south, but the views along that path are disappointing and it gets little or no maintenance, so turn back and return to you car.

Trip 2

Twin Lakes – Palmateer Loop

(Map Area MH-4)

Distance	Elevation Gain	Hiking Time	Optional Map	Difficulty
7.8 miles	1100'	3.5 to 4 hours	Green Trails–Mt. Hood & Mt. Wilson	**

Usually Open	June to October
Best Times	Mid-to-late August
Agency	Zigzag Ranger District (Mt. Hood National Forest)

This popular outing has just about everything you can ask from a hike in the Oregon Cascades. There are two sparkling lakes, lots of attractive forests, acres of berries to pick, and a smashing view of Mt. Hood. About the only thing missing is a wildflower-filled meadow, but to complain about that would really be getting picky. The easy trail makes this an ideal family back-packing trip, with enough to keep both children and adults happy, while not excessively tiring young legs.

Directions: Drive U.S. Highway 26 a short distance east from Government Camp, then exit onto State Highway 35, following signs for Hood River. Just 2.7 miles later, you'll come to Barlow Pass. Turn right here, and drive 0.2 mile on single-lane, paved Barlow Road to the signed Pacific Crest trailhead.

Pick up the Pacific Crest Trail just a few feet east of the parking lot and turn right (south). The wide, gently graded trail gradually gains elevation as it passes through a viewless mountain-hemlock forest. The miles go by quickly as you climb into more open terrain and reach a junction with the return route of the loop. Go straight, sticking with the PCT, and gradually go down through open forests with lots of huckleberries lining the trail. The delicious fruit of these plants ripens in the second half of August, a particularly good time for this hike. Just 0.6 mile later is a second junction, where you once again go straight on the PCT. After another 1.4 viewless miles you arrive at a third junction. Turn left and climb this path over a low rise, then drop gradually to some excellent camps at the north end of lovely Lower Twin Lake. Even though it is crowded on weekends, this is a good place to spend the night, partly because the greenish waters of this deep lake are great for swimming.

To continue the loop, bear left at a junction just above the lake and loop back to the north, climbing two switchbacks, to shallow Upper Twin Lake. This tranquil pool has adequate camps, lots of huckleberries, and a view of the top of Mt. Hood. You go right at a junction at the south end of the lake and follow the east shore for 100 yards, then bear right at a junction with the Pal-

Mt. Hood from viewpoint northeast of Upper Twin Lake, Oregon

mateer View Trail. After about 0.4 mile, don't miss visiting a superb viewpoint at a small rock outcropping atop the cliffs on your right. The view from here of Barlow Butte, the Barlow Creek Valley, and towering Mt. Hood is classic. If you stop for lunch, you may also be rewarded with a visit from friendly rufous hummingbirds feasting on the pink cliff penstemon that clings to these rocks.

After reluctantly leaving this idyllic location, you soon hit a junction where you go right and drop to a lush little meadow with adequate camps and a nice creek. Shortly after the easy creek crossing, you have the option of turning right on a 0.3-mile side trail leading to the fine view from Palmateer Point. This is worth a visit, even though the view is not as photogenic as that at the trailside location described above.

The main loop goes left at the Palmateer Point junction and climbs a gentle slope in an interesting forest of mixed conifers. Unlike the rather monotonous mountain-hemlock forests in most of the Cascades, here there are open woods of Alaska yellow cedar, western white pine, lodgepole pine, Douglas-fir, Pacific silver fir, and Engelmann spruce, along with the hemlocks. Partway up the slope, you go straight at the junction with a trail to the right, which leads to Devils Half Acre, and continue uphill to close the loop at the junction with the PCT.

Trip 3

Twin Lakes from Wapinitia Pass

(Map Area MH-4)

Distance	Elevation Gain	Hiking Time	Optional Map	Difficulty
5.6 miles (to Upper Twin Lake)	900'	2.5 hours	Green Trails–Mt. Hood & Mt. Wilson	*

Usually Open	June to October
Best Times	Mid-to-late August
Agency	Zigzag Ranger District (Mt. Hood National Forest)

This is a good option for hikers with children or pedestrians who just want to visit the Twin Lakes without the added miles of the approach from Barlow Pass (Trip 2). By starting from Wapinitia Pass, your drive is a little over the one-hour drive limit for the hikes in this book, but since you save almost two hours of hiking, that is a reasonable tradeoff. This approach is less scenic than the one from the north, but if your goal is to spend more time fishing or swimming at the lakes, then this is the superior choice.

Directions: From the U.S. Highway 26 junction with Highway 35 east of Government Camp, drive south on Highway 26 toward Bend. After 6 miles, you arrive at the enormous Frog Lake sno-park on your left. In summer this sno-park serves as the Pacific Crest Trail parking lot.

You will find the PCT a few feet north of the lot, near a brown marker for skiers. You turn right on the PCT and, in 120 yards, go straight at the junction with a trail that heads south to the busy car campground at Frog Lake. The gently graded PCT climbs gradually, in one very long switchback, up a slope covered with mountain hemlocks and firs. Nearer at hand are dense thickets of huckleberries, which ripen nicely in late August. After 1.3 miles, you reach a trail junction where you leave the PCT and turn right. Follow this path as it crosses a saddle and begins a gradual descent toward Lower Twin Lake, which is visible through the trees on the right. Just after crossing the often-dry inlet creek, a signed trail drops to the right and leads to some large camps at the north end of the lake. A fisherman's path goes around the lake, while the trail to Frog Lake Buttes climbs away from the lake's eastern shore. To reach Upper Twin Lake, which has poorer camps but fewer people and a partial view of Mt. Hood, hike past the signed turnoff to Lower Twin Lake, round a ridge, and climb two well-graded switchbacks to the shallow upper lake.

Views from both lakes are limited, so hikers who want to see Mt. Hood, or who simply want more exercise, must take one of two options. Most hikers head south from Lower Twin Lake to Frog Lake Buttes on a rather dull, woodsy route that tops out at a decent viewpoint but one whose immediate surroundings are rather ugly. A much better and quieter option follows the Palmateer View Trail from the eastern shores of Upper Twin Lake. After 0.4 mile, you reach an unmarked viewpoint just a few feet off the trail with outstanding views of the Barlow Creek Valley and Mt. Hood.

Trip 4

Pacific Crest Trail – North of Barlow Pass

(Map Area MH-4)

Distance	Elevation Gain	Hiking Time	Optional Map	Difficulty
7.4 miles	1100'	4 hours	*Green Trails–Mount Hood*	**

Usually Open	July to October
Best Times	July
Agency	Zigzag Ranger District (Mt. Hood National Forest)

This convenient segment of the Pacific Crest Trail is not noticed by most hikers, who typically head for the more popular destinations on Mt. Hood. The thinking seems to be that if it is possible to drive to both ends of a trail, then there isn't much point in hiking it. Nonsense! Granted, you might not drive four or five hours out of your way to take this hike, but for a simple one-hour stint in the car, the scenery and exercise are ample compensation.

Directions: Drive U.S. Highway 26 a short distance east from Government Camp, then exit onto State Highway 35, following signs to Hood River. Just 2.7 miles later, you'll come to Barlow Pass. The Pacific Crest Trail crosses the highway about 0.2 mile beyond the pass, but it is quieter and safer to park at the Barlow Pass sno-park. To reach it, turn south on a single-lane, paved road from Barlow Pass and drive 0.2 mile to the signed Pacific Crest trailhead.

From the north end of the parking lot hike due east on the signed tracks of the Oregon Trail, then, after a few yards, come to a junction with the Pacific Crest Trail. Turn left on this gentle path, which wanders through a dense forest of mountain hemlock, Douglas-fir, and noble fir on an old roadbed for 0.1 mile before arriving at Highway 35. You cross the highway and pick up the well-marked trail on the other side.

Mt. Hood from PCT above White River, Oregon

The road is a noisy intrusion, but you soon leave its sight and, not long later, its sounds behind as you climb west across a woodsy hillside. The trail rounds a ridge marking the crest of the Cascade divide, then curves north, as it continues its ascent. There are no views along the way, but the forests are pleasant, with a few shade-loving wildflowers in July and some huckleberries in late August. The trees become generally smaller in size as the trail curves west to reach a small campsite beside a tiny creek in a gully. As you continue to gain elevation, the flowers become increasingly abundant, and the views improve, making for very enjoyable hiking throughout the summer. Shortly after reaching the edge of a meadow, you come to a junction with the Timberline Trail.

You now have a choice. Those looking for a good workout should continue straight on the PCT to historic Timberline Lodge. This often exposed path stays in timberline meadows for most of the next 1.4 miles on a tiring, sandy ascent overlooking the glacial and volcanic mudflow material in White River Canyon. The scenery along this path is very good, but it is no better than what you can obtain without this extra effort. If you've had enough exercise (or you simply have no desire to fight the tourist crowds at Timberline Lodge), then turn right at the Timberline Trail junction and walk for a couple hundred yards to a lovely, flower-filled meadow with a view of Mt. Hood.

Clackamas River Area

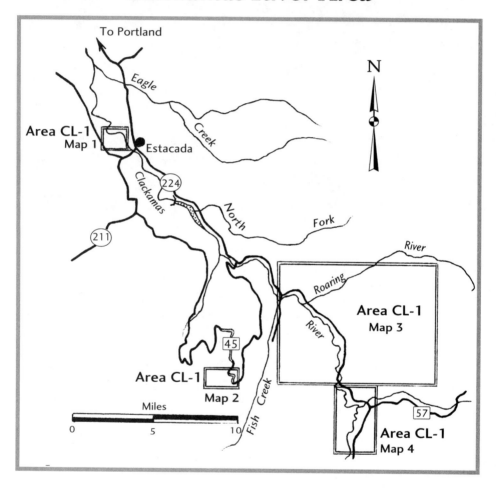

To Portland

Eagle

Creek

Area CL-1
Map 1

Estacada

Clackamas

224

North

Fork

River

211

Roaring

Area CL-1
Map 3

River

45

Fish Creek

Area CL-1
Map 2

57

Area CL-1
Map 4

N

Miles

0   5   10

Clackamas River Area

Area CL: Clackamas River

RISING IN THE FORESTED HIGHLANDS AND WILDERNESS AREAS OF THE CASCADE MOUNTAINS, THE STRIKINGLY BEAUTIFUL CLACKAMAS RIVER IS PERHAPS THE MOST LOVELY STREAM IN OUR REGION—AND THAT'S A CATEGORY WITH LOTS OF COMPETITION. Everything seems designed to add to this river's scenic attributes. With no glaciers in its watershed, the river's water is free of any glacial silt and incredibly clear. Over the millennia the river has cut a twisting canyon that screens the stream from the clearcuts on surrounding ridges and provides close-up looks at many scenic basalt cliffs and densely forested slopes. The forests right beside the river have escaped the chain saw, and represent some of the most impressive, and accessible, old-growth forests in the region. Rollicking rapids between glassy eddies give the stream a wide variety of moods, all of which put the visitor in a perpetually good mood.

To give visitors the chance to enjoy these attributes, the Forest Service has developed several comfortable campgrounds and picnic areas along the river. There are also developed launch sites for rafters and kayakers, and even a fishing pier specifically designed for the disabled. And, of course, most relevant to this book, there are trails. You will find easy paths beside the river's waters and, in the surrounding hills, more challenging trails that lead to viewpoints on ridgetops and to sparkling mountain lakes. While it is true that compared to Mt. Hood or the Columbia River Gorge these trails are relatively few in number, every trail here is worth hiking and, for that matter, rehiking. What more could you ask for?

Like so many other place names in our region, the name *Clackamas* has Native American origins. The Clackamas Indians were once a large tribe who lived along the banks of this stream. Lewis and Clark were familiar with them (spelling the name *Clackamus*), and most other early explorers and settlers had friendly contact with this tribe. Unfortunately, repeating the sad history of Native Americans throughout this continent, most of the tribe was wiped out by disease or pushed off their homeland by white settlers. The remnants of the tribe were relocated to the Grande Ronde Reservation in the Oregon Coast Range.

Most people also assume that the town of Estacada, which serves as the gateway to the Clackamas River region, also has a Native American name. Actually *Estacada* is a Spanish word meaning something like "marked with stakes." This name was chosen for this town for no better reason than that the early residents thought it had a pleasing sound.

Trip 1

Milo McIver State Park Loop

(Map Area CL, Map 1)

Distance	Elevation Gain	Hiking Time	Optional Map	Difficulty
4.3 miles	250'	2 hours	Use park brochure	*

Usually Open	All year
Best Times	Late October to mid-November
Agency	Milo McIver State Park

Milo McIver State Park is a quiet tract of land along the Clackamas River near Estacada. The park is surrounded by farms and woodlands that give the area a tranquil, rural setting rather than the feeling of true wilderness. The state parks department has developed an extensive network of trails in the park, although hikers generally have to take a backseat to equestrians, picnickers, and disc golfers. The best way to appreciate the wilder parts of this park is to follow the outer equestrian loop, which explores the forests, riverbanks, and open fields in the southern part of the park. The heavy emphasis on hooves makes the recommended path wide and easy to follow, but it also

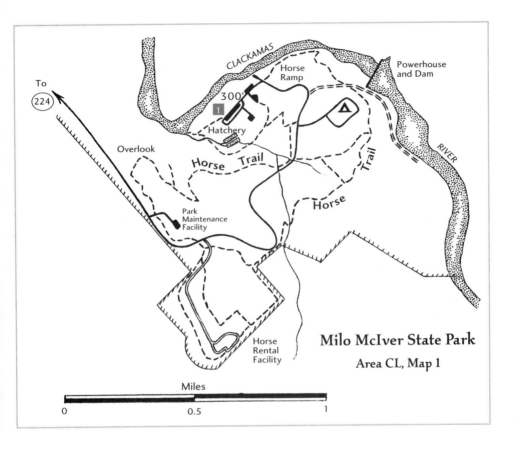

To
(224)

CLACKAMAS

Horse
Ramp

Powerhouse
and Dam

300'

1

Hatchery

Overlook

Horse   Trail

RIVER

Horse   Trail

Park
Maintenance
Facility

Horse

Horse
Rental
Facility

Milo McIver State Park

Area CL, Map 1

Miles

0   0.5   1

turns the trail into a chewed-up quagmire during the rainy season. Summer and fall are better, especially the latter, when the many deciduous trees add color and a seasonal bed of fallen leaves on the trail.

Directions: To reach the park from the Portland area, take exit 12 off Interstate 205 and drive east on State Highway 224/212. Turn right (south) where these roads split, following Highway 224 and signs to Estacada. About 1.5 miles later, bear right at the town of Carver and cross a bridge. At a junction on the other side of the bridge, turn left, then simply follow the signs for the next 10 miles directing you to McIver Park. Once you turn into the park, pass the entrance station, where a $3.00 day-use fee is charged, and follow the signs to the fish hatchery at the south end of the park. Leave your car in the large equestrian overflow lot near the hatchery.

The horse trail departs from the fish hatchery directly across from the parking area. A slightly longer hiker approach, however, is worth the extra 0.1 mile of walking. To find it, follow a well-beaten path from the southwest end of the parking lot and walk past mixed conifer and deciduous woods to a short spur trail, which leads to a river-bend fishing hole on the Clackamas River. The main loop goes left from the short

Fisherman on Clackamas River, Milo McIver State Park

spur to the river and immediately crosses a culvert over the outlet creek from
the hatchery. In spring, expect thickets of tall, pink-blooming corydalis to
brighten the woodsy scene of moss-draped red alder, black cottonwood, western red cedar, and bigleaf maple.

You cross a bridged tributary creek as you loop around the hatchery, then
pick up the horse route at a junction. Turn right and go uphill on a wide trail
that is pleasant despite being chopped up by hooves and made aromatic by
horse apples. The loop route goes right at the next junction, following the
small posted markers for the horse loop. Hummingbirds, warblers, sparrows,
chickadees, and other birds twitter away, taking the edge off the quiet of the
open woods.

The horse trail travels near the park's access road for a short stretch, then
veers away and follows near the edge of some bluffs overlooking a large bend
in the Clackamas River. You'll enjoy occasional glimpses through the trees
down to the stream and out to the surrounding rural landscape, as the wide
trail makes one long switchback up an embankment covered by red alder,
bigleaf maple, and sword fern. Partway up this short climb, you keep straight
at a junction with the Vortex Trail, which is often closed due to landslides. At
the top of the 100-foot ascent, you reach a wooden bench and scenic overlook
of the river. This is a nice lunch or rest stop, with the snowy foothills of the
Cascade Mountains providing a scenic backdrop for the raging river. You may
hear trains in the distance and see a few farms and homes, but none of this
really detracts from the scene.

Shortly after the bench, the path emerges from trees and follows the edge
of a mowed grassy area, where you can see a nearby highway and farmhous-

es outside of the park. Your trail goes in and out of forested areas and through more lawns, then crosses the entrance road to the park maintenance buildings. After this, you pass through a wet area, which is home to false hellebore, and cross the park access road.

About 100 yards after crossing the road you come to yet another junction, where you bear right and soon arrive at a spot where the trail is regularly closed for the wet season. An alternate, drier route goes left, crosses a gravel access road, and passes through a huge grassy area as it works toward a large barn. You turn left a bit before reaching the barn—a private facility providing horse-riding opportunities—and enjoy nice looks at Mt. Hood over the wild grassy expanse directly ahead of you. After looping around the barn, the obvious, but not terribly wild, route turns left to follow a fence line at the edge of the park. The trail turns 90 degrees to the left, following a hedgerow along a property boundary, then comes to a T-junction, where you turn right and walk through stunted woods and brushy areas popular with nesting birds.

The pleasant path winds downhill in deciduous woods to a bridge over a small creek, then levels off in lovely deciduous forests taking you to a junction. Go right again and pass through a semi-open area with very tall Oregon grape plants, which bloom from mid-April into May. You pass several junctions with hiker trails, then once more follow a fence with the commercial activity of a dam and powerhouse on your right and car campsites on your left.

After leaving the campground area, cross a confusing old road at a left diagonal, then saunter through more mixed woods. The trail now drops to the banks of the Clackamas River, where you can enjoy the soothing sounds of rushing water, or take any of several short side paths that tempt you to visit the riverbank. The final short portion of this loop leads through deep woods near the river before arriving back at the road and parking lot.

Clackamas River from trail overlook, Milo McIver State Park

Trip 2

Memaloose Lake &
South Fork Mountain

(Map Area CL, Map 2)

Distance	Elevation Gain	Hiking Time	Optional Map	Difficulty
4.6 miles	1350'	2 to 3 hours	*Green Trails–Fish Creek Mountain*	**

Usually Open	Mid-June to late October
Best Times	June
Agency	Estacada Ranger District (Mt. Hood National Forest)

The popular hike past Memaloose Lake to the top of South Fork Mountain is a simple, unassuming walk that has no single outstanding feature but many worthwhile attributes. Lovers of big trees will delight in traveling through an isolated stand of old-growth Douglas-fir. People who enjoy mountain lakes (and who doesn't) can relax by the shores of a clear pool tucked in a little basin beneath a scenic rockslide. Finally, those who revel in expansive views can take in the scene from an old lookout site. Other hikes in this book include better old-growth forests, better mountain lakes, and better viewpoints, but this hike is one of the few to include good, if not outstanding, examples of all three.

Directions: Drive State Highway 224 southeast from Estacada 9.4 miles, then turn right on Memaloose Road 45, which immediately crosses a narrow bridge. Stay on paved Road 45 for 11.3 miles to the end of pavement and a junction, where you turn right and drive a final 0.9 mile to the trailhead.

The gently graded trail makes a steady climb up a hillside above Memaloose Creek, where the trees are the most noteworthy feature and will impress even the most jaded hiker. Take the time to snap a photo of the kids next to one of these old-growth giants to teach them a lesson in both conservation and humility. The mostly open forest floor has very little brush but lots of low-growing wildflowers, including oxalis, vanilla leaf, and bunchberry. As it climbs, the path crosses several small creeklets and goes up a few short switchbacks before making a final series of longer switchbacks that takes you up to the shores of Memaloose Lake.

There is an old picnic table here and several good campsites for hikers who are looking to make this an easy overnight trip. In late summer, this shallow, 5-acre pool is also good for swimming. If you prefer more exercise, go straight through the camping area and pick up the 0.9-mile path that climbs 16 switchbacks to the top of South Fork Mountain. The views along this trail

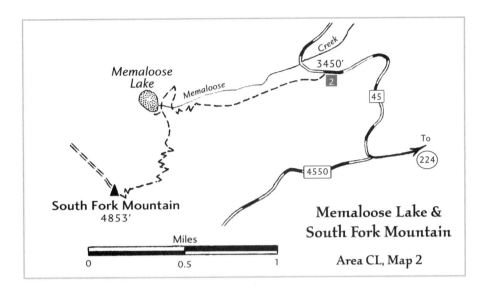

Memaloose Lake &
South Fork Mountain

Area CL, Map 2

are limited by trees. The last bit of the climb is along a high ridge leading to the summit. You may have to share the view with car-bound travelers, who can access this high point via a rough dirt road, but console yourself with the knowledge that these "cheaters" missed the lovely forest and lake below. From the summit, you can see Cascade snow peaks from Mt. Rainier to the Three Sisters, and look west to the Willamette Valley and the rolling green hills of the Coast Range. On perfectly clear days, those with binoculars can even pick out the familiar skyscrapers of downtown Portland.

Trip 3

Clackamas River Trail

(Map Area CL, Map 3)

Distance	Elevation Gain	Hiking Time	Optional Map	Difficulty
7.8 miles (one way)	1300' (one way)	4 hours (one way)	Green Trails– Fish Creek Mountain	***

Usually Open	All year
Best Times	All year
Agency	Estacada Ranger District (Mt. Hood National Forest)

The best way for hikers to enjoy the beauties of the Clackamas River is to take an extended walk along its shores. There is no better option for that than the segment of the Clackamas River Trail that goes upstream from Fish Creek.

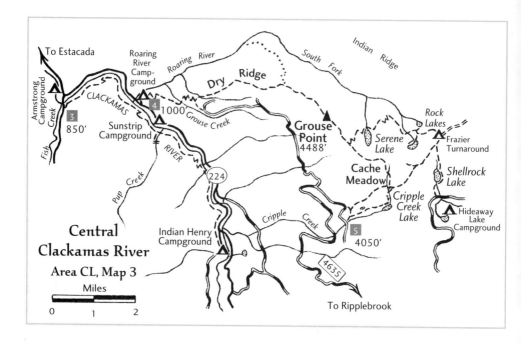

Central Clackamas River

Area CL, Map 3

Miles

0   1   2

With easy road access to both ends, this hike is ideal for a car or bicycle shuttle. The hike is probably most enjoyable in late winter and early spring, when the trees lack their summer leaves and allow you to see the many wispy seasonal waterfalls dropping from trailside cliffs. Unfortunately, the path gets very little sunshine in winter, which makes for chilly temperatures, so bring a coat.

Directions: Drive State Highway 224 southeast from Estacada 15 miles to the Fish Creek Road. Turn right on this road, cross a bridge, and reach the large trailhead parking lot on the right. The newly rerouted start of the trail is across Fish Creek Road from the south end of the parking lot.

If you are doing the trip one-way, you can leave a second car (or bicycle) at the Indian Henry trailhead. To reach it, continue on Highway 224 another 7 miles, then turn right off the main road just before it crosses a bridge. Drive this route 0.6 mile to the trailhead on the right.

From the Fish Creek trailhead, the wide path begins by going through a forest of western hemlock and western red cedar. The forest floor is covered by sword fern, various mosses, salal, and lots of April-blooming oxalis. In a few hundred yards you bear right at a junction with the old trail coming in from the left and hike a wide, smooth path up the Clackamas River Canyon. Unless you are an angler, you can ignore the several side trails that drop to fishing spots on the river.

The trail crosses a small feeder creek, then begins a series of miniature ups and downs. Although the highway is never far away across the river, the intervening sounds of rushing water and the rollicking songs of small birds provide a more pleasant experience for the ears. If you are lucky, you may get a glimpse of the source of these songs, the diminutive, brown, winter wren. Be prepared to be surprised by the small size of this amazingly powerful songster.

To avoid mossy, river-level rocks and cliffs, the trail takes you up a slope almost 200 feet above the water. It then contours briefly before using two short switchbacks to descend to a camp on the riverbank. The road's sights and sounds are more intrusive for the next 0.6 mile, as the river is more placid and the road is especially close. More ups and downs takes you past a tiny sloping falls, just above the trail, then you descend to a comfortable riverside camp in a nice grove of cedars. Past this camp, you climb two steep switchbacks to a viewpoint of the Roaring River Canyon to the northeast. Here you stay high for a while. Then you will come close to a set of powerlines, which follow the Clackamas River up the canyon. You will play hide and seek with this powerline for much of the rest of the hike.

When you reach the powerlines a second time, there is a well-signed junction with a 0.1-mile side trail to Pup Creek Falls. Don't miss the chance to

Pup Creek Falls along Clackamas River

347

visit this impressive 100-foot-tall falls, which is set in a dramatic grotto. Unfortunately, the falls is almost perpetually in the shade, so photographers will need either a tripod or very fast film.

Back on the main trail, you cross Pup Creek on a set of strategically placed stepping stones. Then you go through a partially cleared area near the powerlines to a junction with a short side trail to a good riverside beach and campsite. From here, you climb over a small knoll, then descend in small switchbacks back to river level. At this point, a short side trail goes left to the river at The Narrows. The name isn't very original, but it *is* an accurate description of this place, where the river cuts through a 20-foot-wide chasm between large mossy rocks. The Narrows are ideal for sunbathing and they make a great place to eat your lunch while watching rafters pass through the narrow opening. Beyond this point, the trail is less interesting as it either stays in heavy forest or goes beneath the powerlines for about 1 mile. You then pass through a cavelike grotto that has been carved out of a cliffside and travel along a hillside above a paved road before the trail ends at Indian Henry Campground.

Trip 4

Dry Ridge to Grouse Point

(Map Area CL, Map 3)

Distance	Elevation Gain	Hiking Time	Optional Map	Difficulty
12.2 miles	3600'	7 hours	*Green Trails–Fish Creek Mountain*	***

Usually Open	June to mid-October	
Best Times	Mid-June to mid-July	
Agency	Estacada Ranger District (Mt. Hood National Forest)	

The most popular trails in the Clackamas River country stay at low elevations right along the river, but there are also options for hikers looking for more exercise. The attractive trail up Dry Ridge is a good workout for any hiker. While most of the long climb is in viewless woods, those up for the challenge can end the hike at a good viewpoint, featuring part of Mt. Hood and the many wooded ridges of the Clackamas River country.

Directions: Drive State Highway 224 southeast from Estacada for 17.5 miles to Roaring River Campground. Turn left into this camp and find the signed trailhead at the end of the campground loop near campsite #8. This campground is closed until about June, so if you are visiting before then, you will have to park along Highway 224 and walk about 0.1 mile to the trailhead.

The trail begins by briefly following the bank of the sparkling Roaring River, then it cuts back to the right away from the water. Almost immediately thereafter, you cross beneath a set of powerlines, the last manmade intrusion on the hike. The forest canopy here is almost uniformly Douglas-fir, with some massive old-growth specimens to admire. Below the firs are the more shade-tolerant western hemlock, which, given a few more centuries of undisturbed growth, will take over as the dominant species. The forest floor is more varied than the trees, with lots of vanilla leaf, both sword and bracken fern, moss-covered rocks, and an abundance of white, five-petaled anemones.

After the powerlines, the trail begins switchbacking on a relentlessly steady but not overly steep climb. The ascent is best done in the morning, when the weather is cooler and the trail is well shaded. Near the top of the first 12 switchbacks, the trail reaches a small grassy glade, where tiny white iris bloom in early summer. Above this glade the trail makes a final turn and takes you to the top of a rocky slope with a good view of the Clackamas River Canyon. This viewpoint is about 1.5 miles from the start, and it makes a good stopping point for off-season hikers because the trail is usually snow-free to here for most of the winter.

Those continuing beyond this point must make an uneven, but generally uphill, traverse on the north side of Dry Ridge to a crossing of splashing Grouse Creek, which may get your boots wet in early summer. Beyond the crossing the trail continues its generally uphill traverse to the base of a small rockslide and the start of a second set of switchbacks. There are eight this time, which lead you up to a rockslide and to a trail junction. Going straight at this junction takes you 0.3 mile to Forest Road 4635, a possible starting point for hikers who care only about the view from Grouse Point.

The main trail turns left at this junction and soon demonstrates that most of the climbing is over. The grade of the ascent is much more gradual now, with many level sections mixed in with the uphills. You step over a small, seasonal creek and follow the edge where Dry Ridge's gentle slope suddenly drops off to your left. Views are limited by the forest cover, which is now made up of much smaller hemlock, cedar, and fir trees. The mostly open forest floor features scattered beargrass and rhododendrons, both of which bloom nicely from mid-June into July.

You bear slightly right at the signed junction with a sketchy, unmaintained trail that goes back to the left, then steadily ascend in forest for about another mile. Eventually you break out of the trees and reach the partially obstructed views from the beargrass meadows atop Grouse Point. For the best views, leave the trail and bushwhack a few dozen feet to the left. From here, you can sit and enjoy a marvelously wild landscape featuring the South Fork Roaring River Canyon and the top third of Mt. Hood peeking over Indian Ridge. Best of all, there isn't a road or a logging scar in sight.

Backpackers can extend this outing another 2 miles to scenic Serene Lake. This area is easier to reach, however, by shorter routes, such as that described in Trip 5.

Trip 5

Cripple Creek – Serene Lake Loop

(Map Area CL, Map 3)

Distance	Elevation Gain	Hiking Time	Optional Map	Difficulty
11.0 miles	1800'	6 to 8 hours	*Green Trails–Fish Creek Mountain & High Rock*	***

Usually Open	Mid-June to October
Best Times	Mid-June / Late August to September
Agency	Estacada Ranger District (Mt. Hood National Forest)

This outstandingly scenic loop includes a sampling of all the things that make hiking in the Cascade Mountains such a joy. There are scenic lakes tucked away in old glacial cirques, lush mountain meadows carpeted with wildflowers, lovely high-elevation forests, high viewpoints where you can look out to snow-capped volcanic peaks, and fields of huckleberries that provide tasty treats in late summer. The hike makes a perfect short backpacking trip, as all the lakes have good campsites. Wildlife enthusiasts might be interested to know that the author has been fortunate enough to observe both black bear and mountain lion in this area. Keep your eyes open and hope for similar luck. The drive here is actually slightly longer than the self-imposed one-hour limit for this book. The trip was included to ensure complete coverage of the hiking opportunities in the Ripplebrook vicinity. **Warning:** In early summer, mosquitoes can be *terrible* around the high lakes. To avoid them, try to visit during a two-week window of opportunity in June just *after* the snowmelt and *before* the bugs hatch. Since it is difficult to time this exactly right, it may be easier to visit in late August or September, when most of the bugs are gone and the huckleberries are ripe.

Directions: Drive State Highway 224 southeast from Estacada 25.5 miles to the Ripplebrook Guard Station. Just beyond the station, turn left on paved Forest Road 4631. Stay on this road for 2.6 miles, past several minor intersections, to the end of pavement. At a fork 0.4 mile later, bear left onto Forest Road 4635, and climb for 9.8 miles on this narrow, twisting, gravel road to a fork. Bear right and, exactly 1.8 miles later, just before a culvert over Cripple Creek, park in a small pullout on the left with room for about two cars.

The unsigned, but obvious, trail departs from the left side of the trailhead pullout. Just 50 yards from your car, you come to an unsigned junction. Either route will get you to the destination, but it is slightly easier to navigate this loop if you go straight. This path gradually climbs through a lovely, high-elevation forest dominated by Pacific

Pond in Cache Meadow

silver fir and mountain hemlock. On the generally open forest floor are bear-grass and huckleberry bushes, with a few flowers like blue and white ane-mone and yellow wood violet for color. This general description of the flora holds true throughout this hike.

You pass a shallow, marshy lake, then continue slowly ascending in the open forest. The rarely used trail is reasonably easy to follow, but even if you temporarily lose it, you can quickly relocate the tread by using the yellow paint marks on trees along the route. After a little over 1 mile, the trail arrives at shallow, 15-acre Cripple Creek Lake, where brook trout and rough-skinned newts rise to the surface, breaking the glassy stillness of this forest-rimmed lake. After working its way along the north shore of the lake, and passing two good campsites, the trail curves left and goes gradually uphill beside the inlet creek. The path is a bit sketchy, but experienced hikers can easily follow it, especially with the help of the many orange survey tapes tied to tree limbs along the route.

After about 0.3 mile, you arrive at the lower end of marshy Cache Meadow. Just as the snow melts in June this meadow comes alive with white marsh marigolds, while a bit later in the season pink shooting stars put on a nice show. Throughout the season you'll enjoy the serenade of frogs, which live in the shallow ponds of this meadow.

The trail seems to end at the meadow. To continue the hike, simply cross the seasonal creek that runs out of a pond and, 20 feet later, arrive at Cache Meadow Shelter, a dilapidated wooden structure that no longer provides much shelter. The main loop trail passes just in front of this shelter. To do a clockwise loop, turn left and walk 200 yards to a confusing junction. The loop trail, marked only with a tiny wooden sign stating "517," turns right. You pass a couple of small meadows and a bubbling spring, before climbing fairly steeply for 0.8 mile to a wonderful clifftop viewpoint. The ancient glacial basin of Serene Lake spreads out below you like a geology classroom display. Easiest for the amateur to recognize are the old glacial features that are now filled by the Serene Lake or covered by forests. Towering in the distance are Mounts St. Helens, Adams, and Hood, where glaciers still do their work and the Ice Age continues.

To make the loop, continue hiking northwest across a high forested table-land, then descend to a junction in a small saddle, where there are lots of rhododendron bushes. Going straight would take you to Grouse Point and Dry Ridge (Trip 4). For the loop, you turn right and descend four quick switchbacks, then make a downhill traverse to lovely Serene Lake. This deep, 20-acre lake has several popular and comfortable camps, one of which includes a seemingly out-of-place wooden picnic table.

The trail curves around the northwest shore of the lake, crosses the outlet stream, and veers away from the water to go around a low, forested ridge. On the other side of this ridge, a series of switchbacks descends about 300 feet, elevation which you partially regain on a subsequent uphill traverse. You pass above a tiny pond, hop across the headwaters of South Fork Roaring River, then come to a junction. To the left, a 0.1-mile spur trail goes to Lower Rock Lake, which is worth the trip, if you have the time. The main trail goes right and quickly meets a second spur trail, which goes straight and, in 0.2 mile, reaches Middle Rock Lake, a large, swimmable mountain gem with nice camps.

To continue the loop, you turn left at this junction and gradually climb to a primitive and waterless car campground at Frazier Turnaround. This is where most people begin this hike, although the miserably rock-strewn dirt road you must drive to reach this trailhead would make you wonder *why* it is so popular. You turn right and follow a wide trail that leaves the camp area and gradually ascends a ridgeline. After 200 yards, a side trail drops to the left on its way to scenic Shellrock Lake. Backpackers with more time to do this loop, or very athletic dayhikers, will want to take the 1.1-mile side trip to this beautiful lake, which is backed by a scenic talus slope.

The main trail, actually an ancient jeep road, crosses an open rockslide with good views of pointed Mt. Jefferson, before topping out on a small forested plateau. A little after the almost straight old road begins going downhill, you turn left at a sign for Grouse Point Trail 517. This narrow foot trail winds fairly steeply downhill, all the way back to the broken-down shelter at Cache Meadow.

For a slightly different route back to your car, go 200 yards past the shelter to the junction you passed earlier in the day, and veer left. This attractive trail lazily loses elevation for 1.7 miles, traveling through narrow meadows and along the rocky bottom of seasonal streambeds, where the trail is easy to lose. You pass a lovely lakelet, then, just in front of a second shallow lakelet, turn left at an unsigned junction. About 0.1 mile later, you return to the junction just 50 yards from your car.

Trip 6

Alder Flat Trail

(Map Area CL, Map 4)

Distance	Elevation Gain	Hiking Time	Optional Map	Difficulty
1.8 miles	250'	1 hour	Green Trails–Fish Creek Mountain	*

Usually Open	All year
Best Times	All year
Agency	Estacada Ranger District (Mt. Hood National Forest)

This easy route gives hikers the opportunity to experience an increasingly rare ecosystem, the low-elevation, old-growth forest. Most of these forests were cut down decades ago, but here you can enjoy a small sample of what is still left. If this short path does not provide you with enough exercise, then consider doing this trip in conjunction with the nearby Riverside Trail (Trip 7) for a full day of hiking.

Directions: Drive State Highway 224 southeast from Estacada for 25 miles to milepost 49, just past the Timber Lake Work Center. The well-signed Alder Flat trailhead parking lot is on your right.

The gentle Alder Flat Nature Trail descends through a peaceful, old-growth forest of Douglas-fir and western hemlock, where small numbered posts mark places of interest. A thick mat of mosses crowds the forest floor along with Oregon grape, sword

Forest along Alder Flat Trail

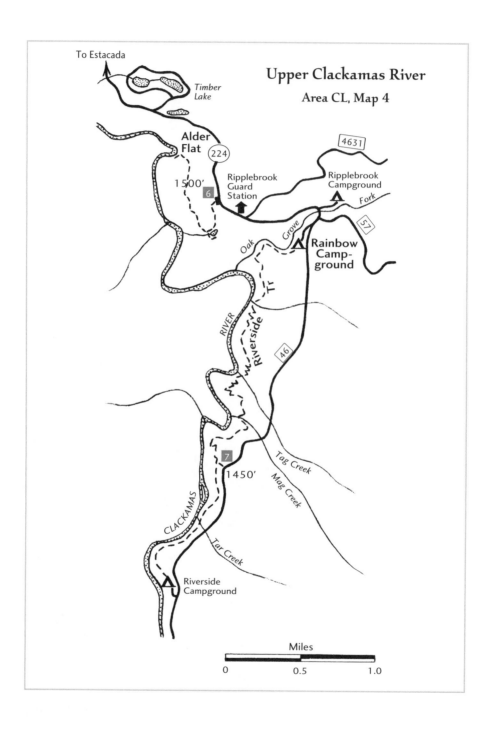

To Estacada

Timber
Lake

Upper Clackamas River

Area CL, Map 4

Alder
Flat (224)

4631

1500' 6

Ripplebrook
Guard
Station

Ripplebrook
Campground

Fork

57

Oak Grove Tr

Riverside Tr

Rainbow
Camp-
ground

RIVER

46

7

Tag Creek

1450'

Mag Creek

CLACKAMAS

Tar Creek

Riverside
Campground

Miles

0   0.5   1.0

fern, and downed nurse logs. After just 0.2 mile, you pass above a medium-sized marsh created by beavers. From the lower end of the marsh, a worthwhile 0.1-mile side trail goes to the left. Along this route you will find evidence of beaver activity and several nest boxes for wood ducks.

After the marsh, the main trail curves right and goes slowly downhill through a glorious forest of big trees covered with draping mosses. Near the bottom of the hill, you will find a marshy area and a sluggish creek as well as an ever-increasing number of western red cedar. The trail crosses a couple of wooden boardwalks before ending at Alder Flat, an attractive river-level bench with wooden picnic tables and metal fire pits. Here, you can enjoy a fine lunch or dinner beside a lovely stream before returning to your car.

Trip 7

Riverside Trail

(Map Area CL, Map 4)

Distance	Elevation Gain	Hiking Time	Optional Map	Difficulty
4.8 miles	400'	2.5 hours	Green Trails–Fish Creek Mountain	**

Usually Open	All year
Best Times	Late September
Agency	Estacada Ranger District (Mt. Hood National Forest)

This short and pleasant outing is a winner at any time of year, but it is probably most interesting in September, when the hiker has the opportunity to watch salmon spawning in the Clackamas River. In any season, however, you will enjoy stately old-growth forests, quiet trails, and some excellent high viewpoints above the water. The scenery is not as dramatic as on higher-elevation routes, but this is an excellent option for the quiet contemplation of nature.

Directions: Drive State Highway 224 southeast from Estacada for 25.5 miles to the Ripplebrook Guard Station. A little past the station, the road crosses a bridge, immediately after which you bear right at a fork. The new Riverside trailhead is on the right about 1.6 miles from the bridge.

The path from the trailhead leads down 150 yards through a pretty forest to a junction with the main Riverside Trail. At this point, you can turn in either direction, but the route to the right is much more attractive and is the one described here.

The trail travels downhill through low-growing western red cedars and western hemlocks to the first of many viewpoints, this one above a bend in the Clackamas River. Still traveling downhill, you follow small Mag Creek to a bridged crossing of that stream, then begin the up-and-down pattern that will soon become this trail's trademark. The path ascends a ridge, then drops to a rocky beach beside the river, which is an ideal rest stop.

Next, you cross on a bridge over the often dry Tag Creek, then climb four short switchbacks to another viewpoint well above the river. From here the path wanders around in circuitous ups and downs through the hills above the river, before dropping to a superb rocky beach beside the water. You can eat lunch here or take a dip in the water, but you'd better make it a really *quick* dip, because the water is awfully cold!

Leaving this inviting beach, you cross a wooden boardwalk and climb to a final excellent viewpoint at the top of a cliff overlooking the river canyon. Stay well back from the drop-off, as the edges of this cliff are crumbly and unstable. This is a good turnaround point, but if you want to finish off the distance to Rainbow Campground, then follow the path as it goes up and down through a forest of western red cedar and Douglas-fir beside splashing Oak Grove Fork. It ends at a tiny parking area at the far end of the campground.

View of the Clackamas River from the Riverside Trail

Appendix A

Recommended Reading

Bookstore shelves are overflowing with books about the Pacific Northwest outdoors. It seems we Portlanders have an inexhaustible appetite for information about our beloved wilderness. Some books are better than others, of course, and owning them all would involve a lot of redundancy. Here are the author's recommendations for the best local books to have in your outdoor library.

Dayhiking Guides

With this book, you already own the most comprehensive guide to dayhikes close to Portland. You really don't need anything else—except for updates to this book as changes occur in the future. There are, however, other good books with different purposes.

For coverage of hikes somewhat further from Portland—up to two hours' driving time—your best choice is *100 Hikes in Northwest Oregon* by William L. Sullivan. It includes places like the east side of Mt. Hood, further up the Clackamas River, and the Indian Heaven and Mt. St. Helens areas in Washington. If you are headed for the coast, Sullivan's *100 Hikes/Travel Guide Oregon Coast & Coast Range* is the best book covering this popular area.

If you want a different perspective on the wonderful trails of the Columbia River Gorge than what you find in this book, look for *Columbia Gorge Hikes: 42 Scenic Hikes* by Don and Roberta Lowe, the deans of Oregon guidebook authors. This old favorite has been updated with beautiful, all-color photographs, but it is in a large format that is awkward to carry on the trail. One useful and quaint book on the southern Mt. Hood area is *Hikes & Walks on Mt. Hood* by Sonia Buist and Emily Keller. Produced by LOLITS Press (an acronym for Little Old Ladies in Tennis Shoes), it covers unique hiking options on old and little-used roads, ski runs, and cross-country ski trails clustered around Government Camp and Timberline Lodge. It is a good choice if you are willing to expand your ideas about what qualifies as a "hiking" route.

Other Travel Guides

If you are interested in outdoor sports other than dayhiking, you might want to pick up some of the following:

Long-distance backpackers looking for the best places to go for that 3-day-to-2-week hiking vacation should pick up copies of this author's *Backpacking Oregon* and *Backpacking Washington*.

Wildlife enthusiasts will get good value from two skinny volumes that designate areas for viewing wildlife in Oregon and Washington. Although far from a comprehensive list, the sites are usually reliable places to visit. *The Oregon Wildlife Viewing Guide* is written by James A. Yuskavitch, and the author of the *Washington Wildlife Viewing Guide* is Joe La Tourette.

The bible on winter sports is Klindt Vielbig's *Cross-Country Ski Routes: Oregon*, which is consistently updated and valued by those who love this sport. The book covers southwest Washington as well as Oregon.

All the water in our area makes this a paradise for river runners. *Soggy Sneakers: A Guide to Oregon Rivers* by the Willamette Kayaking and Canoe Club and *Oregon River Tours* by John Garren are the two most useful books.

Those who prefer to power themselves along on two wheels will want *Bicycling the Backroads of Northwest Oregon* by Philip Jones and Jean Henderson.

Natural History

Two good, general-interest, natural history guides, which give an overview of the most common varieties of plants and animals are *The Audubon Society Nature Guide—Western Forests* and *A Field Guide to the Cascades & Olympics*, both by Stephen Whitney. The former has lovely color photography, but does not include fish. With such wide coverage, it has room for a woefully inadequate number of mushrooms and wildflowers. The latter book is more specific to our region, but has only black and white drawings of many of the wildflowers, and leaves out the mushrooms and fungi.

The best field guide for identifying birds is the *National Geographic Society's Field Guide to the Birds of North America*. Only the common species of reptiles, amphibians, and mammals are likely to be seen by most hikers, and these are adequately covered in the general-interest Whitney guides.

Trees get adequate coverage in the general-interest guides, but if you are looking for more detail and comprehensive coverage, then your best choice is probably *Northwest Trees* by Stephen Arno and Ramona Hammerly.

From the average hiker's point of view, almost all wildflower guides have one major flaw—they follow a format originally developed for professional botanists, resulting in an overemphasis on Latin names, an obsession with minute distinctions between virtually identical species, and, worst of all, an organization based on taxonomic families rather than something useful for amateurs like habitat or color. Unfortunately, most of the flower guides with more useful organization seem to have been written for children. The best comprehensive guide to wildflowers in our area is probably *Wildflowers of the Columbia Gorge* by Russ Jolley. It completely covers the rich diversity of this remarkable region and, in doing so, it includes most of the species found in the rest of our area. It has excellent color photography and useful recommendations on where to go in each season for wildflower viewing.

A fun guide you might consider is James Luther Davis' *Seasonal Guide to the Natural Year*, which you can use to plan trips around natural events such as animal migrations, fall-color, and wildflower-blooming.

Finally, an informative and endlessly fascinating book for history lovers is *Oregon Geographic Names* by Lewis A. McArthur. This classic is full of things like the meaning of the word Wahtum and how Starvation Creek got its name. It is more interesting to read than any other reference book you will probably ever own.

Information Sources

Local Organizations

Friends of the Columbia Gorge
522 S.W. 5th Avenue, Suite 820
Portland, OR 97204
(503) 241-3762
www.gorgefriends.org

Friends of Powell Butte
3908 S.E. 136th Avenue
Portland, OR 97236

Friends of Tryon Creek State Park
11321 S.W. Terwilliger Boulevard
Portland, OR 97219
(503) 636-4398

The Mazamas
909 N.W. 19th Avenue
Portland, OR 97209
(503) 227-2345
www.mazamas.org

Portland Audubon Society
5151 Cornell Road
Portland, OR 97236
(503) 292-6855
www.audubonportland.org

Ptarmigans Mountaineering Club
PO Box 1821
Vancouver, WA 98668
www.ptarmigans.org

Trails Club of Oregon
PO Box 1243
Portland, OR 97207 ʼ
(503) 233-2740
www.trailsclub.org

Sierra Club, Columbia Group
2950 S.E. Stark Street, Suite 110
Portland, OR 97214
(503) 231-0507
www.oregon.sierraclub.org

Parks and Land Agencies

Baskett Slough National Wildlife Refuge
10995 Highway 22
Dallas, OR 97338
(503) 623-2749

Beacon Rock State Park
34841 State Route 14
Skamania, WA 98648
(509) 427-8265

Clark Parks & Recreation Department
603 West Evergreen Boulevard
Vancouver, WA 98668-1995
(360) 696-8171
www.ci.vancouver.wa.us/parks-recreation

Columbia River Gorge National Scenic Area
902 Wasco Avenue, Suite 200
Hood River, OR 97031
(541) 386-2333
www.fs.fed.us/r6/columbia

Gifford Pinchot National Forest
www.fs.fed.us/gpnf

Wind River District
1262 Hemlock Road
Carson, WA 98610
(509) 427-3200

Jackson Bottom Wetlands Preserve
123 W. Main Street
Hillsboro, OR 97123
(503) 681-6206
www.jacksonbottom.org

Mt. Hood Information Center
65000 E. Highway 26
Welches, OR 97067
(503) 622-7674

Mt. Hood National Forest
www.fs.fed.us/r6/mthood

Estacada Ranger District
595 N.W. Industrial Way
Estacada, OR 97023
(503) 630-8700

Zigzag Ranger District
Use Mount Hood Information
Center

**The Nature Conservancy
of Oregon**
821 S.E. 14th Avenue
Portland, OR 97214
(503) 230-1221
www.nature.org/states/oregon

**Nature of the Northwest
Information Center**
800 N. Oregon Street
Portland, OR 97232
(503) 731-4444
www.naturenw.org

Oregon State Parks
1115 Commercial Street, N.E.
Salem, OR 97301-1002
(503) 378-6305 or (800)551-6949
www.oregonstateparks.org

Milo McIver State Park
(503) 630-7150

Silver Falls State Park
(503) 873-8681

Oxbow County Park
3010 S.E. Oxbow Parkway
Gresham, OR 97080
(503) 663-4708

**Portland Parks
& Recreation Bureau**
1120 S.W. 5th Avenue, #1302
Portland, OR 97204
(503) 874-8793
www.parks.ci.portland.or.us/parks

**Ridgefield National
Wildlife Refuge**
PO Box 457
Ridgefield, WA 98642-0457
(360) 887-4106
www.rl.fws.gov/ridgefield

Santiam State Forest
22965 N. Fork Road S.E.
Lyons, OR 97358
(503) 859-2151

Sauvie Island Wildlife Area
18330 N.W. Sauvie Island Road
Portland, OR 97231
(503) 621-3488

Tillamook State Forest
www.odf.state.or.us/tsf

Tillamook District Office
4907 3rd Street
Tillamook, OR 97141
(503) 842-2545

Forest Grove District Office
801 Gales Creek Road
Forest Grove, OR 97116
(503) 357-2191

Tualatin Hills Park & Recreation District
15707 S.W. Walker Road
Beaverton, OR 97006-5941
(503) 645-6433
www.thprd.com

Washington Department of Natural Resources—Central Region Yacolt State Forest
1405 Rush Road
Chehalis, WA 98532
(360) 748-2383

Map Sources

Captain's Nautical Supply
138 N.W. 10th Street
Portland, OR 97209
(503) 227-1648

Nature of the Northwest— see previous section

Pittmon Map Co
732 S.E. Hawthorne Blvd
Portland, OR 97214
(503) 232-1161

REI—Recreational Equipment Inc.
1798 Jantzen Beach Center
Portland, OR 97217
(503) 283-1300

REI—Recreational Equipment Inc.
7410 S.W. Bridgeport Road
Tigard, OR 97224
(503) 624-8600

Appendix C

Friends of Forest Park

Several of the hikes in this book explore the beautiful trails through Forest Park. Like all urban preserves, this park needs committed and involved citizens to help maintain trails, keep out invasive non-native plants, restore damaged habitats, and otherwise protect and preserve this irreplaceable treasure of the city of Portland. The Friends of Forest Park have done all of these things and more since 1946. I encourage hikers who enjoy the wild trails of this magnificent park to support and join this non-profit organization and lend a hand in helping to protect, preserve, and enhance Forest Park.

Mailing Address
Friends of Forest Park
P.O. Box 2413
Portland, OR 97208

Office Address
2366 N.W. Thurman Street
Portland, OR 97208
Phone: (503) 223-5499
FAX: (503) 223-5637
info@FriendsofForestPark.org
www. FriendsofForestPark.org

Friends of the Columbia Gorge

More of the trails described in this book travel through the Columbia River Gorge than any other area. The magnificent landscapes of this nationally significant scenic treasure remain largely unspoiled and open to the public due, in part, to the tireless efforts of people dedicated to protecting this special place. Friends of the Columbia Gorge is a grassroots organization that works to protect and enhance the unique scenic, recreational, and biological features of this area and it deserves your support.

Mailing Address
Friends of the Columbia Gorge
522 S.W. 5th Ave, Ste. 820
Portland, OR 97204
(503) 241-3762
www.gorgefriends.org

Index

About the Author

Doug Lorain, a resident of Portland, has lived in Oregon for 35 years and has spent a large percentage of that time exploring the trails and backcountry of his home region. Since beginning his trail-stomping efforts at the age of 5, he has hiked over 25,000 miles in Oregon and Washington, and is constantly seeking out new trails to explore. As this comprehensive guide demonstrates, almost no path has escaped his notice.

He is the author of *Backpacking Oregon* and *Backpacking Washington*, both with Wilderness Press.

The author holding up an old Cedar Tree on the Old Salmon River Trail near Zigzag, Oregon